Library of
Davidson College

VOID

JAMES MCCOSH
AND THE SCOTTISH
INTELLECTUAL
TRADITION

James McCosh (about 1870)

JAMES McCOSH AND THE SCOTTISH INTELLECTUAL TRADITION

from Glasgow to Princeton

J. DAVID HOEVELER, JR.

PRINCETON UNIVERSITY PRESS
PRINCETON, NEW JERSEY

Copyright © 1981 by Princeton University Press

Published by Princeton University Press, Princeton, New Jersey
In the United Kingdom: Princeton University Press, Guildford, Surrey

All Rights Reserved

Library of Congress Cataloging in Publication Data will be
found on the last printed page of this book

Publication of this book has been aided by the Whitney Darrow
Publication Reserve Fund of Princeton University Press

This book has been composed in Linotron Bembo

Clothbound editions of Princeton University Press books
are printed on acid-free paper, and binding materials are
chosen for strength and durability

Printed in the United States of America by Princeton
University Press, Princeton, New Jersey

*This book
is for my parents—*

JOHN HOEVELER AND
VIRGINIA THORNBURGH HOEVELER

Contents

List of Illustrations	viii
Preface	ix

Part I SCOTLAND

Chapter One • THE HEIRS OF KNOX	3
Chapter Two • A SCOTTISH EDUCATION	33
Chapter Three • THE GOSPEL MINISTRY	66

Part II IRELAND

Chapter Four • INTUITIONAL REALISM	111
Chapter Five • PROTESTANT SCHOLASTICISM	147
Chapter Six • NATURE AND NATURE'S GOD	180

Part III AMERICA

Chapter Seven • ACADEMIC REFORMER	215
Chapter Eight • ACADEMIC POLITICIAN	272
Chapter Nine • THE NEW PRINCETON	312
McCosh Bibliography	351
Index	361

List of Illustrations

James McCosh (about 1870). British Museum

1. Thomas Chalmers. National Galleries of Scotland	51
2. Sir William Hamilton. John Veitch, *Memoir of Sir William Hamilton* (Edinburgh and London: C. Blackwood and Sons, 1869)	56
3. Thomas Guthrie. National Galleries of Scotland	76
4. James McCosh (about 1845). National Galleries of Scotland	92
5. Robert Chambers. National Galleries of Scotland	182
6. Hugh Miller. *My Schools and Schoolmasters* (Boston: Gould and Lincoln, 1864)	185
7. James McCosh (about 1890). Wheaton J. Lane, ed., *Pictorial History of Princeton* (Princeton: Princeton University Press, 1947)	336

Preface

JAMES MCCOSH'S LIFE spanned most of the nineteenth century. It embraced three countries and concluded with two decades of leadership at one of America's most renowned institutions of higher education. It also interacted critically with major intellectual and cultural movements of his period: the Scottish philosophy, in whose tradition McCosh was reared; Protestant evangelicalism, for which he prepared a philosophical foundation; and evolutionary science, which he set in a theistic framework. To this extent, the prolific McCosh commands our attention as a subject of intellectual history. He is clearly the last major voice of the Scottish Enlightenment and the system of philosophical realism for which it is best known. McCosh stands squarely in the tradition of Thomas Reid, Dugald Stewart, and, more uncertainly, Sir William Hamilton. But he was an independent thinker as well and recast older molds of thought to meet the challenges of new philosophical currents. He is, in fact, our best vehicle for answering the question, What happened to the Scottish intellectual tradition as it confronted the new direction of ideas in the middle and later nineteenth century?

McCosh was a product of lowland Scotland. From his youthful experience in the farming life of the southwest he acquired his keen observation and the practical sense of things that animate even his most technical philosophical works. He pursued an educational course that was typical of his time and place, passing from the local parish school on to Glasgow University and the University of Edinburgh. McCosh thus knew firsthand the commercial and industrial life of Scotland's largest city and the intellectual vitality of its cultural and political capital. His experience with both shaped his religious and philosophical careers. At Edinburgh, McCosh threw in his lot with the insurgent reformist party in the Church of Scotland. The Evangelicals, under the organizational and spiritual leadership of Thomas Chalmers, McCosh's mentor at the university, were enjoying their greatest gains in the 1830s. Under Chalmers, McCosh imbibed the neo-Puritan faith of the rising party and after a decade of agitation joined with the ministerial ranks who formed the Free Church of Scotland.

Conceivably, McCosh might have lived the remainder of his life a servant of the Scottish parish. But he had a restless intellect and read prolifically in philosophy and other fields. At Edinburgh, another influence, that of Sir William Hamilton, was crucial. Hamilton was achieving his brilliant merger of Reid and Kant and taking the Scottish school in a significant new direction. Indeed, McCosh spent years wrestling with the implications of Hamilton's ideas. McCosh's first effort was a massive contribution, *The Method of the Divine Government*, published in 1850. It won him immediate attention, both in Britain and in the United States, and it led directly to an academic career, launched at Queen's College in Belfast, Ireland, the following year.

His sixteen years as professor of logic and metaphysics at Queen's embroiled McCosh in the most lively philosophical disputes of the day. In this, his most productive period, McCosh gave his attention to the ideas of Kant, the German idealists, Hamilton, and John Stuart Mill and sought to counteract their influence by redrawing the outlines of Scottish intuitionism and realism. His most profound work, *The Intuitions of the Mind*, systematically summarized these positions, and, more than any other product of the Scottish school, employed realism to outline the intellectual possibilities of theism. Also at Queen's, with the collaboration of Professor George Dickie, McCosh wrote *Typical Forms and Special Ends in Creation*, a scientific treatise. This large tome contributed significantly to an issue in which McCosh became conspicuous. In the United States he was known to many as an important religious thinker who welcomed the insights of evolution.

In 1868 McCosh began a twenty-year presidency of Princeton College. From the moment of his inauguration, McCosh was a reformer at Princeton. As this study explains in detail, McCosh pushed Princeton in new directions. He built a faculty without the inbred and parochial character of the one he inherited. Scholars with advanced European training arrived at Princeton and helped McCosh expand and modify its traditional curriculum. McCosh organized new fellowships for Princeton's best students, sent many of them to London, Berlin, and elsewhere, and then, in the second half of his administration, brought them back to Princeton as allies in the conflict that had grown at home over the nature, purpose, and future direction of the school. Also, because McCosh encountered such heavy opposition, he found it necessary to redefine Princeton's external relationships. He made new contacts in the world of American money, he cultivated regional alumni groups, he organized feeder schools for Princeton, and he toured the country many times over to gain money and students for his school. By the end of his administration he had set the stage for another classic battle at Princeton. As this study concludes, an assessment of McCosh's transforming role at Princeton must take account of the efforts of Woodrow Wilson, and other students of McCosh, to give substance to his academic ideals in the years that followed.

But at no time was the situation at Princeton a simple one. Although McCosh might appear to certain members of Princeton's board of trustees as a dangerous modernizer, compared to such contemporaries as Charles William Eliot at Harvard or Andrew Dickson White at Cornell, he may look quite the contrary. McCosh encouraged religious revivals at Princeton. In his debates with Eliot, he urged that religion have a central place in American colleges, and he required all Princeton students to study the Bible. He believed that no gentleman was truly educated who did not know the classical languages. For all his flexibility and skillfulness at adapting, McCosh could be arrogant, prideful, and stubborn. He who gave quiet encouragement to the scholarly careers of some of Princeton's leading future academics, could also be a tyrant in the classroom. Altogether, I have found McCosh a fascinating individual, and a challenging one. His life—his career in the church, his intellectual evolution, and his academic leadership—is, I believe, a story worth telling.

I would like to add that what I have attempted here is something more than an intellectual biography. Very early in my study of McCosh it became clear that critical to the history of the Scottish philosophy were the changing social and institutional arrangements of Scotland, to which I give much attention in the opening chapter. Most students of ideas in America know the general place of the Scottish philosophy within the intellectual climate of the eighteenth century and appreciate the dominant place that philosophy came to have in American academic thought in the early and middle nineteenth century. Less appreciated, however, is the genesis of the Scottish system within the reconstructed Scottish society of the earlier period and the attendant cultural divisions within the nation. But this background permanently affected McCosh's intellectual and administrative career. The years of his university training at Glasgow and Edinburgh saw the culminating warfare between Scottish Moderatism, represented by the philosophes of the universities and the rational ministry in the Church of Scotland, and Scottish evangelicalism, represented by the pietistic ministry and its occasional academic allies. These persons disparaged the Enlightenment and decried its social effects. At Edinburgh, McCosh saw these contending factions in the ideas and writings of the dynamic neo-Puritan, Thomas Chalmers, and the cerebral Sir William Hamilton. Always McCosh felt the pull of each and carved his unique place in the Scottish school through his efforts to merge the two cultural traditions of his native country that these men represented. Those efforts bore results not only in McCosh's writings on epistemology, metaphysics, ethics, religious experience, and evolution, but in his institutional rearrangement of Princeton College. The intellectual work in fact is the indispensable background for McCosh's career at Princeton.

I have tried to keep two large concerns in focus in this biography. The recently published volume of essays, *New Directions in American Intellectual History* (Baltimore, 1979), urges in several places that historians of ideas demonstrate the organic character of their subject, the relation of thought to its extended milieu. We need to know, many of the contributors urge, how ideas become incorporated into the various categories of human life, how they move from their contemplative to their activist habitat. Biography is perhaps the best vehicle we have for fulfilling this command. There is a striking unity in McCosh's career, but it is not a mere unity of ideas. It is one, rather, of ideas and institutions, and it is evidenced by his ministry in the Free Church of Scotland, his academic and social concerns at Belfast, and, most strikingly, his presidency at Princeton. For McCosh assured his legacy at Princeton not so much by the system of philosophy he erected over the years, but by the institutional reorientation that registered the impact of his entire Scottish experience.

Second, I have endeavored to address in this work an issue of concern to scholars of American higher education. One school of thought, best articulated by Daniel Boorstin, describes the American university with reference to the flux and formlessness of American society in general. American colleges and universities, he believes, have been characterized by a certain amorphous quality, one derived from their inconstant and uncertain interaction with the pluralistic world around them. In short, they have lacked institutional identity and purpose; they are more the shaped forces of American society than the self-defined autonomous creations of their own wills. On the other hand, Laurence Veysey believes that American universities achieved their distinction precisely because they maintained aloofness from the anti-intellectual or indifferent world outside them. At a critical period in the late nineteenth century they had a unique opportunity for self-definition and made significant achievements when they seized it. Both historians thus raise critical questions about the American university in American society. (See the first section and note 1 of Chapter Eight for further remarks and references.)

McCosh's Princeton provides us with only one example, but I think it is instructive. McCosh brought to Princeton in 1868 a fairly clear conception of his presidential role and the institution he hoped to fashion. Gradually he gave that ideal concrete form. But at a critical juncture he met virulent opposition from a powerful group of Princetonians. McCosh then achieved his critical reforming role when he brought Princeton into an extended network of new external alliances. The heterogeneous character of these individuals and groups is rather bewildering and may appear to confirm Boorstin's thesis of institutional confusion. But the process was executed with a clear sense of purpose, one that extended directly, in fact, from McCosh's unique philosophical position and the academic program drawn out of it. Princeton in the McCosh years reflected, in its style and character, both of the cultural traditions of McCosh's native Scotland. But in the very act of extending the college's environment in order to achieve these purposes, McCosh introduced new forces into the college, ones that took Princeton in a direction he could not have anticipated and would not necessarily have endorsed.

MY ACCUMULATED DEBTS in this study are many, and it is a great pleasure to acknowledge them. Over the several years of my work I have visited libraries, archives, and other depositories of needed materials. For their cheerful and competent assistance, I wish to thank the individuals of the following institutions: the British Museum, London; the Center for Historical Research, University of London; Colindale Newspaper Library; British Museum of Natural History, London; National Library of Scotland, Edinburgh; General Register House, Edinburgh; Scottish Record Office, Edinburgh; University of Edinburgh Library; Edinburgh Central Public Library; Scots Ancestry Research Library, Edinburgh; New College Library, Edinburgh; Arbroath (Scotland) Public Libary; Mitchell Library, Glasgow; Glasgow University Library; Brechin (Scotland) Public Library; Carnegie Library, Ayr (Scotland); National Library of Ireland, Dublin; Trinity University Library, Dublin; Queen's College Archives, Belfast; Yale University Library; Princeton University Library and Archives; Harvard University Archives; The Johns Hopkins University Archives; Library of Congress.

I owe a special, personal acknowledgment to three individuals: Mr. and Mrs. Alexander Lowson of Arbroath and Mr. A. M. Lawson of Brechin. They gave of their time and efforts to assist me in obtaining church records of McCosh's ministry and are a reminder to me of the kindliness and goodwill of the Scottish character.

The graduate school of the University of Wisconsin—Milwaukee provided me with summer salary in 1972 to begin research for this book. Its assistance was of critical importance. I also thank the American Council of Learned Societies for a valuable contribution to travel expenses in pursuit of my research.

In 1973-1974 I was a fellow in the Institution for Social and Policy Studies at Yale University and participated in the program in Historical and Comparative Study in Higher Education, organized by Professors Burton Clark and George Pierson. This unique opportunity for research and discussion aided me immeasurably, and I am most grateful for it.

At a late stage in the preparation of the manuscript, Professor Harold Wechsler of the University of Chicago gave it a careful reading and made useful suggestions. And for their painstaking care and conscientiousness in typing the manuscript I am most appreciative of Mrs. Ilga Strazdins, Ms. Pat Checkvala, and Ms. Jacqueline Sokol.

For all the labor and inevitable frustrations that one encounters along the way of scholarly research, I shall nonetheless cherish many memories associated with this work, above all because of my wife, Professor Diane Long Hoeveler. We shared a summer of travel and investigation in the British Isles, and here and elsewhere she was a masterful historical sleuth. Her encouragement and intellectual interest in this work have sustained my efforts throughout.

Finally, the dedication of this work to my mother and father expresses a long-standing debt of love and gratitude.

Milwaukee
October 1979

Part I

SCOTLAND

Chapter One

THE HEIRS OF KNOX

IN THE FIFTH DECADE of his life James McCosh embarked on "a labor of love." It was a work of history and philosophy, and McCosh gave to it the care and concern demanded by an age straying dangerously from "first and fundamental truths." He required more than twenty years of work, crowded into a busy academic career, to complete the project, but McCosh's *The Scottish Philosophy, from Hutcheson to Hamilton* is even today one of the richest and most reliable guides to that incredibly fruitful period of Scottish intellectual life. McCosh wrote and searched widely to obtain details of genealogy, biography, personality, and local and regional history, but the work was above all an exploration of the Scottish mind. When it appeared in 1875, McCosh had moved another step from his native land, coming from Ireland to the United States as president of one of America's oldest colleges. So he offered the book to the world, he said, as the only remaining means "of testifying my regard for my country—loved all the more because I am now far from it—and my country's philosophy." But there was something else at stake. McCosh wished "to make my work a contribution to what may be regarded as a new department of science, the history of thought, which is quite as important as the history of wars, of literature, or of civilization."[1]

THE WORLD that McCosh described in his *Scottish Philosophy* was one corner of the cosmopolitan eighteenth-century culture known as the Enlightenment. It was the age that brought international renown to the Scottish universities, secured Edinburgh's label as the Athens of the North, and of course gave a national designation to the ideas of its leading philosophers. In its cultivation of reasonableness, its obsession with social and civic virtue, its concern for improvement and faith in progress, its confidence in human nature, and its generally benevolent spirit, the Scottish Enlightenment

---

[1] James McCosh, *The Scottish Philosophy, Biographical, Expository, Critical, from Hutcheson to Hamilton* (New York, 1875), pp. iii-iv.

shared the intellectual temper of its age. But we shall observe presently some of the unique characteristics and distinguishing features of the Enlightenment in Scotland. Its relationship to the Church and the universities was especially significant and affected McCosh's own social attitudes. The names of Francis Hutcheson, David Hume, Thomas Reid, and others will recur frequently in this study, but it is important to introduce them in this chapter. American students are less familiar with Reid, Dugald Stewart, and Hamilton than they are with Locke, Voltaire, and Rousseau, although it is undeniable that the Scots exercised a profoundly greater influence in this country than any other group of Enlightenment spokesmen. From the introduction of Hutcheson's works to Harvard College in the mid-eighteenth century, through John Witherspoon's appearance at Princeton, through the extended use of Reid's, Stewart's, and Hamilton's writings in countless American colleges, to McCosh's own twenty-year tenure at Princeton, the Scottish thinkers were familiar to five generations of American college students. Indeed they dominated American academic thought for almost a century.[2] But the social context of the Enlightenment in Scotland, the burden of this chapter, is especially important and provides the setting for McCosh's early career. The background is Scottish religion.

Presbyterianism impressed itself indelibly on Scotland in the sixteenth century, but it had to fight for its birth and later for its right to live. Even when it secured that right it continued to think like an institution at war and left a permanent mark on the Scottish population. This had not been the case with the Kirk in Catholic Scotland. In 1500 wealth and power lay with the Church and nobility, and increasingly ecclesiastical life became remote from the middle and lower classes. Bishops came largely from the noble and landed classes, and this group allied itself with the Church. The Church was also an avenue for ambitious careerists, and many employed their titles to accumulate benefices or to become commendators of abbeys and priories. They also found the means to acquire heritable rights to ecclesiastical wealth and property. The royal line too found the Church, which owned more than half the real estate in the country and possessed twenty times greater wealth than the crown, an obvious source to tap. No less than six of King James

[2] See D. H. Meyer, *The Instructed Conscience: The Shaping of the American National Ethic* (Philadelphia, 1972) for the development of American moral philosophy, and Sydney E. Ahlstrom, "The Scottish Philosophy and American Theology," *Church History*, 24 (September 1955), 257-72, for that subject.

V's illegitimate sons held abbeys as commendators. Here as throughout Europe the low moral condition of the Church was becoming a public scandal or at least causing much of the population to become indifferent to its spiritual offerings. The twelve of the seventeen Scottish bishops who had fostered illegitimate children at the time of the Reformation openly invited the moralistic reaction that followed.[3] But these reasons alone do not explain the rapid Protestant takeover in the 1560s.

Middle and lower classes alike aided the Reformation in Scotland. As the medieval social structure weakened in the sixteenth century, the newer merchants, master craftsmen, and some of the lairds and gentry became rivals of the upper nobility. While that group tightened its grip on the state and the ecclesiastical offices, the gentry, finding resistance to increased rents and services from their tenants, turned to the affluent bourgeoisie for loans. Alienation from society and the Church was most acute in this new educated middle-class element. Far too often the local churches had been entrusted to impoverished, poorly educated vicars. "Neither intellectually nor religiously," writes John Knox's most recent biographer, "was the church speaking relevantly to the energetic burgesses," and these were the first people to receive the Protestant reform ideas from Germany. Suffice it to add that the Church was further negligent in its responsibilities to the poor, and this at a time when poverty, in the north especially, was severe. Church reformers pointed to the contrasting conditions of prelatical wealth and apostolic wretchedness, and the poor resented the comfortable friars who professed the ethics of poverty.[4]

That bitterness, even among the middle classes, often took the form of violent acts of public hostility against the churches, and the flames that began in Dundee soon spread to Edinburgh and other places, where destruction of church buildings showed the extent of Protestant wrath. But there was also a quiet revolution taking place, and it left a permanent legacy in Scottish social life. The Reformation was a popular movement and was accompanied by clear democratic consequences, especially in the religious life of the nation. As the movement spread throughout the country, it left ecclesiastical disorganization in its wake; formal authority broke down, to be reconstituted at the local level. After 1558 a congregational

[3] Gordon Donaldson, *Scotland: James V to James VII* (Edinburgh, 1971), pp. 12, 135; W. Stanford Reid, *Trumpeter of God: A Biography of John Knox* (New York, 1974), pp. 7-9.
[4] Reid, *Trumpeter of God*, pp. 2-3, 9; Donaldson, *Scotland*, p. 138.

system of church polity exercised an informal authority, and kirk sessions assumed some of the functions of the old church courts. Ministerial authority derived directly from the local flocks, and when the distinguishing mark of the Church of Scotland, the presbyterial system, emerged, the laity played a prominent role. While supporting a new democratic structure the Reformation church breathed venom against royal authority, and a distinctly liberal political movement paralleled the religious. From John Knox (1505?-1572) through George Buchanan (1506-1582), Andrew Melville (1545-1622), and the Covenanters, the defiance of kingly prerogative attained legendary proportions. Buchanan's *De Juri Regni* (1579) took the uncommon position that the king rules by popular will and for the good of the people. And Melville, who inherited the mantle of Knox and stands in several respects as the commanding figure of the Scottish Reformation, paid often for the sins of royal rebuke. Melville reorganized the Scottish church and the universities and outspokenly attacked prelacy and royal supremacy, while asserting the independence of the Church.[5]

It was Melville also who instituted reforms of the ministry that actually anticipated the substantial part the liberal clergy would later play in the Scottish Enlightenment. The Scottish preacher quickly secured his reputation for hellfire sermons and a moral vigilance that could tyrannize a neighborhood, but in educational attainments he was probably the equal of his counterpart anywhere in Christendom. Melville himself led the General Assembly, the governing body of the Church of Scotland, in instituting requirements that each minister have a knowledge of the Latin language, and in the second Book of Discipline imposed strict, high educational standards as prerequisites for the profession. These included "sufficient testimonials of . . . time well spent in Dialectick, Mathematics, Physics, Ethics, Economics, and Politicks, and the Hebrew tongue," and further outlined a course of study that pointed to six years' work. Similar standards were redefined a century later in 1696, although there is evidence that they were not always enforced. Nonetheless, new conditions did prevail in the ministry. Not only was its moral and educational stature enhanced, its social situation also changed. The earlier disparity between the upper nobility that staffed the episcopate, and the humble elements that staffed the rank and file, yielded to a clergy of the middle classes.

[5] G. D. Henderson, *The Burning Bush: Studies in Scottish Church History* (Edinburgh, 1957), p. 121; Donaldson, *Scotland*, p. 103.

The economic attractions improved immensely overall, but no longer included the easy and lucrative posts that had lured the aristocracy heretofore.[6]

The zeal for reform of course touched more than the churches, though the reinvigoration of religious life was the key to new Protestant ambitions. The Reformation sought the conversion of the country, and not by the gospel word alone. Although Catholic efforts at education had achieved creditable results and several of the cathedrals had attached schools, among the poor and in the countryside the record was not so good. Knox's ambition to see a parish school in every community made remarkable strides over the years, and the first Book of Discipline supported the goal by prescribing, in every town, a schoolmaster competent to teach Latin. In country parishes the minister himself, or the reader, would assume the task of elementary education.[7] The results were impressive, though the schools did as much to extend the word of John Calvin as to teach Latin and arithmetic. McCosh considered himself a direct beneficiary of this Reformation ideal and accounted it among the major blessings of Scottish Protestantism.

The Book of Discipline further outlined the specific ecclesiastical and social reforms for the new order. It called for the abolition of all abbeys, friaries, nunneries, and cathedral kirks. The local church was to be the arm of reform, supplementing the magistrate in securing good moral behavior. Drinking, brawling, swearing, licentious living, and fraud against the poor: these social and personal lapses could be controlled by private admonishment, public censure, or excommunication. And this disciplining was taken up with energy and dispatch by an eager ministry, so that by the early part of the seventeenth century few parishes lacked a kirk session. Gordon Donaldson writes: "Thus the people were being exhorted, instructed and disciplined as never before."[8] This tradition persisted tenaciously over the succeeding decades and was the central occupation, often to his regret, of James McCosh's early ministry.

Lutheran works had introduced Scotland to Reformation ideals by the time of John Knox's famous address to the St. Andrews University faculty in 1547. But ultimately Scottish Protestantism was of the Calvinist variety. Knox and Melville took much from

---

[6] Stewart Mechie, "Education for the Ministry in Scotland since the Reformation, I," *Scottish Church History Society, Records*, 14 (1963), 115-16, 123; Donaldson, *Scotland*, pp. 150-51.

[7] Donaldson, *Scotland*, pp. 262-63.   [8] Ibid., p. 150.

Theodore Beza in Switzerland and incorporated ideas of divine initiative in salvation into the Scots Confession of 1560. And Knox, the fiery "trumpeter of God," denied that the pope was head of the Church, rejected any religion not based on the single authority of Scripture, labeled the mass an abomination, and devised his own format of worship emphasizing the centrality of the sermon. Furthermore, the Scottish Reformers went the full route against civil authority in ecclesiastical affairs by proclaiming Christ "the onlie Head of his Kirk, our onlie hie Priest, Advocate and Mediator." A history full of trouble was anticipated in these words from the Confession. James McCosh prepared to sacrifice his place in the Church of Scotland to defend them.[9]

McCosh always looked back with pride to his country's heroic age. King James I of England cried "No bishop, no king" as he contrived to enforce episcopacy and the Book of Common Prayer on his reluctant neighbors to the north. His son Charles was no less unrelenting. But the Scots were of a different mind, and protesters became martyrs. Popular rebellion showed the depths of Reformed sentiments in Scotland and joined religious ideals to patriotism in the National Covenant of 1637. Twelve years later the Westminster Confession made Scotland the world's preeminent Calvinist country.[10]

The remaining years of the seventeenth century, however, did not bring religious peace to Scotland. Charles II reaffirmed the belief that Presbyterianism was inconsistent with monarchy, and his foes concurred. For "the peace of the realm" he was resolved to restore the true church of the bishops; hereafter only recognized synods and religious meetings were tolerated, and all acts favorable to Presbyterianism rescinded. In the area of McCosh's birth the new policies raised again the standards of rebellion and throughout southwestern Scotland open meetings defied the law. James II, seeking to remove all restraints against Catholics, intensified the wrath against the Stuarts, in England and north of the Tweed. His forced departure not only secured repeal of the Act of Supremacy in 1690, along with the approval of the Westminster Confession in Scotland and the reestablishment of presbyterian polity, it also introduced a decade of zealous, even vengeful religious reaction in

[9] Reid, *Trumpeter of God*, pp. 48-49, 76; Philip Schaff, ed., *The Creeds of Christendom with a History and Critical Notes, 1877*, 3 vols., vol. 3, *The Evangelical Protestant Creeds, with Translations* (Grand Rapids, Mich., 1966), pp. 437-85.

[10] J.H.S. Burleigh, *A Church History of Scotland* (New York, 1960), pp. 204-14; Donaldson, *Scotland*, pp. 313, 316.

Scotland. In the universities, and at Edinburgh especially, there began a thorough housecleaning as Anglican sympathizers confronted a "Presbyterian inquisition" determined to purge the land of all prelatical influences.[11] But as religious extremism flourished in the 1690s there was little indication how near at hand was the great transformation of Scottish life and culture. In fact, though, Scotland was at the dawning of a new age.

SEVERAL DEVELOPMENTS explain the emergence of the Scottish Enlightenment, but we notice first that nearly all its participants were weary of the religious warfare that had so long marked Scottish life. They reacted, however, not so much against religion itself as against the petty debates over doctrinal small points, and proposed instead to elevate religious considerations to the more worthy issue of the spiritual nature of humanity. As McCosh noted in discussing the background to the Scottish Enlightenment, the first part of the eighteenth century saw serious attacks made on Christianity, but those years also produced the first great modern defense of religion. The new grounds of discussion "led the great thinkers of the age, such as Samuel Clarke, Berkeley, and Butler, to spend their strength, not so much in discussing doctrines disputed among Christians, as in defending religion in general, and in laying a deep foundation on which to rest the essential principles of morality and the eternal truths of religion, natural and revealed."[12] These considerations in fact governed the Scottish Enlightenment more than any other concern, for of all the national phases of that intellectual movement in Europe, the Scottish was most sympathetic to a theistic interpretation of life, and its leading spokesmen were major influences in eighteenth- and nineteenth-century religious philosophy.

The warmer winds came first from the south. It was the English thinker Anthony Ashley Cooper, third Earl of Shaftesbury (1671-1713), who, McCosh believed, "exercised the most influence on the early philosophic school of Scotland." Shaftesbury's outline of the moral sense, which he linked to the aesthetic faculty, anticipated a major emphasis in the later writings of the Scots. But McCosh detected also in this early forebear the pretentiousness and affectation

---

[11] Burleigh, *Church History*, pp. 236-54; D. B. Horn, *A Short History of the University of Edinburgh, 1556-1889* (Edinburgh, 1967), pp. 36-37; William Ferguson, *Scotland: 1689 to the Present* (Edinburgh, 1968), pp. 103-7; Mechie, "Education, I," 3.

[12] McCosh, *Scottish Philosophy*, pp. 13-14.

of the Enlightenment, a style toward which he was ever cool. Shaftesbury, he said, "has the jaunty air of one who affects to be a man of elegance and fashion." After all, as the earl himself conceded, "to philosophise . . . is but to carry good breeding a step higher."[13] His ideas clearly impressed Gershom Carmichael (1672-1729), on whom McCosh penned an appreciative chapter in his book, and whose "Notes and Supplements" for an edition of Pufendorf's *De Officio Homines et Civis*, was, Francis Hutcheson believed, more valuable than the original work.[14] The connection was important in McCosh's intellectual genealogy, for it was Hutcheson whom he labeled the founder of the Scottish school. And with Hutcheson's career at Glasgow, Scotland began to emerge from the glacial age of Calvinism.

The "founder" deserved the title in part because his influence on Scottish thought and on Scottish religion was so great. Francis Hutcheson (1694-1746) was born to a family that had long roots in Ayrshire in the southwest but with thousands from that area migrated to Ulster. Both his grandfather Alexander and his father John were Presbyterian ministers. Francis studied at Glasgow, then taught at a private academy in Dublin, returning to Glasgow in 1729 to succeed Carmichael in the chair of philosophy. Among his writings, three contain his major ideas: his *Inquiry into the Original of Our Ideas of Beauty and Virtue* (1725), the *Essay on the Nature and Conduct of the Passions and Affections, with Illustrations of the Moral Sense* (1728), and his lectures, edited by his son and published in 1755 as *A System of Moral Philosophy*. When McCosh gathered materials for his section on Hutcheson he found among Hutcheson's letters one that was especially revealing, for it announced as the author's purpose, to "put a new face upon theology in Scotland."[15] What Hutcheson had in mind was intimated in his early works by a reference to philosophy and religion, which he says, we have made into so "austere and ungainly a form that a gentleman cannot bring himself to [them] . . . so much have they changed from what was once the delight of the finest gentlemen among the ancients." For Hutcheson, the concerns of philosophy were beauty, reason, utility, and morality, and he unquestionably looked to a new society wherein those principles would govern. Such a state was surely within reach; but it required first that we gain a just understanding

---

[13] Ibid., pp. 29-30; John Herman Randall, Jr., *The Career of Philosophy: From the Middle Ages to the Enlightenment* (New York, 1962), pp. 742-52; the quotation is on p. 743.

[14] McCosh, *Scottish Philosophy*, pp. 36-42.   [15] Ibid, p. 64.

of human nature. Indeed, we could know the human constitution as we know the Newtonian universe, by careful inquiry into its internal structure, its multiple component parts of the conscience, reason, intellect, will, and imagination. From these we can gauge the purpose of the whole and the proper course of action that God intends. Hutcheson therefore began his *System of Moral Philosophy* by directing his readers to observations and conclusions discoverable from the constitution of nature, "without any aide of supernatural revelation."[16] The nature of man was sufficient for theology.

Hutcheson's moral philosophy was a distinct movement away from the Calvinistic understanding of human nature, for the Scottish philosopher believed that individuals naturally aspire to selfless motives and that aesthetic perception is a uniform condition in all beings. But though Hutcheson was breaking new paths (or at least giving a more systematic outline of Shaftesbury's ideas), the continuity with Scotland's intellectual past has been clearly overlooked in the several commentaries on Hutcheson. The critical point of Hutcheson's moral philosophy was his idea of disinterested benevolence, though he was not the first to employ it. But for the moralist, this idea had all the self-effacing qualities that defined the Calvinist theology, especially its virtual extinction of the self in the face of a magisterial God. For Hutcheson, attaining the moral state, though human nature tends toward this supreme good, involved a conscious struggle against the individual's lower but powerful and irrational drives. The sinful nature of a fallen humanity, which, in the Calvinist account could be relieved only by the supernatural grace of God, was still, in a naturalistic sense, a reality for Hutcheson. For "appetites and passions" arise constantly, "and the checking, examining, and balancing them, is a laborious exercise." True benevolence cannot come from the will and its self-interested concerns; Hutcheson's "grace" derives from an independent faculty, the moral faculty, which is a pure and natural instinct wholly divorced from the human ego. We therefore approve of good acts independent of how they affect us, and the most selfless motivations always appeal to our consciences as the purest. But Hutcheson dared not allow the conscience too great an independence; it had to find its way with the other faculties as their governing control. Moral considerations must touch the heart and its "affections" so

[16] Francis Hutcheson, *An Inquiry Concerning Beauty, Order, Harmony, Design* (1725; The Hague, 1973), p. 25 n (vol. 1 of the two-volume *Inquiry into the Original of Our Ideas of Beauty and Virtue*); idem, *A System of Moral Philosophy* (1755; New York, 1968), p. 1.

as to check the countervailing forces of the lower self. It is important therefore that Scotland's illustrious moralist was also its chief architect of an aesthetic philosophy. The good and the beautiful were the twin ideals of his new system, and Hutcheson hoped they would provide the basis for a new social culture.[17]

Hutcheson was indeed a major influence, and no less in the Church than elsewhere. A whole generation of students for the ministry, coming from Scotland and Ireland, studied under Hutcheson at Glasgow and absorbed his dispassionate ethics. Alexander Carlyle, a major voice in the age of the Moderates, had found the divinity professor at Edinburgh "dull and Dutch and prolix" and went over to Glasgow to pursue moral philosophy with Hutcheson.[18] And there is no doubt that Hutcheson had the Church in mind when he looked to new liberalizing influences in his country. At the university he gave Sunday lectures that reached outside the regular curriculum, but afforded him the opportunity to illustrate the "truth and excellency of Christianity" and to draw the New Testament into his own moral system. Hutcheson tried especially to involve the divinity students. He urged that they deemphasize speculative essays delivered from the pulpit, and try instead to inspire moral activity, "which is the main thing the sacred orator should be concerned about." In this way, Hutcheson wrote in another of his letters, "I hope I am contributing to promote the more moderate and charitable sentiments in religious matters in this country, where yet there remains too much warmth, and commonly about matters of no great consequence to real religion."[19] He was doing that, and more. For Hutcheson's lectures cast a wide net that included reflections on politics and just govern-

---

[17] Hutcheson, *Moral Philosophy*, pp. 37, 55-58; W. Leechman, "Preface," in *Moral Philosophy*, p. xxxi. (Leechman was a contemporary of Hutcheson at Glasgow.) These norms were also important to Hutcheson's theology, though they need not greatly concern us here. The principle of benevolence, Hutcheson believed, was the quintessential quality of the Creator, who, out of disinterested love, wills and works for the happiness of his creatures. The human exercise of this quality does itself, therefore, make us like God. Hutcheson used this suggestion to bridge the chasm that separated human nature from divine nature in Calvinist theology. Hutcheson's point of view, though, was clearly humanocentric, for, besides conceding to "design" a method of demonstrating God's existence, he argues that it is from human nature that we deduce the existence of a benevolent deity who fashions us after himself. Hutcheson, *Moral Philosophy*, pp. 174-76.

[18] Andrew L. Drummond and James Bulloch, *The Scottish Church, 1688-1843: The Age of the Moderates* (Edinburgh, 1973), p. 47; Mechie, "Education, I," 121-23.

[19] Quotations from Leechman, in Hutcheson, *Moral Philosophy*, p. xxxviii (the first); and McCosh, *Scottish Philosophy*, p. 67 (the second).

ment; he articulated for his readers the ideals of civil and religious liberty, and he broadened young horizons by quoting widely from the rich and eloquent literature of ancient Greece and Rome. He numbered among his students Adam Smith and Matthew Stewart, father of Dugald, and the son later credited Hutcheson for spreading "a liberality of sentiment, and a refinement of taste, unknown before in this part of the island."[20]

But it was just this influence, from the perspective of a hundred years, that disturbed McCosh and largely determined his assessment of Hutcheson. For Hutcheson helped to inaugurate a movement whose worst effects McCosh spent a lifetime combating. The confident optimism of the Moderates, their cult of social decorum as the greatest of virtues, and the mild and secure sense of a benevolent deity: all these were later writ large in the generation of ministers who learned from Hutcheson. Among some in the wealthier and learned classes that influence led to an abandonment of the Church altogether. Reflecting back on Hutcheson in his *Scottish Philosophy*, McCosh described the development metaphorically: "The moderate party in the Church of Scotland is being crystallized by coldness out of the floating elements." It was Hutcheson's impact surely that blinded McCosh to the self-negating qualities of his system. McCosh saw too little of the Christian virtues of repentence, humility, and meekness in Hutcheson and labeled his philosophy "self-righteous in its injunctions, and pagan in its spirit." It was surely dangerous to ally the conscience to the "animal organism," not simply because it prepared the way for a naturalistic ethics, but because it left too little place for the reason and the "higher intelligence." What McCosh saw in Hutcheson he saw later in all the Scottish philosophers: a correct emphasis in defending the moral nature of man, but an insufficient grounding of that nature. McCosh himself tried to fill this deficiency, but at the very least he found something suspicious about a system that could inspire David Hume to write Hutcheson saying that "I hope [your views] will next get into the world, and then into the churches."[21] There was too much true prophecy in that.

While these quiet changes in Scottish intellectual life laid foundations for more spectacular developments to follow, visible outward manifestations of a new society appeared. For the eighteenth

[20] Dugald Stewart, "Account of the Life and Writings of William Robertson . . . ," in *The Collected Works of Dugald Stewart*, 11 vols. (Edinburgh, 1858), 10:105.
[21] McCosh, *Scottish Philosophy*, pp. 66, 85-86. The quotation of Hume is on p. 86.

century was Scotland's "age of improvement." As never before the country was prosperous, and if wealth does not always love culture, the two at least coexist handsomely. Greatly responsible for the transformation was the famous 1707 Act of Union that joined Scotland and England into Great Britain. One parliament and one flag united the countries; complete freedom of trade guaranteed the entrance of Scottish textile and agricultural products into English markets; coinage, measures, and weights were now uniform. The act, however, preserved much of Scottish law and officially recognized the Church of Scotland. Evidence of Scotland's emergence from the economic dark ages appeared everywhere, perhaps most strikingly in the rural areas where agricultural improvements made Scotland the envy of Europe. New, roomier, and more comfortable homes dotted the landscape where the huts of impoverished tillers and shepherds had prevailed a few decades before. But the capital city itself advertised best the increased affluence. Edinburgh witnessed an architectural revolution that introduced splendid Georgian structures and generated a passion for English fashion and styles. In fact the aping of English and also continental tastes was one aspect of the drive for improvement, sparked frequently by embarrassment about things Scottish and their reminders of cultural and social inferiority. More critically, the years following the Union saw the steady departure for London of much of the high Scottish nobility, while many who stayed behind indirectly partook of the anglicanizing influences by joining the Church of England.[22]

These facts are worthy of our attention for they explain the social roots of the Scottish Enlightenment and even much of its intellectual temper. The departure of the high nobility left Edinburgh as the resort of the minor nobility and gentry, suddenly thrust into the uncertain position of social leadership in the community. But these individuals assumed this position with a sense of cultural inferiority, for they lacked the traditional institutions of church, court, and cosmopolitan connections familiar to a governing elite. Nicholas Phillipson has written a provocative essay showing how this group consequently needed and sought a new social identity and public function, and came to find that identity in an alliance with a new literati drawn from the universities, the legal profession, and the Church. And here was an even more significant source of the quest for improvement, generated now by new societies of letters, sci-

[22] Ferguson, *Scotland*, pp. 48-50; Drummond and Bulloch, *Scottish Church*, pp. 83-84.

entific and mercantile organizations, salons, lodges, theaters, libraries, and patronizing academies. In all of this activity was a self-conscious effort, a quest for a collective identity and a distinct national style peculiar to this provincial culture—cosmopolitan, rational, and tolerant, but also local and particular. The social sources of the new literati in fact were manifold; coming from the rootless elements of the city were students, the younger ministers, doctors, schoolmasters, lawyers, the rising bourgeoisie, and others on the threshold of the professions. They played a critical role in a yet unshaped, new aristocratic city, and their alliance with the new social elite gave a distinct sense of purpose to that group also.[23]

Outlets for this enthusiasm abounded, and among the most interesting was the Select Club. Organized in 1754, its members included David Hume, Adam Ferguson, William Robertson, Adam Smith, Allan Ramsay, Lord Monboddo, and later Henry Home (Lord Kames). McCosh called them "the bright literary constellation of their age and country."[24] A large number of the group went into state bureaucratic positions where the passion for progress seemed to afford a practical arena for their ideas. The publications of the Select Club confronted social rather than metaphysical problems and soon won it a national reputation with many requests for admission. The interest it generated led the following year to the establishment of the Edinburgh Society for the Encouragement of Arts, Sciences, Manufactures and Agriculture, and it too bore witness to the cult of modernization. Under the leadership of the duke of Hamilton and Lord Kames, the Edinburgh Society incorporated multipurpose committees that offered prizes in chemistry, belles lettres and criticism, mathematics, history, and politics.[25] This energy, furthermore, illustrated a reformist spirit in the Scottish En-

[23] N. T. Phillipson, "Culture and Society in the 18th Century Province: The Case of Edinburgh and the Scottish Enlightenment," in *The University in Society*, 2 vols., vol. 2, *Europe, Scotland, and the United States from the 16th to the 20th Century*, ed. Lawrence Stone (Princeton, 1974), pp. 410-12, 421-25. Phillipson also suggests, though this idea is questionable, that the popularity of philosophy at the University of Edinburgh derived from the new and uncertain social situation that prevailed in that city. "The intense and continuing preoccupation of students with rationalist and empiricist metaphysics and with the foundations of knowledge was expressive of a society anxious to acquire through philosophy the certainty and stability that seemed to be absent from the wider world in which they moved." Ibid., p. 429. For another effort to explain the Scottish Enlightenment with reference to its social origins, see John Clive and Bernard Bailyn, "England's Cultural Provinces: Scotland and America," *William and Mary Quarterly*, 3rd ser., 11 (April 1954), 200-213.

[24] McCosh, *Scottish Philosophy*, p. 256.

[25] Phillipson, "Culture and Society," pp. 444-46.

lightenment that nonetheless shunned the radical and fervent anti-institutional character that often appeared elsewhere. From the time of Carmichael and Hutcheson the Scottish philosophes merged metaphysics, moral philosophy, politics, and economics; and were it more appropriate to this study, a thorough review of the Scottish Enlightenment would certainly include the pioneering work of Adam Smith, the moral philosopher and author of *The Wealth of Nations* (1776), and Adam Ferguson, whose *Principles of Moral and Political Science* (1792) many credit as a seminal work of sociology.

But how did these social changes affect the Scottish Church, in which McCosh spent his early career? The prominent place of the Scottish Enlightenment in the Church critically altered the religious style of the country and generated a reaction that brought schism in the nineteenth century; but it also gave to the Enlightenment in Scotland its distinguishing qualities. Here we must recall another important event of the early century, the Patronage Act of 1712. By this highly controversial enactment, Parliament restored the ancient patronage of the heritors, the Protestant nobles, and confirmed their power to nominate ministers to the local congregations. Although the congregations could still exercise the right of vetoing the designees, that right languished until it became the center of the storm that split the Church later. The act was intended to buttress the local power of the lairds and compensate for alleged deprivations suffered in 1690. It was an imprudent measure, and its effects quickly became clear. It afforded a happy occasion for the nobility and gentry, looking for a cultural leadership worthy of their elite status, to ally themselves with the reformist ministry that inclined to the moderate views of Shaftesbury and Hutcheson. This marriage of taste and convenience also blessed the other party, who now found the means to voice their liberal sentiments within this institutional structure of the Church. For McCosh later, and for many throughout the rest of the century, the results were all too clear: "Young men [now] sought the office [of the ministry] because of its respectability and with no zeal for the conversion of souls."[26] But this group, the new party of "Moderates," clearly intended to put a new face on the Church. It wished to be done with the pounding of the pulpit and the theology of damnation; it sought to liberate the Church from the popular prejudices of the masses, and in concert with the cultured and educated, it wished to ex-

[26] Burleigh, *Church History*, pp. 277-78; Ferguson, *Scotland*, pp. 100-111; McCosh, *Scottish Philosophy*, pp. 13-15; idem, *John Witherspoon and His Times* (Philadelphia, [1890]), p. 14.

pound the practical duties of the Christian life. The Church, too, would be a party to the age of improvement.[27]

For a portrait of the Moderate clergy most chroniclers find that Hugh Blair (1718-1800) supplies the essence. He does so, but only in the most extreme manner, sometimes to the point of caricature. Blair does inform us greatly about the new religious style in Scotland. A product of the University of Edinburgh, he was inspired to classical literary tastes by John Stevenson's lectures on Aristotle's *Poetics* and Longinus's writings on the sublime. Alexander Carlyle, John Witherspoon, and William Robertson also sat in Stevenson's classes. Blair's dissertation in 1739, describing benevolence as one of the natural laws of our moral nature, showed the influence of Shaftesbury, Hutcheson, and Joseph Butler. We may discover these laws without the aid of Christian scripture, though that source facilitates the growth and exercise of the moral nature. After a term of service in Collessie, Blair assumed the pulpit in the fashionable Canongate section of Edinburgh, and there presided over a congregation characterized by its distinctly non-Scottish gentility. Indeed, Blair outdid the other Moderates in aping English styles, including the accent. He was anxious to purge the local culture of embarrassing provincialisms and like Adam Smith, Hume, and Robertson, sought to import models of English taste. Blair made his own contribution by editing in 1754 the first complete edition of Shakespeare to be published in Scotland. This love of literary eloquence led Blair to polish his sermons and reflected a Moderate motto, expressed by Robertson, *Vita sine litteris mors*.[28] Blair moved over to the St. Giles Church, the church of John Knox, but the changed style was obvious. Blair shunned the Calvinistic doctrines of original sin, divine election, reprobation, and arbitrary grace, and "never harrangued his parishioners with fire-and-brimstone oratory." He avoided any manifestations of "enthusiasm." And surely Blair found his true calling when he assumed the professorship of rhetoric and belles-lettres at the University of Edinburgh in 1760. Here he became the high priest of Scotland's improving taste, for his own *Lectures on Rhetoric and Belles-Lettres* (1783) incorporated the essential theses of Lord Kames's *Elements of Criticism* and endeavored to show, as Hutcheson had shown with the moral faculty, that standards of high taste had a foundation in human nature and

---

[27] Drummond and Bullock, *Scottish Church*, p. 37.
[28] Robert Morell Schmitz, *Hugh Blair* (New York, 1948), pp. 11, 15, 18, 20, 61; McCosh, *Scottish Philosophy*, p. 108. Blair's expression is "Life without literature is death."

could be discovered by observing the common aesthetic sense of mankind throughout the ages. Fifteen of the forty-seven chapters of Blair's book dealt with "style" and ten with "eloquence."[29] And Blair's easy gravitation from the pulpit to the university introduces one of the fascinating aspects of the Scottish Enlightenment.

James McCosh was a graduate of two Scottish universities, both of which had helped give Scottish higher education its international renown in the eighteenth century. St. Andrews University was the oldest in Scotland, founded in 1411, Glasgow University following in 1451. The University of Aberdeen comprised King's College, established in 1483, and Marischal College, 1593. The youngest institution was the University of Edinburgh, founded in 1583 and directly under the jurisdiction of the Edinburgh Town Council. As did the Scottish Church, so also did the universities in Scotland provide an important institutional setting for the Enlightenment. To a remarkable degree, the spirit of improvement that generated the various societies for arts and industry was directly reflected by the curricular innovations that brought students to Scotland from many parts of the world. The Glasgow Chemical Society, for example, met in the university and included leading Glasgow industrialists as well as professors like Adam Smith and students from the campus. This was a major point of contrast to the English universities, where a heavily classical curriculum maintained its hegemony throughout the eighteenth century, especially at Oxford, and restricted devotees of practical science and technological research to the scientific clubs and societies outside the universities. Scotland's outstanding contributions to medicine in the eighteenth century came through the work of her universities, Glasgow at first, then Edinburgh, where William Cullen and James Alexander added genuine luster to each. The medical chair at Edinburgh had been established in 1685, but accomplished instruction began with Alexander Monro's appointment to the anatomy chair in 1720. Scotland thereafter attracted an international student body, as the University of Edinburgh matriculated more Englishmen than Scots, and a notable handful of Americans, including Benjamin Rush.[30]

Out of the medicine program crystallized a host of new academic

[29] Schmitz, *Hugh Blair*, pp. 66, 98.

[30] Douglas Sloan, *The Scottish Enlightenment and the American College Ideal* (New York, 1971), pp. 11-13. The Scottish universities drew heavily from the nonconformist ranks of the English and Irish population. Barred from Anglican Oxford, Cambridge, and Trinity, these sons from middle-class homes predominated heavily in the north. Ibid., p. 65.

branches of the sciences, and materia medica, chemistry, and natural history emerged as separate disciplines. The practical bent of the Scottish universities became more pronounced with the establishment of new academic chairs at Edinburgh, including ones in natural history, astronomy, agriculture, and even, in 1739, midwifery. Actually, these reforms derived from other Scottish innovations. Since the early Reformation period when Andrew Melville's reforms took effect, specialized professors had been replacing, slowly at first, the "regent"system by which one instructor guided the same class through the entire college course. Although this system lapsed for a while, William Carstares (1649-1715), a leading figure of the Church and principal of the University of Edinburgh, cooperated with the Town Council in 1708 to place the arts curriculum under six specialized professorships. This change meant that students could take the courses they chose, creating a kind of "elective system" that reinforced the practical tendencies of Scottish higher education and helped break the hold of the classics. By 1731 probably more than half the students at Edinburgh had not studied Greek and Latin, and many, from home and abroad, were taking advantage of opportunities to pursue rhetoric and belles-lettres, mathematics, and "universal civil history," each of which had become separate subjects. While elsewhere the Enlightenment was inspired by the pagan spirit of the ancient classics, the tendency in the Scottish universities was away from that emphasis, which diminished, though of course did not eliminate, the influence of Greece and Rome in the national culture.[31] Furthermore, we should not be surprised to find that in the Scottish universities, where the bent toward the practical and the empirical was so strong, and a concern for the ideal and theoretical far less pronounced, a parallel quality emerged in the Scottish philosophy, with its concern for "common sense" and its faith in the veritable report of reality provided by the senses. McCosh later hoped that that characteristic could be the basis of a reconstructed American philosophy.

In the age of the Moderates the Church was a partner with the universities in providing the forum for Enlightenment ideas. We have seen that the prominence of the liberal clergy brought the Church out of its Calvinist intellectual past, but its influence in the universities also preserved in the Scottish Enlightenment a posture friendly to religion. Freedom of discussion at Edinburgh, Lord Cockburn recalled, "was not in the least combined with scepticism

[31] Horn, *Short History*, pp. 40-41, 48, 53; Sloan, *Scottish Enlightenment*, pp. 18, 23.

among the students."[32] We will notice presently how important to the development of the Scottish philosophy were intellectuals who launched their careers in the Protestant ministry and maintained a cordial connection with it. But this important institutional alliance is best reflected in the person who, as much as any other, provides us with an individual portrait of the Scottish Enlightenment. William Robertson (1721-1793) was the principal of the University of Edinburgh for thirty years after 1762, and, after Gibbon, the most famous historian of the eighteenth century. But he was also the highest authority in the Church of Scotland, where he firmly defended the right of patronage. Robertson was born in Borthwick in Midlothian, and his early interest in intellectual matters led him to follow his father into the ministry. He typified the many liberal clerics who joined the Select Society, and he himself founded the Royal Society of Edinburgh, "for the cultivation of every branch of science, erudition, and taste." He moved easily into the principalship of the University of Edinburgh where his scholarship immensely enhanced his prestige. Robertson had published in 1759 his *History of Scotland during the Reigns of Queen Mary and King James VI,* and this he followed by his three-volume masterpiece, *The History of the Reign of Charles V,* and, later, the *History of the Discovery and Settlement of America* (1777). Though Robertson engineered a more liberal Church policy, which terminated religious tests for new professors and relaxed the Church's moral prescriptions, he nonetheless rigorously enforced church discipline and defended the Westminster Confession. His twin position of leadership in the churches and universities in Scotland was by no means exceptional, and in fact Robertson continued his Sunday preaching in the Edinburgh churches throughout his tenure as head of the university.[33]

If the Church and university gave birth to the Scottish Enlightenment, what then of David Hume (1711-1776)? If the spirit of the European Enlightenment was the spirit of criticism and skepticism, then certainly Hume was its purest voice. Peter Gay's celebrated interpretation of the Enlightenment calls Hume "the first modern pagan" and concludes with a special section on Hume's critique of religion. And this consideration gets us to the heart of the matter; for the Scottish Enlightenment was almost everything that Hume was not, and Gay's thesis seems quite plausible only because he virtually ignores the other Scottish philosophers; Hutcheson, Reid,

[32] Henry Cockburn, *Memorials of His Time* (Edinburgh, 1856), p. 38.
[33] Stewart, "Account of Robertson," 10:103-12, 134, 185-90; Horn, *Short History*, p. 76; Drummond and Bulloch, *Scottish Church*, pp. 65-66.

and Stewart receive no consideration in his treatment. Hume was much influenced by Hutcheson and enjoyed intimate friendships with Blair and Robertson. But it was Hutcheson who countermined Hume's effort to gain a philosophy chair at Edinburgh when he sought it in 1745. And Hume despised the churches as much as they feared him. In fact he left a deathbed regret that he had not liberated his native country from "the Christian superstition." No doubt, Hume was utterly out of place in Scotland, intellectually above all. McCosh attributed to Hume's happy years in France his materialism and skepticism and regretted that Hume did not live to see the terrible legacy of his philosophy in the social disorders and degeneration of that country. McCosh need not have been so severe, for the good-natured Hume suffered in loneliness and lived "affrighted and confounded with that forlorn solitude, in which I am plac'd in my philosophy."[34] Hume lamented that his famous *Treatise on Human Nature* came "dead-born from the Press" in 1739, but we need feel no pity on this count. More than any other work, it set the stage and defined the terms for the second phase of the philosophical movement in Scotland.

The subtitle of Hume's work was "An Attempt to introduce the experimental Method of Reasoning into Moral Subjects." The inspiration of Newton and the new vogue of the inductive sciences set Hume, and after him the other Scottish philosophers, to erecting a science of human nature by an empirical and introspective methodology. Hume and the others reached dramatically different conclusions, but McCosh to the end of his life defended the method that Hume forced onto the Scottish school. Hume's discoveries, shocking to his own generation, need not detain us here, for they are a shadow that hangs over much of this history. We note only that Hume described a most uncertain world, for his thinking disposed with all general abstract or intuitive ideas, made light of all epistemological theories that tried to confirm the certitude of our knowledge of the external world, and deprived that world of first and last causes. For Hume there were no absolutes; he was a thinker who found it far easier to doubt than to believe. Hume's ethical theories actually took their cue from Hutcheson's contention that moral thinking is grounded in the affections, but he then ran to the extreme with that hypothesis. In the end he had no use for Hutcheson's moral faculty and derived benevolence from sympathy and social utility, and justice from utility alone. But Hume too rejected

[34] Peter Gay, *The Enlightenment: An Interpretation: The Rise of Modern Paganism* (New York, 1968), pp. 401, 403, 65.

the simplistic self-love theories of morality, and his thoroughgoing skepticism was intentionally constructive, seeking the surest grounds for philosophizing. Though Hume's "Essay on Miracles" and his powerful *Dialogues Concerning Natural Religion* (1779) confirmed his enduring reputation as a critic of theism, McCosh, at least, feared these works less then Hume's others. For like the rest of the Scottish school, McCosh looked for a defense of religion through a more careful inquiry into "fundamental truth." Hume, though, was setting the terms of the debate.

MCCOSH'S HISTORY tells how the Enlightenment entered a second phase when the Scottish northeast became philosophically articulate. The Highlands, and its cultural center at Aberdeen, had long exercised independence in political and religious matters. Cut off by mountains and firths from the south, the northern region communicated directly by sea with England and France. Here also Jacobinism and Episcopalianism flourished, for the strong Calvinistic and Covenanting principles that reigned among the Lowlanders had made little advance beyond the Grampian Mountains. Only when the counterrevolutionaries breathed their last at Culloden in 1745 did the northern region become one with the rest of the country. In the meantime, the graduates of King's and Marischal spread their influence.[35] McCosh greatly appreciated the work and significance of the early leader of this group, George Turnbull (1698-1748), and regretted that his name had gone the way of his discarded study on ancient paintings, as depicted by Hogarth's famous "Beer Street" painting. McCosh credited Turnbull's works as the first full commitment to the inductive method in the investigation of the human mind. Yet another admirer of Turnbull was his student Thomas Reid.[36]

Thomas Reid (1710-1796) also constructed a science of the human mind and hoped that it would undo that of David Hume. Reid

[35] H. Trevor-Roper, "The Scottish Enlightenment," *Studies on Volatire and the Eighteenth Century*, 58 (1967), 1651-52; McCosh, *Scottish Philosophy*, pp. 91-95; Sloan, *Scottish Enlightenment*, p. 24. Trevor-Roper strains to show that nearly every inspiration for the Scottish Enlightenment came from the periphery of Scottish culture and society and hence emphasizes the Jacobite north as a major influence. His argument is clearly overstated, and this chapter reflects my belief that the Scottish Enlightenment came overwhelmingly from liberal elements that grew out of the Scottish Presbyterian culture and the tensions within it. Even the major figures of the Aberdeen school, Turnbull, Campbell, Reid, and Beattie, all served in the Presbyterian ministry. But see Trevor-Roper, "Scottish Enlightenment," 1652-58.
[36] McCosh, *Scottish Philosophy*, pp. 99-101.

The Heirs of Knox

was born in Strachan, Kincardineshire, not far from Aberdeen. Here in the Grampian Mountains his father for fifty years had presided over a parish, continuing a family affiliation with the ministry that extended back to the Reformation. His mother, Margaret Gregory, was descended from one of Scotland's most famous intellectual families, and two of her younger brothers pioneered in physics at St. Andrews and Edinburgh. Reid entered Marischal College at the age of twelve and there studied under Turnbull. He served as college librarian for two years afterward and in 1737 began a ministry at New Machar. Not until 1752, after Reid had read and published on mathematics and ethics, did he gain an appointment as professor of philosophy at King's College. Despite its curricular innovations, King's still employed the regent system (one that Reid, incidentally, defended because he believed it afforded greater opportunity for the instructor to influence the moral growth of his students), and this enabled Reid to teach mathematics and physics, two favorite subjects.[37] But like other Scottish professors, Reid worked outside the university too, and he was one of the founders of the lively Aberdeen Philosophical Society.

Established in 1758 with six members, including Reid, John Gregory, and George Campbell, the society expanded, adding James Beattie in 1760, and became the major forum for a surprisingly large number of philosophers in the Aberdeen region. It made precise provisions for its activities, meeting twice monthly in an appropriate tavern in one of several towns, and securing ample provisions for culinary enjoyment. (Half the funds were earmarked for the port.) Regulations also allowed that "any member may take a glass at a by-table while the president is in the chair, but no health shall be drunk during that time." Members of the society took turns reading philosophical dissertations. Examining the records of the society, McCosh noted that "many of the speculations of the Aberdeen philosophers, afterwards given to the world in their published writings, were first laid before this society." Among the most suggestive of the records he found was a letter that Reid penned to Hume in 1763; it tells us much about the emerging course of Scottish philosophy.

> Your friendly adversaries, Drs. Campbell and Gerard, as well as Dr. Gregory, return their compliments to you, respectfully.

[37] Ibid., pp. 194–95; Dugald Stewart, "Account of the Life and Writings of Thomas Reid, D. D.," in *The Works of Thomas Reid, D. D.*, ed. Sir William Hamilton (Edinburgh, 1854), pp. 3–5.

A little philosophical society here, of which all three are members, is much indebted to you for its entertainment. Your company would, although we are all good Christians, be more acceptable than that of Athanasius; and since we cannot have you upon the bench, you are brought, oftener than any other man, to the bar; accused and defended, with great zeal, but without bitterness. If you write no more in morals, politics, or metaphysics, I am afraid we shall be at a loss for subjects.[38]

Reid removed to Glasgow University in 1764 where he succeeded Adam Smith in the moral philosophy chair. One year later he published his *Inquiry into the Mind on the Principles of Common Sense*. In moving to the growing Glasgow metropolis, Reid was entering a different society, and his reaction reflects the differences of the northern and southern culture. For Hutcheson and the Moderates notwithstanding, south of the Grampians in lowland Scotland, the popular culture of Calvinism still flourished. Reid reacted harshly to the tastes of the general populace and the "fanatic" character of its religion. It was even more regrettable that "the clergy encourage this fanaticism too much, and find it the only way to popularity."[39] Reid therefore fell in easily with the Moderate party, and the second phase of the Enlightenment continued like the first to be reflected in the style of the Church. Reid's affiliation with the Church may have been a disturbing factor to Hume, who wished at first to dismiss Reid's *Inquiry* when the author sent him a copy and asked if he had done justice in the work to Hume's ideas. Hume wished that the "parsons" would leave him alone and in peace, but conceded on reading the *Inquiry* that it had much merit, even if it was not ultimately convincing. Reid published his major philosophical works, *Essays on the Intellectual Powers of Man* and *Essays on the Active Powers of the Human Mind*, in 1785 and 1788 respectively.

Reid's ideas, like Hume's, will be an important theme in this work, and it is better to explore them in greater detail later. We note here only that Reid, like Kant, awoke from his dogmatic slumber by reading Hume; he conceded in his introduction to the *Inquiry* that he had been at one time wholly persuaded to Berkeley. But if Hume and the European Enlightenment register the will to skepticism, then Reid and the Scottish Enlightenment register the will to believe. Reid took up Hume's epistemological challenge and carefully distinguished between perception and sensation to break

[38] McCosh, *Scottish Philosophy*, pp. 227-29.
[39] Quoted by McCosh, *Scottish Philosophy*, p. 205.

the Humean confinement of our knowledge to our impressions of external objects. He also clarified the distinctions, inherited from Locke, between primary and secondary qualities. McCosh would find both distinctions suggestive, if not entirely accurate. Reid was moving in an important direction in trying to show that we know the external world directly, and he even went so far as to demonstrate that we have no reason at all to believe in the "mental states" that theoretically separate us from external objects; yet another distinction, between conception and other mental acts, was needed to allay the confusion. Baruch Brody has shown that Reid's most important effort transcended the debate with Hume, since that skeptic merely registered a long tradition that dated from Descartes. For Descartes wished to get along with as few intuitional judgments as possible, and Reid insisted that such a meager residue as he left could not be the basis of a constructive philosophy; it could never tap all the resources of our knowledge. For these judgments of common sense, though usually incapable of proof, were the essential constructs of all our reasoning and knowledge.[40]

The flowering of the Scottish intellect in the last decade of the eighteenth century brings our subject back to Edinburgh. Sooner or later all intellectual movements become fashionable, objects of finery to be consumed and flaunted. The capital city was now flourishing as never before, the winter home of Scotland's wealthiest families and the receiving port of their sons, who came to the university. Over this happy society presided the high priest of the Scottish Enlightenment in its last years, Dugald Stewart (1753-1828). Stewart in fact brought together many of the themes we have outlined so far, and, more than any other individual, he personified the society and culture of his country. Stewart was born in Edinburgh where his father, the mathematician, taught at the university and where Dugald enrolled at the age of twelve to pursue

[40] Baruch A. Brody, "Introduction," Thomas Reid, *Essays on the Intellectual Powers of Man* (1785; Cambridge, Mass., 1969), pp. x-xvi, xxxiii. Two other products of the Aberdeen Philosophical Society reinforced the Scottish philosophy's case against Hume. George Campbell (1719-1796) was the son of an Aberdeen Presbyterian minister and entered the ministry himself in 1746. He graduated from Marischal and became principal of the unversity in 1759 after having already succeeded Reid in the philosophy chair. His *Dissertation on Miracles* (1763) was a direct reply to Hume's piece on that subject. James Beattie (1735-1802) was also a Marischal graduate and professor of moral philosophy and logic there after 1760. His *Immutability of Truth, in Opposition to Sophistry and Scepticism* (1770) was an intemperate attack on Hume that made Beattie as renowned as any of the philosophers in his day. McCosh, *Scottish Philosophy*, pp. 239-45, 230-38.

studies with John Stevenson and Adam Ferguson. The latter was the greater influence, for Ferguson's instruction embodied ethics, history, and politics, and Stewart tried later to make his political philosophy extend directly from moral philosophy. It was Stevenson's encouragement, however, that sent Stewart to Glasgow for a year to learn what he could from Reid. Stewart returned to Edinburgh after one semester to assist his ailing father in the mathematical courses and took over the chair in 1775. A decade later he was appointed to the chair in moral philosophy, but the versatile Stewart continued to teach math and astronomy. In 1792 appeared his *Outlines of Moral Philosophy*, which followed by a year the first volume of his *Elements of the Philosophy of the Human Mind*. He was a member of the General Assembly of the Church of Scotland where he acted as representative elder for the university. But it was in the classroom that Stewart made a truly unforgettable impression.[41]

McCosh thought Stewart representative of the best and the worst of Scottish society and taste in the age of the Moderates. Stewart cultivated language and style to the point of ceremony. Lord Cockburn remembered that "his gesture was simple and elegant . . . and his whole manner that of an academical gentleman . . . there was eloquence in his very spitting." His home was the resort of the best society of Edinburgh. "The weekly reunions in his house," McCosh wrote, " . . . happily blended the aristocracies of rank and letters [and] were for many years the source of an influence that most beneficially affected the society of the capital." At a time when revolution and war ravaged the Continent, sons of aristocrats departed from tradition and stayed in Scotland for their education. Others came from England and some even from abroad. The well-to-do and the usual middling ranks that characterized the Edinburgh student body all had their rough edges smoothed by Stewart's polished decorum and rhetorical grace. From his classroom went some of the most influential men of British culture and politics: Lord Palmerston, Earl Russell, Sir Walter Scott, Sydney Smith, Francis Jeffrey, Cockburn, Thomas Brown, James Mill, Henry Brougham, Thomas Chalmers, and Henry Jardine. But they received more than eloquence from Stewart. Cockburn found him "uniformly great and fascinating" and relished his lectures on ethics, economics, and politics. "He breathed the love of virtue into the whole generation of his pupils."[42]

[41] John Veitch, "A Memoir of Dugald Stewart, with Selections from His Correspondence," in *The Collected Works of Dugald Stewart*, 10:vii–xxxii.

[42] McCosh, *Scottish Philosophy*, pp. 282–83; Cockburn, *Memorials*, pp. 19–22.

He breathed more than that. Stewart reflects better than any of the other Scottish thinkers the opposing spirit of the Scottish and French enlightenments. French philosophical materialism, religious skepticism, and the temper of revolution were the lurking menaces that Stewart resolved would never despoil his native land. He was the veritable temper of the Whig conscience, devoted to liberty in politics and trade, obsessed with social order. His aristocratic clientele worshiped him, but he was the voice of the aspiring British bourgeoisie. His philosophy came from Reid, but he did more than the teacher to spread the Scottish philosophy. Stewart's lectures pressed indelibly on his students the moral and spiritual nature of man, defended natural religion, and, McCosh believed, thoroughly discredited the "low sensational, materialistic, and utilitarian" viewpoint. In fact McCosh credited Stewart with almost singly checking the radical spirit in Scotland.[43]

THE WORLD of the Moderates and the philosophers was the happy and benevolent exterior of a nation whose inner soul lived with all the uncertainties of life and feared desperately for its salvation. The popular mind of Scotland was on the whole unconcerned with the comfortable culture of the Enlightenment and listened instead to its own ministers pronounce upon the terrible fate that awaited the sinners of this world. Civic virtue and the accoutrements of taste loomed far less consciously in the minds of Scotland's rural farmers and small traders, its common housewives and cotters, for they had long heard other voices than those who cultivated decorum and literary fashion. We misconstrue the cultural picture of Scotland, in fact, if we lose track of the persistence of older habits and ways of thinking throughout the eighteenth century. McCosh knew too well that in a sense the Enlightenment was largely irrelevant to the Scottish population. There were always elements who kept alive the old Covenanting spirit—Ralph and Ebenezer Erskine, Thomas Boston, the Calvinist Seceders, plus a dedicated party of Evangelicals. And, wrote McCosh, "from the time of Hutcheson, there is a felt and known feud . . . between the new philosophy and the old theology."[44] The Erskines had no time for "the dry sapless harangues of a heathenish morality," and the popular preachers generally stressed the fallen and corrupted state of humanity, the need for repentance, and the divine mercy of God. Like Boston they

[43] James McCosh, "Introduction," "Outlines of Moral Philosophy by Dugald Stewart," in *Outlines of Moral Philosophy* (London, 1865), p. iii.
[44] McCosh, *Scottish Philosophy*, p. 86.

looked to Scripture for its saving knowledge, which no ethical account of human nature could furnish, and emphasized "converting grace" as the critical element of experiential religion. The Moderates, Boston charged, knew no more of Christ than a man knows of honey and vinegar without tasting the two. And of Ebenezer Erskine it was said that if you never heard him preach, then "you never heard the gospel in its majesty."[45]

In the eighteenth century all the tensions between Moderates and Evangelicals that would later split the Church were festering. The Patronage Act was never popular outside the ranks of the Moderate ministers and aroused bitter opposition from the beginning. John Bisset's *Modern Erastianism Unveiled* (1732) proclaimed that patronage made the churches slavishly dependent on the aristocratic and powerful, and insulted the dignity of the popular ministry by requiring refinement and polished prose in the pulpit. Splinter groups emerged, as well as independent praying societies like those in Glasgow. Ralph Erskine's party, suspended from the Church by the Moderates in the General Assembly, formed the "Associate Presbytery" and recalled the memory of the Covenanters in asserting the right of congregations to elect their ministers.[46]

Nor should we forget the immense esteem in which the popular preachers were held by many in the lower ranks of the Scottish population. These surprisingly literate and educated people knew Scripture to a degree that was legendary. John Wesley's Arminianism could not dent their stubborn Calvinism. Nor did the popular minister of Scotland confront what plagued his English counterpart, a tradition of popular disdain for the cleric that made him, if not an object of neglect, an object of ridicule. Liberal historians like Buckle too easily dismissed the Scottish ministry for its narrowness and bigotry. McCosh thought otherwise. "The evangelical and the seceding ministers of these days are quite as erudite as the academic men who despised them, and are holding firmly by old truths which the new philosophy is overlooking." Nor did the moralism of the popular preacher make him as drab as the familiar caricature, for many congregations thought their minister "nane the waur for his tunes on the wee sinful fiddle."[47]

Many of our familiar impressions of the Scottish folk derive of

---

[45] Ferguson, *Scotland*, p. 121; Henderson, *The Burning Bush*, pp. 141-42, 148-49.

[46] Henderson, *The Burning Bush*, p. 129; Drummond and Bulloch, *Scottish Church*, pp. 41-42, 50-51.

[47] Peter Bayne, *The Free Church of Scotland: Her Origin, Founders, and Testimony* (Edinburgh, 1893), pp. 22-24; Burleigh, *Church History*, p. 294; Ferguson, *Scotland*, p. 109; McCosh, *Scottish Philosophy*, p. 89.

course from the earthy poems and songs of Robert Burns (1759-1796). He was the voice of the people in their secular habitats and culture, and he provides us with another perspective of the world beyond the philosophers and Moderates. McCosh recalled that "in my boyish days" he had " 'kissed the cup to pass it by' " with those who had drunk and been drunk with Burns. Kissed but not consumed, he said. For the evangelical McCosh laid on Burns much responsibility for the "national vices" of the late eighteenth century.[48] Burns did speak for a lively, ribald, fun-loving strain in the Scottish population, and certainly for many whom the Moderates in the Church never reached. For McCosh this neglect was the most serious mark against the Church in the era of high culture, and one for which it paid dearly. But as a witness to his times and his people, Burns's insights are wonderful, his poetry a delightful, refreshing, unforgettable portrait of the age and place. For example, probably no description, however much a caricature his may be, can match the parade of popular preachers that Burns summons in his "Holy Fair." There is "Moodie."

> Here how he clears the points o' Faith
>   Wi' rattlin and wi' thumpin!
> Now meekly calm, now wild in wrath,
>   He's stampin, an' he's jumpin!
> His lengthen'd chin, his turned-up snout,
>   His eldritch [unearthly] squeel an' gestures,
> O how they fire the heart devout,
>   Like cantharidian plaisters

And there is "Russell."

> But now the Lord's ain trumpet touts,
>   Till a' the hills are rairin
> And echoes back return the shouts;
>   Black Russell is na sparin:
> His piercin words, like Highlan' swords,
>   Divide the joints an' marrow:
> His talk o' Hell, where devils dwell,
>   Our vera "sauls does harrow"[49]

Joy and sorrow, the hedonism that the Church disdained, the plight of the poor and the heavy burdens of life: as do people everywhere, Scotland lived with these realities, and Burns sketched them in memorable rhyme. The preachers preached the straight and nar-

---

[48] McCosh, *Scottish Philosophy*, p. 270n.
[49] *The Poems and Songs of Robert Burns* (London, 1906), pp. 51, 54.

row path and warned against the broad one that leads to perdition, while the poor lived with reminders of their mean estate. And there is a simple wisdom, perhaps, in the philosophy of "The Jolly Beggars."

> What is title, what is treasure,
>   What is reputation's care?
> If we lead a life of pleasure,
>   'Tis no matter how or where![50]

But we find these respites of pleasure but seldom. Burns set one of his famous poems, "Man Was Made to Mourn—A Dirge" "along the banks of Ayr," where McCosh grew up. The poet meets an aged traveler who sobers the young man's blithe spirit by reminders of the cruel injustices of life.

> See yonder poor, o'erlabour'd wight,
>   So abject, mean, and vile,
> Who begs a brother of the earth
>   To give him leave to toil;
> And see his lordly fellow-worm
>   The poor petition spurn,
> Unmindful, though a weeping wife
>   And helpless offspring mourn.[51]

Sometimes a kind of secular Calvinism comes through in Burns's perspective. The ways of God are arbitrary and not accountable to human reason; divine justice is not of this world. So Burns concludes his poem by a stark reminder that if there is any universal justice, it comes in a cruel way, in death.

> O Death! the poor man's dearest friend,
>   The kindest and the best!
> Welcome the hour my aged limbs
>   Are laid with thee at rest!
> The great, the wealthy fear thy blow,
>   From pomp and pleasure torn;
> But, oh! a blest relief for those
>   That weary-laden mourn![52]

Thus the popular ministry and the secular Burns stood as notable exceptions to the prevailing confident and optimistic mood of the Enlightenment in their country.

[50] Ibid., p. 85.
[51] Ibid., p. 11.
[52] Ibid., p. 12.

McCosh made it the central purpose of his early career to reconcile these opposing movements in Scottish culture, to infuse Moderatism with the spirit of the Gospel and the sense of human sin and need for grace, to smooth the rough edges of the popular preaching by a respect for culture and high taste, and to enliven the work of the churches where the injustices that Burns decried frustrated the ideal of a Christian society. But for all the intellectual luster of the Moderates, McCosh believed that the popular preachers, the children of this world, were wiser in their own generation than the children of light. "The philosophers were laudably engaged when they were unfolding man's intellectual, esthetic, and moral nature; but they missed the deepest properties of human nature, when, in the fear of the ghosts of fanaticism, they took no notice of man's feelings of want, his sense of sin, and his longing after God and immortality." In their confidence and faith in moral human nature, the Moderates overlooked the darker personality of the human soul, and its irrational strain. The evangelical preachers on the other hand, "erred so far as they opposed the refinement and liberal sentiments which the moral philosophers were introducing."[53] But Scotland was now entering a new period when these less attractive realities could not be ignored. The first inroads of the Industrial Revolution in Great Britain were manifest in Edinburgh, and especially in Glasgow's Clyde River region. A swelling population, much of it coming from Ireland, crowded the city districts and spread violence and immorality, to say nothing of poverty, among the working classes. How remote was this world from that of the Moderates in the Church, and how neglectful toward it was the Church, were all too clear. "These things," write Drummond and Bulloch, "were to bring to an end the world which [the Moderates] knew."[54]

McCosh later experienced the effects acutely. At the very same time that Dugald Stewart was dissertating with eloquence on the beauty of moral virtue, there was growing up around his university a new population, "sunk in vice and degradation . . . which is not to be arrested by any remedy which the mere philosophic moralists have propounded."[55] In its social consequences but also in its intellectual, McCosh believed, this was the severest shortcoming of the Enlightenment in his country. "The Glasgow professors may not have been directly responsible for the growing wickedness; but

[53] McCosh, *Scottish Philosophy*, pp. 86-87.
[54] Drummond and Bulloch, *Scottish Church*, p. 68.
[55] McCosh, *Scottish Philosophy*, p. 299.

there was nothing in their teaching, moral or theological, adequate to the task of purifying the pollution coagulating all around them."[56] For these reasons, we shall see, McCosh joined the evangelical ministry.

And so had McCosh's predecessor at Princeton, John Witherspoon (1723-1794). McCosh in fact delighted to quote from Witherspoon's famous *Ecclesiastical Characteristics* (1753), a sharp satirical offering that measures the depths of the cultural and social warfare of Scotland's two religious parties. With tongue clearly in cheek, it summarizes the Moderates' "credo":

> A minister must endeavor to acquire as great a degree of politeness in his carriage and behavior, and to catch as much of the air and manner of a fine gentleman as possibly he can.
>
> Good manners is undoubtedly the most excellent of all accomplishments.
>
> A moderate man is quite at liberty to indulge in what his forefathers regarded as sin, but which have now been called by a hopeful youth *good-humored vices*.
>
> You must be very gentle in dealing with heretics, and speak of them as men of exalted genius.
>
> As to preaching, you should not dwell much on sin and repentence: these topics may be liked by the vulgar, for whose favor we do not care, but they are obnoxious to the upper classes, with whom the patronage of the kirks lies and with whom we wish to associate.
>
> You must, above all things, use refined and polite language, and not talk of grace, but of virtue—not of conviction of sin, but a sense of honor and beauty.
>
> You must speak with Francis Hutcheson on morality, . . . order, proportion, taste, and the nice balance of the affections.
>
> It is thus we do all we can to make religion respectable, especially to the better classes. We never mention hell or damnation in the ears polite of my lords and ladies.[57]

Not to make religion respectable, but to make it respected. That was one goal of the new religious party, and it was now its turn to "put a new face" on the Church.

[56] Ibid., p. 206.
[57] Quoted by McCosh, in *Witherspoon*, pp. 14-17.

Chapter Two

A Scottish Education

THE SOUTHWESTERN PART of Scotland is a land of rolling hills and meadows, small valleys intermixed with rugged moorland terrain. Here for centuries farmers had struggled to wrest a living from stubborn but not unfruitful soil, and here shepherds tended their numerous woolly flocks. Here too the enduring characteristics of the lowland Scot are writ large. Over many years the people of this region had won for themselves a reputation for dogged determination, for dour resolution, and for an obstinateness equal to the land they tilled. Such is the naturalistic root of their character. It shows in this description of the Lowlanders: "severe in aspect, restrained in manner, serious in thought. . . . At the same time they are full of deep feeling which is sometimes shown in a passionate and silent concentration of their energies, their spirit, and their intellects upon some task."[1] In the extreme far west of this lowland territory is the town of Ayr, nestled comfortably on the Firth of Clyde and looking out to the southern tips of the Western Isles. Twenty miles inland is the village of Patna, where, just above the banks of the River Doon, stands a sturdy stone farmhouse, where James McCosh was born on April 1, 1811. McCosh long retained in his memory the peaceful bucolic setting of these Ayrshire environs, but his life and personality reflected another quality of the region—the religious tenacity, the defiant Protestantism for which the people of the southwest had once been famous. For in this region a formidable dissenting tradition dated back to the Lollards of Kyle, renewing its vigor later when Knox's reforms led to prohibitions against the celebration of mass. Presbyterianism here, in defying the Stuarts, produced many martyrs, and McCosh, ever ready to invoke the memories of the Covenanters, could recite the names from the very tombstones of the parish church where he was baptized.[2]

[1] Moray McLaren, *The Scots* (Harmondsworth, England, 1951), p. 63.
[2] W. Stanford Reid, *Trumpeter of God: A Biography of John Knox* (New York, 1974), p. 22; Gordon Donaldson, *Scotland: James V to James VII* (Edinburgh, 1971),

McCosh was born fifteen years after the death of Robert Burns, whose poems and songs have provided lively and lasting impressions of the Ayrshire region. Burns knew both the people and the landmarks of the territory and gives us in "The Bridge of Ayr" a quaint little dialogue about the old and new monuments on the river of that same name. The word derives from the Celtic "ar," meaning "clear," in contrast to the Celtic "dhu," or "dark," the origin of "Doon." This river, flowing just down the hill from the McCosh farm, wanders through deep bog at its head, acquiring a black, mossy tinge that it retains the rest of its course. Almost within sight of the McCosh farm was Loch Doon, once the seat of one of Scotland's ancient castles, but later destroyed by Robert the Bruce in 1298 to keep it from the possession of an invading English army. Here, where McCosh fished as a boy, stood the ruins of an important memorial to the distant history of his country.[3]

The McCoshes of Scotland follow an uncertain line of descent that traces back to Ireland. Black's *Surnames* finds the earliest use of the name in Erad MacCoise, the first of several of this family listed as voters in the parish of Quilton, in the sixteenth century. "McCosh" means "son of the footman," or "courier." It is not uncommon in the southwest of Scotland, but not usually found elsewhere. The earliest traceable ancestor of James was Jasper McCosh, who died in 1729. He is buried with his son John and wife Janet Nivan in the small cemetery of the Straiton parish where McCosh attended with his family. But interestingly, the inscription on the

p. 338; J.H.S. Burleigh, *A Church History of Scotland* (New York, 1960), p. 246; Andrew L. Drummond and James Bulloch, *The Scottish Church, 1688-1843: The Age of the Moderates* (Edinburgh, 1973), p. 40.

[3] *New Statistical Account of Scotland* (Edinburgh, 1846), 6:1-3, 21; James McCosh, "Incidents of My Life in Three Countries," unpublished typescript in the Princeton University Archives, 9. This is apparently the original and only typescript of McCosh's autobiography, and its history is rather mysterious. It arrived at the Princeton University Archives in February 1974, sent by some very distant relatives of McCosh. There is no indication of its whereabouts before this time. One can recognize readily that it is the basis of William Milligan Sloane's *The Life of James McCosh: A Record Chiefly Autobiographical* (New York, 1896). Sloane, who edited and rearranged the work, was on McCosh's faculty at Princeton and published the manuscript two years after McCosh's death. The front page of the work has a large gold seal and bears a very large signature of McCosh. It also has this curious inscription: "Young Men of Princeton! This I leave for thee upon the occasion of my visit to the Saturn Club of Buffalo on April 18, 1888—for I see that you will call for it twenty years hence, to the hour, being in the vicinity of midnight April 18, 1908. Dean Murray is with me." "My Life," the form used in future citations, contains some details that Sloane omitted from his edition.

tombstone refers to John McCosh of "Carskeoch," an indication that the farmhouse of that name, owned by John's son Andrew, James McCosh's father, was long in the family possession. The McCoshes had no aristocratic titles and seemed quite typical of the large group of prosperous, rural, and middle-class Presbyterians in the southwest. McCosh's mother was Jean Carson McCosh, also of Straiton parish, who married Andrew July 19, 1796. She gave birth to seven children including a son who died after three years in 1811, leaving James the only surviving male. James was the fifth oldest of the children. Jean's father, John Carson, had large farm holdings in the moorland area of Loch Doon. On her mother's side, the McClymonts, she was joined to a family with strong connections to the earlier Covenanters.[4]

Andrew McCosh was unquestionably an enterprising and hardworking farmer who did much to improve his family's condition. The home, still standing today in Patna, has had only a small addition since his day, and, with its sixteen rooms and the small servants' quarters that run down from the house along both sides of the driveway, it suggests that one reference to James's father as "wealthy" is not inappropriate.[5] The later eighteenth century saw important changes in Scottish agriculture and the rise of a class of farmers who made their work a scientific art, employing technology for greater efficiency and farming for profit. Andrew McCosh typified this business-minded group and shared the advantages of those in the southwest who had a ready access to the booming Glasgow market in the Clyde district to the north. The breakdown of the older ways meant also that smaller farms were being absorbed into larger ones. Many landlords went to London or Glasgow and left their property under the management of larger tenants, finding it easier to collect their rents from one large tenant. Andrew McCosh managed a considerable amount of property and, it appears, was able to draw enough remuneration to purchase additional lands for himself. In any case, as the documents of the Scottish Record Office indicate, he accumulated not only new lands, but two houses in Maybole and Whitehall.[6] In the Patna area Andrew

[4] George F. Black, *The Surnames of Scotland* (New York, 1964), p. 477; "Parochial Register of Straiton, County of Ayr 1644-1819," in the Register Office, Edinburgh; McCosh, "My Life," 1-4, 9.

[5] J. M. McBain, *Eminent Arbroathians: Being Sketches Historical, Genealogical, and Biographical, 1178-1894* (Arbroath, 1894), p. 317.

[6] William Ferguson, *Scotland: 1689 to the Present* (Edinburgh, 1968), pp. 171-74; McCosh, "My Life," 3-4; "Sasines, Ayrshire, 1781-1806," in the Scottish Record Office, Edinburgh.

McCosh, or "Carskeoch" as he was always called by his neighbors, was both well-known and well liked.

Andrew McCosh died when James was only nine years old, but the son retained some memories of his father and the family's life together on the farm. James remembered "an intelligent man, much addicted to quiet reflection." He was modest in taste and moderate in style despite his affluence, traits that probably owed much to his strict Presbyterian habits. Andrew "took the book" every Sabbath evening and held family worship with the children and servants gathered in attendance. "I remember the graphic expressions which he often used in his prayers," McCosh later wrote, "especially in confessing his shortcomings." McCosh recalled with even greater intensity the weekly trek that the family made over hill and dale to the nearest parish church in Straiton. This village, from the Gaelic word meaning "deep valley," lay five miles to the south of the McCosh farmhouse and required a painstaking journey of several hours through rocky moorland. "Some of my most interesting recollections gather round these Sabbath excursions. My father and mother who went regularly to the house of God, rode on horseback. We young people walked on foot (except that after my father's death I rode on his pony)."[7] From his father also McCosh derived some of his intellectual interests. Many years later he told a Yale College commencement audience that his first acquaintance with America came through a large book that his father brought home one day, a copy of Timothy Dwight's *Systematic Theology*.[8] A generous man, Andrew McCosh shared his prosperity with others. James remembered that almost nightly a beggar, sometimes families of beggars, appeared at the farm. These unfortunate products of a changing economy were always sure to receive a bed in the stable and a "substantial supper and breakfast" from the proprietor.[9]

Young James assumed important responsibilities at an early age, for upon his father's death he took charge of the sheep and cattle and learned through this and other tasks the business and workaday aspects of farming. He never came to love the work, but he always credited the experience with giving him a practical sense of things and sharpening his observation. Perhaps from this early training comes that remarkable quality of McCosh that none can miss, even when reading his most complex philosophical works. For always his writing was leavened with the graphic and ordinary example

[7] McCosh, "My Life," 20-21
[8] *New York Observer*, July 28, 1870.
[9] McCosh, "My Life," 5-6.

from everyday life, but never so as to spoil the technical treatment of the issues under consideration. Even with the pressing demands of the farm, however, McCosh found time for self-indulgence and for a romantic abandonment amid the rivers, hills, and glens that he always cherished. "There I wandered at my own free will, following my thoughts and fancies among green and heather hills and valleys, among trees . . . and brooks. . . . Here I became interested in wild plants, such as lillies, roses, meadow-sweet and foxgloves." There were auditory pleasures to be had also. "I was accustomed to hear a flock of geese cackling in my father's house, and on the romantic hills in the neighborhood I ever heard the lapwing, the curlew, and the grouse." All around Carskeoch scurried hens, ducks, geese, and turkeys. And to complete this circle of intimates the Scottish lad enjoyed a collie named Famous and a pony called Cuddy.[10]

Andrew McCosh did not intend his son to be a farmer, and the intellectual encouragement he gave him anticipated a career in the ministry for James. Preparation for that career was a long-established pattern that led through a parish or burgh school to one of the Scottish universities. The parish school was one of Scotland's celebrated institutions, long esteemed as an emblem of the nation's social democracy. These schools were egalitarian in their social composition, for with the exception of a distinctly wealthy class, both the rich and poor of Presbyterian Scotland took it for granted that they would be educated in the same classroom. The long legacy of Knox had secured the attendance at schools of the children of Scotland in every region, and in far greater proportion than their English counterparts. This fact made entry of the poorer classes into the business and professional ranks more open than anywhere else in Europe. The parish schools were neither compulsory nor free, but they were an honored tradition and universally recognized as a parental obligation.[11]

The quality of any individual school depended of course on local conditions, especially since the Education Act of 1803 confirmed parish control of the schools and entrusted their well-being to the local patrons. Some patrons took great pride in their trusts, and this

---

[10] James McCosh, "The Association of Ideas, and Its Influence in the Training of the Mind," in *Lectures Delivered Before the Dublin Young Men's Christian Association* (Dublin, 1862), 16; idem, "My Life," 2, 22.

[11] Ferguson, *Scotland*, p. 204; Laurence James Saunders, *Scottish Democracy: The Social and Intellectual Background* (Edinburgh, 1950), p. 242; Drummond and Bulloch, *Scottish Church*, p. 187.

seemed to be particularly the case in Ayrshire. McCosh provided few details of his parish school education, referring only to the intense study of catechism and Scripture, with Latin also a major focus of the curriculum. But it was likely that he reaped some of the advantages of the changing educational patterns in the late eighteenth century. Many schools were now introducing practical instruction in such techniques as bookkeeping, surveying, and navigation. Inculcation of a literate piety, however, remained the fundamental aim of the schools, so the intellectual and moral emphasis persisted. Schools like McCosh's were typically one-room structures, and in Ayrshire were often under the direction of a recent Glasgow University graduate who taught all subjects. William Boyd's history of education in Ayrshire cites a local advertisement that gives us some indication of prevailing practices: "Wanted for the parish of Dundonald, a schoolmaster qualified to teach English grammar, writing, arithmetic, book-keeping, Latin, and the elements of mathematics: if French and Greek, an additional recommendation. Correct principles and moral character are indispensable."[12] The parish school education, McCosh noted, was not likely to produce the genius of a Burns or Carlyle, but it did instill logical and commonsensical habits of mind.[13]

McCosh always boasted that he knew the Scottish character well and was never at a loss for illustrations drawn from the rich store of memories from his youth. Centuries of struggle with a harsh climate and stubborn soil had given the Ayrshire people a kind of grim tenacity that perfectly complemented their stern religion. McCosh admired the sober habits of work that prevailed in his region, but admonished his countrymen for their excessively dour exterior. Later the American New Englander would suggest to him an appropriate comparison, the more so when the distinctive canniness of each type was considered. The Scot exuded a dogged and stubborn independence at times and went to extremes to contain his feelings within. If he had better self-discipline than the Irishman, he was the latter's inferior in displaying warmth and love to his friends and neighbors. The trait rankled McCosh, who recalled an incident when he went to console a bereaving father at the funeral of his son. The man's only comment: "This is a fine day Sir!" But McCosh knew that a tender heart and fierce loyalty thrived beneath the cold outer surface. Nor did he find his community lacking in

[12] Ferguson, *Scotland*, p. 201; Saunders, *Scottish Democracy*, pp. 242-43; William Boyd, *Education in Ayrshire through Seven Centuries* (London, 1961), pp. 96-98, 101.
[13] McCosh, "My Life," 13.

intellectual nourishment outside the home and school. On the farms and in the village shops he encountered minds that engaged him in profound subjects, mundane and metaphysical.[14]

But in the long run, McCosh's assessment of his early situation was a negative one. This owed nothing to his personal situation, which was happy; rather it was a judgment that grew with the years. For even in his youth McCosh sensed the contrast of ideals and fact, of past and present. Everywhere in the Patna and Straiton region were memorials of a heroic past, and beyond, where he visited with his father, were Drumclog and Bothwell Brig, where, he was told, lay the ashes of his valiant forefathers. But now the local tombstones "were moss grown and little attended to." The people were mostly immersed in the cultivation of their land. They admitted that these old worthies were good men, but congratulated themselves on living in more enlightened, more "moderate" times.[15] McCosh had additional visible evidence of the local and disquieting impact of Moderatism. The minister who baptized him, later a moral philosopher at St. Andrews, "never pressed home the doctrines of grace in his hearers," and religion waned in his parish. McCosh preserved a volume of the man's sermons and found "not one word of gospel from beginning to end." Nowhere in his district did the ministers preach of sin and salvation, and this group of ministers, "commonly well-educated and of good manners," had no moving influence on the general populace. McCosh knew even at this time that here was the surest legacy of the Patronage Act of 1712.

Here also were the roots of his own concerns for the ministry and his eventual involvement in the evangelical cause. More was at stake, however, than the mere fact of religious decline. The level of moral values was low, by-product of a smug and comfortable age. Intemperance had become fashionable, McCosh lamented. A farmer could not sell a horse or cow without being obliged to offer a drink to the buyer, and teachers gave toddy to the students who presented the largest Christmas gifts. McCosh even recalled, with dead seriousness, a situation in which people gathered for a funeral in such a state of inebriation that they forgot to bring the coffin and corpse. Almost as bad was the prevailing "illicit intercourse" among the younger set. Local standards did not permit open courtship, so uncompromising lovers took a cue from Robert Burns, and

---

[14] Ibid., 13-14, 20.

[15] James McCosh, *Christ the Way, the Truth, and the Life: A Sermon* (London, 1867), p. 24; idem, "My Life," 10.

"whistle and I'll come to you, my lad" secured the means for undetected romance.[16] McCosh's judgments came from a later perspective, but his prejudices were clearly set by the time he set off for Glasgow to begin his university education. Vexed at the signs of declining times and troubled about the state of his own soul, young James now entered a world far removed from the rural familiarity of farm and community.

McCosh's student career spanned eight years at Scotland's two most famous universities. If we are looking ahead to his years at Princeton, we can see in his academic experience of two European institutions the seeds of some of the significant reforms that McCosh tried to introduce in the American school. But those efforts at reform derived in part from the particular nature of the Scottish universities, distinct in some important ways from both the British and the Continental. Moreover, McCosh pursued his studies amid an intensive cultural debate that raised fundamental questions about the nature and purpose of university training. Although only much later did the significance of this debate become apparent to him, it was by then clear that McCosh had internalized much of the Scottish style of higher education, and he rejuvenated Princeton with its spirit.

McCosh was completing his third year at Glasgow University in 1826 when a British Royal Commission issued a lengthy report that summarized its investigation of the four Scottish universities. The controversy surrounding this report only brought into sharper focus a long-standing quarrel of cultures. The report was detailed and precise, giving accounts of the administrative structures of the Scottish institutions and very specific data about individual professors, courses, and pedagogical arrangements.[17] But for most interested persons the heart of the matter was the ancient question of the classical languages. The contrasts between the British and the Scottish universities can easily be overstated, and studies such as G. E. Davie's *The Democratic Intellect* often err in that direction. But Davie is right to the extent that the Scottish institutions and their defenders often did conscientiously articulate ideals by which they distinguished a northern educational emphasis from the English. Their objective, specifically, was a democratic system that stressed

---

[16] McCosh, "My Life," 16-18.
[17] See *Report Made to His Majesty by a Royal Commission of Inquiry into the State of the Universities of Scotland* (London, 1831).

philosophy and professional training in contrast to a heavily classical program appropriate to social-class elitism. A well-known work in Scotland was the *Outlines of Philosophical Education, Illustrated by the Method of Teaching the Logic Class in the University of Glasgow*, (1818) by Professor George Jardine (1742-1827). McCosh probably met Jardine, though he had retired from the logic and metaphysics chair in 1824. McCosh certainly knew Jardine's work, however, and endorsed it strongly. Jardine was a strong advocate of including English literature and composition in the curriculum and successfully defended the Scottish preferences in education against the "almost exclusive" degree of attention given to the classics in England. The Scots, Jardine said, believe it to be "of greater consequence to the student to receive instruction in the elements of science both physical and mental, than to acquire even the most accurate knowledge of the ancient tongues, when all that is most valuable in them may . . . be obtained without so great a sacrifice of time and labour."[18]

The Scottish universities by no means ignored the Greek and Latin languages, but they cultivated them less intensely and even judged them to have a function different from that assigned by the English. Davie argues that "in Scotland . . . the national taste for philosophy, aided by a fairly thorough training in it, coloured the whole approach of the native classical and mathematical Professors to their respective subjects, and gave their teaching . . . a characteristically humanist flavor."[19] Some Scots criticized the English classics-dominated curriculum as excessively philological, too much a study of words and language at the expense of intellectual content. The Royal Commissioners, on the other hand, believed that the Scottish curriculum plunged too fast into stressing mastery of concepts; they even denied the premises of philosophical culture as the substance of a university education. But the Scots did emphasize a philosophical underscoring of their professional preparation, making education an exercise in mastering first principles. Francis Jeffrey, editor of the *Edinburgh Review*, defended the universities of his country. Their broad and philosophical program, he said, coincided with a democratic concern that education be accessible to a fairly large portion of the population. The need was for an education to

---

[18] Quoted in Drummond and Bulloch, *Scottish Church*, p. 191; James McCosh, *The Scottish Philosophy: Biographical, Expository, Critical* (New York, 1875), p. 316.

[19] George Elder Davie, *The Democratic Intellect: Scotland and Her Universities in the Nineteenth Century* (Edinburgh, 1961), p. 13.

liberalize and promote the intellectual advance of "the mass of our population."[20] To the English, who often judged the strenuous Presbyterianism of their neighbors from the rational and milder perspectives of Anglicanism, classical education in Scotland was shallow. The Royal Commission undoubtedly felt that the rough edges of the people beyond the Tweed might be honed and refined by the mellowing influence of ancient civilization.

Young James McCosh surely bore many rough edges himself when he arrived from the rolling farm country of the Doon in the booming metropolis of Glasgow. As recently as the early eighteenth century Glasgow had been a small and very lovely town. Daniel Defoe could still call it the most beautiful little town in Great Britain, and Tobias Smollett concurred. Noted for its cathedral and its university, Glasgow evidenced the tone and tenor of a church and academic community. But already the traders of Glasgow, small businessmen and craftsmen, were turning the town into a port and setting its face westward toward the new world and southward toward England. The Union of 1707 in fact soon proved to be a boon to Glasgow commerce, opening the markets of England to free trade. By mid-century Glasgow merchants were at the height of their prosperity, importing heavily from the American colonies and shipping on to France and the Netherlands. The tobacco trade, especially, spawned a hardy new aristocracy, quite distinct from the landowners, who regarded this new elite as upstarts. The new group did win a reputation for haughtiness and arrogance, flaunting their brash new clothing styles all over the city, but out of their investments developed another phase of Glasgow's economic explosion. Now new industries in clothing, furniture, footwear, glassware, and hardware intensified the commercial and industrial spirit of the place. Cotton too played an important role, giving birth to spinning mills all over the Clyde River region, and in the rest of the country also. These mills drew workers from the rural

---

[20] Saunders, *Scottish Democracy*, pp. 307-9, 358-59; Davie, *Democratic Intellect*, pp. 16, 27-28, 31-32, 212. Further indication of British, and especially British aristocratic opinion of Scottish higher education, is supplied by John Hamilton Grey, who attended both Glasgow and Oxford in this period. The Scottish universities, he said, "were good for imparting general knowledge to the middle and lower classes . . . but they are not calculated to educate gentlemen. . . . The English system is more successful in giving to the student the tone and style of learning and literate association." Quoted by W. H. Mathew, "The Origins and Occupations of Glasgow Students, 1740-1839," *Past and Present*, 33 (1966), 79. For a dissenting British opinion, one that disparages an archaic British system and praises the Scottish, see "State of the Universities," *Quarterly Review*, 36 (1827), 216-68.

areas and produced another group of ambitious and talented capitalists exemplified by the industrious Montieths. Meanwhile, the efforts of James Watt and William Murdoch, plus a host of others, confirmed Glasgow's reputation for mechanical genius. The city's business classes were a sophisticated lot, entrepreneurially and socially. The famous Tontine Hotel in the city gathered proud and black-velveted merchants into its coffeehouse exchange and witnessed the grandest balls of the century. Many citizens met in weekly political and economic clubs where the spirit of Adam Smith and the passion for improvement were manifest.[21]

These tendencies had accelerated in Glasgow by the time of McCosh's arrival in 1824. The population had expanded from 43,000 in 1780 to about 175,000 in the latter year, making it Scotland's largest city and securing it the name "second city" of Great Britain. The Napoleonic wars had impaired Glasgow's economy, but the marks of recovery were evident soon thereafter. Now another boom period was underway; the spirit of the place was buoyant and optimistic, self-confident, aggressive. "Ambition . . . animated all classes." There were examples everywhere of prosperous captains of industry who had once walked the city streets barefoot, and who now inspired lofty hopes in the imaginations of thousands who came from Highlands and Lowlands, Border Hills and the Hebrides.[22] (Soon thousands more would come from Ireland out of sheer economic necessity.) Glasgow also boasted of its democratic spirit. Its society was in constant flux; it had little of the reserve of Edinburgh nor the stability that moderated the pace of change in that city. Naturally it became the arena of larger ambitions, but these dangerously concealed the appalling and oppressive conditions that lurked beneath, and the invariable outlets for human despair that grew in their midst. Few took note of the fact that every twelfth house in Glasgow had become a drink shop.[23]

These conditions were more apparent though, to one in McCosh's situation. McCosh arrived in the city with his older cousin Samuel Walker McCosh who was appointed to help the thirteen-year-old through his adjustment to his new situation. The two found a room together in a "confined and unhealthy" part of the city. This was normal procedure for the Glasgow scholars. The Scottish universities had not adopted the residential college system of Oxford and Cambridge, and students traditionally fended for

[21] C. A. Oakley, *The Second City* (Glasgow, 1967), pp. 2-3, 6-7, 15, 24-27, 87.
[22] Ibid., pp. 31-32, 82, 152.
[23] Ibid., p. 41; Saunders, *Scottish Democracy*, pp. 97, 109-10.

themselves by finding quarters in the city. McCosh from the very beginning then knew firsthand what was becoming one of the major social problems in the country. The city swelled with the new industrial working classes whose arrival, compounded by the precarious situation of labor in the early phase of the Industrial Revolution, created conditions of extreme poverty and crowded housing equal to any in Great Britain. The humble student quarters of McCosh and his cousin set him in close proximity to the poor districts and the appalling squalor they displayed. Their memory never left him, and they influenced significantly his own career in the Church of Scotland. Soon McCosh was to be one of a growing number of Evangelicals who flayed the Church for its indifference to these conditions.[24]

McCosh vaguely anticipated a career in the ministry as he began his course of studies at Glasgow. No other profession, at least, appealed to him. And though confirmed in his religious convictions, he needed conscientiously to cultivate piety. He prayed "earnestly but not regularly and systematically" and was conscience stricken over his lack of consistency.[25] If McCosh ever underwent a conversion experience he never mentioned it; yet by the time he finished university training there was no want of faith in his outlook.

McCosh spent his first year at Glasgow in the preparatory department, then matriculated in the Greek class with Professor Daniel K. Sandford. His academic program took him through Greek and Latin and the usual double philosophy dosage of the Scottish universities, which embraced separate courses in logic and metaphysics, plus moral philosophy. He also pursued mathematics and physics. The classics did not come easily to him, though he did not complain that he was ill-prepared. He preferred Greek to Latin and relished Homer for his superb portrayal of human types. For the most part, though, he judged the curriculum uninspiring, a fact that owed much to the timidity of the professors, who drew fees from each student and feared dissolution of their sustenance by expansion of the curriculum. James did well in his courses, but was not overall a stellar student, a fact he attributed later to his young age. The prize lists of Glasgow University mention McCosh twice, in his junior and senior years. They indicate, interestingly, that he excelled most in mathematics and natural philosophy.[26]

[24] Saunders, *Scottish Democracy*, p. 113; McCosh, "My Life," 30-31.
[25] McCosh, "My Life," 22.
[26] Ibid., 24-25; Saunders, *Scottish Democracy*, p. 317; *Prize Lists of the University of Glasgow, (1788-1833)*, collected by W. Innes Addison (Glasgow, 1902), pp. 295-96, 308.

The Glasgow years were a turning point in McCosh's life in at least one important respect, for they produced an intellectual awakening, and a love for philosophy especially, that carried him through his ministerial career and into university teaching. James Mylne was the professor of moral philosophy, toward whom McCosh remained somewhat ambivalent. He was one of the few political liberals on the faculty, and by the strongly religious minded was labeled a Socinian. Mylne's analysis of the human mind, McCosh believed, was "meagre," and there was little that was stimulating in his system of ideas or his manner of presenting them. But in a narrow sense Mylne, who held the chair from 1797 to his death in 1839, fulfilled his task. He covered a wide range of philosophy, and McCosh found much "wisdom" in his treatment and critique of the different schools. Mylne also employed a technique popular among many Scottish professors, the requirement that students prepare weekly essays, some presenting them to the class. McCosh believed the practice highly useful, keeping his mind sharp and active. Interest in philosophy at the university was such that this class had its own ample library.[27]

But beyond Mylne's classroom there was much more to explore. McCosh was discovering Thomas Brown's sophisticated treatises on metaphysics and mental science, and, in his fourth year, plunged into Hume. Here he recognized immediately his greatest intellectual challenge, one that haunted him the rest of his life and energized his own philosophical efforts. McCosh cultivated philosophy amid the quiet inspiration that comes in solitude. He was a large, shy young man, who made no permanent friends at the university. But he was also a young man of drive and resolution. His insatiable appetite for books prompted impatient demands of the librarian that the newest works be immediately at his disposal. These efforts of course were unproductive, so when the desire demanded instant satisfaction, he dipped into his own pockets for the pennies to borrow from the city's circulating libraries. By this means he also succumbed to a persistent romantic bent. He devoured the novels of Scott and the poetry of Byron, and this indulgence supplied some of the most exciting material for his education.[28]

As McCosh remembered the institution, Glasgow University exuded the spirit of Moderatism. Thomas Chalmers's movement

---

[27] *Royal Commission Inquiry*, p. 247; James Coutts, *A History of the University of Glasgow: From Its Foundation in 1451 to 1909* (Glasgow, 1909), pp. 349-50; McCosh, *Scottish Philosophy*, p. 365.

[28] McCosh, "My Life," 25, 28.

had struck the city only recently, and the new generation of Scottish academics that would introduce evangelical influences into the universities had not yet made an impact. Two Presbyterian ministers who taught at the university were uninspiring and "jejune" in their instruction, typical, for McCosh, of the Moderate style. The university had a chapel for students and faculty, but services were so bland and unnourishing that McCosh, with several other students, attended the Glasgow churches on Sundays and there found spiritual nourishment. The divorce of religiosity from the life of the university, a legacy, McCosh judged, of the Moderate era, remained for a long time a troublesome factor for him, and it was a tendency he struggled energetically to resist when he himself exercised academic responsibilities.[29]

McCosh perceived the disturbing influence of Moderatism in the lives of the students themselves. That influence was not the sole cause of the students' moral laxity, but it did promote a general indifference toward their welfare. McCosh's own situation, as we noted, was typical of the Glasgow undergraduate, cast into the city to provide for feeding and clothing himself. The complete lack of any *in loco parentis* supervision on the part of the faculty allowed dangerous vices to flourish among this very youthful student population. McCosh saw the results firsthand. He was one of about two dozen students who had come up from the land of Burns to the big city, all acquainted with each other. One evening several of them met in one of the students' homes and began a card game that led to a resolution to convene nightly for this purpose and to play for money. McCosh discovered pervasive cheating among his friends when these winnings became substantial and noticed shortly that this evening indulgence was inaugurating a lapse into worse habits. "It is one of the bitterest recollections of my life," he later wrote, "that of those who associated together, more than one-half fell into vice of various kinds, such as drinking, licentiousness and gambling, and never came to hold any position of importance."[30] McCosh undertook to rescue his friends by alerting some of his professors, but he met universal indifference. Most said directly that it was not their business. Writing at Princeton many years later McCosh recalled these events and asked: "Whose business was it?"[31]

[29] Ibid., 28-30.   [30] Ibid., 31.
[31] James McCosh, *Religion in a College: What Place It Should Have* . . . (New York, 1886). This pamphlet, abstracted from McCosh's debate with President Eliot of Harvard, summarized McCosh's lifelong belief that college students must be constantly under the moral and religious surveillance of their professors.

McCosh left Glasgow University in 1829. He had made considerable strides in his intellectual growth, though by his own admission had achieved nothing that made a lasting impression on his professors. Mostly he had acquired from the Scottish university what the Scottish universities were best at providing—an education in philosophy and the sciences. Much of the effort, to be sure, was his own, but Glasgow generally made the human and instructional resources available. He had also learned and perceived enough to recognize that a social and spiritual crisis was mounting in his own country. In many ways Glasgow was uniquely situated to magnify and dramatize that crisis. McCosh could see already the revitalized role the churches would have to play to meet the problems at hand. But the public policy of both church and state, he believed, hinged on the resolution of fundamental intellectual questions. The warfare of skepticism and faith already attained in his thinking broad philosophical and scientific outlines. James McCosh, the Glasgow University graduate, would be a minister in the Church of Scotland, but he would first equip himself with the most advanced education he could obtain. That resolution now took him forty miles eastward, down the road to Edinburgh.

McCosh spent five years in Scotland's great capital city. These were years that were to prepare him for a ministerial career in the Church of Scotland, and McCosh at that time could not anticipate that the intellectual experience would lead further to an academic life and to a college presidency. But preparation for the Scottish ministry did not lead along a narrow path of theological studies. McCosh found his richest rewards at the university in the opportunities it afforded for advanced studies in science and philosophy, and so thoroughly did he immerse himself in these fields that by the time he left Edinburgh in 1834 he had outlined the general philosophy that he labored thereafter to expound. In fact, the University of Edinburgh during the years McCosh attended gave the young scholar a unique opportunity to develop his system. The evangelical movement was exploding everywhere in Scotland, and at the university its most dynamic leader and its most important intellectual defender, Thomas Chalmers, occupied the chair of divinity. But the Moderate era was also entering its last illustrious phase, and Sir William Hamilton, in the chair of universal and civil history, assured Scottish preeminence in philosophy. McCosh, who was influenced by both these men, would ever after mediate their thought. Chalmers and Hamilton, the one profoundly spiritual, the other the pure breath of intellect, virtually exemplified two models of life. McCosh drew upon both and wove Chalmers and Hamilton together in such a way as to make evangelical religion and Scottish Moderatism compatible. That was to be his own contribution to the Scottish intellectual traditions.

McCosh always thought Edinburgh "the grandest city in the world." Indeed, few who visit it ever forget the magisterial splendor that is Edinburgh. "With its imposing castle rock; with its picturesque mountain, Arthur's Seat, overlooking it; with its deep ravines on which its ancient city is built; its historical palace of Holyrood; its massive university," Edinburgh, McCosh believed, was a visual distillation of Scottish history. The eastern "haar" (fog) that "creeps up from the sea and searches us through and through with its chilliness" oozes into the eerie atmosphere that envelops much of this country of the far north.[32] Whereas Glasgow had become the city of commerce and industry, Edinburgh was the city of the professions. Glasgow looked out to the Atlantic and to the new world; Edinburgh, tucked under the Firth of Forth a few miles to the north, looked out to the North Sea and back to the old world. Only forty miles apart, the two cities sat with their backs to each other. Glasgow was buoyant, bustling, volatile; Edinburgh, serene, imperturbable. A visitor once contrasted the shouting, laughing, jostling, and unselfconsciousness of the street crowds of Glasgow to the stiff rectitude of the strollers on Princes Street, the formal air of the bankers, lawyers, financiers, and scholars of Edinburgh. The very mood of Edinburgh takes its note from the massive castle that surveys the city from on high and sets the moderate and even-tempered pace of its life. Merely to walk the streets of Edinburgh is to be conscious of the long, long past.[33]

The young divinity student at the university experienced Edinburgh during a second phase of its great cultural century. The city had lost some international prestige, but remained wholly secure as the cultural and political capital of Scotland, center now of its educational, religious, and legal institutions. And even within Great Britain, Edinburgh was the publishing leader, publishing more than all other places combined. In literature the great age of Sir Walter Scott was enjoying its last years. No one thrilled with greater excitement to that writer's resurrection of Scotland's romantic past than McCosh. He never met Scott personally, but remarked that he saw him occasionally at his clerical desk at the Court of Session.[34]

[32] McCosh, "My Life," 33.   [33] McLaren, *The Scots*, pp. 83-84, 88-89.
[34] Ferguson, *Scotland*, p. 219; McCosh, "My Life," 34.

But the enduring legacy of Edinburgh's age of splendor lies about the city in its architectural monuments. Great public buildings and magnificent private homes, most of them concentrated in the New Town, described the social aspirations of the capital. The Georgian classical revival enhanced the disciplined and controlled exterior of the city, but these new edifices, Moray Place, Anslie Place, Saxe-Coburg Place, unquestionably denoted an aspiration for elegance that was Edinburgh's distinguishing mark. McCosh could see all this firsthand, for the university too shared in the classical renaissance. The famous Robert Adam had laid plans for the university before the French Revolution, but these had to wait until 1816 for Robert Playfair to complete. Now a spectacular library, with heavy square and circular columns lining the upper interior, and a magnificent museum, combining elevated Venetian windows with Corinthian columns, embellished the campus around Charlotte Square.[35]

As a student McCosh found the mood of Scotland's two main cities roughly represented in the academic life of their universities. The atmosphere of Edinburgh, he wrote, was "literary and philosophical, and to a small extent scientific." There was less here of the "commonplace" than at Glasgow University. On the other hand, the Edinburgh campus was more personal, especially in the divinity department, where a corps of students met frequently and discussed intellectual matters at professors' homes. McCosh partook of these events, even carried his concern and interest into some of the student societies. Outside, momentous issues were pressing, especially in the Church's impending crisis, and the divinity students, through the Theological Society which McCosh joined, had a ready forum for debating all of these. McCosh was already taking the radical stand of the Evangelicals, and argued with fellow students the merits of the congregational veto and the spiritual independence of the Church. In his five years at Edinburgh, McCosh matured from the shy and timid student of Glasgow, to a formidable and self-confident thinker. He won increasing respect from classmates and from his professors.[36]

Chalmers and Hamilton were the two focal points of McCosh's academic life at Edinburgh, but there were other opportunities to be had, and McCosh seized them. Students were free to take a great

---

[35] A. J. Youngson, *The Making of Classicial Edinburgh, 1750-1840* (Edinburgh, 1966), pp. 193-202. This entire work is a full, beautifully picturesque treatment of the subject.

[36] McCosh, "My Life," 41, 44-45.

variety of courses and, next to philosophy, McCosh found the sciences most stimulating. McCosh, who collaborated later at Queen's College on a lengthy scientific treatise, and who was renowned in the United States for his evolutionary views, found Edinburgh alive with pre-Darwinian scientific hypotheses. James Hutton first articulated the uniformatarian theory of terrestrial evolution and with John Playfair's vigorous efforts to disseminate that theory, gave the Scots a prominent place in the controversy. But Scotland reflected diverse views, and while McCosh attended the lectures of Robert Jameson, he heard the theories of a Wernerian, or catastrophist, geologist. Jameson was something of a local celebrity, and townspeople, from silversmiths to civil engineers, joined students at his lectures. Drawing fees from all who attended, Jameson put together a popular course of no less than 273 lecture topics, covering an incredibly wide array of scientific subjects. He was also keeper of the Natural History Museum, giving it a deservedly high reputation at home and abroad. And only his students enjoyed free access to it. Another eminent scientist at Edinburgh was Sir John Leslie, who made significant strides in physics, though it is not clear whether McCosh studied with him. McCosh studied with him. McCosh did, however, read Lyell's *Principles of Geology*, whose three volumes appeared while McCosh was still at Edinburgh. Already it was becoming clear to him that science was immensely useful to the defense of faith.[37]

Besides Chalmers, another partisan of the evangelical movement in the universities was David Welsh (1793-1845), professor of church history. McCosh knew Welsh before his arrival in Edinburgh in 1831, for Welsh preached at St. David's Church in Glasgow, drawing McCosh and several others of the students into the town. Welsh, the son of a sheep farmer in the Clyde region, had studied under Thomas Brown at Edinburgh and later became his biographer. He, like Chalmers, was joining in the effort to combine piety and intellect, to offer a reasoned defense of evangelical religion. McCosh described him as "a philosopher, teaching, not philosophy, but the doctrines of the cross, always in a philosophic manner and spirit." Welsh's major influence and his role in the disruption of the Church lay ahead, but McCosh found his work with Welsh at the university extremely satisfying. He received from the professor enthusiastic encouragement for his scholarly efforts.[38]

[37] J. B. Morrell, "Science and the Scottish University Reform: Edinburgh in 1826," *British Journal of the History of Science*, 3 (1971), 48-51; McCosh, "My Life," 43.

[38] McCosh, *Scottish Philosophy*, pp. 408-9; idem, "My Life," 37-38, 41.

Thomas Chalmers

ON GEORGE IV STREET in Edinburgh, one of the city's main thoroughfares, stands a large statue of Thomas Chalmers (1780-1847), who ranks with John Knox as the most commanding figure in the religious history of Scotland. More secular times have made both of these men seem rather quaint, but the nineteenth century, which witnessed such spectacular gains in science, technology, and material culture, also witnessed, especially in the English-speaking countries, a pervasive revival of religion. In Scotland, in fact, Chalmers was merely the most strategic personality in bringing into a sustained movement the popular religiosity that had endured, even in the Moderate era. He was already nationally known when McCosh entered Edinburgh University; indeed his very presence there first motivated McCosh to continue his studies at that university. "I am inclined to look upon Chalmers as upon the whole the greatest man I ever met with," McCosh said. He was "the most eloquent preacher of his age." But Chalmers was more than the popular orator. He was "the scientific inquirer, the philosopher and divine, standing firmly on earth while he measured the heavens." This was always critical for McCosh, for "it was an age that boasted of its science," and it was thus imperative that the spiritual leader of the age should be the master of mundane learning as well. "It was in combining and harmonizing philosophy and revelation that his genius as a deep and original thinker was chiefly drawn." An impassioned preacher and lecturer, Chalmers projected himself into his subject, using a rough and distinct Scottish brogue that often rankled finer Moderate sensibilities. That never bothered McCosh: "I embraced every opportunity of hearing him. I was more moved by him than any man I have ever listened to." Chalmers indeed was almost a father figure to the young man of nineteen, and their relationship extended beyond the classroom. McCosh had an open invitation from the Chalmers family for Friday dinner or Sunday breakfast. Certainly Chalmers excited McCosh about the work of the ministry. While Chalmers was still living, his protégé could conclude that "he has given Evangelical fervor to a cold and secular age."[39]

Chalmers was born at Anstruther, where the Firth of Forth loses itself in the North Sea. He attended St. Andrews University, only ten miles from his home, and was classmate to John Leslie and James Mylne. Only later did Chalmers realize how much he had imbibed the spirit and "chilling influence" of Moderatism, although his journal up to 1825 shows the strains of his quest for spiritual growth. That effort led him in intellectual directions and to the publication of his *Astronomical Discourses*. It also led into the great evangelical campaign that took Glasgow by storm. Chalmers wanted the churches to take up the challenge of urban poverty before the state made it its business. A superb organizer, he was well-equipped to lead that task, and he energized the churches for that difficult challenge. McCosh did not share Chalmers's outspoken

---

[39] McCosh, "My Life," 35-37; idem, *The Method of the Divine Government, Physical and Moral* (New York, 1851), p. 102; idem, *A Tribute to the Memory of Dr. Chalmers, by a Former Pupil* (Brechin, 1847), pp. 4, 6.

Toryism, but he wholly endorsed the new social role for religion that Chalmers was charting.[40]

What did McCosh acquire from Chalmers as a student at Edinburgh University? Chalmers assumed the chair of divinity there in 1827 and delivered the famous Bridgewater lectures during McCosh's last year at the university. McCosh, though, thought that his later *Natural Theology* had far more substance. Chalmers placed himself in the natural theology tradition and believed that the scientific structure of the universe illuminated divine design and presence. But it is clear, especially from students' notes of Chalmers's lectures, that he used such stalwarts of natural religion as Joseph Butler (1692-1752) and William Paley (1743-1805) as foils for a neo-Calvinist portrait of God. Both the *Analogy of Religion* and the *Evidences of Christianity*, which McCosh read in Chalmers's classes, could give some useful examples of the external evidence of God. But Paley, for one, rested theology on little more than expediency and morals. Chalmers then threw out to his students the essential challenge of religious thought, the internal evidence of spiritual reality. Jonathan Edwards was introduced to meet this need, and McCosh recalled later that Chalmers never spoke of Edwards without "an enthusiasm which communicated itself to his pupils." Reading Edwards in fact was momentous for McCosh, though he would never accept Edwards's rigid determinism. But there was a heavy dose of Puritan literature, besides Edwards, that students received from Chalmers. His constant advice to his students, McCosh said, was to "fill their hearts with the practical writings of the great Puritan divines." Baxter, Howe, Owen, Charnock, Marshall—all were useful.[41] And, as one study has made clear, Chalmers accepted the Scottish philosophy as perfected by the Moderates, but insisted that the moral and spiritual reality it described merely prepared the way for the realization of the Christian notions of grace, atonement, and repentence.[42]

---

[40] Quoted by McCosh, *Scottish Philosophy*, p. 394.

[41] "Notes from Dr. Chalmers's Lectures on Theology, 1827," in the University of Edinburgh Department of Manuscripts and Rare Books; William Hanna, ed., *Memoirs of the Life and Writings of Thomas Chalmers*, 4 vols. (New York, 1851), 3:279, 388n; *New York Obsever*, July 28, 1870; James McCosh, *Whither? O Whither? Tell Me Where* (New York, 1889), p. 15.

[42] See Daniel F. Rice, "Natural Theology and the Scottish Philosophy in the Thought of Thomas Chalmers," *Scottish Journal of Theology*, 23 (February 1971), 23-46, for a complete statement of this theme. One distinction between Chalmers and McCosh is the rather greater willingness of the student to use philosophy in the defense of biblical truth. Chalmers seems to be more reluctant to allow the fallen

Here was not only the great challenge that the Edinburgh divine threw out to the Moderates, it was also the challenge that McCosh himself picked up. When McCosh wrote his first philosophical work, he dedicated the 600-page tome to Chalmers, for it was the result of his own grappling with the problems Chalmers had outlined. But in fact McCosh always had more confidence in philosophy, and in the Scottish tradition especially, than did the evangelical leader. That McCosh stayed much more closely within the intellectual tradition of his own country was due to another major influence on his life and thought, one that came during the Edinburgh years. Sir William Hamilton was the intellectual giant of his day, as McCosh very soon acknowledged.

EDINBURGH continued to to be an intellectually exciting place in the early nineteenth century, for now the Scottish Enlightenment was moving in a new direction. From the classroom of Dugald Stewart emerged an ambitious group of young men, lawyers not ministers, who took the ardent liberalism of their mentor into the political campaigns of the new century. Their youth and their passion for literary expression often set them apart from the Whig establishment of Scotland, but the power of the pen soon made them the voices of that party. Their vehicle of influence was the widely read and always stimulating *Edinburgh Review*, which came from the designs of Francis Jeffrey, Henry Brougham, Sydney Smith, and Francis Horner, all former students of Stewart and all, except Smith, Edinburgh attorneys. The *Review* entered the political fray with an ardent plea to end the slave trade and emancipate the Irish Catholics. It waved the banner of free trade and spoke increasingly for the economic interests of the commercial and industrial elements against landed wealth and the interests of protection. But most important, the *Edinburgh Review* pursued new standards of public seriousness, moral energy, and literary tastes in Britain. It castigated the aristocracy and the gentry for their indolence and backwardness, their effete cult of fashion, and their lack of moral fiber. Though the new Scottish reviewers chided the middle classes for their indifference to the poor, at the same time they opened their pages to Thomas Malthus and proclaimed the inutility of outdoor relief. Unquestionably, the commercial and industrial groups, admired for their drive, ambition, and practical talents, had the best

---

human intellect to wander freely from the tether of revealed truth. Again, see Rice, "An Attempt at Systematic Reconstruction in the Theology of Thomas Chalmers," *Church History*, 48 (June 1979), 175-88.

A Scottish Education

press. The *Review*'s yardsticks for social approbation, as John Clive has noted, were culture, virtue, and industry. With respect to religion, skepticism was the prevailing tone, a fact, however, that only suggests a secularization of the moral rigor that Presbyterianism had fostered in Scotland. Even Jeffrey remarked that "our fashionable readers may detect the extreme rigour of our Calvinistic education." The Whig liberals were by no means levelers. They defended the alliance of wealth and culture, and scenting heresy in the perversion that would find wisdom in the intuition of shepherds and peddlers, gave a hostile reception to Wordsworth and the romantic movement in its early stages.[43] McCosh, who eagerly consumed each issue of the *Review*, recognized, as others did, that the secular Whig movement formed a counterpoint to the evangelical reform efforts that he was now joining.

One of the major voices of the Scottish Whigs during McCosh's Edinburgh years was Sir William Hamilton. Hamilton in fact had a distinct place within this circle, for he was Scotland's most formidable philosopher, and in a certain sense, the last great voice of the Moderates. Hamilton was born in 1788 in Glasgow University where his father, a professor of anatomy and botany, had won a distinguished reputation, and where his grandfather, holder of the same chair, had pioneered with Cullen to establish the medical school. But because his father died when William was only three, his upbringing and education were entrusted to his mother, to whom William had a lasting attachment. He attended the Glasgow public schools and entered the university in 1803, studying philosophy with George Jardine and James Mylne, but still anticipating a career in medicine. He won a Snell Exhibition scholarship to Oxford and during his years at Balliol became a brilliant student of the highest rank. He astonished his examiners with the scope of his mastery of the Latin classics, in which he was examined in four times the usual number of books. Interestingly though, Hamilton gave little credit to Oxford. Its instruction, even in the classics, was trivial and uninspiring. In philosophy, where Hamilton was now discovering his true love, its efforts were negligible, furnishing him nothing in logic, ethics, or metaphysics. Here too Hamilton was essentially self-taught, but the job was brilliantly done.[44]

---

[43] John Clive, *Scotch Reviewers: "The Edinburgh Review," 1802-1815* (Cambridge, Mass., 1957), pp. 27, 84, 87, 131, 139, 141, 145, 149, 164-69. The quotation is on p. 145.

[44] John Veitch, *Memoir of Sir William Hamilton* (Edinburgh and London, 1869), pp. 1-6, 8-12, 18, 20-21, 23-24.

Sir William Hamilton

When he returned to Edinburgh, Hamilton entered the legal profession and joined with the bright young set that included Jeffrey, Brougham, and Henry Cockburn. Though the dread fear of the French Revolution hung heavy on the city and made the young Whigs virtual outcasts in this Tory-dominated establishment, the group nonetheless espoused liberal views and tried to remind its contemporaries of some of the positive benefits of that great event.[45] But not for political reasons alone did Hamilton fail to

[45] Ibid., pp. 76-78; Clive, *Scotch Reviewers*, p. 95.

flourish as a lawyer. He was not a great speaker, and more, his fastidious temperament and a passion for exhaustive, detailed research, were frustrated by the need for summary preparation of legal briefs. Hamilton, in fact, increasingly succumbed to the appeal of abstract thought, and more and more he gave his mind to the rarefied and esoteric. Even before he published, Hamilton was known as a great philosophical thinker, and in 1810 he emerged as a strong, perhaps even the obvious choice to succeed Thomas Brown in the moral philosophy chair at Edinburgh. But this was not an issue to be decided on merit. The contest became one of the most celebrated in the history of the university, Hamilton opposed by John Wilson, the "Christopher North" of *Blackwood's* magazine. North had already helped establish *Blackwood's* as a deliberate rival of the *Edinburgh*, and now the Tory majority on the Town Council, vigorously backed by Sir Walter Scott, pushed Wilson's candidacy. Dugald Stewart himself supported Hamilton, but that did not prevent the twenty-one-to-eleven vote in favor of his opponent. Nonetheless, the next year Hamilton, through an appointment that came from the Faculty of Advocates, took the chair in universal and civil history. Later in 1836 he won a more prestigious post, the professorship of logic and metaphysics.[46]

In 1829 Hamilton became a cause célèbre in the philosophical world with his famous review, his first published writing, of Victor Cousin's *Cours de Philosophie*. This *Edinburgh Review* essay introduced Hamilton's "Philosophy of the Unconditioned," and it demonstrated that philosophy in Scotland had taken a new turn. It was neo-Kantian in its critique, but used this perspective to question some of the more ambitious transcendentalist directions that Germany had taken since Kant's own famous efforts to circumscribe the realm of the knowable. The larger outline of the essay will concern us later, for McCosh made painstaking efforts to show its limitations and thereby made himself a party to a major controversy that involved Hamilton, Henry Mansel, and John Stuart Mill. Hamilton, however, did not seek to undo the Scottish school, and in some significant ways actually extended it. His writings show him to be a follower of Reid, and later in his Edinburgh career Hamilton gave several years of hard work to editing the writings of Reid and Stewart. Until his death in 1855 Hamilton perpetuated the prestige of Scottish philosophy.[47]

[46] Veitch, *Memoir*, pp. 74–75, 97–107; Alexander Grant, *The Story of the University of Edinburgh During Its First Three Hundred Years*, 2 vols. (London, 1884), 2:332-35.
[47] Veitch, *Memoir*, p. 207.

What kind of a person was Sir William and why did he so much impress McCosh? His Edinburgh follower had no reservations about the great man. He was "the most eminent man in Philosophy," McCosh wrote, "not only in Scotland, but throughout the world." He preserved a "very vivid" recollection of Hamilton in the classroom.[48] "There was an evident manliness in his person and his whole manner and address. His features were marked, he had an eye of a very deep lustre, and his expression was eminently intellectual. He read his lecture in a clear, emphatic manner, without show, pretension, or affectation of any kind." His lectures were in fact intellectually rigorous and difficult. McCosh observed that a flurry of scribbling pens accompanied the beginning of the lecture, but as Hamilton proceeded the slower students fell one by one by the wayside.[49] McCosh was not alone in his enthusiasm for Hamilton. The philosopher James Ferrier said of Hamilton: "I knew him in his glorious prime, when his bodily frame was like a breathing intellect, and when his soul could travel, as on eagle's wings, over the tops of all the mountains of knowledge."[50] With Hamilton the love of knowledge was contagious; he was the living model of the cerebral man. Hamilton's passion for books was limitless, and from his very early youth he amassed a collection drawn from dark and hidden corners of old bookstores. He had an irresistible urge for the antiquarian, and his expanding stock included ancient German

[48] It has been very difficult to determine exactly what was the relationship between Hamilton and McCosh while McCosh was a student at Edinburgh. I have found nothing to suggest that McCosh was actually a student of Hamilton. On the contrary, a few references force the conclusion that he was not. Thus, McCosh wrote in his autobiographical memoir that when his first book, *The Method of the Divine Government*, was published, Hamilton and Hugh Miller received gift copies. Hamilton apparently sent favorable comments to the publisher, comments that McCosh quoted in the memoir, and that appear in advertisements of several of McCosh's works. But McCosh wrote of these two men: "with neither of whom I was at that time acquainted, but with whom I now became intimate." "My Life," 107. Also, before he described Hamilton's classroom appearance, as quoted next in the text, McCosh wrote: "The writer of this article has a very vivid recollection of Sir William Hamilton in happening to pass into his classroom a year or two after his appointment." That date would have been 1837 or 1838, three or four years after McCosh's graduation from Edinburgh. And finally, in a letter dated March 11, 1850, Hamilton supplied some sentences to be used in promoting McCosh's book. At the end he says, "It would give me great pleasure to become personally acquainted with Dr. McCosh." W. Hamilton to ?, in the "Correspondence of James McCosh." Department of Rare Books and Special Collections, Princeton University Library.

[49] McCosh, "My Life," 39; idem, *Scottish Philosophy*, p. 428; see also Veitch, *Memoir*, p. 202.

[50] Quoted by Davie, *Democratic Intellect*, p. 261.

theses and rare editions of classical and historical authors. He delighted to discover an unknown or forgotten thinker, and to trace the history of an idea back to its origins. Hamilton the bibliophile assembled one of the most valuable private philosophical libraries in Great Britan. His total collection of works McCosh remembered as about 10,000 volumes. And to McCosh it seemed that Hamilton had mastered them all. "No man has ever done more in clearing the literature of philosophy of commonplace mistakes, of thefts and impostures."[51]

Nor did any man probe the past more deeply to bring fresh thoughts on a matter of increasing concern in his country. The Scottish universities had long been the pride of the nation, but charges circulated during McCosh's years at Edinburgh that they were in a state of decline. McCosh himself concurred in these suspicions, from the perspective of his Glasgow experience especially. Edinburgh had a few academic stars to uphold the standards, but even here McCosh experienced some glaring weaknesses. A decline in enrollment complicated the discussions of university purpose, furthermore, by inducing calls for greater practical emphasis in the curriculum. But an offsetting force came from the growing prestige of the German universities and the principles of pure learning and research that they exemplified. Hamilton, who had already introduced the Kantian ideals of German philosophy, now appealed to German academic standards, albeit not uncritically, as a means to reconstruct the British institutions. Beginning in 1836 he wrote a series of articles for the *Edinburgh Review*, most of them centering on Oxford University, that enabled him to outline a broad university philosophy, with special attention to the curriculum in the British and the Scottish institutions. The articles brought Hamilton still greater fame. They were hard-hitting and forthright, and the public attention they received influenced the decision to appoint a Royal Commission to investigate Oxford and Cambridge in 1850.

Hamilton's critique of higher education reflected his own personality and life. He drew the lines of university purpose narrowly, proscribing both the utilitarian and the professional emphasis. Students must come to the university motivated by a love of knowledge for its own sake and determined to discipline their intellects by the rigors of academic pursuit. The university itself must be so constituted as to make these ends feasible, and thus must purge itself of any possible competing interests. Hamilton wanted a tightly

[51] Veitch, *Memoir*, pp. 23-24, 38, 45-46, 75-76; McCosh, *Scottish Philosophy*, p. 416.

knit academic community and reproved the Scottish universities, more than the English, for allowing students to live in scattered communities beyond the campus. Hamilton was clear on one point: the end of education is mental discipline, and whatever course of study assists that end is justified. "Knowledge," Hamilton wrote, "is only valuable as it exercises, . . . develops, and invigorates the mind." This standard enabled Hamilton to plead against the vogue of practicality, but also to delineate the points of distinction between his model and the German. Hamilton never venerated as valuable in themselves the possession of scientific truth or the accumulated minutiae of knowledge that new tools of research and investigation made available in the world's storehouse of learning. Too little of this learning, he believed, resulted from worthwhile mental effort. Hamilton wrote that the contribution of education is to narrow and refine the sense of what is truly valuable in life, but there was for him little of worth beyond the cerebral pleasures. To save us from the worldly snares that seduce and dissipate the mind, the thousand petty amusements that detract us from the pursuit of wisdom: that was education's essential function.[52]

His essays on university education made Hamilton known as a critic of the national culture, and when these essays are supplemented by his views of religion they add an important element to the history of Scottish Moderatism. Hamilton was not at all a religious polemicist. He was not sympathetic to Calvinism, but, significantly, respected its intellectual rigors as a form of systematic theology. In the emerging schism of the Church, Hamilton played only a small role, but one that showed him partisan to the Moderates. Hamilton's concern centered on the philosophical foundations of religion, for like all aspects of life and learning religion presented itself to him under that consideration, and in pursuing this question, Hamilton further embellished the Moderate critique of the popular culture. For Hamilton's essay on classical learning was also asking the question, Why had Scotland so little distinguished itself in theology? The religious fervor of its clergy or populace had seldom been in doubt, of course. But Hamilton observed that Scotland's religion was imported; it did not spring from indigenous roots, but came ready-made. Also, it never found itself in the polemical position of the Church of England, surrounded in a hostile

---

[52] Veitch, *Memoir*, pp. 163–67; Sir William Hamilton, "On a Reform of the English Universities: with Especial Reference to Oxford; and Limited to the Faculty of Arts," in *Discussions of Philosophy and Literature, Education and University Reform* . . . (London, 1852), pp. 674–77, 694.

atmosphere by other Protestant churches whose theological perspectives radically opposed it. Scotland's religious wars, Hamilton implied, were popular struggles, not intellectual encounters. More instructive by comparison was the Reformation in Germany, so much an affair of the intellectuals and academical divines. There, in contrast to Scotland, the determination of religious dogma was the privilege of erudition, and in Germany religion remained a subject of learned investigation.[53]

It was clear where Hamilton was directing his essay, for he echoed sentiments to which Moderates had long been sympathetic. The Reformation in Scotland, he said, was the choice of an unlettered people. It originated neither in native learning nor in the learned authority of its propagators, though Melville, educated abroad, was the possible exception. Scottish religion had always shown the marks of popular belief and assent, defending itself by the dogged tenacity of dogma or the violence of the sword. The Covenanters, wrote Hamilton, "were unlearned as they were enthusiastic" and so smug and satisfied were their people with their political victory that their clergy had no occasion to invite them to the table of learned disputations. The standards of Scottish orthodoxy remained so clear and lucid in the public mind that they foreclosed any adventures of the intellect into the realm of the speculative.

Hamilton's main point was to show that in Scottish religious controversy, when it existed at all, popular opinion was always the final arbiter, the last and highest tribunal. The preaching of a popular sermon was judged the mark of clerical accomplishment. "Theological learning remained superfluous, if not unsafe." The Scottish clergy were not, of course, defective in learning (and their English counterparts were generally more ignorant), but they were certainly undistinguished. Hamilton, it should be noted, wrote his essay shortly after the passage of the Veto Act that confirmed congregational control over ministerial selection and dealt a severe blow to the Moderates. Nor could Hamilton have failed to be aware that the Evangelicals were at the same time appropriating the Scottish philosophy, with its emphasis on common sense and moral intuition, to defend the right of the plain untutored conscience to exercise judgment against a higher social wisdom. Here was both a kind of romanticism and provincial philistinism that

---

[53] Sir William Hamilton, "On the Conditions of Classical Learning," in *Discussions*, pp. 334-36, 340.

never sat well with the Moderates, the devotees of the *Edinburgh Review*, or Hamilton, the protagonist of high intellect.[54]

Hamilton was an enduring influence on McCosh. He represented the finest achievements of Scotland's later philosophical age and upheld uncompromising, high standards of intellectual life and performance. For the time being it was Chalmers who captured the imagination of the young divinity student, but even as McCosh looked toward a career in the Church of Scotland, the challenge that Hamilton threw out to him, the challenge to unite a tradition of learning to the religious life of the country, would bear fruit in McCosh's life. In fact, even before McCosh left the University of Edinburgh, he entered the popular religious controversies of the day. His earliest published writings show McCosh clearly a partisan of the evangelical reformers, but McCosh chose to enter the fray by bringing to that side a precisely reasoned defense of its religious principles. McCosh's first effort to explore the nature of religious experience reflected his training under Chalmers, but the terse academic style reflected his immersion in philosophy.

MCCOSH WON HIGH DISTINCTION for his academic work at Edinburgh and was proud to win honors through Hamilton's endorsement of his master's thesis on Stoic philosophy. The attention drawn to McCosh, even at this time active among the local Edinburgh divines, led to a request that he undertake the review of a new publication, John Howard Hinton's *The Work of the Holy Spirit in Conversion*, for the *Edinburgh Christian Instructor*, the major popular and intellectual publication of the evangelical party. Hinton was a Baptist minister, trained at Edinburgh and at that time preaching at the Hosier Street Chapel in Reading. This work was one of several that marked a productive career of writing on religious philosophy. McCosh used the occasion to draw some fine distinctions respecting the nature and means of experiencing divine grace. His perspective at this time was clearly neo-Calvinist in contrast to the Arminianism of Hinton. Thus although Hinton conceded that a man cannot repent and be converted by his own efforts, or without the influence of the Holy Spirit, he rejected the stricter view that no effort to this end is even possible without such assistance. McCosh put the question this way: "Can any man come

---

[54] Ibid., pp. 337-39; Veitch, *Memoir*, p. 274; Davie, *Democratic Intellect*, pp. 288-90, 309.

to Christ except the Father draw him?" Hinton affirmed; McCosh denied.[55]

Conforming to the general practice of the day, McCosh used the review of Hinton's work to embark on an independent course and present his own analysis of an intellectual problem. He wished to delineate the distinction the Evangelicals were drawing between the divine and the natural and thus undercut the natural theism that inspired much of the Moderates' religious philosophy. For McCosh this was no small issue. He was bringing to bear on this question the whole weight of his culminating academic career and the serious and often disturbing efforts he had made to confront the intellectual challenges these issues presented. But the essay was surely anticipatory as well as retrospective. McCosh was mapping out in rough outline the challenges of the religious life as the future preacher would confront them, and in a profound way the essay struck at the heart of the widening divisions of the two religious parties in Scotland.

McCosh began by saying that God works in the world and deals with human beings by two methods—by natural means and by miracles or special acts. The one is distinguished from the other by law, that is, by events that occur according to the pattern ordained by God for the normal conduct of his world and the pattern by which man accommodates himself to it. We find nothing miraculous here because by familiarity with this pattern we see a universe of order, law, and rational behavior. But McCosh was anxious especially to show that into this class falls the experience of what he calls "natural grace." Natural grace, which, like the phenomenon of gravity or any natural event, indicates a certain way by which God has arranged things, is capable of producing highly useful effects, and is effective in inducing a higher spirituality. It proceeds by natural causes, and its results are clearly evident. But natural grace is not "efficacious grace." McCosh reproved Hinton for making no real distinction here and for suggesting that natural grace automatically brings full conversion. This equation was not acceptable to the evangelical McCosh, who judged the attainment of grace impossible by any such natural course. A fallen and depraved human nature could not generate of itself the means of complete transformation; the stubbornness of the human heart and the

---

[55] James McCosh, Review of *The Work of the Holy Spirit,* by John Howard Hinton, *Edinburgh Christian Examiner,* 2, n.s. (December 1833), 831-32.

resistance of natural man to spiritual influences precluded such a course. Yet McCosh could not deny that grace was irresistible, that even sinful human nature must succumb to God's reaching out. Therefore, we can only conclude, he said, that natural grace, because it does not produce a total conversion of the heart, was never intended to do so. It produces only the effects intended.

And what are these effects? McCosh believed that God used natural grace for important purposes—to increase morality, to advance human wisdom, to ameliorate social intercourse, even to advance civilization. McCosh did not have to belabor the point. He was making an oblique reference to all the celebrated virtues of Moderatism, all the effects that the devotees of the Enlightenment described as the essence of the religious life, the general improvement of social well-being and the cultural and moral advancement of the individual and the race. These of course have a kind of divine sanction, for even the ordinary and natural working of things expresses divine intention. But miraculous grace is something quite different. It does not have a cause or an invariable antecedent in nature; instead, it uses "occasions" that are not joined to a chain of causal sequences. McCosh thus said that two persons in the same natural state may hear the same reading of the Word, sing the same hymn, attend the same religious ceremony. One may yet remain estranged from God, or, he may even be inspired to good works and Christian benevolence. The other, however, may experience the sense of total and absolute regeneration, the consummation of the self in the divine presence. And to reinforce the earlier point, McCosh maintained that this experience of divine grace does not derive from natural man's sense of the beauty of nature or from any merely aesthetic response to the world. True holiness comes only when the breath of God infuses the heart of natural man and effects a total transformation of the inner being. McCosh's analysis of this point shows the unmistakable influence of the Puritan tradition and of Jonathan Edwards especially, and it strikes one very definitely as a paraphrase of Edwards's *A Divine and Supernatural Light*.[56]

McCosh also drew upon some of his own philosophical training to bolster the evangelical theology. Hinton left a wide door open for human initiative in the quest for divine grace, to which McCosh countered that "it is vain to think that anything can change the natural state of man, short of the direct interferences of God in the very processes of our mental nature." The problem is a simple one of

[56] Ibid., 832-35.

causation. No state of the unconverted man has the power to make him converted; the sinner cannot of himself effect regeneration. Every effect must contain within itself the qualities and characteristics of its causes, and no causes of the natural world and natural man suffice therefore to produce effects denoted by the attainment of distinctly nonnatural and spiritual qualities.

Or put the matter another way. The unconverted man cannot have a love of holiness for its own sake; in a state of sin he must be blind to God's beauty, having a love of natural things, but no more. Natural man, that is, cannot desire what his own heart knows not, a fact that negates the efficacy of human initiative in renewing the individual's heart. We conclude, McCosh said, that in the transformation of the natural man "God is the real physical cause, not intermediately, but immediately and directly." In this part of the essay McCosh quoted directly, and several times, from Edwards. And he concluded on a note similar to that by which Edwards had earlier made himself America's most thoroughgoing critic of the age of reason. Those who act only under the direction of natural grace will imagine nothing higher at stake in the religious life than the experience of its normal effects. These people, McCosh noted, are usually good churchgoers, and practitioners of good deeds; they do much to embellish the world with art and culture and to improve and refine its taste. There were, to be sure, many positive benefits to be had from this "mere worldly honesty and amiability."[57] But McCosh, leaving the University of Edinburgh, was now looking out on a world he believed was spiritually dying. It needed more than what natural grace could offer. He had seen the blight of the cities in Glasgow and Edinburgh, and he recalled from his youth the religious indifference of the older rural populations. But a new movement was stirring in Scotland and resolving to change all this. McCosh was ready to lend his hand to the cause.

[57] Ibid., 3, n.s. (January 1834), 34-36.

Chapter Three

THE GOSPEL MINISTRY

IN THE PERIOD between his graduation from Edinburgh and his first academic appointment at Queen's College in Ireland, McCosh became embroiled in Scotland's greatest religious controversy of the nineteenth century. This controversy produced schism in the Church of Scotland and the establishment of a new ecclesiastical order. Unquestionably the evangelical movement that spawned these events reinvigorated the religious life of the country and brought the gospel message to areas where it had long been in decline. New church leaders, Thomas Chalmers, Thomas Guthrie, and others, carried Scotland from its age of Moderatism to a new era of revivalism, from an age of decorum and gentlemanly manners toward a new middle-class democracy. James McCosh grew to maturity amid these changes. More than that, he worked actively to bring them into being.

The seventeen years of McCosh's service in the gospel ministry critically shaped the contours of his entire career. The Church struggle that consumed his energy and emotions became a permanent legacy of his personality and his social attitudes. Even his work in the Princeton presidency is incomprehensible without knowing the early background whose shadow extended to the end of his life. At no time was McCosh more immersed in the life of his native land, in the hopes and fears, the sorrows and sins of the masses among whom he lived. The proverbial Scottish preacher, justly renowned for his grim determinism, his often cold exterior, and his rigid dogmatism, was nonetheless educated by the world as well as the Book. In his daily ministerial routine McCosh came to know the strengths and frailties of human nature. There was little occasion for idealism to thrive amid the grim realities of life. The man of the cloth taught the later philosopher to keep a grip on the world of experience.

But this period was important to McCosh for yet another reason. Although he forsook for a while the comfortable and cerebral confines of the university, he looked on his gospel work as an extension of his education. It was not always easy to do that, and Mc-

Cosh admitted as much. But he did try to keep the two worlds together, and the end of this period, concluding his formal career as a preacher, saw the publication of his first book. The lengthy treatise, bearing the ideas of the academy but also the vigor and color of the preacher's rhetoric, not only marked his transition from the pulpit back to the university, but prefigured the essential outline of his intellectual life. The work unmistakably exuded the spirit of Chalmers on the one hand and Hamilton on the other. For even in the gospel period McCosh was attempting the difficult reconciliation of the Scottish Enlightenment with the neo-Calvinism of the evangelical movement. In a large sense, McCosh's ensuing career in philosophy was a refinement and enlargement of this initial outline of his ideas.

McCosh's career in the Church began with the onset of the Victorian age. The era of England's great financial splendor and imperial world leadership was, in its cultural, social, and intellectual characteristics, also one of grandeur and accomplishment. Marked by an immense diversity, Victorian culture embraced a variety of antithetical spirits: the Brontës and Dickens, Arnold and Pater, Mill and Newman, Coleridge and Huxley. Historians have looked for the elements of unity through themes that cut across these contrasting patterns and give us the sense of "Victorianism." Walter E. Houghton's superb study, *The Victorian Frame of Mind*, successfully taps the mood and outlook of this age by identifying prevalent ideas, concepts, emotions, locating their sources in the several corners of the culture and society. Prominent among these coexisting elements, Houghton finds "optimism," "anxiety," "fear of revolution," "the strain of Puritanism," "the danger of atheism," "reliance on authority," "anti-intellectualism," "the will to believe," "dogmatism," "the commercial spirit," "earnestness," "enthusiasm," "hero worship," and, alas, "hypocrisy." Any culture will have these elements in various degrees, but they stand out somehow with special relevance in the Victorian period. Certainly the major social and intellectual movements of the era furnish the reason. Democracy, utilitarianism, industrialism, Darwinism, imperialism, and evangelicalism—all of these gave Victorianism its personality and spirit.[1]

No movement more inclusively embraced Houghton's characteristics than evangelicalism. Although its zealous partisans could be found all over the world, it had particular force in the English-

---

[1] Walter E. Houghton, *The Victorian Frame of Mind, 1830-1870* (New Haven, 1957).

speaking nations. And among these, Scotland, Ulster, and the United States emphatically felt its impact. McCosh, in each of these places, participated actively. Evangelicalism everywhere joined with other forces of a romantic age to reject reason as the arbiter of all things. Its gospel-centered religion pursued a new authority, renewed a special kind of dogmatism, and flourished often in an antiintellectual medium that it had helped to create. It could denounce with one voice the godless inroads of modernism, a concept that the evangelical mind made elastic enough to include everything from avowed atheism to Unitarianism. To recall Houghton's terms once more, evangelicalism did furnish a new will to believe, often translating the articles of faith into the promise of a new millennial kingdom of God. It did supply earnestness and enthusiasm to refuel a world it saw numbed by rationalism, scientism, and materialism. Its Puritan strain, joined to a middle-class spirit of uplift, made the gospel preacher an activist social reformer, for the new Kingdom would not come by God's hands alone. It even molded its own kind of hero worship as it recovered the temper of radical Protestantism, looked back to the model of the early church, and found in Christ of the New Testament a personal model for the regeneration of a fallen world.

Evangelicalism inaugurated a religious revival while it played a very definite social role. By the nineteenth century Methodism and other dissenting bodies in England had lost their radical reputation without compromising their antiaristocratic prejudices. Evangelicalism, in short, had found a new alliance with the rising middle classes. Entirely comfortable with its Puritan strain, equally obsessed with social uplift through ambition, moral reform, industry, and work, the bourgeoisie pursued evangelicalism's ideals as aspects of a worldly and spiritual faith. To this extent, moreover, the Evangelicals became complements to the other side of the middle-class ethos, the utilitarian vogue. So seemingly dissimilar—evangelicalism's emotionalism and supernaturalism, utilitarianisms' analytical and rational temperament—the two nonetheless shared a feeling for social efficiency and improvement, for order over class warfare. Utilitarians knew that moral character would turn the wheels of industry, that a sober working class put its money in the bank, not in the local pub. Both elements therefore had a stake in the great temperance crusade. The Evangelicals pursued many social reforms, from the abolishment of slavery to the eradication of cockfighting, bullbaiting, and bare-fisted boxing, but none so motivated their reformism as the crusade against liquor. Cheap gin may have been the quickest way out of Manchester for the working classes, but its role in murder and social mayhem was abundantly evident. Whether one spoke of a moral Christian society or the spirit of enterprise and commerce as the ends of this world's work, apologists for both stood on a common platform for reform.[2]

In 1844 the evangelical *Free Church Magazine*, summarizing the events that had produced the Disruption of the preceding year, described "God's quarrel with the Church of Scotland." For over a decade before this pronouncement, anyone could read, in countless samples from the prolific religious literature of the day, similar judgments. The *Magazine* here pointed to "the long and dreary period of spiritual lethargy in which [the Church] lay supine." Over the long reign of Moderatism the Church produced many ministers who were "strangers to real, personal religion" and therefore incapable of inspiring it in others. Evangelicalism everywhere expressed these feelings, but in Scotland they flourished in a particular context. Thus in another essay, "The Banner of the Covenant," the *Magazine* recalled the memory of the heroic fighters for true religion in Scotland and contrasted their unyielding resistance to the king with the pliant Church of the latter day.[3]

Antagonists debated the ecclesiastical issues largely on these terms, but all knew that in Scotland, as elsewhere, the pervasive forces of social change now made these matters acute. As much at issue as church law was the question of religious styles. McCosh, from the time of his college days at Glasgow, knew that the price of Moderatism was the decline and neglect of religion beyond the comfortable circles of fine taste and cultural refinement. The Evangelicals of his kind approached the religious question with a sense of desperation. They looked out on the cities and declining rural regions and saw the worsening condition of the poor. In their midst spread radical reform societies that promised bread without the cup. With a mixture of fear and genuine concern the Evangelicals undertook to win these masses back to the Church and to revitalize the gospel among them. Now in the fourth decade of the century the work that Chalmers helped to spread found a whole new generation of ministers armed with the cause of religious and social reform. Glasgow now teemed with industrial workers, many of them Irish immigrants. The versatile weavers faced a dreary future, and

---

[2] For a general outline of the evangelical ethos, see Richard D. Atlick, *Victorian People and Ideas* (New York, 1973), pp. 165-85.

[3] *Free Church Magazine* (June 1844), 134-45, (October 1844), 289-96, (November 1844), 342-43.

the coal industry was introducing Scotland to the age of gray and black. The Church's response to the new social conditions, the Evangelicals believed, must be the democratization of religion. They would make the gospel message intelligible by whatever means. They would broaden its base by a huge missionary effort. This was by no means simply a measure to win votes. The *Free Church Magazine*'s plea for the Factory Bill sought to prevent the waste of God-given faculties that occurs when workers are thrown into endless toil. "Existence," it reminded its readers, "was not intended to be a ceaseless round of animal effort," and woe to him who caused his brother to hew wood and draw water to the neglect of the contemplation and love of his Maker. The Evangelicals pursued a Christian economics while a very dismal science proliferated elsewhere.[4]

The emotional zeal of the Scottish Evangelicals, their commitment to missionary work and church extension, and their puritanical streak very likely suggest a movement best described in terms of sheer energy. Evangelicalism has always carried that suggestion, one that is true enough, though it unfortunately belies other qualities in its leaders. In England John Henry Newman dismissed the pietism of Methodism and Puritanism as essentially nonintellectual, and somewhat later Mark Pattison cited "the professed contempt of all learned inquiry which was a principle with the Evangelical school."[5] Much truth may lie in these statements as general descriptions, but they will not hold up in reference to the Scottish counterparts. The Evangelicals of the Free Church movement, with numerous exceptions undoubtedly, were not prepared to sacrifice intellect to their cause. Their commitment to parish education and university training constituted elements of continuity with their Scottish religious past. The Evangelicals themselves were invariably products of the Scottish universities. Chalmers had an extensive interest in and some mastery of science. Hugh Miller, we shall see, made suggestive contributions to evolutionary theory. David Welsh was Scotland's most accomplished church historian, and McCosh found the influence of these persons most useful. Through the *Witness* and the *North British Review* the Scottish Evangelicals provided learned and scholarly commentary on the developing culture and society of the Victorian era. For all these reasons McCosh would find the Free Church movement, and his participation in it,

---

[4] William Ferguson, *Scotland: 1689 to the Present* (Edinburgh, 1968), pp. 273-77; *Free Church Magazine* (May 1844), 131.
[5] Houghton, *Victorian Frame of Mind*, p. 125.

"the greatest event of my life." As we move now to the inauguration of his own career in the ministry we note this fact. As McCosh graduated Master of Arts in Divinity from the University of Edinburgh in 1834, the swelling ranks of the evangelical party won that year a numerical majority in the Presbyterian General Assembly. Religious developments in Scotland had taken a decisive turn.

THE BOILING CAULDRON of religion and politics that marked the emerging schism in the Scottish churches beset McCosh's ministerial career at its very beginning. As a duly graduated divinity student McCosh was licensed by the Presbytery of Ayr as a member of the Church of Scotland. But McCosh had reservations. He knew the history of his country well and doubted his own ability to translate his university learning into effective popular preaching. For all his sympathy to the evangelical efforts he was nonetheless a product of the age of Moderatism, educated in the universities and inheriting the intellectual apparatus of the eighteenth-century Enlightenment. McCosh lingered in the comfortable and cultured environs of Edinburgh for nearly a year before pursuing a parish appointment. When finally he looked out to the provinces he hoped at least to receive a call from one of the churches in his old territory of Ayrshire. But when that event occurred it was quickly marked by disappointments. The young minister made a favorable impression on his prospective new flock, but his association with Chalmers and his declared preference for the Evangelicals raised the opposition of the local patron who vetoed the appointment. For a while McCosh filled a parish vacancy in Kirkmichael, and that too seemed to promise a full-time appointment. But everywhere in Scotland by now the divisiveness of the religious parties complicated the normal procedures. Here again the congregation of this village of farmers and tradesmen recommended the appointment of the young Edinburgh graduate only to provoke the interference of the Tory heritors. McCosh was still without a parish.[6]

Renewed hope came in June 1835 when McCosh received a request from the kirk session of the Abbey Church in Arbroath to preach before the congregation. The Arbroath church was following the standard form for announcing a vacancy and inviting candidates to try for the position. In this instance McCosh was one of

---

[6] James McCosh, *For Love's Sake: Being a Farewell Sermon Preached in the West Free Church, Brechin, August 24, 1884* ([Brechin], 1884), p. 11; idem, "Incidents of My Life in Three Countries," unpublished typescript in the Princeton University Archives, 49-53.

seven persons so invited. The event also had more than the usual seriousness and scrutiny that surrounded such procedures, for this kirk had recently endured a nasty affair that brought the dismissal of its preacher, Rev. James J. McFarlane, after a trial for attempted rape, falsehood, and chronic acts of drunkenness. The evangelical sympathizers most actively pursued these charges, believed by the historian of the church to have been mostly trumped up.

But even in the age of Moderatism the act of selecting and judging a minister often had the aura of sacred rite in Scotland. From Edinburgh to the distant countryside the process was marked by solemnity and vigilance. In a period before electoral democracy, no event was dearer to the hearts of a people than the selection of the local pastor. Nor should any preacher, whether visitor or candidate, ignore the local ways and the provincial wisdom. Thomas Guthrie told an anecdote about a visitor to Glenisla who preached in the absence of the infirm pastor. Calculating that here was a small pastoral parish, he figured that the twenty-third psalm would surely be appropriate. But he failed to detect that the sheep of this area of moist green herbage attended to the streams only when sick and went on at length about the "still waters" and their necessity for the flocks. As they stopped on leaving the service to light their pipes, one of the farmers said to another, "Puir bodie! Hear ye ever the likeo'yon about the sheep drinkin?" McCosh may not have been learned in the local ways at Arbroath, but at least he made no such faux pas as Guthrie's example. When all candidates for the Arbroath position had been heard, a direct vote of the proprietors of pews found McCosh with forty-six votes to fifty-two votes for a Mr. Bell and forty votes for a Mr. Burns. These formed the top three in the circle of candidates, and each was invited to return. Bell either chose not to return or fared miserably. McCosh emerged a clear choice at a meeting that selected him on October 13 by a vote of eighty-two to twenty. A copy of the letter informing McCosh of his success remains in the Abbey Church minute book. It promises him a salary of £100 annually and conveys the hopes that his heavy majority in the election will help "to consolidate and keep together, or rather bring back, the congregation."[7]

Arbroath is an attractive and quiet little seacoast town that lies

---

[7] Andrew Douglas, *Centennary of Arbroath Abbey Church: Outline of the History of Abbey Church, Arbroath* (Arbroath, 1897), pp. 33-34, 51-52; "Minute Book of Abbey Church, 1829-42," at the Abbey Church, Arbroath, June 10, 1835, July 15, 1835, October 13, 1835, October 28, 1835; Thomas Guthrie, *Autobiography of Thomas Guthrie and Memoir by His Sons . . .* , 2 vols. (New York, 1875), 1:107.

about one hundred miles northeast of Edinburgh. Its population of about 7,000 today is barely larger than at the time of McCosh's arrival in 1835. Readers of Sir Walter Scott's novel *The Antiquary* may recognize Arbroath as the "Fairport" of that work. As one walks along the coast north of the harbor one encounters the awesome cliffs that rise high above the rough waters of the North Sea. Scott aptly chose this location, where McCosh recalled walking often and surveying the Bell Rock Lighthouse in the distance, to set the dramatic scene of the novel where Sir Arthur, Miss Wardour, and Ochiltree are precariously entrapped below and face impending death from the rising tide of the rainy day and windy night. But Arbroath has other distinctions as well. Here lie the ruins of a magnificent abbey where in 1320 the celebrated Assembly of the Estates declared the independence of the Scottish Church and Kingdom in the historic Declaration of Arbroath. William the Lion, founder of the abbey in 1178, lies buried within. The Abbey Church, which still stands directly next to the abbey, was built in 1797 and rebuilt in 1831 in a peculiar neo-Gothic style, described as "one of the most elegant structures of its kind to be seen in Scotland."[8]

McCosh was arriving in a community with a very pronounced working-class social climate. It boasted no family of noble blood, though landownership by absentee aristocrats affected the economic life. Nearly all families depended on their own businesses for a livelihood. The Parochial Register for Arbroath in the County of Forfar tells some important facts about the community and even about the kind of work in which McCosh was soon involved. Listing the death records and occupations of the deceased, it indicates the prevalence of independent tradesmen—carpenters, grocers, shoemakers, farmers, mill spinners, vintners, masons, wrights, seamen, carters. But clearly the most prevalent, numbering a full 30 percent of the listed occupations, were the weavers. And these especially were the most seriously afflicted by the changing patterns of the English Industrial Revolution. The independent weaver in Scotland had long enjoyed a comfortable life. Weavers were often amateur students of the sciences—botany, ornithology, geology —and were known for their inquiring minds. But in the 1830s they

---

[8] Sir Walter Scott, *The Antiquary* (1816; New York, 1967), pp. 68-82; George Hay, *History of Arbroath to the Present Time* . . . (Arbroath, 1876), n. pag.; J. M. McBain, *Eminent Arbroathians: Being Sketches Historical, Geneaological, and Biographical, 1178-1894* (Arbroath, 1897), p. 320; idem, *Bibliography of Arbroath Periodical Literature and Broadsides* (Arbroath, 1889), p. 60; *New Statistical Account of Scotland* (Edinburgh, 1846), 11:74-82.

faced declining markets, an overcrowded vocation, and above all the cheap competition of the new mills. Many lost their homes, gave up their activity in literary and cultural events, and left the Church. Theirs was an increasingly depressing lot, and drinking often took its toll. The writer for the Arbroath section of the *New Statistical Account of Scotland*, betraying a ministerial perspective that nonetheless seems not to have misconstrued the facts, wrote with respect to the community that "in a great many cases where extreme poverty is observable, the people are the main cause of their own wretchedness. The head of the family frequents the tippling-house, where he spends no inconsiderable portion of his earnings; and this while the wife and children are left in misery. Young men and women in the 'operative' classes never think of saving any part of their earnings." The result also was a generally poor diet. Potatoes sprinkled with salt sometimes constituted the entire meal. But for all his gloom, the writer of the account perceived signs of moral improvement. Thirty or forty years ago, he remarked, smugglers of gin from the Continent were held in such social esteem that they could marry very well. Now they were subjected to public scorn. A financial class of would-be aristocrats then mocked religion with "vulgar scorn," but were now no longer heard. Voluntary giving for benevolent and public purposes was recovering from earlier neglect. The evangelical movement had already begun to make an impact in Arbroath, but the challenge that McCosh faced was still a demanding one.[9]

In contemplating the life of a minister in nineteenth-century Scotland, we are likely to reflect exclusively on the endless round of sermonizing and the incidentals of keeping the parish life in motion. But attention to these details alone obscures the immense human challenge involved. This was not a life for weak hearts and refined sensibilities. Any research into the local history of Great Britain, whether the smoky towns of the industrial midlands or the remoter dens of the bleak and misty Highlands, becomes very soon a reminder of the precariousness of life at this time. Ours is an age that easily becomes numb to violence because it is broadcast loud in the public media. But there is nothing new under the sun. Local Scottish newspapers contemporaneous with McCosh's early ministry are replete with assaults on life. The death of children from a

---

[9] *New Statistical Account of Scotland*, 11:84–87; "Parochial Register of Arbroath, County of Forfar, 1825-54," in the Register Office, Edinburgh. I have taken the figures from the records for the year 1835-1836, coinciding with McCosh's arrival in Arbroath.

multitude of diseases, the almost weekly news of robbery, murder, and suicide, industrial accidents and drownings at sea, acts of madness and insanity—all these recur with arresting frequency in the chronicles of local life. Journalistic reports bring these reminders with the cold realism that one finds in Michael Lesy's *Wisconsin Death Trip*. In Arbroath, the wave of influenza that struck the community in 1837 was only one variety of the many dangers that beset the people of this area. More familiar to the daily routine of the young minister were the special hazards of a fishing town. McCosh knew these hazards and recalled later: "At one part of my life it was my painful duty to intimate to many a poor woman who thought herself a sailor's wife, that she was a widow, that her husband had perished in the waters of the Baltic Sea."[10]

Increasingly, McCosh's pastoral work involved him in the larger organizational structure of the Church. Within the Presbytery of Brechin and the larger Synod of Angus and Mearns, McCosh joined a party of the younger ministers eager to reform the Church and make it "thoroughly evangelical and popular." The clear leader of this religious circle was one of the most striking figures in Scotland, the energetic and charismatic Thomas Guthrie (1803-1873). Already, Guthrie had taken the lead among the local Evangelicals in the fight against patronage, and this nonintrusion issue, as it was called, united McCosh and Guthrie in common cause. They became intimate colleagues and friends. McCosh often invited the fiery Guthrie to charge his own parish against patronage, and McCosh, "whenever I had an idle half-day," walked the several miles over to Guthrie's place. There they spent an afternoon of discussion and laughter as they sat amid the yellow fields and enjoyed the warmth of a sunny Scottish day.[11]

Thomas Guthrie, whose statue stands today along Edinburgh's famous Princes Street, was the product of one of the most remarkable families of the northeast. The Guthries had been farmers of the "braes of Angus" for many generations until David Guthrie came to Brechin, about fifteen miles inland from Arbroath. Here he applied his keen business sense to become the town's leading merchant and one of the few men of wealth who owed nothing to lineage. His family of fifteen also included the son Alexander, who

---

[10] McCosh, "My Life," 56; idem, *The Ulster Revival and Its Physiological Accidents* (Belfast, 1859), pp. 3-4.

[11] McBain, *Bibliography of Arbroath*, pp. 40-41; James McCosh, "Dr. Guthrie's Early Ministry," *New York Observer*, August 14, 1873; Guthrie, *Autobiography*, 1:324, 338-40, 343-44.

Thomas Guthrie

pursued a highly successful career in medicine. Their mother was the daughter of the Reverend James Burns of Brechin and with her husband contrived to run a household on the strictest lines of puritan discipline. Parents and children met together mornings and evenings at the family altar and, Thomas recalled, "no departures from the strictest habits of virtue and religion would have been tolerated for an hour."[12] With these influences, Guthrie became a

[12] *Genealogy of the Descendants of Thomas Guthrie* . . . (Edinburgh, 1902), pp. 17-19; Guthrie, *Autobiography*, 1:18-19, 248-49. McCosh's career almost took a signif-

The Gospel Ministry 77

lively example of the Scottish provincial character, a major ingredient of the evangelical movement. He pursued an active ministry in Brechin before transferring to Edinburgh and launching a spectacular career at the Old Greyfriar's Church. Guthrie here led the evangelical movement in a major new direction with his program of ragged schools, for which he is today best remembered.

The McCosh-Guthrie friendship was in many ways a friendship of opposites. McCosh remembered that Guthrie wholly disdained "metaphysical disquisitions," for which McCosh had a consuming love. Moreover, McCosh saw in Guthrie the vigorous and charismatic preacher that he knew he could never be. Even Sir William Hamilton, who liked his religion in milder doses, called Guthrie the best preacher he had heard. Guthrie, sporting heavy leather country boots and trousers bespattered with mud, truly appeared a man of the people. He interspersed his gospel sermons with local colloquialisms, and, McCosh swore, he could move an audience from tears to laughter within minutes. But Guthrie also had "sound common sense [and] a profound knowledge of human nature." He was generous with his possessions, and, as McCosh found when the two were visiting some poor children, generous with the possessions of others. Guthrie gave them McCosh's dinner![13]

The Arbroath period of McCosh's career was a brief one. His pastoral work was energetic, and he proved to be popular with his flock, winning the confidence of the congregation. In Arbroath he became an active partisan of the evangelical movement, but, save one instance when he made the church available for a public meeting on the patronage issue, his pastorship was devoid of bitterness.[14] It was already clear, as the Church moved toward crisis, that

---

icant turn in 1837. In June he recieved a request from the prestigious Old Greyfriar's Church in Edinburgh to preach on the Sabbath of the twenty-fifth. The Town Council was anxious to fill an opening in the church, and McCosh's former professor, David Welsh, saw an opportunity to enhance the Evangelicals' strength in the city by urging McCosh's consideration. But McCosh, only twenty-six at the time, lacked the self-confidence to pursue this opportunity, and strongly pushed the name of his older friend Guthrie. Then began Guthrie's energetic ministry in the slums of the Cowgate section of the capital city. Letter from the kirk session clerk, Old Greyfriar's Church, June 20, 1837, in the "Correspondence of James McCosh," Department of Rare Books and Special Collections, Princeton University Library; McBain, *Eminent Arbroathians*, pp. 320-21; McCosh, "My Life," 64–66; Guthrie, *Autobiography*, 1:370.

[13] Guthrie, *Autobiography*, 1:259, 352, 338n-339n; McCosh, "Guthrie's Early Ministry."

[14] Douglas, *Centennary*, p. 56. The issues surrounding the meeting are described in the "Minute Book of Abbey Church," May 9, 1838.

McCosh would excel not as the zealous popular preacher of the Thomas Guthrie kind, but as an organizer and administrator. His next appointment tested those skills to the fullest.

BRECHIN was to be McCosh's home for the next twelve years. From here he joined with hundreds of his pastoral brethren to bring the Free Church of Scotland into being, and from here he pursued an arduous itinerant ministry that took him to villages and farms in the eastern coastal region and into the Grampian Mountains to the north of the town. McCosh's new position again owed something to the efforts of David Welsh, although by virtue of his own work in the area he was not an unfamiliar figure. At the Cathedral Church of Brechin McCosh now became first charge and had as a colleague the Reverend Alexander Leith Ross Foote, a resourceful man, graduate of Aberdeen, and later author of four books on religion. On January 24, 1839, the Presbytery of Brechin gathered to ceremonialize McCosh's new ministry, and Rev. Mungo Parker from the neighboring East Church of Brechin delivered the sermon.[15]

Thomas Guthrie, who grew up in the center of this small community of 6,500 persons, remembered "a noisy street, with dull grey houses on either side, in an old provincial town." Brechin had long been a familiar sight to travelers on the old coach route north to Aberdeen, but the new East Coast Railway soon diminished its prominence, passing four miles to the west and affording only a glimpse of the town. McCosh thought Brechin perfectly typical of provincial Scotland. He remembered a flax mill, a bleach field, several linen manufacturers, a whiskey distillery, three banks, and the usual number of shops and stores. The single Episcopal Church in the community served most of the gentlemen's families in the town, and some of lesser ranks as well. The Reverend Mr. Burns drew an uneven portrait of Brechin's inhabitants in the *New Statistical Account of Scotland* in 1833. "Not much can be said in favor of the habits of the ordinary class of inhabitants as to cleanliness in their persons and habitations." Inns and public houses proliferated to a scandalous degree, and "their effects on morals are in many cases very bad." Nonetheless, the writer found a fairly well disciplined population, much of it shrewd and intelligent, with many

---

[15] Thomas Brown, ed., *Annals of the Disruption* . . . (n.p., 1843), p. 5; "Report of the Actings and Proceedings of the Presbytery of Brechin, From February Third One Thousand Eight Hundred and Thirty Years," in the Scottish Record Office, Edinburgh, January 8, 1839.

readers of history and practical theology. The available temptations notwithstanding, the populace generally rated high on temperance, certainly better than most places of its kind.[16]

Brechin also had some prominent historical monuments. The town slopes down to the River South Esk, which, widening, flows on past the precipitous rock on which stands Brechin Castle. This edifice, then the home of the powerful Panmure, was earlier the site of Thomas Maule's unsuccessful defense against the invading English armies of Edward III. In the upper region of the town stood the ruins of the ancient chapel Maison Dieu. Brechin indeed had deep roots in the Protestant and pre-Protestant periods of Scottish history. In the tenth-century reign of Kenneth II, the Scottish king gave "the great monastery of Brechin to the Lord." The *Pictish Chronicle* suggested that the king either founded a religious community here or gave his blessings to one already established. David I in 1153 made Brechin the see of a new bishopric for the several towns in north Angus. Then the early decades of the thirteenth century saw the first construction of the Cathedral Church (known later as the West Church), one of the country's finest examples of the Scottish Gothic style. For three centuries this structure remained a bishop's see in the Roman church. In the Reformation period and through the Anglican wars when Brechin was the headquarters of the Covenanters in Angus, the cathedral lost its prestige and much of its wealth. By the nineteenth century the original medieval fabric had clearly deteriorated. The heritors and private seat holders made extensive alterations but at the price of the original character. Nonetheless, in visiting Brechin today one can still appreciate the beauty and traditional Gothic richness of this site of McCosh's second ministry. The nave and chancel beautifully reflect the medieval splendor of their original design. Also, the adjacent eleventh century Round Tower makes Brechin nearly unique in Scottish architecture.[17] Strange it is to reflect that this ancient edifice was, in 1839, about to become the center of an experiment in radical Protestantism.

McCosh's new ministry had all the characteristics of that experiment. His religious style, reflected in his "gospel sermons," offered

---

[16] Guthrie, *Autobiography*, 1:241, 243; McCosh, "My Life," 68; *New Statistical Account of Scotland*, 11:134-41.

[17] *New Statistical Account of Scotland*, 11:129-33; The Society of the Friends of Brechin Cathedral, *A Guide to Brechin Cathederal* (n.p., 1972); D. H. Edwards, *Historical Guide to Brechin with Notes on the Scenery, Antiquities, and Traditions of the District* (Brechin, n.d.), p. 105.

a Christocentric message and emphasized the conversion experience as the necessary condition of salvation. His energetic social work in Brechin carried the banners of temperance, Sabbatarianism, and educational efforts that motivated the evangelical movements in Scotland and elsewhere. And a special kind of domestic missionary work gave a democratic accent to McCosh's activities that also reflected the spirit of uplift in the reviving religious age. On his arrival in Brechin the twenty-eight-year-old minister established a fairly constant routine, setting aside one day a week for general visits to his parishioners, another for calls upon the sick. Other days he gave to itinerant work in neighboring communities and to visits to the townspeople generally, making it a point to call on persons outside his fold. Mostly, though, his work involved him with the artisan classes, and, outside the town, with farmers and servants. He did of course have business with the middle-class merchants and bankers, but virtually none with the wealthy, the younger Fox Maule, son of Lord Panmure, being an exception. The affiliations were important, for both in Scotland and America, though he may have seemed to these groups an incessant and often cranky moralist, McCosh judged these middling elements the hope of the world. Their puritan virtues and hard work, when he could bring them into play, their mixture of gospel faith and appreciation of science, good literature, and secular learning generally, later became ingredients in the models of his social and educational work.[18]

McCosh's visitation program and his growing immersion in the life of the community brought to his attention one fact that vexed and troubled him profoundly. The profuse drinking habits of the town blighted the morals and sapped the energy of its inhabitants and insulted its Christian pretensions. McCosh's lament was not merely the agonizing of a perfectionist-minded minister. Brechin's historian refers to the nearly ruinous drinking habits that had set into the town earlier in the century. These had improved somewhat, as he and the *Statistical Account* noticed, but among the working classes the persistence of the pattern caused concern. McCosh thought the issue had become serious enough to warrant a special session to confront it, so he called his own congregation and as many of the townspeople as he could assemble to a meeting. "The evil in this parish [a reference to the general area, not the congregation] and elsewhere," he warned, "has grown to an extent that

[18] McCosh, "My Life," 70-72.

must astonish all." Nothing impresses like statistics, so McCosh did some research. He paced the area and counted fifty-one places where liquor was sold (the *Statistical Account for 1833* counted more than sixty). "Now, what a lamentable view does this very circumstance give of the moral and spiritual condition of the people." A spirit shop for every thirty-six adults! McCosh also calculated the "lamentable and appalling fact" that Brechin citizens spent £1,000 a year on intoxicants. That was forty times their gifts to the church. But these were statistics only. The real evil, McCosh asserted, lay in the lives lost, the children rendered orphans, the wives made widows. It was time that drinking ceased to be an expected ritual at social gatherings. Must we "tip" at every occasion? No remedies could produce deep and radical change except the spreading of the gospel and the grace of God. Any others would be palliative only and short-lived. A revival of religion would mean the conversion of the sinner's state of being and the spiritual reconstruction of his personality. That alone would be equal to the challenge at hand.[19]

It may appear that McCosh was employing the method of social improvement for which the Evangelicals have often been criticized. Religious conversion of the kind he pursued looked to an individual salvation that made it possible to avoid any confrontation of the underlying social and economic roots of the evils in question. That the Evangelicals did bring moral improvement in their works cannot be denied, but no fundamental reconstruction of class and economic power was born of their reforms. Their activism was of a different kind, but McCosh at least did not choose to rest his efforts for social betterment on exhortation alone. His work with the Mechanics' Institute in Brechin consumed as much of his energy as any other project and constituted an important adjunct of his ministry. The Mechanics' Institute, completed in 1833, was the gift of the inhabitant of Brechin Castle and patron of the Cathedral Church, Lord Panmure. His endowment provided a meeting hall, a library, and other rooms. The institute, typical of the many of its kind that were popular in Britain in this period, was part of a wider effort of the middle and upper classes to channel the frustrations and boredom of the workers away from the pub and toward useful activities. Its recreational, leisure, social, and cultural activities made the institute a kind of surrogate for the church in its social functions,

[19] David D. Black, *The History of Brechin to 1864* (Edinburgh, 1867), p. 186; *Report and Addresses by the Kirk-Session of the Old Church, Brechin, on the Subject of Intemperance, April 18, 1841* (Brechin, 1841), pp. 1-10.

although, as in McCosh's case, these institutes had the cooperation and support of the religious interests in their communities. McCosh not only organized a great variety of cultural programs in the institute, sponsoring individuals who spoke on psychology, history, art, and nearly anything else, he himself was a frequent speaker. He wished to make the institute a center of humanistic-religious culture and to that extent secured himself a position on the library committee, perusing the shelves to weed out "infidel" books and some of the too plentiful novels. Every indication suggests that the institute was highly popular with a sizable portion of the community.[20]

Were there little more than this to the business of social and moral improvement the work might have been rather pleasant. But the burden of this work was centered in the local congregation and honored a sacred Scottish tradition that made the minister the vigilant and omnipresent disciplinarian of his flock. There is no reason to assume the churches where McCosh served were untypical. Kirk session minutes in every village and hamlet in Scotland recount an unchanging pattern. It is striking to read through the Brechin Cathedral Kirk Session Records and confront the endless procession of cases of moral delinquency that passed under the review of McCosh and the session meeting. These invariably fell to the minister for action. Time and time again McCosh had to deal with cases of "pre-nuptial fornication." At the West Free Church of Brechin, where McCosh was serving in July 1843, for example, a young woman, Ann Young, who had given birth to a child with a partner whom she identified as John Buile, appeared before the session. McCosh, adhering to usual procedure, admonished her and ordered her to report to the next meeting. She did so and McCosh "dismissed her from the discipline of the Church," meaning only that she was pardoned and restored to the list of communicants. That same July day McCosh had no less than four other moral offenses to consider. The extensive and endless recurrence of these cases must speak for the remarkable, and, one suspects, often morbid vigilance of the good men of the church regarding the personal conduct of their members. McCosh fulfilled his assignment dutifully but found the incessant routine trying and tedious. Eventually he decided there were better things to do with his life.[21]

---

[20] Black, *History of Brechin*, p. 205; *Brechin Advertiser and Angus and Mearns Intelligencer*, December 5, 1848, April 3, 1849; *Dundee Warder and Arbroath and Forfar Journal*, December 17, 1844.

[21] "Records of the Kirk Session of Brechin: Beginning with the Year 1821, at the

With a vigorous ministry such as his, McCosh could not expect to escape some of the perils of preaching. He wanted to bring everyone in Brechin to church and boasted that he nearly succeeded. But village atheists and local scoffers remained beyond his reach. Two such persons, McCosh later related, were a pair of wealthy women who kept a pawnshop that lodged vagrants. McCosh did not like the appearance of this arrangement and resolved on a bold course of action. He persuaded the two women to allow him to hold a meeting in their place and to invite the neighbors to attend. Some told McCosh that this was quite unbecoming, and McCosh had no idea that the two pawnbrokers were planning some entertainment of their own. McCosh had barely begun his talk when he noticed that a large monkey, the possession of one of the lodgers and obviously well trained by his owner, was precisely mimicking every movement and gesture of the preacher. Whether lifting his hand, moving his head, or stomping his feet, McCosh found the monkey in perfect cadence, and all "with a face of deepest gravity." Muffled laughter soon spread over the room, and it was clear that the simian was stealing McCosh's show. Some thought McCosh deserved as much for bringing the gathering to so unsavory a place. But the minister emerged triumphant. With a sudden jerk to the side, he threw his shadow violently to the floor, from which he was carried in disgrace by his owner. McCosh garnered respect for his resourcefulness and even some admiration from the attending vagrants. He even claimed that the incident enabled him afterward to win converts among some of the lost souls in the area.[22]

But beyond Brechin the evangelical cause fared not so well. While gaining in numbers it was losing in the courts. In the famous Auchterader case of 1838 the Court of Session in effect declared for the legal right of patronage, and the next year the House of Commons did the same. But Scotland was only divided all the more. Thomas Chalmers, more vigorously than ever, protested against establishment, and his "Claim of Right" made the most elaborate case yet for the spiritual independence of the Church. That case met the rebuttal of Chalmers's university colleague Sir William Hamilton. In a pamphlet entitled *Be Not Schismatics, Be Not Martyrs By Mistake*, Hamilton employed his own legal expertise and carefully

---

Brechin Cathedral," located at the Brechin Cathedral; "Minutes oif the West Free Kirk Session" (Brechin), in the Scottish Record Office, July 31, 1843, August 28, 1843.

[22] McCosh, "My Life," 73-74.

demonstrated the state's legitimate authority in ecclesiastical affairs. By mistake or not, however, it was clear that schismatics were in the making.[23]

While the Evangelicals found their victories rebuffed at the national level, they rallied their forces in scores of towns and villages throughout Scotland. McCosh's work in Brechin was a small but effective part of the total effort. He counseled his congregation and guided them through the conflict and collaborated closely with others in the region. Although the situation for the Evangelicals was grim, Guthrie wrote to McCosh from Edinburgh, urging that they not yet "rashly proceed to dissolve the connection" with the established Church. Yet in the long run, schism seemed unavoidable. "Unless the Government and the Legislature shall, within a given and specified time, redress the wrongs we complain of, we shall dissolve the union, and leave all the sins and consequences at the door of an Erastian and oppressive State." In the meantime a united front was needed. "I pray you," Guthrie urged McCosh, "turn over the subject, and talk of it with your friends, and let us pray that the Lord will bring us all to one opinion."[24]

To the Evangelicals, steadfastness on the Headship principle (that Christ is the only head of the Church) invoked a whole wider array of ideas. At stake was the entire religious heritage of their country, so the warfare of the 1830s was not a new battle but an old one. While the Auchterader case went before the Court of Session the bicentenary of the Covenanting Assembly of 1638 celebrated the heroes and martyrs of an earlier age, and Thomas McCrie's lives of Knox and Melville enjoyed wide circulation. Thomas Guthrie best summarized the feelings of his party as they rallied to save the Church and spread a revival of religion over the land: "There was no mistake about the matter. The controversy was neither new to us nor new to Scotland. For one long and weary century, from the days of Popish Mary down to the blessed Revolution, our stout fathers had fought the very same battle. The whole blood of the Covenant has been shed on this field. We had nought else to do but pluck the weapons from the dead men's hands; and when the State came down on us in its pride and power [we had only to] man once more the moss-grown ramparts where our fathers had bled and died."[25]

[23] J.H.S. Burleigh, *A Church History of Scotland* (New York, 1960), p. 349; Andrew L. Drummond and James Bulloch, *The Scottish Church, 1688-1843: The Age of the Moderates* (Edinburgh, 1973), p. 241; John Veitch, *Memoir of Sir William Hamilton* (Edinburgh and London, 1869), pp. 267-69; McCosh, "My Life," 76.

[24] Guthrie, *Autobiography*, 2:40-41. [25] Ibid., 2:12-13.

Beginning late in 1842 McCosh and Foote called a series of meetings with their congregation to review with them the developments within the Church and the principles at stake in the conflict. McCosh wished to impress emphatically on the minds of his parishioners the magnitude of the ideals at stake. At the first meeting he summarized the main point concisely: "We find it written in the Confession of Faith, also ratified by the Act of Parliament, that Christ is the only King and Head of the Church: that he hath therein appointed office-bearers distinct from the civil magistrate, and not subject to the civil magistrate; and we find the civil power forbidden to the power of the keys or of discipline." It was on this understanding, he said, that he and other ministers entered the church. "We cannot continue in a church which does not act on these principles. We believe them to be Scripture principles." But principles aside, the state hindered the church's work of moral and social improvement. "When we would shut out the drunkard from the communion table," McCosh said, "he appeals to the civil courts, and because we cannot follow him there, his request is granted, and we are commanded to throw open our table to receive him."[26]

McCosh was clearly intimating a break in the Church. By January of 1843 that event seemed unavoidable, and people everywhere were talking of the forthcoming meeting of the General Assembly in March. McCosh knew what was in store and now sought to rally the Cathedral Church by an appeal to religious patriotism. A meeting to discuss the issues again on January 29 was followed by another the next week. This one witnessed an emotional address by the head pastor. The Church of Scotland, McCosh said, is "the fairest daughter of the Reformation." "It may be said of us, as it was said of Israel of old, God never so dealt with any people." Scotland has been blessed with the fruits of the earth and with high intellect in its people. But McCosh did not so much intend to flatter as to warn. Has God a quarrel with Scotland? "Have we improved so much as we should have done the privileges we enjoy? Or have we become wise in our own esteem? Have we been trusting in our privileges instead of trusting in God?"[27]

McCosh did not say so specifically, but his remarks expressed his condemnation of the age of Moderatism in its social and religious consequences. The principles were important, but significant

---

[26] James McCosh, *Recollections of the Disruption in Brechin* ([Brechin, 1842]), pp. 1-2. This is a compilation of several essays by McCosh.
[27] Ibid., p. 5.

mostly within the context of the power of the upper classes through their patronage privileges in the Church. At first that effect meant the steady advance of religious indifference among the middle and lower classes of Scotland, and now, with the evangelical revival making great strides among those elements, patronage was the surest obstacle to its complete success. So McCosh added his voice to the vast chorus of religious propagandizing that fanned the quarrels in this highly literate nation. The immense proliferation of the religious literature astounded even Guthrie. "Think of seven hundred and eighty pamphlets on this one subject, printed during three years, and falling like snowflakes all over the land."[28] In the midst of the crisis McCosh added a tract of his own, entitled *Does the Established Church Acknowledge Christ as Its Head?*[29] McCosh here claimed that the Church operated through a spiritual authority vested in it by Christ. The magistrate can claim none of that authority. Rather, Christ continues in the Headship by ruling through laws and discipline drawn from the Bible. Nor could the Church give up any of that authority to the state, for it was not the Churh's to give. Hence, no "marriage" of Church and state, as the Evangelicals' opponents wanted, was possible. But even if it were possible, McCosh said, what now prevails is certainly no marriage of equals. The Church betrayed its own trust in yielding so much to the state, while the state has yielded nothing in return. What then of the state endowments that supported the whole ministry of the Church of Scotland? They are "the collar which the dog wears," McCosh said. And here he assumed a clearly more radical position than Chalmers. If endowments to the Church come only with patronage attached, then damn the endowments. It would be far better to have a free church.[30]

Amid the heated exchanges McCosh went off to Edinburgh in March to attend the General Assembly meeting. By now it was clear, however, that the two parties had reached a complete im-

---

[28] Guthrie, *Autobiography*, 2:17.

[29] I quote here from the second printing of the pamphlet, dated 1843. The first 2,000 copies of the pamphlet, according to this edition, sold out quickly and the second appeared after the Disruption took place. In the absence of a copy from the first printing, I have been unable to determine its exact date of publication.

[30] James McCosh, *Does the Established Church Acknowledge Christ as Its Head? . . .* (Edinburgh, 1846), pp. 4-9. The *Free Church Magazine* took note of McCosh's essay, judged its argument "completely incontrovertible," and expressed the hope that McCosh would continue as a "vigorous polemicist" for the Free Church. *Free Church Magazine* (March 1846), 94-95. For an elaborate statement of the Established Church's position on this issue, see *Blackwood's Edinburgh Magazine*, 50 (1841), 127-42.

The Gospel Ministry

passe, and compromise on principles so heavily supported by each was out of the question. All looked with a quiet dread to the May meeting which they knew would register the complete break. McCosh convened his congregation after the March breakdown and reported on the failure to make any progress. The outcome now, he told the gathering, was inevitable. "We must throw up all the benefits of an Establishment, because we can no longer hold them without changing our principles." But he urged the people to welcome the new challenge before them: "to build up what I shall ever regard as the true Church of Scotland."[31]

In the few days before May 18, 1843, ministers from all over Scotland, many with heavy hearts, prepared for the trip to Edinburgh. McCosh packed for a four-day visit and boarded the coach for the capital city. Thomas Guthrie left his home there on Lauriston Lane and remarked to his wife: "Well, Anne, this is the last time I go out at this door a minister of an Established Church!" The events of this General Assembly meeting were dramatic, even if foretold. The gathering was centered at St. Andrew's Church on George Street where Moderator David Welsh convened the meeting at 2:30. After completion of the services at the High Kirk of St. Giles, a procession accompanied by military band brought the Lord High Commissioner to St. Andrew's. Already thousands of people lined the streets along the way. Inside St. Andrew's Welsh read the opening prayer, but then broke from all normal procedure, and instead of constituting the Assembly, read a statement of protest against infringements of the Church's liberties. He announced that he would proceed no further. Chalmers was in attendance and rose to join Welsh in the march out of the church. Quickly one whole side of the crowded building was emptied, as hundreds expanded the exiting throng. McCosh had awaited this momentous turn and marched with the protesters as they squeezed through the waiting audience outside. From there a walk of nearly a quarter of a mile took the group down George Street, then north on Hanover to Canonmills, and into Tanfield Hall, which had been prepared for it and now filled with 3,000 people more. When a measure of repose finally settled on the mass, Welsh opened the new Assembly with prayer and called for the election of Chalmers as moderator. At the meeting's end each of the party signed the Act of Separation and Deed of Demission. Affixed thereon were the signatures of the two ministers of the West Church of Brechin.[32]

---

[31] McCosh, *Recollections of the Disruption*, p. 7.
[32] Drummond and Bulloch, *Scottish Church*, pp. 246-49; Norman L. Walker, *Chapters from the History of the Free Church of Scotland* (Edinburgh, [1895]), p. 17.

Thus occurred the Disruption, and thus was born the Free Church of Scotland. For those involved it was an unforgettable event. Others thought it foolish, a rash and headstrong defense of principle. But for the duration of his life McCosh was proud to have been one of the participants. Even those remote from the incident or indifferent to the issues at stake were often highly impressed by the courage and resolution of the Free Churchmen. Witness Lord Cockburn: "I know no parallel to it. Whatever may be thought of their cause, there can be no doubt or coldness in the admiration with which all candid men must applaud their heroism. They have abandoned that public station which was the ambition of their lives, and have descended from certainty to precariousness, and most of them from comfort to destitution, solely for their principles."[33] Cockburn effectively summarized the predicament of the seceders. Back in Brechin a multitude of new challenges awaited the man who was now without a church.

THREE TIMES in his life James McCosh confronted a situation marked by institutional disorganization. The Disruption of the Church of Scotland dissevered hundreds of ministers and thousands of people from their local and national church structures and required everywhere the construction of new institutions. In Brechin and in the whole central northeast area of Scotland McCosh had to take steps to fill the vacuum left by the schism. Similar challenges awaited him in the years ahead—one when he undertook an academic appointment at a newly created institution in Ireland, and another when he assumed the presidency of an old but declining college in the United States. But in conditions like these McCosh thrived. He became a master at using the skills and abilities of different people and at coordinating their efforts, and he was expert at planning and administering. One of the local church historians of Brechin, reviewing the years after the Disruption, concluded from his survey of McCosh's work that he was "a born organizer."[34]

Both McCosh and his colleague Foote returned to Brechin immediately after the Disruption. They had now relinquished their state stipends and had forfeited their rights to minister in the West Church. Calling another meeting for May 21, McCosh and Foote told their parishioners that they were free to follow their own con-

[33] Quoted in Drummond and Bulloch, *Scottish Church*, pp. 248-49.
[34] An unpublished, handwritten history of the East Free Church, Brechin, by a relative of Thomas Guthrie, in the possession of Mr. A. M. Lawson, session clerk of the Cathederal Church, Brechin (n.p., n.d.), 22.

sciences. They could remain as members of the established Church, or they could join them in the Free Church. The two ministers would begin right away to plan for the construction of a new church in Brechin and the raising of funds to support it. The West Church had already pledged its support to the Claim of Right, and McCosh was counting on a majority to walk out with him. That he secured. About 800 persons in the West Church joined McCosh, while 600 remained behind. But the numbers obscure the genuine hardships of the decision. Families, friends, and lovers split over the issue, and McCosh recalled "painful scenes" in a community where many practiced their faith with utmost seriousness and dedication. One young woman, McCosh related, told him that her father was threatening to give her only bread and water until she returned to the established Church. On June 4 McCosh rallied those who supported him. Amid the prevailing uncertainty, and even unhappiness, he tried to impress on his friends the significance of their new undertaking. He believed earnestly that the growing revival had reached its natural fruition in the Disruption and that Scotland was recovering her sacred past. In an impassioned conclusion to his address, McCosh revealed all his dedication and emotional commitment to the cause before the new church. Summoning his followers to that cause, the minister announced: "It is our earnest and burning desire to preach the everlasting Gospel throughout the length and breadth of the land, in every city, and village, and glen, of our beloved country."[35]

Within his own area of the country McCosh himself came close to doing that. But for the moment pressing problems were growing in his own backyard. Hundreds of congregations throughout Scotland now lacked church buildings, and everywhere necessity gave birth to invention. In one place parishioners used a herring store for a church, in another an abandoned public house, and in another nothing less than a distillery of the John Grant Company.[36] After McCosh and Foote duly constituted their new body as the West Free Church of Brechin, they divided their membership into two groups and availed themselves of the generous offer of the two Secession churches in the town. These offers were apparently judged more suitable than that of the North Port Distillery Company, which offered its ample granaries and melting barns for tem-

---

[35] William Ewing, ed., *Annals of the Free Church of Scotland, 1843-1900*, 2 vols. (Edinburgh, 1914), 1:n. pag.; McCosh, "My Life," 79-81; idem, *Recollections of the Disruption*, pp. 9-10.

[36] Drummond and Bulloch, *Scottish Church*, p. 252.

porary accommodation. McCosh and Foote preached separately in the two small churches in the morning, switching in the evening.

McCosh in the meantime had undertaken a campaign to raise funds for the new church building that John Eaton, a local citizen, had designed. He had superb success in his efforts, securing £500 in his first contacts and gaining supplementary money from the Central Building Fund of the Free Church Central Organization in Edinburgh. Construction of the building began immediately and progressed rapidly, and by November the new edifice, combining what one local newspaper called "Scotch cheapness and utility with English elegance," received its first worshippers. One cannot fail to be impressed by this example of local energy and sacrifice, and especially so when one considers that on the other side of town, the East Church of Brechin underwent a similar division that resulted in the construction of another new building, the East Free Church of Brechin. On November 13 the two Free Church congregations held a joint communion in the East Free Church, and two weeks later the West Free Church held its first services. Twelve hundred persons heard Foote preach in the morning, and 1,400 listened to McCosh that afternoon. The new era now dawning, he proclaimed, was akin to the great periods of the Reformation, the Covenant, and the Glorious Revolution. And the gathered people responded with equal enthusiasm. The session minutes list some of the donations to the church by its members, among these a "splendid pulpit Bible and Song Book, a Baptismal Fountain, Four Valuable Communion cups." It was a memorable day in the little town beneath the Grampian Mountains.[37]

Efforts like these were duplicated all over Scotland. By 1845 about 500 new churches were in use; 700 were finished by 1848. But to reach the people of the very small villages often required heroic dedication. In recalling his travels to the upper hinterlands and his effort to preach and raise new church buildings there, McCosh remarked that "the work of Moses in the desert was scarcely a more difficult one." "I preached in places of which I believe I may truly say that the pure gospel of Jesus Christ had never been pro-

---

[37] *Brechin Advertiser and Angus and Mearns Intelligencer*, [1843], (a clipping in the possession of A. M. Lawson); "Deacon's Session Records, Brechin, West St. Columba's Church" (an introductory section outlines these events), June 26, 1843, October 30, 1843, November 27, 1843; "Minutes of the Presbytery of Brechin Free Church," August 1, 1843; *Montrose, Arbroath, and Brechin Review*, [November 1843], in the possession of Mr. Lawson; McCosh, *Recollections of the Disruption*, p. 8.

claimed there before." McCosh, the preacher on horseback, would have certainly been taken in America for a backwoods Methodist circuit rider. But the experience furnished McCosh lasting memories of his native country and indulged his love of the outdoor's natural beauty. And as early as August of the Free Church's first year, McCosh was reporting to the new presbytery that he had preached in Menmuir to a hundred persons, one group gathered by the side of the road, another in the more comfortable quarters of a tent. Other services took place in the open fields, in barns, or from the elevated pulpit of a prominent doorstep on a local main street. McCosh's work, joined to that of a large and omnipresent party of evangelizers in Scotland, led the *Free Church Magazine* to boast in 1844 that the message of God now reaches to "many a forgotten inlet and neglected corner" of the country.[38]

McCosh had no qualms about preaching in his impromptu chapels, but always looked for the means to erect new churches. Such an effort automatically made him the enemy of the local lords and factors, the heritors who held patronage rights in whatever local churches existed. Everywhere in Scotland the refusal of those parties to grant the use of their lands raised major obstacles to establishing new church sites. In the central northeast, Panmure's lands were extensive. McCosh was reporting to the presbytery in September of 1843 on the obstacles he encountered in his work among the surrounding villages. But in many cases his resourcefulness prevailed. McCosh secured the sites and helped to raise the funds for new churches in Fettercairn, Menmuir, Lochlee, Fourdoun, Lawrencekirk, Bervie, and Stonehaven (scene of the novel *Sunset Song* by James Leslie Mitchell). McCosh's organizational talents were widely recognized, and his appointment by the Free Church General Assembly as convener of supply for the whole synod area of Angus and Mearns entrusted him with a heavy responsibility for the work of church extension. He also headed a committee to study the best means of making presbyterial visitations to the new sites.[39]

McCosh conducted most of his home missionary work after his transferral to the East Free Church of Brechin in 1844. That call fol-

---

[38] Walker, *Chapters*, p. 47; James McCosh, *The Duty of Irish Presbyterians to Their Church at the Present Crisis in the Sustentation of the Gospel Ministry* (Belfast, 1868), pp. 13-14; idem, "My Life," 97-98, 93; "Minutes of the Presbytery of Brechin, Free Church" (August 1, 1843); East Free Church History, 23.

[39] "Minutes of the Presbytery of Brechin, Free Church," September 5, 1843, November 5, 1844; Ewing, ed., *Annals of the Free Church*, 1: n. pag.; McCosh, *For Love's Sake*, p. 11.

James McCosh (about 1845)

lowed the increasing mental deterioration of Rev. Mungo Parker in the East Church, and the kirk session, which was thoroughly familiar with McCosh and his work, looked no further than the other side of town for a replacement. McCosh spoke to his own congregation in a New Year's address in 1844 and announced that he was accepting the call. He feared that the still unsettled condition of the

The Gospel Ministry

Free Church would possibly lead to a request that he locate elsewhere. The removal to the East Free Church would fill a needed position and enable him to remain with friends and continue his association with Foote. Further inducement may have come in the form of a £160 annual salary.[40]

But even stronger incentives possibly affected McCosh's decision. His close association with Thomas Guthrie and his work in the town where the Guthries were the leading family had introduced McCosh to the lively daughter of Thomas's older brother Alexander, the famous physician. Isabella Guthrie reflected all the energy and vitality of her notable family and was a woman of enormous resourcefulness. She was gifted with remarkable practical talents and had served with her father a rudimentary medical apprenticeship. Friendship with the soft-spoken minister of the East Free Church led to marriage on September 29, 1845; their love and mutual respect lasted throughout the remainder of McCosh's life. Isabella was a stabilizing force in McCosh's life, and her own expertise assisted their domestic existence and played an important part later in the Princeton community. Mary Jane McCosh was the first child of this marriage, born in July 1847. But the McCoshes soon were victims of the kind of tragedy James had witnessed on many occasions in his ministry. Their son Andrew, born in April 1848, died in October of the next year. In January of 1850, the year of the publication of McCosh's first book, Alexander Guthrie McCosh was born.[41]

THE ART of the sermon: none was more sacred to the Protestant tradition of Scotland. From the early days of John Knox's preaching, the mastery of popular rhetoric had always been the means of any minister's appeal to the hearts of his people. In the practice that the Free Church of Scotland fought vigorously to revive and defend, the pulpit performance marked the first and major trial of any candidate for the local kirk. Provincial Scots, however, looked for more than flash. Inspiration without illumination was nothing. The minister needed to demonstrate the force of his own convictions and the activity of the holy spirit within him, but he also needed to supply his listeners with some reflections worthy of the learned tradition that produced him. McCosh well knew this middle line that

---

[40] "Minutes of the Presbytery of Brechin, Free Church," November 9, 1843; "Deacon's Session Records," (West Free Church), December 17, 1843, January 1, 1843; unidentified newspaper clipping in the possession of Mr. Lawson.
[41] McCosh, "My Life," 75.

he needed to walk. The Church had suffered badly in forsaking the power and vigor of the older style for the elegance and informality that spoke only to "the polite, the gay, and the refined." The Moderates had betrayed their calling in pursuing so narrow an audience. The minister, McCosh believed, must wear the dress of his age, "but he must never forget that he is a minister of the Word," and must deliver the goods unransomed. McCosh, reared on the literature of an earlier Puritanism, looked back to its healthy blend of learning and enthusiasm as useful guidelines for this middle way. "The preachers who have caught the spirit of the Puritans, but have avoided their technicality and mannerism, have commonly been the most successful in rousing the sunken and dead from their apathy, and in stirring them to anxiety and prayer." Had the Puritan tradition survived more generally, McCosh believed, we should not now have in our midst the ills of the new age: a populace that takes its pleasure in reading novels, a business class devoted only to its shops and its amusements, and a neglected rural population growing up in ignorance.[42]

McCosh believed he knew what had to be done. He wished earnestly to be a successful and popular preacher, but wishing did not make it so. His first years in the provinces steered him through a sometimes painful process of trial and error. For he too was partly a product of the age he wished to undo. He had absorbed much of the smooth and sophisticated style of the capital city, its love of learning and culture. In the course of his studies, immersed as he was in the philosophical tradition of the Scottish Englightenment, McCosh prepared several sermons that he was anxious to make a part of his preaching repertoire. But the results were disastrous. Out of this package of twenty sermons, McCosh found to his distress that some fifteen of them "would not preach." They moved nobody. McCosh therefore burned them and began the process anew. This time he was precise and systematic. He took a cue from his friend Guthrie, who painstakingly worked and reworked his sermon the Saturday night before the delivery, memorized and recited many times over the key passages, and carefully drew out practical and lively illustrations of his ideas. McCosh now took this pragmatic approach. He learned to watch his audience as a chemist watches his bubbling test tubes. He observed the lines that made no impact. He marked the sections that opened eyes, and those that his listeners seemed to retain in their minds. (His parishioners were not

[42] James McCosh, "Introduction to Charnock's Works," in *The Complete Works of Stephen Charnock, B.D.*, 4 vols. (Edinburgh, 1864), 1:xxx-xxxiii.

slow to tell him which these were.) But if this kind of dedication helped make McCosh a more popular preacher, it nonetheless never made him a Guthrie. A historian of Arbroath charitably described McCosh as "too solid and able to be what is called popular." McCosh later was his own severest critic. He was far too serious, he said, too stern and strict to laugh at the follies of the world and live with its ways. He believed he was too much like Paul, not enough like John or Jesus, "wanting in tenderness," he later admitted.[43]

The Scottish Evangelicals sought to revive the style of the older Reformers and much of their message as well. Here as elsewhere the religious revival turned back to the Protestant emphasis on the scriptural foundations of the faith and invoked a pronounced sense of the sinfulness of man and the power of a wrathful deity. But the later standard-bearers softened the harsh determinism of Calvinism. The conversion experience was still decisive, but its occurence was not left wholly to the whim of an arbitrary deity. Christ worked to bring grace to the hearts prepared to receive him, to persons who forsook the love of the world, abandoned the pride of self, and acquiesced fully in the will of God. The Evangelicals preserved all the tensions and fears that ruled the Calvinist sense of life, but they outlined a more certain world. For McCosh, a decade and a half in the ministry had mellowed the rigid intellectualist Calvinism of the Edinburgh review of Hinton. He and the other Evangelicals delivered a message of voluntaryism that merged with the advancing democratic temper of the age and the spirit of assertiveness and uplift. Nonetheless, as McCosh's early sermons show, the whole weight of the religious past of Scotland bore heavily on the new movement. But also in McCosh's early sermons we perceive the rough outlines of his ensuing intellectual career, and the essential structure here emerges in the large treatise that marks the end of the ministerial period of his life. The young preacher in Arbroath and Brechin reflected both the spirit of Knox and the spirit of Reid.

A strongly Christocentric emphasis pervaded nearly all McCosh's sermons. Faith in Christ was the essence of the Christian life, and McCosh warned his popular audiences against extending the gospel authority by human reason and the creeds of men. In our faith in Christ we receive from Christ, and we thereby make the first critical transcendence of our fallen human nature. But we are

[43] James McCosh, "Relation of the Church to the Capital and Labor Question," in *Problems of American Civilization* (New York, 1888), p. 117; idem, "Guthrie's Early Ministry"; idem, *For Love's Sake*, p. 24; idem, "My Life," 53.

nothing without this source and drift aimlessly at the natural human level. Further, McCosh made much use in his sermons of the divine and spiritual realms, themes important to his later writings too, and here especially the mediating role of Christ was essential. How can man, so enfeebled by natural sin, relate in any useful way with the awesome and majestic deity? How is any reconciliation between them possible? The Calvinist, so overwhelmed by the very question, could appeal only to the occasional mercy of an arbitrary God and his special and gratuitous providences. The Calvinist therefore was less inclined to use Christ than were the later Evangelicals. McCosh's sermon "The Lamb in the Midst of the Throne" stressed the critical office of Jesus. "In the Mediator the divine and human offices are united in such a manner that the one does not destroy or overpower the other, but each retains its own properties, while the whole is a unity." We are not so awed therefore in coming to Jesus, for here is man coming to man and also finding divine nature. But the knowledge and discovery of Christ were still the greatest challenge to the Christian. The means were important, and McCosh stayed within the Calvinist context at least to the point of making no appeal to good works as the sure path to salvation. None of his sermons stressed the Christian life in its external manifestations. McCosh the preacher became instead the prober of the inner soul.[44]

In this endeavor McCosh wanted first to rip the mask off the face of the Moderate age. The essential feature of the Moderate man was his self-righteousness, the title of one of McCosh's sermons. The self-righteous person pursues his religion earnestly and with good intention. Every good deed done warms his heart and is a source of self-congratulation. He takes pride in his service to the world and the improvements he furnishes. But the life centered outward obscures from his attention the life within. An easy comfort with one's self follows, and it obviates the need to probe inside. But this was the real stubbornness of heart that most besets all human behavior. Perhaps we are all Moderates by nature. Even so, McCosh was unsparing in his assault. "Determined to cherish thy self-righteousness, thou art waiting for self-indulgence, waiting for earthly goods and pleasures. God offers thee grace, but thou wishest to remain graceless. Thou mightest be made humble, but thou art determined to remain proud. . . . Friend, I would strip thee of these false pre-

[44] James McCosh, *Christ the Way, the Truth, and the Life: A Sermon* (London, 1867), pp. 13-14; idem, *Gospel Sermons* (New York, 1888), pp. 21, 145. This work contains many of McCosh's early sermons and is a very useful guide to his ministry.

tenses by which thou art deceiving thyself, but by which thou cannot deceive God."[45] There is something in the Scottish soul that delights to be told how sinful it is.

We are often imperceptive of the state of original sin, McCosh said, but even our consciousness of this fact too often leads to an exercise of our human powers to overcome it. Those powers are not unavailing if properly employed. But for McCosh and the Evangelicals the first step to personal salvation was a supreme act of self-effacement. Preparation for salvation, in the language of the Puritans, was preparation of the heart. Mere good works too often conceal "a self-righteous spirit unconsciously cherished" and one that crowds out the love of God. No other motivation, though, is possible or necessary. In the end, McCosh said, we will find relief only in trusting in Christ, relinquishing all faith in ourselves. "The crowded bosom now finds an outlet, the confined heart experiences enlargement, and the fettered spirit is free." Indeed the discovery of our own wretchedness may be the mark of the quickening spirit within. But we must be constantly on guard, we must look for the marks and stains of sin in our constant and vigilant self-examination. McCosh entitled one of his sermons after the Syrophoenician woman whose display of humility ultimately wins Jesus' healing of her daughter. But such humility assuredly heralds the conversion of the sinner and the building of the "new man." Indeed it is a new personality that results and even the full restoration of the self and its place in the world. The new man, McCosh said, "takes a new view of every object. He takes a new view of himself. Before, he may have regarded himself with complacency . . . now he sees that his heart is corrupted, and ever tempting him to evil. He takes a new view of God. Before he was alienated from him and did not care for intercouse with him; now he is reconciled to God in Christ. . . . He takes a new view of the world. He lived for it and sought as many of its pleasures and honors as possible; now he sees that these cannot satisfy the immortal soul, and he is seeking for higher enjoyments and more enduring." The new man is also renewed by a new love for his fellows, a new benevolence that springs not from abstract love but from the new knowledge that they like he are immortal beings.[46]

McCosh's gospel sermons are not characterized by any remarkable innovations of thought. Certainly he was telling his audiences what they expected to hear. Many of the sermons are graphically

---

[45] McCosh, *Gospel Sermons*, pp. 247, 105-6.
[46] Ibid., pp. 112, 91, 154-56.

written, especially those in which McCosh explores the heart and mind of the sinner. The anxiety, the fear, the moroseness, the ambition and self-love—these McCosh liked to probe in all their nuances. It can be no surprise that the gospel minister who employed these tools gravitated easily in his later life to the study of the human mind and its infinite facets. The McCosh who introduced the new methods of empirical psychology to students at Princeton descended from the pulpit preacher of eastern Scotland.

Finally, it must be noted that even at this point in his career McCosh's life reflected both of the main cultural forces of his country. The Moderates of the Church in the age of the Scottish Enlightenment could get along very well without the sense of sin and the God who condemns it. They were far more impressed with the achievements of man's rational faculties, his creative ability, his good and charitable deeds. Here, to be sure, the divine and human natures blended, for what was man but the noblest reflection of God's own being? McCosh's sermons were also a dialectic of these two traditions. The recognition of sin was the beginning of wisdom, but it was not the end of living. The Calvinist's gloom mixed with the philosopher's optimism in McCosh's preaching. For it is Christ's love that wins us. The Lamb is as important as the throne; it is the symbol of God's gentleness and his promise to save all who seek him. "God gives grace, and to those who ask it, more grace." But more than this McCosh shared the rationalist's sense of the magnificence of the human condition when all its fine powers have been put to work. Nothing in all God's creation outshone man. "Ye are of more value than mere sparrows," he told his congregation. "[Man] is of more value than all the beasts and planets of the earth, of more value than the sun or moon and all the stars of heaven; for when all living things have died and the heavenly bodies have been changed as a garment thrown aside when it has served its purpose, this soul shall be in its youth, its infancy still, with an eternity before it." So what then is human existence? A wavering struggle between the two awesome extremes of depravity and grandeur. We all occupy middle positions, yet more than this life alone is at stake. In a passage that anticipates the substance of McCosh's own career in philosophy, the minister described the Christian life. "It is a contest between the lower principles of man's nature and the higher, quickened and sanctioned by the Spirit of God. It is a struggle between the animal man and the spiritual man; between pleasure and duty; between selfishness and benevolence; between appetite and conscience; between lust and reason; between love of ease and zeal for good; between deceit and candor; between selfishness and love; between the fear of man and the fear of God; between earth and heaven."[47]

MCCOSH'S ACTIVITY as a Scottish Evangelical and his efforts to win the victory of evangelical principles in the early years of the Free Church absorbed his time and energies. He believed these were heroic ventures, and he thrilled ever afterward to their memory. But in the later 1840s much of this work was becoming routine; furthermore, that work alone had never wholly commanded his spirit. McCosh had departed the University of Edinburgh excited by the love of knowledge. The heady metaphysical atmosphere of the place had enriched his youth, and his intense philosophical interest survived. Although he burned the early sermons born of his thoughts on divine and supernatural things, McCosh eagerly hoped that the pastoral life would have its own intellectual excitements. Throughout his years in Arbroath and Brechin McCosh made every effort he could to squeeze into the rounds of local visitations and horseback itinerary a time for concentrated reading in philosophy. Usually he was quite successful and nearly every week liberated at least a day or two for reading and writing. In this period, and extending into his years in Ireland, McCosh collected his outlines and reflections from different works and placed them into what he labeled "Notes on Books." These files, now in the Princeton University Library, indicate the considerable range and depth of his study program.[48] But McCosh kept all of these pursuits to

[47] Ibid., pp. 16-17, 20, 23, 163, 268-69, 160.
[48] Except in a few cases, it is not indicated exactly when McCosh read a particular item. But the extensive notes show that McCosh read heavily in philosophy and religion, and much poetry as well. The "Notes" contain, among other items and in no discernible order, the following authors and titles: *The Life of Schleiermacher*; Comte, *Cours de Philosophie*; J. S. Mill, *Political Economy*; Mansel on Hamilton and J. S. Mill; Bacon, *Logical Treatises*; Faraday, *Lectures on Non-Metallic Elements*; Ruskin (four works are listed); Carlyle, *Frederick the Great*; Wordsworth's *Life*; Whatley's *Autobiography* and *Logic*; Jeremy Taylor's *Sermons*; Hume's *Essays*; Cuvier, *Theory of the Earth*; Malthus on population; Cicero, *De Natura Deorum*; John Taylor on original sin; *Literature of Geology*; *Playfair's Illustrations*; Magee on the atonement; Newton's *Dissertations*; *Literature of Predestination*; Dwight's *Life of Edwards*; Brougham, *Discourse on Natural Theology*; Jouffroy's *Mélange Philosophique* ("finished 19 June 1848"); Whewell, *Philosophy of the Inductive Sciences* and *Elements of Morality*; Hugh Miller, *Footprints of the Creator*; Carlyle, *Heroes and Hero-Worship*; Coleridge, *Aids to Reflection*; Brown on Puseyite episcopacy; Grote's *Greece*; Lyle's *Travels in America*. Perhaps what is conspicuous in this list is the absence of German philosophical books. McCosh once said that he could barely stand to read Hegel.

himself. He did not tell anyone that he was writing a book, and when the volume appeared the *Free Church Magazine* registered surprise that so hefty and ponderous a work had come from the pen of one heretofore unknown. The reviewer said he had heard McCosh's name before, but nothing more than that.[49]

The Method of the Divine Government appeared in 1850 and brought McCosh immediate and wide acclaim. And although it led directly to an important academic appointment for McCosh, this work properly belongs to his life in the gospel ministry and stands as the terminal landmark of that period of his life. The work, first of all, received far greater consideration in the religious press than in the academic. The *Free Church Magazine* judged it "the most valuable contribution to natural theology with which we are acquainted." It valued the work as a useful reply to Robert Chambers's *Vestiges of Creation* and Auguste Comte's *Positive Philosophy*. According to McCosh, the work, as McCosh may have intended, found its audience among the nonacademic public—ministers, lawyers, teachers, businessmen, and at least one high and influential man of state. It sold extremely well, with the largest consumption in the United States. The first edition was exhausted in six months, and seven more followed. And it is the most readable of McCosh's books. It bears all the marks of the rhetorical style of his ministry. It shuns the scholastic rhetoric and abounds in lively and practical illustrations from the commonplace of life. It is wordy, but fluent. Above all, it occupies a significant, transitional place in McCosh's intellectual life. For despite its popular style and manner it did investigate some weighty problems, and *Divine Government* was McCosh's first effort to correct the premises of the Scottish Enlightenment from the perspectives of the evangelical movement.[50]

McCosh had read widely in the physical and natural sciences, and the first part of his work was an effort to relate these to his religious understanding of the world. His effort to move beyond the kind of evidences of design for which William Paley had become famous took McCosh eventually to an apologetic science that was fully outlined in his philosophy of evolution. Already McCosh was calling for a more thoroughly organic sense of the creation, a unity not of mechanical parts but of progressive and systematic transformation of typical forms. In later works McCosh illustrated these patterns with immense scientific detail, so we will postpone for a while the richer analysis that ensued.

[49] McCosh, "My Life," 105; *Free Church Magazine* (April 1850), 101.
[50] *Free Church Magazine* (April 1850), 97-98; McCosh, "My Life," 108.

The Method of the Divine Government is essentially a book of evidences. Unlike McCosh's later works, it is a religious rather than a philosophical work. But McCosh deliberately avoided specific scriptural references because he did not wish to link the fate of his theistic arguments to the authority of the revealed Word, which held an autonomous status. He did intend of course to bolster the Christian world view and to show that God's goverance of the world paralleled a particular kind of Calvinistic Christianity compatible with his own evangelical perspective. The book divides into two sections, one exploring the external, the other the internal evidences of God's existence and activity. Both parts were drawn in large outlines that became increasingly technical in succeeding works. In each of them McCosh wanted to explore with his readers the possibilities of an ordered universe that allowed both for God's sovereignty and man's freedom. He wished to show both the majesty and meanness of the human condition, its freedom and dependence. He wished to demonstrate the necessary compatibility of a rational and moral human nature, and the important corollary of the will's freedom, with the fact of a controlling, independent deity. McCosh would show that there was something to be said for both of Scotland's intellectual and religious traditions, and that each needed the support and refinement of the other.

The second part of his book explored the subjects of mental and moral science, psychology, and ethics. Here too McCosh outlined issues and answers that he refined and elaborated in later, more technical works. A glance at his views at this point, however, shows clearly how much the neo-Calvinism of the gospel minister informed the views of the early philosopher.

McCosh inherited from his Scottish philosophical predecessors not only the introspective method of that school but the faculty psychology that characterized its analysis of the human constitution. By this approach the mind was divided into its several components or "faculties," and mental philosophy became the science of these faculties, the nature of each and its interaction with the other parts. Intellect, will, conscience, imagination, the sensibility, or emotions, constituted the major divisions and were often the subject of separate treatises. Investigations of these faculties were often highly technical and today seem antiquated and somewhat tedious. But much was at stake in the various interpretations. Was the moral faculty an independent faculty, and did its status as such confirm the freedom and moral independence of human nature? Was the will determined, and what then became of individual moral responsibility? Often at stake were important religious issues. Does the existence of moral laws pronounced by the conscience confirm Christianity's contention that we inherit from God a certain ethical framework that it is our obligation to obey? In answering these questions, McCosh introduced two considerations that merit attention here. They concern the nature of the will and the nature of conscience.

McCosh believed that despite their contrasting points of view, both the naturalism of French thinkers like Condillac and the determinism of the neo-Calvinist Jonathan Edwards did equal violence to a correct understanding of the human will and the attendant question of moral freedom. Recently Cousin and Jouffroy in France and Thomas Brown in Scotland had endeavored to explain the will in terms of sensibility, or emotion, and to reduce its status from an independent faculty to the sum product of the prevailing inclinations of the whole psyche. A crude determinism would seem by this effort to undermine any plausible notion of human responsibility derived from a condition of freedom and capacity to choose. But McCosh did not want to discount the role of some causal factor. McCosh wished to eschew both the naturalistic determinism of the French thinkers and the logical determinism of Edwards. We can imagine a condition in which thoughts and volitions follow each other at random, but we cannot assign to a being in that condition either rationality or moral responsibility. Like the universe at large, the human condition rests in a middle position between determinism and flux. "Human nature expects and finds that the law of causality reigns among the wishes of the heart and the purposes of the mind, as it reigns in every department of the soul." Furthermore, we cannot expect that the law of cause and effect, assigned to us by God, could be the grounds for undermining, through an unyielding determinism, our moral responsibility. But in what sense can it be said that the will is under this law, yet also free?

Here McCosh placed himself again directly in the Scottish tradition by appealing to a radical dualism of spirit and mind. That dualism derived in part from the critical distinction between spirit and mind as "self-acting substance" and inert matter. Reverting to Plato, McCosh argued that any body that is moved from within and of itself possesses a soul, while every body that can be moved only from without possesses no soul. Such is the nature of the human soul that its will is free, not determined by other agents.[51] This

[51] James McCosh, *The Method of the Divine Government, Physical and Moral* (New York, 1851), pp. 279-88. McCosh did not anticipate here the possible objection that

is not the same thing, McCosh insisted, as saying that it is uncaused. Causation applies to the human soul as it does to everything in creation. We assert only that changes in the mind can be produced by the mind itself and according to "mental laws." It is the nature of God alone to be uncaused, but in having the attributes of self-action the mind shares an attribute of divinity. These links in fact regress again to the "eternal self-operating causes in the Divine mind" and are extensions, like the physical laws of nature, of that mind. McCosh in this manner preserved the identity of God as sovereign creator, but also preserved man's moral freedom. To define the situation in different terms: God's nature as pure spirit is to be free acting, and in creating spiritual man in his own image, he imparts to human nature the same quality. McCosh thereby affirmed not only a radical dualism in the human constitution (one central to Scottish philosophy) but further outlined the elements of freedom and contingency in the human will.[52]

To give the science of ethics a secure foundation McCosh, like many in the Scottish school, felt that he needed to demonstrate the independent authority of conscience. Its status, he believed, was like that of reason, which gives us certain axiomatic ideas or laws that "admit of no demonstration" and cannot be challenged. All reasoning proceeds on these principles. But philosophers have readily conceded this truth while they have been reluctant to allow a similar authority to the moral judgment. The two faculties, however, are analogous, even though strictly independent. The moral faculty is not the product of the sensibility or the intellect, nor any hybrid combination. No combination of colors in nature can produce sound, and no composition of odors can produce color. The mind, through the conscience, declares an "indelible distinction between good and evil" in the same manner it declares a distinction between truth and error. Laws of the conscience even hold the same authority as such intuitive truths as cause and effect; they too are bestowed by God as the certain means by which he assures the harmony of his creatures and his creation. Moral laws have an inflexible character that confirms the supremacy of God's decrees and that lifts these laws "above everything that is fleeting and variable."[53]

McCosh's assertions merely recapitulated the essential outline of the Scottish philosophers, Hutcheson especially. He pursued the

---

the soul, consisting of the sum of its faculties, or parts, acted of its own but in a manner determined by those parts constituting a self-acting whole. He did not, in short, wholly overcome Edwards's case for a determinism of this kind.

[52] Ibid., p. 291.   [53] Ibid., pp. 297-303.

question, though, with a particular interest in the functioning of the conscience and the conditions that make the moral life possible. The Scottish tradition, he felt, had done much good in defending the moral authority of the conscience, but that won only half the battle. For McCosh's evangelicalism there was something too automatic and superficial in a mere defense of moral principles and their inviolable place in the human constitution. Hutcheson's disinterested benevolence remained only an instinctive element whose operation could render much good when fully exercised. But McCosh suspected that unless the moral faculty was united with the other components of the soul, it was likely to be inefficacious and dormant. It was likely also to be brought into operation only as it related to special social situations, to have a merely utilitarian value and work for social convenience only. Nor could it effectively withstand the countervailing power of an essentially sinful human nature. Hutcheson had correctly defined the moral qualities in terms of personal disinterest, but he and his followers had insufficiently fortified the soul against countervailing forces.[54] The Enlightenment and Moderatism had left the moral life in a precarious condition.

The moral faculty can exercise true authority only when it unites with the affections and the will. Indeed it must dominate both. McCosh was taking an interesting position here, because although he inherited from the philosophers the structure of the faculty psychology and the habit of viewing the elements of the soul in their distinctive characteristics and functions, he also inherited from the religious thinkers, and probably Edwards especially, a sense of the entire internal state of the individual. The Evangelicals, specifically, wished to describe the person only in terms of his status as converted or unconverted, in or out of grace. The distinctions were emphatic; we live either as "natural" men and women, or we live in the transformed state of grace.

In uniting this perspective to Scottish psychology, McCosh saw that it was inadequate merely to defend the conscience and the possibility of an absolute moral authority. The conscience could derive

---

[54] Hutcheson had done no such thing, as we noted earlier. McCosh too readily exaggerated the Enlightenment's confidence in human nature, a confidence that Hutcheson, for one, severely qualifed as he pointed to a passionate self-interest and intemperate expansiveness that pervade the human soul. McCosh and Hutcheson, in fact, differed only with respect to the means of overcoming these characteristics and locating the moral base from which to do so. As shown in Chapter 5, the evangelical McCosh argued for a biblical foundation as the only ground of moral certitude.

its power and fulfill its assignment only when linked to a particular inward condition of the individual. Conscience must dominate and join with the other faculties, the emotions, the intellect, the will, even though these have independent status, in order to produce the fully transformed person whom the Evangelicals described as in a spiritual state. McCosh readily admitted that this interplay occurs in any human behavior; emotions attend many actions as a kind of echo of the conscience. The moral faculty "is the master power of the human soul, and it is fitting that it should never move without a retinue of attendants." McCosh's evangelicalism led him then, to move beyond a description of ethics in terms of the outward behavior of the benevolent principle. He wished to shift attention inward, to the whole internal makeup of the individual. In this way, too, not deeds alone, nor any doctrine of works, could be the criteria of moral value and ultimately meritorious. The motivation and intentions of the heart were critical, for if these did not receive primary attention, any ethical theory was likely to become a utilitarian one measuring not intentions but results. It was not legitimate to call a person virtuous merely because he did right. Virtue is not an action but a quality. McCosh hoped here to discredit the Moderates in their preoccupation with decorum and civilized behavior, and his account confirmed the challenge that the Evangelicals set for themselves in undertaking the full transformation of the individual. Centering on the will and the affections in their alliance with the conscience, the ethical life emerged as a rough description of what the religious party called the state of conversion.[55]

McCosh's views paralleled Hutcheson's more than he realized. Both pursued an ethical system in which behavior motivated by the least degree of personal interest was the most virtuous. But once more the evangelical perspective influenced McCosh. The sinfulness of human nature complicated any ethical situation. For the interaction of the conscience with the other faculties embroils it in the self-interest and attendant deception of the fallen personality. Pride, vanity, and passion prevent the pure voice of the moral faculty from having its say. Though it may try to rule over the emotions and the will, it may even obscure its own intentions by its involvement with these other faculties. "Much of human wickedness is displayed in the ingenious schemes which are contrived to deceive the moral faculty, and avoid its humbling judgments." McCosh was no longer asking with the philosophers whether the moral life

---

[55] Ibid., pp. 303-34, 316-17.

was possible; he was asking with the religious thinkers whether it was probable. McCosh then once more linked the philosophical concepts with the religious. Ethics does consist in disinterestedness, but because the human constitution makes disinterestedness so difficult to attain, God has provided a more certain means. Virture in its highest form, McCosh wrote, exists "when the will is exercised in reference to the Divine Being." That reference comes first in our obedience to the highest impersonal source of authority, the will of God as expressed in Scripture. This "voice from heaven" provides a "pure and holy law" that transcends the compromises that human nature forces on the voice of conscience, and it alone can furnish a motive power sufficient to counteract the appeal of self-interest. When the human soul has lost its direction, it needs the magnetic attraction of a force outside itself. Hutcheson's quest for a self-effacing ethical philosophy pursued not the wrong ends but the wrong means. The human soul should find its fulfillment in the only effective means available to transcend and delimit our own concerns and interests. The Bible to that extent, McCosh said, "restores to the conscience its own primitive discernment and sensibility, and it becomes a constant monitor against evil." This appeal alone sufficed to complete an ethical philosophy for a fallen human nature, and it joined the moral life to biblical faith.[56]

This summary of McCosh's first major publication describes his efforts to correct the Scottish philosophy's rationalism and confidence by the Evangelical's sense of human sin and the fact of an omnipotent deity who judges sin. His loyalty to the first tradition should not be neglected, even though McCosh perceived its weaknesses. Hutcheson was much preferred to Hobbes or Hume for he and the other Scots had rescued humankind from the pit of a relentless self-interest that recognized no transcendent moral realities. Our sense of human weakness and depravity need not fall into a pervasive cynicism. Can we not have a realistic sense of human nature without yielding to a flattering and overconfident portrayal of its manifold virtues? McCosh intimated his own position concisely: "Every thinking mind has felt as if there were a gap to fill up between such writers as Hutcheson, Reid, Stewart, Brown, Mackintosh, Kant, Cousin, and Jouffroy, on the one hand; and the common treatises of divinity, such as those of Augustine, Calvin, Owen, and Edwards, on the other." Thus spoke the Scottish philosopher and the Scottish preacher.[57]

James McCosh, who celebrated contrivance and arrangement in

[56] Ibid., pp. 339, 486, 317-18, 323-25.   [57] Ibid., p. 408.

the ways of God's governance, found himself the lucky beneficiary of timely events. The publication of *Divine Government* brought him considerable fame, and in recognition he received an honorary doctorate from St. Andrews University. But events probably quite beyond his awareness coincided with his advancing reputation and accrued to his advantage. One of the readers of McCosh's book was the earl of Clarendon, entrusted with the approval of academic assignments to the new Queen's College in Belfast, Ireland. The story of his reading McCosh's work is cited by so many sources as not to be judged apocryphal. Clarendon became so absorbed in *Divine Government* one Sunday, the story goes, that he wholly neglected to go to church.[58] He immediately judged McCosh suitable for the open philosophy position at the college and offered it to him.

McCosh seems not to have hesitated in accepting. He had served the ministry with dedication and energy, but had not attained the kind of prominence that foretold any great renown in ecclesiastical circles. Already he was witnessing a different kind of struggle in the world, a battle of ideas that promised as much for good or ill as any work the churches might undertake. But mixed feelings attended McCosh's departure. He was devoted to Scotland and to Scottish things. For nearly seventeen years he had lived and worked happily among the people of the eastern regions. And when McCosh announced his intention to leave, his friends and acquaintances responded with love and kindness. His Bible classes presented him with a farewell gift of two handsome religious books beautifully inscribed in gold with the words, "in testimony of their esteem and gratitude for his indefatigable labors in the promotion of their eternal welfare." The Brechin citizens made McCosh a life member of their Mechanics' Institute and gathered for a farewell service for him in the West Free Church. The meeting, as the local newspaper reported, was open to the public and attended by all the denominations in town, and "was crowded to the doors by an immense assemblage." McCosh reviewed some of the trials and successes of his ministry and the events of the Disruption. The next Sunday, December 29, 1851, he delivered the traditional farewell sermon to his congregation. He closed the message saying: "Finally brethren, farewell. Be perfect, be of good comfort, be of one mind, live in peace; and the God of love and peace will be with you."[59]

[58] Among the sources giving this account are *The Northern Whig* [Belfast], November 19, 1894; McBain, *Eminent Arbroathians*, pp. 324-25; *New York Sun*, November 17, 1894; and also McCosh, "My Life," 110.

[59] *Brechin Advertiser and Angus and Mearns Intelligencer*, January 6, 1852.

Part II

IRELAND

Chapter Four

INTUITIONAL REALISM

🌿 JAMES MCCOSH trod a well-worn path in his removal from Scotland to northern Ireland. Since the days of the Tudor monarchs, the efforts of the English crown to establish a Protestant stronghold in Catholic Ireland had promoted the settlement of Scottish Lowlanders across the North Channel. Cut off from the rest of Ireland by a natural barrier of mountains and lakes, Ulster became an area of Presbyterian strength. Only recently, however, had the Presbyterian party felt its real muscle. Long excluded from full economic, political, and educational opportunities, the dissenting Presbyterians had endured an often bitter enmity with the privileged Anglicans. But in the late eighteenth century, when Daniel O'Connell joined a vigorous Irish nationalism to the Catholic cause, the unfriendly Protestant sides forgot their quarrels. The 1800 Union immensely benefited the commercial and industrial north and by the middle nineteenth century, when McCosh arrived, Belfast had become the leading exporting city of the north and a major manufacturing area. Less dependent than the rest of the country on potato agriculture, it was spared the horrors of the 1840s famine, and its economy enjoyed boom years for the next two decades.[1]

Higher education felt the effects of this new spirit of uplift. The establishment of Queen's College in 1846 testified to that spirit and also proclaimed the institutional gains of Presbyterianism. To be sure, the issue of its founding registered all the political antagonisms and the tragic religious rivalries that marked the history of Ireland. And with its nonsectarian policies the college was intended to bypass these. But it signaled a triumph for the Presbyterians who had long called for a college in the north. They were expected to dominate the institution, and they did. Nonetheless, other issues motivated the founding. The Belfast campus was part of the new Queen's University system, which also included campuses at Cork

[1] J. C. Beckett. *A Short History of Ireland* (London, 1952), pp. 145-56; F.S.L. Lyons, *Ireland since the Famine* (London, 1971), pp. 15-16, 49.

and Galway. Queen's of Belfast responded to a city noted for its lively intellectual circles and its intelligent working-class population. Protestant young men of Ulster had long pursued higher education in Scotland; now Queen's enhanced their opportunities while perpetuating the major characteristics of the Scottish universities. And it sought to blend the classical with the practical. The first meetings to determine the course of instruction at the new school resolved that, without sacrificing the traditional courses in ancient languages and philosophy, the college should also provide instruction in "those branches of modern literature and science now essential to be known by every well-educated man." The new school, in fact, made the study of Greek optional, and its trustees proclaimed its modernism. Their memorandum remarked that the academic reforms at Belfast spoke to the "practical wants of the middle classes" and to the needs of a community "busily occupied with practical science, with commerce, with agriculture, and with manufacturers."[2]

McCosh's career at Belfast would greatly extend the Scottish intellectual influence in the area. Among some sensitive nationalists his appointment sparked a reaction, and a noted English writer satirized these feelings in verse.[3] Nevertheless, McCosh's reception was enthusiastic. An overflow audience gathered at the college on January 12, 1852, to hear McCosh present an introductory lecture that ceremonialized his appointment.

The address, reported in full by the local *Belfast Mercury*, was an energetic plea for the Scottish method of inductive philosophy, its intuitionism, and its dualistic humanism. The issues and the philosophical warfare of the day, apparently, were not unfamiliar to the assembled group, for the *Mercury* reported that cheering frequently

---

[2] Theodore William Moody and James Camlin Beckett, *Queen's Belfast: 1845-1949*, 2 vols. (London, 1959), 2:1-44. The quotations are on pp. 41 and 43.

[3] Scots at Queen's were highly represented, and the consequent nationalist laments of the Irish inspired Thackeray's "The Last Irish Grievance," which refers in two places to McCosh:

As I think of the insult that's done to this nation
  Red tears of rivinge from my faytures I wash,
And uphold in this poem, to the world's daytistation,
  The sleeves that appointed Professor M'Cosh
....
O false Sir John Kane! is it thus that you praych me?
  I think all your Queen's Universities Bosh;
And if you've no neetive Professor to taych me,
  I scawurn to be learned by the Saxon M'Cosh

The Works of William Makepeace Thackeray, 26 vols. (New York, 1911), 20:185-86.

interrupted McCosh's talk. And the talk itself faithfully anticipated McCosh's philosophical career at Queen's. He would rescue philosophy from its contemporary pitfalls—from the indiscriminate materialism that honors no spiritual reality, and from the overzealous intuitionism that defies experience. He would find a middle course between the old French sensationalists and the romantic Germans, and his fellow Scots must lead the way.[4] The middle path was a difficult path, however. McCosh would find himself caught in the crossfire as he fought the two strongest impulses in the philosophies of his day.

Undoubtedly McCosh did make Queen's Belfast a bastion of strength for the Scottish philosophy. He taught classes in logic and metaphysics there for sixteen years. He usually had from fifty to one hundred students in any given semester, lectured to them twice a week in each course, and held examinations on the other two class days. McCosh defended this approach. The constant examinations, he believed, prevented the students from falling into idle habits; and he judged this device one improvement on the Scottish universities. The student body was religiously diverse, and McCosh had several Catholic students in his courses, including "some of my best." He claimed that he awarded the highest grades to those who demonstrated an independent judgment in their examinations. But McCosh is not to be taken at his word on this issue. Witness this examination question from his metaphysics class: "What service was done to philosophy by Reid, more especially in rescuing it from the defective or erroneous views of Locke, pushed to an extreme by Berkeley and Hume?"[5] Surely there was no doubt as to what the professor was looking for!

McCosh believed that much was at stake in his intellectual work at the college. Beyond its quest for intellectual truth, the new institution, he believed, had a precise place to play in the community at large. The professor of metaphysics looked out on a city consumed by material ambition and enamored of industrial progress. Much hard work and discipline flourished amid the manifest prosperity, and McCosh gave his blessings to these enterprising people. But the materialistic spirit, he feared, threatened to drown the college. It was under continual pressures to make practicality its guiding principle. McCosh counseled resistance to these pressures. Already

---

[4] James McCosh, "On the Method in Which Metaphysics Should Be Prosecuted," *Belfast Mercury*, January 13, 1852.

[5] *The Queen's College Commission Report* . . . (Dublin, 1858), pp. 30-36; *The Belfast Queen's College Calendar* (Belfast, 1853), cxxv.

a stifling materialism dominated the college curriculum, especially in the heavy emphasis on the physical sciences. The school had no established chair of divinity, and philosophy was optional. Too many students, McCosh felt, "devote themselves exclusively to studies which will never bring them near the human mind and its spiritual nature" and pass through their college years ignorant of history's greatest thinkers. And the world could not be made safe for Christianity if higher education did not somehow abate the taste for affluence and infuse the middle-class society of money, trade, and manufacture with a taste for ideas and literature. Such an alliance was McCosh's great social hope. He designed a plan at Queen's by which local merchants were asked to reduce by one year the apprenticeship terms of a boy who pursued classes, even evening classes if necessary, at the school. In the new urban world of industrial capitalism, the modern university had a critical role to play. Mammon must lie down with the muse.[6]

THE BELFAST YEARS soon became a period of prodigious output for McCosh, witnessing the publication of all his major philosophical writings. They were exciting years, too, though hazardous for the tradition he defended. New directions in ideas, several already prevalent in Scotland itself, placed McCosh and the intuitional school on the defensive. But McCosh bound himself to no rigorous system that recalled an earlier age. The task he set himself looked to a flexible stance that could adopt from the new while protecting the best of the older ways. The result was a new formulation and one that gives McCosh a distinctive place among the Scottish philosophers. We may rightly employ the label "intuitional realism" to designate that place.

McCosh's philosophical efforts have a definite context within the

[6] James McCosh, "The Arts Course in the Queen's University and the Queen's Colleges," summarized in the *Transactions of the National Association for the Promotion of Social Science, 1867* (London, 1868), p. 447; Moody and Beckett, *Queen's Belfast*, 1:248–49. *Queen's College Commission*, pp. 36, 43, 352. On the larger curricular issues McCosh also defended the ancient languages and criticized the increasing prevalence of the modern ones. These points addressed a reform effort in the college, one that McCosh dismissed as an effort to "water down" the academic standards of the school. "For the first time in the history of any university," he wrote, "French is put on the same footing as Greek." Idem, *The Mental Sciences and the Queen's University in Ireland: Being a Letter to the Secretary of the Queen's University* (Belfast, 1860). McCosh's conservative stance drew a direct pamphlet reply from Professor William Nesbitt of Queen's College Galway: *A Reply to the Strictures of the Rev. Dr. McCosh on the Recent Ordinance of the Senate of the Queen's University in Ireland* (Dublin, 1860).

literature of mid-nineteenth-century England and one that lends some drama to the great debates of that time. The publication of Sir William Hamilton's *Discussions on Philosophy* in 1852 brought renewed attention to that great Scottish mind, as did his *Lectures on Metaphysics and Logic* in 1859. The *Lectures*, an editing of Hamilton's classroom discourses at Edinburgh, is the most complete synthesis we have of Hamilton's ideas. It clarifies many obscure points, and although at times it is somewhat simplistic, the posthumous volumes bolstered the Scottish methodology against the growing appeal of empiricism. McCosh also made it his avowed purpose to strengthen the Scottish system, and his *Intuitions of the Mind* (1860) constitutes his most exhaustive philosophical treatise. Certainly it was McCosh's most technical work, clearly different from the breezy, evangelical style of the *Divine Government*. But the battle was soon joined from another quarter, for in 1865 John Stuart Mill (1806-1873) employed all his analytical skills in his effort to bring the Scottish intellect under English judgment. Mill's *An Examination of Sir William Hamilton's Philosophy* (1865) registered the alarm of the leading spokesman of the empiricist tradition. He believed that Hamilton's popularity outstripped any warranted acceptance of his system and endeavored to turn philosophical attention from a fruitless concern with the analysis of consciousness to a systematic study of sensations as the only legitimate data of mental philosophy. Mill of course set into renewed combat forces that had warred before. But the struggle did not rest here. With the death of Hamilton in 1856, the Scottish position needed a new defender, and that role McCosh assigned to himself. He followed the *Intuitions* with a direct reply to Mill. In 1866 McCosh published *An Examination of Mr. J. S. Mill's Philosophy; Being a Defence of Fundamental Truth*.[7] McCosh intended not so much to rescue Hamilton, with whom he had several grievances, as to prepare the burial grounds for sensationalism and its attendant dangers. All of these exchanges won considerable attention, and the periodical journals especially charted the progress of the debates by many penetrating reviews.

As the next chapter will show, the religious aspects of philosophy were also very much in view. Hamilton's "philosophy of the unconditioned," probably the most controversial thesis in his writings, had profound theological implications. Henry Longueville Mansel (1820-1871) first realized the full extent of these implica-

---

[7] The London edition of this work inverts the title and subtitle. Mill's work extended many of the points already elaborated in his earlier *A System of Logic*, published in 1843.

tions, and his famous Bampton lectures of 1858, published as *The Limits of Religious Thought Examined*, translated Hamilton's idea of the Absolute as a negation of thought into the essential unknowableness of God. McCosh perceived some disturbing implications here and feared the German idealistic tendencies in these philosophies as much as he feared Mill's sensationalism. Both confirmed in his mind the need to establish antimaterialistic intuitionism on a realistic basis. McCosh published a volume of religious speculations, a sequel to the *Divine Government* entitled *The Supernatural in Relation to the Natural* (1862), and gave considerable space in his philosophical publications to the theological question. The religious reflections, indeed, complete the philosophical system. McCosh, whose career stood at the juncture of the Scottish philosophy and nineteenth-century evangelicalism, integrated the two traditions into a Protestant scholasticism that housed both.[8]

Close inspection will reveal that McCosh modified Reid and Stewart in important ways, though all three faced somewhat similar challenges. For the Scottish philosophy poised itself between what it considered a loose and airy idealism and a low and shallow materialism. The Scottish thinkers intended to discipline the unearthly qualities of one by an appeal to the real world and to common sense; they would check the deadening naturalism of the other by upholding an independent spiritual reality, in man and in the universe at large. In most of their efforts the Scots saw themselves laboring to prove what was obvious to the general sense of mankind. It was only the devious wiles of philosophers that had rendered such an effort necessary. Thomas Reid, in a rare moment of passion, inveighed against the abuses of genius. What are we to think, he asked, when we find intelligent minds asserting that there is no heat in fire, or no color in the rainbow; when men of acumen seek to disprove the existence of a material world, and assert that we ourselves are only ideas in a mind without substance? "I say," Reid lamented, "when we consider such extravagances of many of the most acute writers on this subject, we may be apt to think the whole to be only a dream of fanciful men, who have entangled themselves in cobwebs spun out of their own brain."[9]

Reid mistrusted speculative efforts even when they served the

---

[8] Much of McCosh's theological interest centered in his writings on science, the subject of Chapter 6, where *The Supernatural* and *Typical Forms and Special Ends in Creation* (1855) are discussed.

[9] Thomas Reid, *Essays on the Intellectual Powers of Man* (1785; Cambridge, Mass., 1969), p. 64.

cause of theism. For fanciful or undisciplined speculation of any kind should be discouraged, lest the dangers already apparent in Berkeley and Hume be intensified. So much, then, for all the good efforts of Nicholas Malebranche (1638–1715). He had tried to show that we may know the real world absolutely because all human minds are united with a Being possessed of all perfection, who has in himself the ideas of all created things. But Reid believed that Malebranche failed in the most crucial matter. For his system did not fully certify the existence of a real world. The divine ideas were the same before the world existed and did not necessarily postulate the existence of that world. It was no surprise to Reid therefore that the larger outline of Malebranche's ideas emerged in Berkeley's more aggressive and dangerous idealism.[10]

Reid in fact so despaired of the tortuous and bewildering ways of genius that his appeal to common sense took on a note of urgency. He created for his readers two classifications of men: "On the one side, stand all the vulgar, who are unpractised in philosophical researches, and guided by the uncorrupted primary instincts of nature. On the other side, stand all the philosophers ancient and modern; every man without exception who reflects. In this division, to my great humiliation, I find myself classed with the vulgar."[11] Painful confession indeed, from this voice of Scottish Moderatism!

Far more disturbing to Reid, however, were the gains of an advancing materialism. Reid could choose widely from the French philosophes for examples, but referred specifically to the English physician David Hartley (1705–1757). Hartley's *Observations on Man* (1749) linked the behavior of the mind to the vibrations of the nervous system and thereby suggested a deterministic relation between physical effects on the medullary substance and the mind's thoughts. Reid did not label Hartley a thorough materialist but took issue with a system that seemed to reduce the mind to a "mere mechanism, dependent on the laws of matter and motion." For Reid and for the Scots generally the exemption of mental and spiritual phenomenon from such laws was essential. But Reid also thought Hartley's efforts discredited by the implausibility of uniform vibrations on the brain producing the great plurality of sensations we experience.[12]

[10] Ibid., p. 129.   [11] Ibid., p. 221.
[12] Ibid., pp. 86–87. James Beattie believed that even more momentous issues were at stake in this question: "That I am a free agent, is what I not only believe, but what I judge to be of such importance, that all morality must be founded on it, yey, and all religion too. To vindicate the ways of God to man, is not so difficult

For Reid and others the epistemological question rested on the laws of the mind and consciousness. But McCosh, we shall see, had a more critical problem to meet. For merely to prove against Hume, for example, that our notion of causality is not derived from experience was not to prove that it had any real bearing on the actual world. Hamilton, we shall also see, made much use of his conviction that it did not, and McCosh was left to deal with that assertion too. How can we know that the laws of the mind, certain though we be that they exist, do in fact describe the actual constitution of the world outside, the way that it is ordered and arranged? For the Scots it was essentially a matter of faith that they do. John Gregory said that God has so ordered the world that its laws correspond to those of the mind and we can have certain knowledge of the external creation. For Reid it seemed that we should have no more reason to doubt the authentic report of the intuitions than the report of our senses, which give us the actual object and not some shadowy extraction from it. "The Supreme Being intended," he wrote, "that we should have such knowledge of the material objects that surround us, as is necessary in order to our supplying the wants of nature, and avoiding the dangers to which we are constantly exposed; and he has admirably fitted our powers of perception to this purpose."[13]

McCosh always believed that Reid was essentially correct, but knew that his ideas needed stronger fortification. Challenges came not only from without, but from within Scotland itself, and two philosophers particularly made an impact. Hamilton, we have seen, was one; the other was Thomas Brown (1778-1820). Brown, alluded to earlier, was an imaginative thinker who reached the height of his influence in the 1830s, a full decade after his death. Since then he has suffered undeserved neglect. McCosh thought him highly important to the course of Scottish philosophy and gave him a separate chapter in his book on the Scottish philosophy and additional attention elsewhere. Brown came from Kirkudbrightshire in the south, where his father was parishional minister at Kirmabreck. He attended the university at Edinburgh, and there his genius for poetry flourished, spilling over later into the lively prose of his philosophical writings. Another product of Dugald Stewart's philoso-

---

a thing when we acknowledge human liberty; but on the principle of fatality, it seems to me absolutely impossible." Quoted in Richard Olson, *Scottish Philosophy and British Physics, 1750-1880: A Study in the Foundations of the Victorian Scientific Style* (Princeton, 1975), p. 29.

[13] Reid, *Intellectual Powers*, p. 118; Olson, *Scottish Philosophy*, p. 45.

phy classes, Brown circulated prominently among the rising Whig set of the early century and counted Brougham, Horner, Jeffrey, and Smith among his close friends. He succeeded his mentor in the moral philosophy chair in 1810. But Brown soon demonstrated an independent spirit that vexed the older man, and many others too.[14]

Brown's *Lectures on the Philosophy of the Human Mind* (1820) exudes the typical Scottish disdain for the abstract and remote. Philosophy should learn to get along without all abstractions, Brown believed, and he even lamented the continuing credence given Aristotle's notion of forms and the reality attributed to them.[15] He contributed to the *Edinburgh Review* an article very critical of Kant, which outlined the emerging warfare between the Scottish and the German schools. But in his reaction against one system, Brown opened himself to the influence of another. He was probably the first of the Scots to take Hume positively and seriously, and Mill mentions Brown with approval in many sections of his writings. McCosh thought that Brown's immersion in medical studies bent him toward "French Sensationalism."[16] Brown's fascination with physiology and psychology illuminated his lectures. "Certain states of our bodily organs," he writes, "are directly followed by certain states or affections of our minds;—certain states of affections of our minds are directly followed by certain states of our bodily organs."[17] Ultimately, though, Brown wanted to limit philosophy to the immediately knowable, and that determination seems to have generated his insistence that all we can know are the laws of the mind itself. He therefore assumed a skeptical posture toward knowledge of the external world and acknowledged only that sensations indicate, but do not verify, the existence of a world outside the self.[18] McCosh did not approve of Brown's skepticism, but did value him for his dualism and for some excellent reflections on natural theism.[19]

Brown's ability to bridge different schools of thought is best exemplified by his theory of causality. Most commentators saw in his

[14] James McCosh, *The Scottish Philosophy: Biographical, Expository, Critical, from Hutcheson to Hamilton* (New York, 1875), pp. 317-25.

[15] Thomas Brown, *Lectures on the Philosophy of the Human Mind*, 2 vols. (Hallowel, England, 1835), 1:67.

[16] James McCosh, "Scottish Metaphysicians," *North British Review*, 27 (1857), 404, 408-9.

[17] Brown, *Lectures*, 1:171.

[18] McCosh, *Scottish Philosophy*, p. 334.

[19] McCosh, "Scottish Metaphysicians," 410-11.

theory the direct influence of Hume, for Brown described the notion of cause and effect in terms of a sequence of change. The added notion of power, employed by Reid (and discussed later in this chapter), was for Brown another of those abstractions that philosophy could do without. For power is to relations occurring in time, what form is to objects of similar traits—a meaningless addition. The invariable antecedent is the cause, the invariable consequent the effect, Brown insisted. Nature gives us only substances, not any additional power separate or different from these; no more at least than Aristotle's abstracted forms. The more we study any phenomenon, Brown said, the more we know that all we see in it is the immediate sequence of change with the certainty of the future recurrence of the effect when the antecedent presents itself. This seemed to echo Hume, but Brown chose not to be tied to the Scottish skeptic. For it is a power of the mind, not merely the impact on the mind of repeated experiences, that furnishes the notion of causes and that leads us to perceive as cause and effect what are only relations in time. And lest there by any doubts about God's place in this, Brown added: "It is thus we are able to exercise that command over nature, which *He*, who is its only real Sovereign, had designed in the magnificence of his bounty, to confer on us."[20] Again Brown mixed skepticism toward experience with a strong and positive faith in laws of the mind, the only certainty available to the inquiring philosopher.

That Brown's star diminished later probably was owing both to the fact that many strains of his thought found a more precise formulation in Mill and to the fact that Hamilton, who emerged as the brighter figure, completely disavowed Brown's ideas. And Hamilton is so critical to this study, affecting both McCosh and the detractors of the Scottish school, that his place in that school merits careful attention. Let us consider first the philosophical temperament of the man, and then look more closely at his major ideas.

If one characteristic describes Hamilton's place in the Scottish school, it is certainly his middle position regarding the two traditions we have examined. One of Hamilton's important *Edinburgh Review* essays examined idealism. Hamilton, employing a favorite device, went not to Berkeley for illustration but to the less familiar Arthur Collier (1680-1732), an obscure but very original formulator of idealistic philosophy.

Idealists, Hamilton said, differ from natural realists (like Reid and

[20] Brown, *Lectures*, 1:67-68.

himself), not really in denying the existence of the real world, but in arguing that we do not know it directly. We know it instead through some ideal object (that is, "perception") in the mind itself. That intermediate source is judged variously to be either a veritable or a nonveritable report of the external object in question. These different judgments distinguish between "cosmothetic" idealism and "absolute" idealism, the first of which acknowledges the existence of the external world (and makes the ideal object an empirically derived "representation" of it), the second of which does not. But only absolute idealism, Hamilton believed, is philosophically consistent, even if profoundly wrong. For nearly all cosmothetic idealists confirm that we have a natural belief in the external world (alleging that when we are conscious of self we are also conscious of something that is not-self) even while saying that immediate knowledge of such a world is not available, or more likely, that our immediate conviction that such a world exists can yield only a hypothetical truth. Hamilton replied that the external world cannot be doubted if it is also admitted that we have knowledge of the world as immediately existing (that is, knowledge that derives from immediate consciousness). Cosmothetic idealists, Hamilton said, deny the validity of our natural belief in an external world; yet at the same time, many of them, like Descartes and Brown, allow that we must believe in such a world because our consciousness so dictates. The absurdity, for Hamilton, was all the greater because the belief from consciousness exists "in and through" the perceptions whose reliability are here questioned. Wrote Hamilton: "It might be thought that philosophers, when they maintained that one original belief was illusive, would not contend that another was veracious,—still less that they would assume as true a belief which existed only as a result of a belief which they assumed to be false. But this they did."[21]

This point, however, was preliminary to a larger one. Hamilton wanted to rest all philosophy on the authority of consciousness and on this issue especially carried forth the banner of the Scottish school against new departures in the early nineteenth century. Hamilton, we shall see, was himself influenced by some of these new currents, but they did not compromise his central place in the Scottish school. All philosophy must start with the testimony of consciousness. We cannot explain why consciousness tells us what

[21] Sir William Hamilton, *Discussions on Philosophy and Literature, Education and University Reform* . . . (London, 1852), pp. 192-94.

it does, but the heavier burden rests with those, the cosmothetic idealists, who allege the essential mendacity of consciousness. "The truth of consciousness, is the condition of the possibility of all knowledge."[22]

Hamilton opposed all representative theories of knowledge and dealt an effective blow to their proponents in a devastating article in the *Edinburgh Review*.[23] We need not pause here to review the subtle casuistry of that essay, and merely note for now that Hamilton improved considerably on Reid in making the same points. Ultimately the blow against the representationists fell on Thomas Brown as the most recent proponent of that position. Brown, in insisting that certitude of knowledge can never get outside of the mind and its contents, violated, according to Hamilton, the one absolutely critical law of consciousness itself—that the objects of which we are conscious in perception *are* external realities. Thus, whereas Brown maintained that we are conscious only of our own minds and that consciousness of external things is only consciousness of their modifications of our minds, Hamilton replied that the first dictate of consciousness is the reality of the objects it presents to us. Brown never refuted the reality of the external world; he simply said that consciousness is an insufficient guarantor of its existence. For Hamilton this was the ultimate philosphical sin. "Consciousness, once convicted of falsehood, an unconditional scepticism, in regard to the character of our intellectual being, is the melancholy, but only rational, result. *Any* conclusion may now with impunity be drawn against the hopes and dignity of human nature."[24]

It was noted earlier that Sir William Hamilton first reflected the gains of German philosophy in Scotland. Specifically, it was a Kantian variety of metaphysics with which his shared some affinity. Hamilton did much service to the Scottish philosophy by his defense of direct perception, by his appeal to the authority of consciousness, and by his attack on the subjectivity of Brown's system. But among more direct defenders of the Scottish school, including McCosh, Hamilton was always suspect, specifically because of his connection to German thought. Hamilton's philosophy of the un-

---

[22] Ibid., pp. 62-63.

[23] Reprinted in *Discussions*, pp. 38-97. Representative theories of knowledge are those that maintain that what we can claim actually to know are only representations of possible real objects.

[24] Hamilton, *Discussions*, pp. 55, 94-96; idem, *Lectures on Metaphysics and Logic*, ed. H. L. Mansel and John Veitch, 2 vols. (Edinburgh, 1861), 1:278-79.

conditioned had very important theological implications as we shall see, but it was the heart of his metaphysics also. The philosophy of the unconditioned was a doctrine of the relativity of knowledge. We know all things, Hamilton believed, in relation, and only in relation. Relatedness is involved in consciousness itself, is its very essence. Thus, we know self only as we know not-self. We are always conscious of two existences in "the same indivisible moment of intuition." Likewise, "subject and object, mind and matter, are known only in correlation and contrast—and by the same common act."[25] Therefore, to think is to condition; it is to limit some realm of being by relation to another; thought involves subject and object mutually limiting each other. Consciousness implies differentiation and plurality.[26]

But the corollary is even more important. We cannot know absolute, or *un*conditioned existence at all. For the unconditioned is one, universal, unrelated; it is its nature to be undefined by anything but itself. But therefore the Absolute is not a positive concept; it is not available to human conceptualization. Consciousness, whose essence is plurality, cannot be identified with the Absolute, whose essence is unity. The Absolute then, is, if possible, only a negative idea.[27]

Further conclusions followed Hamilton's destruction of the positive conception of the Absolute. Time, as the notion of an absolute endurance in itself, has no positive status in our mental framework. It has a positive existence only as a relation to things in time, or in temporal relation to each other. It fades into nonentity when we try to conceptualize it as an absolute. Likewise is space, considered in itself, a nonentity. It cannot present itself to our minds as whole, therefore as either absolutely bounded or infinitely unbounded, as absolutely commencing or absolutely terminating. Space is positively conceivable only as a means between extremes, as a relation of actual objects in a spatial relation. We can, to put it simply, conceive space and time only with real things in them, and not without them. This challenge to philosophy was controversial enough, but Hamilton further added, in a manner that suggested his relation to Kant, that although we know positively, we do not know absolutely. We know only the conditioned and not a *possible* realm of the unconditioned. "Beyond these modes we know, and can assert, the reality of no existence." The extent of our mental faculties, it is

[25] Hamilton, *Discussions*, pp. 53, 49.
[26] Ibid., pp. 13-15.
[27] Ibid., pp. 28-30. A similar situation prevailed with respect to the Infinite.

clear, is inadequate for the external world as it might exist in some absolute nature. Lest there appear to be some contradiction between Hamilton's defense of Reid on direct and certain perception and this apparent skepticism, Hamilton reverted in both cases to the common ground of consciousness; for it is consciousness itself that assures us that we know only the conditioned, things that are in relation to others, and not a possible absolute, or self-contained portion of reality.[28]

Finally, the question of causality defines Hamilton's position in the Scottish school. He disagreed emphatically with Hume that experience was powerful enough by itself to generate so implacable a notion of the human mind. But should we therefore, asked Hamilton, conclude that causality is a primary and positive datum of the mind? He thought not, and his provocative analysis further agitated the controversy surrounding his metaphysics. Causation does derive from the nature of the mind, to be sure, but mind, we recall, is restricted to the conditioned; it can think only in certain forms, in the conditioned interval between two unconditioned extremes or poles. "Now the phaenomenon of causality," he asserted, "seems nothing more than a corollary of the law of the conditioned." We cannot conceive or know a thing except under the attribute of existence. But we can know existence only in space and time, and these only under the relative conditions respecting them. If we were to imagine that a thing merely comes into being, then we would have to say that at one time it had no being, that it was out of all relation. But the mind can conceive no such possible absolute fact. So then we say that the object existed under a different form, and here precisely is our whole notion of causality. Causality derives from our inability to think in terms of absolutes, in this case of any absolute commencement in time or any infinite extension backward in time. We can conceive nothing as coming into being uncaused, and nothing as having existed from forever, or noncaused. Causality, therefore, is merely a "negative impotence" of the mind. It cannot be a positive law, as the other Scots believed. Furthermore, as we shall see, Hamilton believed his idea did greater service to theology because it extricated it from the problem of a causal regression to God as an uncaused existence, or "first cause." Hamilton, in fact, made it clear that because causality derives from the very limitations of the mind, because it is able to know only relative and not absolute existence, we cannot conclude anything with re-

[28] Ibid., pp. 581-82; idem, *Lectures*, 1:141.

spect to the actual causal nature of the world itself. Hamilton believed that any theory that so asserted both the positive nature of the causal law of the mind and the rigid play of causation on the world gave credence to fatalism. But as a negative law of the mind and only problematical with respect to the ultimate nature of reality, causality, in Hamilton's description, still preserved the more sacred possibilities of moral freedom and the freedom of the will.[29]

Here in essence was the challenge that Hamilton threw out to his philosophical contemporaries. He had partly confirmed and partly challenged the secure and confident world of the Scottish philosophy by limiting the ultimate authority of mind and throwing into precarious uncertainty the intellectual absolutes long cherished by his countrymen. To a large extent the reconstruction and rehabilitation of the Scottish school undertaken by McCosh was a response to the legacy of this most ingenious of the Scottish thinkers.

In the first few pages of his *Intuitions of the Mind*, McCosh outlined two powerful forces in the contemporary philosophical world and the "struggle for mastery" in which they were engaged. They were the perennial and familiar enemies of the Scots. There was the one, "earth-born, sensational, empirical, utilitarian, deriving all ideas from the senses, and all knowable truth from man's limited experience, and holding that man can be swayed by no motives of a higher order than the desire to secure pleasure or avoid pain." And there was the other, "if not heaven-born, at least cloud-born, being ideal, transcendental, pantheistic, attributing man's loftiest

---

[29] Hamilton, *Discussions*, pp. 585-88, 595-97. To some people reading Sir William Hamilton there must appear, as there did to John Stuart Mill, an apparent discrepancy between the Scot's tenacious natural realism (his presentative theory of knowledge and his faith in the veracity of consciousness), and his Kantian hesitancy to speculate on ultimate reality. I have found only one section in Hamilton's writings where he seems to confront this apparent discrepancy, and it shows Hamilton's resourcefulness. In brief, what Hamilton insists is that the philosophy of the unconditioned must support a natural realism. For just as we cannot present to our minds any object stripped of its qualities and attributes—any "absolute" thing, such as an apple without the color red or without its smooth texture—neither can we present to our minds any quality as absolute in itself, such as the color red. We know red only in relation, and therefore by what is not red. We must posit red in relation, or more generally, we can posit color only as a relation to something else. Hence, we return to real objects and can know qualities only in relation to them. See Hamilton's "Dissertations on Reid," in *The Works of Thomas Reid*, ed. Sir William Hamilton, 2 vols. (Edinburgh, 1863), 2:934-35. We note, however, that once again, although Hamilton fortified the Scottish epistemology, he did so on the basis of mental impotency. McCosh wanted a more positive defense.

ideas to inward light, appealing to principles which are discovered without the trouble of observation, and issuing in a belief in the good, instead of a belief in God."[30]

McCosh in fact found much merit in both these schools. He thought much was to be gained by the many new inroads of physiological psychology, and his interest increased through his years at Princeton. But his willingness to learn never overrode his ultimate reliance on introspection and the laws of consciousness as the proper method of psychological study. And for the transcendental and idealistic systems associated mostly with Germany McCosh also had much praise. Against an advancing materialism they centered human sights on spiritual realms, and against the low course of utilitarianism and relativism they pursued the realm of the absolute and universal. But McCosh feared the ambitious and unrealistic claims of this school. Kant began a dangerous course in modern philosophy when he claimed that the laws of the mind reorder experience by imposing their own special forms on the phenomena of experience. Kant, McCosh believed, merely prepared the way for greater offenses, and Fichte carried the absurdity to the point of imagining the world itself to be a projection of the mind. There seemed for McCosh only one means of avoiding both extremes. One must certify the reality of the laws of the mind and their precise and conjunctive relation to the world of experience. McCosh's efforts to execute such a via media resulted in his own intuitional realism, and it gave him a distinct place in the Scottish school.

Intuitions assume many forms—"primitive cognitions," "primitive judgments," "moral convictions"—but for McCosh they all had a precise relation to experience and did not function merely as laws of the mind independently or autonomously displaced from the real world. All intuitions are of some thing, existing, and on this fact alone is a realistic philosophy possible. "Our intuitive convictions," McCosh wrote, "are thus not ideas, notions, judgments, formed apart from objects, but are in fact discoveries of something in objects, or relating to them."[31] McCosh included a variety of persons among those who he believed had erred fundamentally in their interpretations of intuitions—Locke for saying that the mind looks at ideas and not things, Kant for supplying the mind with a priori forms. Each had constructed a philosophy of mind that prevented mind from penetrating to the real world. But equally deceptive

[30] James McCosh, *The Intuitions of the Mind, Inductively Investigated* (1860; 3rd ed., rev., New York, 1874), p. 4.

[31] Ibid., p. 26.

were those who gave the mind a direct access to some higher or fundamental realm of being behind the phenomenal world. Plato therefore left the Western mind with an impossible confusion when he postulated a reason that contemplates immutable, eternal, and suprasensible entities, and when, furthermore, he made the discovery of these entities the special goal of the philosopher and the contemplation of them the highest act of wisdom. Plato erred not only in setting up this unearthly unreality but in claiming for the mind some overreaching grasp for this transcendent realm of being. Later and more ambitious theories in the Platonic tradition, McCosh noted, gave the mind a direct apprehension of the true, the good, and the beautiful as real entities. "I hope to be able to show," he said, "that these theories are altogether mistaken."[32]

To McCosh the intuitions were analogous to the eye. The eye is a power with a certain function to perform, and it realizes that function under conditions in which light presents objects to the eye from outside. We should see intuitions working in the same manner. The ability to see may antedate the object viewed, as intuitions antedate experience. But intuitions, like the eye, have no content, and consciousness knows nothing of their laws, until it has experience. Intuitions in this sense are really capacities for experience. But they are also restricted to this experience and can claim no special insight beyond the data provided. McCosh illustrated this point in numerous ways, but the special emphasis alone was important. He sought to save the possibilities of an intuitional philosophy from its discredited association with German transcendentalism and to salvage from the materialistic psychologies the derivation of all knowledge from sensations. He further warned that intuitions should not be confused with vague feelings, unaccountable emotions, blind instincts; for intuitions, in contrast to these, are accompanied by knowledge or judgment. Nor are the intuitions special truths of the individual or even the special property of the race; they are truths of reality, and these truths obtain whether or not the human mind seizes them.[33]

A major strain in McCosh's philosophy centers in his effort to preserve a direct relation between the internal world of the mind and the external world. Because so much of his mental philosophy anticipated its application to religious ideas, and because that appli-

---

[32] James McCosh, *An Examination of Mr. J. S. Mill's Philosophy; Being a Defence of Fundamental Truth* (New York, 1866), pp. 259-60; idem, *Intuitions*, pp. 82-83, 27-28. Further elaboration of McCosh's point is in the next chapter.

[33] McCosh, *Intuitions*, pp. 299, 46-48.

cation moved inductively from the certifiable facts of human experience toward the larger truths of moral reality and divine existence, McCosh was actually resting the burden of his religious philosophy on the ultimate validity of his philosophy of mind. To that extent it was imperative not to fall into speculation, to preserve a "marriage of mind and nature," as Bacon put it, to ground the points of his mental philosophy on the hard rock of the real world. Conclusions about divine existence extrapolated from these facts, therefore, would not encounter the charge that they were mere products of the speculative imagination or some untested fabrication of the mind in its independent operations. All laws of the mind, McCosh therefore insisted, are known through their extended media, by the objects through which they operate. But there were dangers here. McCosh insisted with the other Scots that introspection, the examination of consciousness itself, affords the only access to the laws of the mind. His intuitional realism would endorse no wholly sensational basis of psychology however much it insisted on keeping its grip on the real world. Second, in preserving a direct relation between internal and external reality, McCosh had to avoid the danger of a monistic philosophy that would dissolve the spirit-body dualism so central to Scottish metaphysics. He needed to preserve a relational balance between both realms while avoiding a merger of the two.

These concerns necessarily led McCosh into a consideration of the nature of our knowledge of self and our knowledge of the external world, as well as the authority of that knowledge and the relation of these realms to each other. McCosh insisted emphatically that we have a direct and certain knowledge of self as distinct from all else, a separate entity. He believed that his own predecessors had not sufficiently asserted this fact, and failure to insist on it opened the way for numerous errors. Reid, McCosh noted, allowed only that sensations within the mind itself allow us to "infer" a mind and to establish a belief in its existence.[34] And Stewart: "We are not im-

[34] Reid wrote: "It appears, then, to be an undeniable fact, that, from thought or sensation, all mankind, constantly and invariably, from the first dawning of reflection, do infer a power or faculty of thinking, and a permanent being or mind to which that faculty belongs; and that we as invariably ascribe all the various kinds of sensation or thought we are conscious of, to one individual mind or self." Reid disclaimed to know by what rules of logic we make this inference (they are simply "judgments of nature," "immediately inspired by our constitution"). But Reid did insist that the data also carried an inevitable belief in the existence of the faculty and the mind. *Works*, 1:100. However, McCosh, it will be noted, intended his philosophy to discover a precise rule of mind that would serve more positively for a realistic philosophy than Reid's "inference."

mediately conscious of [the mind's] existence, but we are conscious of sensation, thought, and volition, operations which imply the existence of something which feels, thinks, and wills."[35] But from his own mid-nineteenth-century perspective, McCosh believed that such a timid defense of the knowledge and reality of self permitted later heresies. Kant asserted that we know the soul only as a phenomenon and not as it is in itself. Soon the soul lost its autonomy completely, and even in Scotland James Ferrier (1808-1864) at Edinburgh denied absolute existence to mind and matter and contended that both coexist in all experience.[36] Hamilton was a far greater help to McCosh for he had maintained that we do not know attributes without knowing substance, and he had taken Reid to task on this point.[37]

So likewise McCosh insisted, "We know self as having being, existence." And we so know it because consciousness itself dictates it. "The knowledge [of self] we have in self-consciousness, which is associated with every intelligent act, is not of an impression, as Hume would say, not of a mere quality or attribute, as certain of the Scottish metaphysicians affirm, nor of a phenomenon, in the sense of appearance, as Kant supposes, but a thing or reality." Nothing is more surely ascertained by the introspective act than this certification by consciousness of an existing self immediately perceived. But McCosh went one step more than Hamilton too. He maintained that consciousness gives us not only this knowledge of self, but knowledge of self as not dependent on our observation of it and, hence, more positively, knowledge of self as an abiding existence. McCosh, in short, wanted to employ with Hamilton the authority of consciousness but not by means of the dreaded "negative impotency" of relations.[38]

But there was more at stake here on purely metaphysical grounds, and these other points further illustrate McCosh's precarious position between extremes of thought. The Scottish school had traditionally fortified its dualism by contending that there ex-

[35] McCosh, *Intuitions*, p. 128n.

[36] Ibid., pp. 128-29. Probably the point was not lost on McCosh that Ferrier was in the thick of the struggle for power at the university and a leading critic of the evangelical party. Ferrier, George Elder Davie claims, saw the mantle of Reid in Scotland pass to the Evangelicals and saw their kind of common sense gospel wisdom applied against the higher philosophy of him and others of the "Hamiltonian circle." See George Elder Davie, *The Democratic Intellect: Scotland and Her Universities in the Nineteenth Century* (Edinburgh, 1971), pp. 283-84, 288-89, 297, 309-11.

[37] Hamilton, *Discussions*, pp. 46-47.

[38] McCosh, *Intuitions*, pp. 128-30. McCosh elaborates these last points on pp. 130-32.

isted a qualitative difference of mind and matter and consequently, different methods of apprehending them—one by use of the senses, the other by introspection. McCosh wished to do no violence to this dualism, but found it necessary on occasion to narrow it. Increasingly it lost force as a critical element in his thinking. The real existence of both mind and matter, McCosh believed, is known through qualities, for consciousness asserts that we never know qualities without knowing substance. McCosh returned to this idea many times. Furthermore, consciousness also asserts that substance is denoted not only by existence, but by power (which also includes the ability to be acted upon) and endurance as well. Descartes, in maintaining that substance is denoted only by extension thereby set up a radical dualism that excluded consciousness from the category of substance. But the notions of power and endurance, McCosh believed, are in our original cognitions; the mind cannot consider substance as not possessing these. But also, his maintaining that the mind inseparably links qualities with substance enabled McCosh to avoid a dualism so sharp that it would either leave the mind unable to know anything underlying empirical data, or leave the data suspended in a void. He had Hume and Berkeley in mind certainly, but also Kant. There was no ground whatever, he wrote, for believing that there must exist something more internal or central than the substance that is known immediately with and as its qualities. Possibly some "occult powers" do exist in objects, and these we may not wholly know; but to suggest that they constitute something different in kind from the revealed object, some "thing-in-itself," or something inherently necessary to the existence of the object, is to postulate in a manner that is unwarranted, unproductive, and unnecessary.[39]

Both subject and object, then, are substances; they have existence, power, and endurance. But they are not qualitatively the same substances, and any effort to establish the identical nature of the two would certainly give credence to the varieties of pantheism and materialism that had already flooded the philosophical landscape. For to confer on subject and object a common nature is to confer on them a common fate or a relation of mutual dependence. But that was clearly dangerous. Both subject and object exercise autonomous functions independently of each other. Likewise, shifting the meaning somewhat, permanence of body does not depend on mind observing it, and neither, to reiterate, does spirit depend for its continued existence on the bodily frame. But ultimately nothing so

[39] Ibid., pp. 147-48, 148n-149n, 141-43.

strongly certifies the distinct natures of spirit and matter as consciousness itself. Its whole life revolves around them. "In the cognition of the knowing mind, which ever coexists with our cognition of matter, we always know the two to be different." To view the beautiful hills against the sky is to know the hills and sky as different from self, and to know self as viewing them.[40] With these distinctions clarified, McCosh believed that philosophy could stand on more certain grounds than any of his predecessors permitted.

And for this reason McCosh could not help but be critical of Hamilton. He believed Hamilton was early "smitten" with the German spirit and never shook himself free of it. His doctrine of relatives, McCosh believed, was destructive of any positive philosophy and deprived mind of its ability to know fully. McCosh wished to show that mind has cognitions that are positive and complete, that knowledge is not restricted to what we know only in relation, and that we do not know a thing only by what it is not. McCosh took a stronger stand, asserting, in contrast to Hamilton, that consciousness should be considered a separate faculty, capable of knowing itself distinct from its acts and its contents. Consciousness is not consumed by its apprehension of material and spiritual substances; rather it embraces these while certifying their distinctive natures. He believed that Hamilton, in insisting that consciousness cannot be separated from its qualities and faculties, made self-consciousness itself dependent on relations and therefore a negative potency of the mind. McCosh on the contrary claimed that "we hold . . . that by self-consciousness we know self; the thing self, the ego, and not a mere phenomenon or relation of self to the knowing subject." McCosh, again, was not pointing to some occult element behind the mental phenomena, and avoided a Kantian agnosticism by asserting that consciousness is an empirical entity, "the source of important experiential knowledge, which can be submitted to all kinds of logical processes." Further, McCosh said, failure to defend this substantive reality degraded the philosophy of Condillac and other sensationalists and, passing from them to Kant, "has confused the whole philosophy of Germany."[41]

McCosh also challenged Hamilton's claim that he was upholding the Scottish tradition of natural realism. He clearly read into Hamilton more than Hamilton allowed and reacted more to the larger implications of the philosopher's words than to their letter. But his

[40] Ibid., pp. 146-47.
[41] Ibid., pp. 211-12, 212n; idem, "Scottish Metaphysicians," 428-29.

concern registered significant fears. McCosh charged that in Hamilton's system the very notion of substance arose only from a mental impotency, the inability to conceive an object existing absolutely in itself. Substance arises only under the conditions of relation and is therefore not a positive notion in itself. But what then becomes of our whole notion of the external world, for which, as Locke had said, the notion of substance is central? Our very belief in the external world becomes mere mental impotency. And if through this impotency we know nonego as the contradictory of ego, then ego too holds the same status of relation, and "it too, then, is a null notion, the vain issue of incapacity."[42] Hamilton, then, had built a house of cards. It could not protect a natural realism from the violent winds now blowing against it.

McCosh then endeavored to demonstrate the positive nature of our fundamental ideas, showing their content to derive from both experience and intuition and necessarily consisting of both for their operation. We may use his discussions of space and time and causality to illustrate his thesis. Of both space and time, believed McCosh, we have an immediate knowledge. We know all objects as occupying space, and the senses carry convictions with respect to space. Our own self-consciousness supplies through its data a conviction of time inseparable from the property of endurance native to consciousness. Both notions are positive and concrete. But, more important, time and space, McCosh urged, have a reality independent of the perceiving mind. Intelligence does not create space and time and merely establish them as ideas affixed to the data of experience. Intelligence discovers them and knows them as having existence outside and independent of itself. This fact, McCosh believed, is one of the strongest and most compelling native habits of the mind. Furthermore, it is directly related to consciousness's assertion that qualities carry the notion of substance and power. We know substance only as existing in time and space. Anyone, therefore, who denies the independent existence of time and space must also, according to McCosh, deny the reality of the objects in them. He cannot, at least, meet the charge of the skeptic who contends that events in time are quite as unreal as the time in which they are perceived as having occurred.[43]

---

[42] James McCosh, "Sir William Hamilton's Lectures," *North British Review*, 30 (February 1859), 554–55.

[43] McCosh, *Intuitions*, pp. 177–86. Here McCosh fell into using his own construction of mind and its laws as given facts, and showed that any other construction, because it would seem to violate these rules, must be invalid. His case against Kant in the next paragraph depends for its validity on McCosh's original assumption.

McCosh could see no warrant for Kant's describing space and time as forms imposed by the mind on the phenomena presented to the senses. Space and time derived from innate and special powers of the mind, but these merely derive from experience of the structured world as it is and function as the mind's capacities to relate the dimensions of reality to itself. Space and time, as ideas, do not have the same status as those mental images derived from the senses, which are equipped to receive those images directly from the objects of experience; space and time, instead, require native ideas for their realization. Neither mode of presentation to the perceiving consciousness, however, is favored over the other as a veritable report of the real world. To this extent, a theory such as Kant's, which allows no necessary existence to space and time and derives them strictly from the mind itself, played havoc with philosophy. So McCosh lamented: "Those who were taught that the mind could create the space and time, soon learned to suppose that the mind could create the objects and events cognized as in space and time, till the whole external universe became ideal, and all reality was supposed to lie in a series of connected mental forms."[44]

For McCosh, though, Hamilton was still the troublesome factor in his efforts to demonstrate the positive concepts of space and time. McCosh made no ambitious claims for the powers of mind and accepted with other philosophers the impossibility of conceiving time and space as without commencement or termination. To deny this impossibility would be to remove both space and time from all relations and thus, by Hamilton's account, remove them from the realm of the conceivable. For Hamilton, then, space and time were negative concepts, essentially altogether beyond the purview of the human intelligence. But McCosh, who had a theological stake in the possibility of absolutes, also had a stake in the notion of space and time as positive ideas of the mind. Our positive sense of space and time appears in several ways, he said. We know both as continuous, and thereby distinct from empirical objects that are always capable of division. The division of space and time, however, is impossible, for we cannot really divide space from space, time from time; only things in space and events in time make a division possible, but they make no change in the quality of space and time themselves. We know space and time as qualitatively uniform throughout. Further, we know intuitively that space and time are such in their very nature that no further space and time could be added to them. These facts confirm for us a sense of time and space as absolute and positive.[45]

[44] Ibid., pp. 178-79.   [45] Ibid., pp. 182-83.

McCosh did not have definitive answers to the difficult problems in dealing with space and time. Nor, in fact, did he wholly reply to Hamilton's case. For instance, McCosh argued that we can in imagination place ourselves at any point in space and from there project an indefinite beyond so that although we cannot seize in one grasp the infinite nature of space, we can have a sense of it from its segments, segments that the mind, however, cannot link together as whole. Thus we can know the infinite even if we cannot conceive it. Not only did McCosh fail to see that he was slipping here into a kind of Kantian thing-in-itself (we do not know the infinite, but do know its attributes), he also skirted the major point made by Hamilton. Specifically, Hamilton insisted that anything having dependence, or anything consisting of parts that constitute its whole, is definitionally not absolute, is not *un*conditioned. For the absolute must exist out of relation to everything else, and it must be simple, having no plurality, and it cannot be a compound depending for its existence on its several constituents. But by this last method, it would seem, McCosh saw the only effective means to construct the possibility of the Absolute and with it our sense of time having that status.[46]

McCosh first outlined his philosophy of causality in the *Divine Government*, but the intervening years provided the opportunity to refine his thoughts. He believed that Reid was essentially correct in joining power to the notion of causality. His difference was one of emphasis, but it was a critical difference nonetheless. We do not have a complete awareness of the mind's sense of cause and effect, Reid said, unless we observe how the notion of power necessarily accompanies that sense. But Reid believed that the mind derived the notion of power from itself, from an awareness of its own nature and its own operations, and attributed it to the external world as well. "It is certain that we can conceive no kind of active power but what is similar or analogous to that which we attribute to ourselves."[47] McCosh, however, wanted to ground causality in a more certain source, in the realm of experience. Reid's approach, it seemed, was too subjective and depended on analogy. Our notion of power as necessarily contained in causality, McCosh insisted, de-

---

[46] McCosh, "Hamilton's Lectures," 555-56; idem, "Scottish Metaphysicians," 429; idem, *Intuitions*, p. 184.

[47] Thomas Reid, *Essays on the Active Powers of the Human Mind* (1788; Cambridge, Mass., 1969), pp. 267-72. Reid explicitly addressed Hume on this point and insisted that the native notion of power demonstrates that we are not dependent on sensation or impressions for the source of our notion of causality.

rives from the mind's intuitive construction of substance. Substance comes to us from our empirical knowledge of qualities, but substance always carries with it existence, power, and endurance. To be noted first, however, is the fact that our original conviction of causality "is not a general truth, but relates solely to the individual facts presented to or contemplated by the mind." Our judgment, McCosh said, does not assert that every cause has an effect and that every effect has a cause; rather, it asserts that "this thing having power, may produce an effect, and that this thing apprehended as a new thing or as having been changed must have had a cause."[48]

McCosh, essentially, did not wish to divorce the mind's notion of causality too much from its contacts with actual things of experience. He even admitted that experience itself, as Hume and Mill believed, could probably function without the intuitions to provide us the notion of causality. But experience could not provide the full notion and could never furnish the natural and universal manner of causality's operation in our consciousness. "Any experimental conviction would necessarily want certain essential elements ever found in our conviction regarding causation."[49] Nonetheless, causality was wholly misconstrued if described as a law of the mind only. Theories that deny the mind's direct access to reality prepare dangerous conclusions. Kant erred fundamentally in this respect, for in supposing the mind to know only phenomena and not things, he constructed a mental law only, with application to appearances but not to reality, and with power referred only to phenomenal substance. The unhappy result of such metaphysics was the further denial of the fact that intuition informs us that when the effect is real the cause is also real and must be a substance. This fact entitles us to infer a real cause of the world, the world that we know as having substance and existence and not as mere appearance, whose essence and therefore whose cause is known. "Metaphysicians who suppose that the mind primitively knows only phenomena (that is, appearances), can never satisfactorily go beyond a phenomenology, or reach a God who has any other sort of existence than the phenomena, and the mental laws which bind them." No such problem exists for those who adhere to a natural realism.[50]

McCosh used the example of Kant in illustrating some weaknesses in causality theory, but in doing so he hoped to check errors among the Scottish thinkers that reflected or corresponded to the

[48] McCosh, *Intuitions*, p. 228.   [49] Ibid., pp. 228-29.
[50] Ibid., pp. 235, 238 (the quotation).

German's ideas. Hamilton's were the most serious of these, but Brown also illustrated the faults of a system that was at once too materialistic and too subjective. For while Brown gave much space to intuitions in his psychology, he never connected them with real things, insisting that we know sensations only. A large gap existed in his epistemology as a consequence, and his theory of causation demonstrated it. For in certifying the intuition of causality Brown imposed this law of the mind on sensations, not on real things, for we have no knowledge of these. Brown therefore missed the critical factor of power and could come up only with invariable antecedence and consequence as the ingredients of cause and effect. McCosh accused Brown of ignoring the main question of the agents acting as the cause to produce the effect. His notions were hollow and essentially subjective. To derive necessity from antecedence reverses the whole priority of factors in causality. For McCosh, causality "is the result of a necessity arising from the potency of substance."[51]

Finally, we may examine a peripheral conclusion to this discussion by noting that McCosh's efforts to define intuitional realism related directly to a problem that had long agitated and very much divided the Scottish thinkers and the university community generally. This problem was the relation of mathematics to philosophy. For Reid, mathematical reasoning, relying on axiomatic first principles and building carefully on these, was analogous to common sense philosophy. Both confirm inviolable laws of the mind that are the foundations of any knowledge of the external world. "Mathematicians," said Reid, "before they prove any of the propositions of mathematics, lay down certain axioms or common principles, upon which they build their reasonings." These are self-evident, and although the mathematical and philosophical axioms do not have precisely the same status, they differ in nature from the first principles of the empirical sciences.[52] But that very difference raised serious problems for Beattie, Brown, and Hamilton. Brown felt that philosophy's rigid laws are ultimately true because we know them as such, independent of experience, to which they have no application. Brown divided the objects of human thought into separate categories of mental and empirical entities. He was not unique in the Scottish school for doing so, but assumed the more skeptical position that we have certain knowledge of the laws of the mind, uncertain knowledge of things derived from the senses. Conse-

[51] Ibid., pp. 235-36, 238.
[52] Olson, *Scottish Philosophy*, pp. 57-60; Reid is quoted on p. 58.

quently, mathematics is only an exercise of the mind's laws, without relation to experience; mathematics is a certain science because it is wholly divorced from the contingencies of empirical data. "It is from our *ideas* of figure that we reason," Brown said, "and it is of no consequence, whether these resemble real external existences."[53]

Hamilton concurred with Brown that mathematics does not pursue its business among the objects of sense, and that fact fired his celebrated diatribe against mathematical reasoning and his disdain for its place in the university curriculum. For mathematics to that very extent incapacitates us for thinking about life and the world, and just that kind of thinking is the business of philosophy, using the authority of consciousness. Mathematics, characterized by axiomatic absolutes and ironclad principles, deprives us of the mental equipment to deal with the world of contingencies and relativities. Mathematics is deductive and encourages a passive acceptance of first principles, whereas philosophy, properly conducted, builds inductively on the plurality of facts and observations furnished by consciousness and the real world. Philosophy would prosper, consequently, the further it was removed from the method and devices of mathematics.[54]

McCosh wanted to end this feuding not by stating a preference for either mathematical or philosophical reasoning, but by showing their essential kinship. As to whether mathematical axioms are the results of generalizations from experience or separate intuitions of the mind, McCosh answered that both views have merit. If we examine the mental processes by which we arrive at an axiomatic law, such as the statement "if equals be added to equals, the sums are equal," we find that "it has been by the contemplation of individual instances that the mind has attained to the comprehension and the conviction of the general proposition." We can arrive at this conclusion empirically, but that fact does not mean that the axiom, the law of the mind, is a mere generalization from experience. McCosh explained that it is not by experimenting with two straight rods, one or a million times, that we formulate the axiom that two straight lines cannot enclose a space; nor do we need to extend two parallel lines indefinitely to conclude that they will never meet. No, we need the action and participation of intuition to aid in our so construing the world of experience. For intuition seizes the facts before us and on bare contemplation of them declares the laws. "In mathematical truth, the mind, upon the objects being presented to

[53] Ibid., p. 65.
[54] Hamilton, *Discussions*, pp. 274–76, 284–86.

its contemplation, at once and intuitively pronounces the judgment." It concludes immediately that what is true for one is true for all. There thus occurs a generalization that is not a mere summary of experience but a universal extension of it, and the role of the intuition is the agent of the extended generalization. And hence arises the difference between mathematical laws and laws of general observation. We may never have witnessed a horned animal that is not at the same time ruminant, but we would not conclude that such an animal could not exist. We would never, however, reason that two straight lines could in fact enclose a space. Mathematical laws, then, have the same status and characteristics as those intuitive laws of the mind that demand that for every effect we postulate a cause. They represent the precise and critical juncture of the world of experience and the world of primitive judgments, beliefs, and cognitions.[55]

OUR REVIEW of McCosh's philosophy to this point has emphasized mostly the means by which an intuitional realism could save philosophy from a fruitless divorce from experience. McCosh claimed no extraordinary powers for the mind, no transcendental reach into some occult realm of existence. He did try to show, however, that the mind's intuitive powers are necessary for the successful transmission of experience to our total consciousness. But in securing this ground, McCosh had to avoid too strong a pull in the other direction. For the reaction against subjectivism had already gone further than he wished to take it. Significantly, therefore, when John Stuart Mill undertook his *Examination of Sir William Hamilton's Philosophy* he selected for his subject the man who had gone far to merge the tradition of Reid with the tradition of Kant. But both these traditions honored varieties of intuitionism that Mill wished to discredit. His recourse to a strict sensationalism, then, showed the full recoil from idealistic and intuitionist models. Mill would try to rely wholly on the data of experience. McCosh, however, believed that Mill's path made no improvements on the impossible claims of the other parties and in fact resulted in a new subjectivism. For when Mill looked into the mind and found only impressions, he allowed himself no avenue of escape from those impressions to an external objective reality. No more than Kant could he certify a world of real things. But McCosh recognized Mill's book as a deft and trenchant assault on the whole possibility

[55] McCosh, *Intuitions*, pp. 364-66.

of an intuitionist system of knowledge. To that extent the defense of the Scottish tradition was at stake in McCosh's reply.

And there was no mistaking that it was the Scottish tradition especially that Mill went after. For he believed that Hamilton, in his repeated defense of consciousness as the ultimate authority for philosophy, wore the largest label of the Scottish school and surpassed even Reid in his determination to defend it.[56] Mill welcomed Hamilton's *Lectures* for providing the clearest demonstrations of the introspective method of philosophy. And like McCosh and the other Scots, Mill pleaded for an inductive approach to philosophy that used the immediate data of mental experience to formulate larger truths. To this extent McCosh acknowledged Mill's and all other varieties of empiricism as useful allies against deductive philosophies that elaborated grand systems from large and vague principles. Both the Scottish introspective and the British empiricist schools therefore contested for the mantle of Bacon; they would build meticulously from the particular facts of experience. Mill had first outlined his methodology in his *System of Logic* (1843), a major document in the literature of empirical philosophy and one that McCosh so valued that he used it in his advanced classes at Queen's.[57] But what exactly did an inductive study of the mind reveal? On that question waged the whole critical warfare of the two schools.

Mill's major ideas were familiar to his readers by the time of his examination of Hamilton, but he elaborated them now with particular force. The book sparkles with brilliant insights and twists of logic and scrutinizes Hamilton thoroughly, from his law of the unconditioned to his theory of perception. But the starting point is Mill's contention that a thorough analysis of mind, though the only proper basis of philosophical reasoning, cannot determine what truths, if any, are intuitively derived, what ideas are "original" and antedate any experience of the world. In so stating, Mill revived an older issue, one that McCosh would cite also, between Cousin and Locke. Cousin (1792-1867), the major translator of the Scottish philosophy into French, charged that Locke erred significantly in seeking to learn the origin of our basic ideas before he had ascertained what those ideas are. But Mill replied that we have no means whatsoever for doing this. We cannot filter out our acquired knowledge from our original knowledge. We cannot say that what seems certain to us now was always a part of our mental makeup, was there

[56] John Stuart Mill, *An Examination of Sir William Hamilton's Philosophy*, 2 vols. in 1 (New York, 1874), 1:135.
[57] McCosh, *Examination of Mill*, p. 26n.

from the beginning. "The proof that any of the alleged Universal Beliefs, or Principles of Common Sense, are affirmations of consciousness, supposes two things; that the beliefs exist, and that they cannot possibly have been acquired. The first is in most cases undisputed, but the second is a subject of inquiry which often taxes the utmost resources of psychology." Moreover, Mill believed, Locke was right, for because we are unable to study the mind in its earliest and most primitive state, we must retreat to the first stages of consciousness where our basic ideas are fully formed. We cannot study the first, original facts of the mind in the facts of our present consciousness. The original can come to light only from a study of those that are admittedly not original. By a direct comparison Mill believed we might be able "to determine whether some of [the alleged original ideas] may not have been generated in the same modes, so early as to have become inseparable from our consciousness before the time at which memory commences." This method Mill labeled the "psychological," in contrast to the "introspective." "It is the known and approved method of physical science, adapted to the necessities of psychology."[58]

The results of Mill's undertaking are well known. Mill discovered no ideas of the mind that could not be traced to sensations and their subsequent associations. For what we now by habit have learned to equate with universal or original facts of the mind are merely the hardened products of experience, empirical data of consciousness fashioned into laws by the associative powers of the mind. In contrast to Hamilton, who believed that a mental law was established by our inability to conceive its opposite, Mill rejoined that "all inconceivability may be reduced to inseparable association." Mill gave a wide application to this principle. We cannot conceive time or space as having an end because the idea of any portion of space or time is inseparably associated, by our experience, with the idea of a time or space beyond it.[59]

McCosh saw a large symbolical clash in Mill's engagement with Hamilton. Both philosophers, he believed, were the best recent representatives of their schools. McCosh placed Mill in the tradition of Hobbes, Hartley, Priestley, Hume, and James Mill, but believed him especially indebted to Hume. McCosh appreciated Mill's influence at Oxford and Cambridge, where at long last some strong reaction against scholasticism was setting in, and in other places where practical spirits sought escape from the thin air of German

---

[58] Mill, *Examination*, 1:184–85.   [59] Ibid., 1:88–89, 102.

metaphysics. So McCosh too argued for practical thinking, for a philosophy that gave experience its full due, and for an inductive psychology built on the certain facts of consciousness. He ever avowed that his system was positivistic and realistic and met the tests of science that Mill claimed for his own. But Mill and too many of his naive followers seemed capable of understanding only matter and sensations, and if Mill's system gained ascendance the materialistic spirit that wrought such mischief in France would likely recur. McCosh therefore tried to fortify the Scottish system against the new assaults upon it.

McCosh wished first to remove some confusion created by Mill in his discussion of sensations. Mill did not duplicate Hume directly but concurred at least to the point of affirming that we are conscious only of feelings, and of these, sensations, the awareness of the mind as being affected from without, hold the largest place. But at least, Mill believed, of sensations alone are we directly conscious. This fundamental point, McCosh believed, created impossible confusion in the manner of Mill's application of it, and misleading implications arose from it. He replied that we are never conscious merely of an impression or sensation[60] but of a thing impressed, not of a sensation apart, but of self as sentient. Anticipating charges from some who would say that the child, for example, may be aware of impressions without a consciousness that simultaneously affirms "this is I," McCosh observed that neither is the child conscious to the extent of affirming "this is an impression" or "this is a sensation." If one is weak so is the other, but unvariably consciousness of sensation is also and necessarily consciousness of self as sentient. This interplay not only avoids the conundrum of a metaphysical self, a ghostly something behind the data of impressions, it also confirms a self of empirical qualities. If we have real sensations we have a real self that is known in and through them. Thus, "we can never be conscious of the self, except as sentient or otherwise affected." But also, "we can never be conscious of a sensation except as a sensation of a sentient self."[61]

The self, of course, is not, however, constituted by sensations or impressions. McCosh went to some length to show that our thoughts cannot be derived from sensations,[62] nor can memory,

[60] Reid identifies the distinctions between these two terms in his *Intellectual Powers*, pp. 21-28.

[61] McCosh, *Examination of Mill*, pp. 81-83.

[62] McCosh said that a sensation may be the occasion for a new thought, but must not be equated with the thought itself. The same element acting on a plant, or on

belief, imagination, judgment, emotion, or volition, be so confined. All these activities of the mind carry the notion of self as so functioning and behaving, even though they do not bear particular sensations. Here also is the essential clue to personal identity. For in every act of memory we have memory of a past self; we recall not only the trip by coach, but ourselves as making the trip. And this is more than a recollection of a particular fact or feeling.[63]

But just this point raised the real issue between McCosh's school and Mill's. For Mill was reluctant to attribute any such substantive existence to mind and certainly did not believe that we have a ready intuitional apprehension of its existence. Furthermore, his profoundly skeptical stance on the existence of mind paralleled his criticism of Hamilton, and of all philosophers who alleged a direct apprehension of external reality. Mill used the occasion of his critique of Hamilton to outline his doctrine of the belief in an external world in terms of our belief "in the permanent possibilities of sensation." This law seems to be in part a corollary to the law of association. At any rate, Mill recognized that sensations as actually experienced need not be present to the whole sum of our mental activities. We never doubt that the fire continues to burn in the room below, though we have retired to the room above. But we have learned to group sensations around this collective phenomenon in a manner that legitimates an inference as to their continued existence or recurrence. Nature, we therefore learn, consists of such groups of possibilities. In fact, "the sensations, though the original foundation of the whole, come to be looked upon as a sort of accident depending on us, and the possibilities as more real than the actual sensations." We may even say that the possibilities are the real substance of which the sensations are the qualities, appearances, or effects. Mill then summarized: "The belief in such permanent possibilities seems to me to include all that is essential or characteristic in the belief in substance." And, he claimed, it gives us access out of ourselves to an external world.[64]

In a complex section McCosh endeavored to show that Mill failed wholly to bridge the inner and the outer world and could ac-

---

a lower form of organism, would give rise to no such thought as in the human mind. "The sensation can originate the thought only by stirring up a mental capacity in the soul, which mental capacity is to be regarded as the main element in the complex cause. And yet this essential element is inexcusably, culpably overlooked by the Sensational School, when they derive all our thoughts from sensations." *Examination of Mill*, p. 86.

[63] Ibid., p. 90.   [64] Mill, *Examination*, 1:239–46.

complish such a feat only by denying his own principles. For by what means, he asked, do we believe the possibilities of sensation to be different from the sensations themselves? By the "constitution of human nature," says Mill.[65] For this reply McCosh rejoiced, for only by some fundamental law of the mind itself is such distinction possible. Of course, Mill meant no intuitive law and believed his description triumphant precisely because it skirted all such laws, even a recourse to causality by which might be inferred a cause behind our sensations. McCosh said that if the law of our constitution in question is that of the association of sensation it will avail Mill little, for these are all in the mind. Nor do these possibilities of sensations amount to anything like a real notion of an external world; they never stand apart from the mere "series of feelings." Moreover, the possibilities of experience must carry with them the notion of time, a concept that mandates an important intuitive capacity as well as the content, that is substance, that realizes it. Mill, McCosh believed, could derive no such higher thought without damage to his cause. Mill then "has utterly failed to rear up the actual mental idea and conviction [of the existence of an external world] from the postulated materials." Mill never gets us out of the "shell of the ego." For it is only by means of an innate power of the mind that we are able to know material objects as existing, as real as the self but distinct from it.[66]

But what about the mind? What can we say about the spectator mind that assigns permanent possibilities of sensations to sensations? Mill did not wish obviously to describe a mind as something behind or above its phenomena, for it would be as difficult to describe this naked essence as to describe matter without its sensible attributes. Mill did wish to go beyond Hume, however, to some element of greater certainty than the mere manifold of inner feelings and impressions. Mind is indeed denoted by these, but as in the case of matter, we have a belief in something permanent and "contrasted with the perpetual flux of the sensations and other feelings or mental states." But Mill did not mean what McCosh meant when Mill insisted that memory, for instance, is only a juxtaposition of different feelings. Yesterday's experience constituted a particular feeling of that experience, but today it is gone. What exists today is another feeling, different from the other even if it recalls the same experience. Mill made no allowance for any mental state carrying with it a knowledge of self as affected by that state. But

[65] Ibid., 1:241.
[66] McCosh, *Examination of Mill*, pp. 124–31. The quotation is on p. 128.

Mill did grant that we entertain a belief that the mind exists when it is not feeling or thinking, or otherwise conscious of its own existence or operation. In other words, we have a belief in the "Permanent Possibilities of those states." Memory and expectation particularly attend this phenomenon, for each of them, although actually only present feelings, involves a belief in more than its own present existence. Mill himself recognized the "intrinsic difficulties" of this explanation, though he asserted it confidently against all others. For my acts of memory and anticipation refer to my experience and not someone else's. Thus the disconnected series that falls together into such an order as to make permanent possibilities possible implies and requires the very existing ego or self it intends to reach, and must give it its own spatial identification. For this reason, Mill admitted, we must conclude that the mind is a series of feelings aware of itself as past and future. That means either that the mind or ego is something different from any series of feelings, or possibilities of them, or that, paradoxically, something that is a series of feelings can be aware of itself as a series.[67]

McCosh could not suppress a smile at the encumbrances in which Mill entangled himself, and all so needlessly. The second horn of Mill's dilemma he rejected without comment, for clearly any agency aware of itself as a series is more than that series. It follows that the mind is aware of itself as an enduring entity that subsists through the series, "the thread of consciousness," to use Mill's words, by which it is constituted. It is this enduring entity and no more, McCosh believed, certainly not some mysterious or unknown noumenal existence. One can easily fall into this error or the error of Mill, missing the mark on either side, if one fails to see the facts. For Mill had all he needed. He recognized that the series of feelings always travels with a belief in that series. Why did he not look more closely at the nature of this belief? For surely it is as significant and quite as essential to the mind as the feelings themselves. Properly, in fact, this belief is "an immediate decision." The present self known is continuous with the past self remembered. More than mere possibility rules here. We have the assurance that we did exist at a particular time, and that I who then existed do now exist. "I know of no philosopher," wrote McCosh, "who has called in so many unresolved instincts to account for our convictions of memory and personal identity as Mr. Mill has done." But he returned to his fundamental point. In every conscious act we know an existing

[67] Mill, *Examination*, 1:252-53.

thing, which after reflection and experience, we begin to call self. In all actions of the mind—remembering, willing, reflecting, thinking, feeling—we know self as under such modes of existence. But we need a word to denote this abiding existence, and the most suitable one is "substance." For mind, revealed in and through its attributes, is in the same existential condition as matter. It is revealed in and through its attributes and has existence, power, and endurance. No examination of consciousness relying on and reasoning from careful introspection will fail to reach these conclusions.[68]

McCosh believed that much was at stake in this review of Mill, of which we have examined only a few sections. For Mill brought to fruition much fundamental error that had plagued philosophy since the late seventeenth century. Indeed, an errant idealism and a misguided "realism" had both compounded the errors of the other in overzealous efforts to correct them. McCosh censured Locke most heavily, but largely because he was the first of these philosophers. Locke's ideas on substance caused irreparable mischief, for he defined substance as the "unknown" support of qualities. Berkeley to this extent was at least logically justified in discarding substance altogether with respect to matter. But then the "avenger" Hume emerged and removed the unknown stratum from mind. Reid tried to salvage something from this wreckage but was too timid, still giving some credence to Locke's "unknown support of qualities." Kant could not do much better and allowed that by the outward senses and internal consciousness we perceive only the phenomenon, or appearance, that refers vaguely to a possible noumenon beyond. Philosophy has wasted untold energy since then in debating the existence of this other realm of being, McCosh believed. Hamilton confirmed a consciousness that knows qualities immediately and fully, but no more than Kant, whom he combined with Reid, would Hamilton allow us to seize the substratum or unknowable noumenon. Mill combined all of these errors in his own way. McCosh quoted from Mill's *Logic* to make his point "As our conception of body is that of an unknown exciting cause of sensations," wrote Mill, "so our conception of mind is that of an unknown recipient or percipient of them, and not of them alone, but of all our other feelings. As body is the mysterious something which excites the mind to feel, so mind is the mysterious something which feels and thinks."[69]

[68] McCosh, *Examination of Mill*, pp. 96-97, 99-101. The quotation is on p. 100.
[69] Ibid., pp. 104-10. Mill is quoted by McCosh.

But it was time to call the sheep home. Philosophy, McCosh insisted, would do well to abandon the idea of an unknown and unknowable substratum or noumenon, for it has ever proven to be a "foundation of ice." Its insidious ploys were now finding their way into Herbert Spencer's ungodly "Unknown" and forming for modern religion a quiet resting place where it would disturb no souls. McCosh's intuitional realism intended to correct these abuses, for, as his last reflection indicates, when loosed from the tether of first and fundamental truth, these philosophies had already wrought much damage in the realm of divine and moral truth.[70] Let us see how this was so.

[70] We could easily pursue the McCosh-Mill debate. In the third edition of his *Examination of Hamilton's Philosophy* (London, 1867), Mill in a footnote gave extended replies to the major criticisms of his philosophy. Mansel and McCosh received much attention. McCosh then extended the exchange in an article, "Mill's Reply to his Critics," *British and Foreign Evangelical Review*, 6 n.s. (1868), 332-62. Both of the replies are of philosophical interest, but of a narrow and technical nature. None of the points raised by either thinker substantially altered the positions as outlined above.

Chapter Five

PROTESTANT SCHOLASTICISM

THE TRUTH of Sir William Hamilton's dictum that no problem arises in theology that has not first appeared in philosophy was clearly evident to those who wrestled with the broad implications of his system. For McCosh, Hamilton's philosophy of the unconditioned could only bear bad fruit, for it was planted in the meager soil of Kantianism and nourished by waters from the wells of the critical philosophy. When Henry Mansel of the Hamilton camp pushed the master's philosophy to its full theological conclusions, he produced, in his Bampton lectures of 1858, a major and controversial document. But the work merely demonstrated, for McCosh, the essential incompatibility of the Scottish and neo-Kantian philosophies. For by the time McCosh was concluding his years in Belfast he had already witnessed the gains of this philosophy in his native country and counted them as loss. But no less in the nineteenth century than in the Middle Ages must philosophy be the handmaiden of religion. The Scottish philosophy would suffer in usefulness if it could not demonstrate how a philosophy of mind helped to certify the reality of a divine ruler and the existence of moral law.

But much more was at stake than the mere possibilities of theism. The German thinkers, philosophers and theologians both, had done much to discredit materialism, but their radical constructions did little to bolster the religious life as McCosh defined and cherished it. Indeed, as we noticed earlier, the Scottish philosophy itself was woefully deficient in this respect. Once again, therefore, McCosh's evangelical perspective was critical. On almost all occasions where he saw fit to modify the thought of his predecessors in the Scottish school, McCosh looked to the means by which the reconstruction could serve the needs of evangelical religion. That effort, to be sure, did not lead him very far from the Scottish system, and intuitional realism, he believed, was quite adequate for a religious understanding of man and the world. Precisely, that philosophy enabled McCosh once again to steer a middle course. It could set practical limits to the unbridled expansiveness of pantheism while defending a spiritual plateau amid the "low" materialistic philosophies of the day. In an age of religious diversity, McCosh's efforts to define the religious meaning of his philosophy constituted his own variety of Protestant scholasticism.

McCosh was careful to point out the relation that philosophy should have with religion. Christianity, he believed, should value nothing more than a sound metaphysics, particularly a true understanding of human nature itself, to undergird its strength. But Christianity had always been sociable and too often friendly with philosophies that could only injure it. For better or worse, Christianity would be known by the company it kept. McCosh noticed that Christianity at an early age mingled indiscriminately with Eastern theosophies and certain forms of Platonism. In the Middle Ages it allowed itself to be befriended by Aristotelianism, and later the rigid deductive method of Descartes tied the faith to a radical skepticism that soon undermined it. But these were alliances of the past. To any concerned Christian of the present, McCosh believed, cause for concern was writ large in the theological vogue for German thought. Kant had set some legitimate bounds to the speculative intellect, but his impatient followers refused to be tied down. In their ambitious outward reach they gave a new coloring to Christianity or went beyond Christianity to "pantheism." "The theologies which have ramified from the trunk of Kant," McCosh wrote, "or sprouted from the germ of Schleiermacher, have laboured to move Christianity from the old foundation of faith in the testimony of God, on to a new ground in the Practical Reason or a God-consciousness."[1] At this stage, he believed, the place of theology had been usurped entirely by philosophy, a fact that well illustrated the dangers of a practical identity of the two. "Can no method be devised," McCosh asked, "of making philosophy and theology coöperate without their being confounded?"[2]

McCosh went on to describe how a sound metaphysics might correct an errant one. Its role in this case is a corrective one only, and the new does not stand in the place of the old as a sufficient basis of faith. Metaphysics may also be used as its own check on itself. Especially, it could demonstrate that human knowledge does have limits. This question above all raged violently in the quarters where McCosh's ideas circulated. Further, metaphysics, without

[1] James McCosh, *The Intuitions of the Mind, Inductively Investigated* (1860; 3rd ed., rev., New York, 1874), pp. 413-16. The quotation is on pp. 415-16.
[2] Ibid., p. 416.

entering theology, could lend it some aid. The skill with which philosophers handle fundamental intellectual problems prepares them for every aspect of divine knowledge. "The difficulties which spring from the doctrine of the Divine Sovereignty are no other than the old ones which philosophers have met with from the beginning, as they sought to reconcile freedom with causation." But even as McCosh took up the challenge of liberating the religious mind of his day from the quicksand foundation of German idealism, he made no loud boasts about the expected results. For having outlined the theological uses of metaphysics he undertook with equal care to mark the two off from each other. He was confident that an intuitional realism, extrapolated from the Scottish philosophy, would do much to defend sound faith. But always the danger persisted that Christianity, joined inseparably to a particular philosophical system, would be joined to a sinkable ship.[3]

Despite these strictures McCosh looked for a religious faith bolstered as far as possible by intellect. He furthermore believed that he pursued the Protestant inheritance in doing so, remarking, perhaps too boldly, that although great Catholic thinkers such as Abelard wished to find reasons for demonstrating the truth of Christianity and for building a larger faith on these, most Romanists and High Churchmen gave precedence to faith. Protestants gave it to knowledge. That was especially true of that Protestant tradition in which McCosh stood, and he quoted the Puritan divine Stephen Charnock: "Knowledge is antecedent to faith in the order of nature."[4] McCosh wished to build in the same manner. Although the mind may not attain from its own powers a wholly adequate notion of God and divine being, it is mentally equipped by its primitive cognitions and judgments to secure the foundations for belief. His primary challenge, we shall see, was to demonstrate the positive nature of these cognitions and judgments.

Much was to be won in this enterprise. McCosh believed that a rampant subjectivism that was destructive of biblical authority and universal moral law had found its way into modern religious belief. By securing the foundations of faith on an intuitional realism that links knowledge with real things, philosophy might discourage a religiosity derived from and restricted to the feelings alone. The subjective faith, McCosh feared, is too much the captive of personality, and the designs of the ego, acting like concealed iron inside the ship's compass, lead us astray. McCosh warned against a faith that

[3] Ibid., pp. 421-24.   [4] Ibid., p. 170n.

gave too much room to "the pride of the self-righteous temper ... the conceits of the fancy or the wishes of the heart."[5] He believed modern religion had successfully weathered this storm, however, and, in the white heat of battle, gave most of his attention to a greater nemesis. An intuitional realism might secure a positive intellectual dimension for faith, but to do so it must overcome the prevailing philosophies of "nescience." Hamilton, with his doctrine of the unknowableness of the Absolute, had fired the first shot, but the battle was fully joined when Mansel translated Hamilton's philosophy into a comprehensive outline of epistemological theology. We shall examine the challenges posed to the defender of the "true" Scottish school by the German system and by Hamilton and Mansel who tried to undo it by a different method.

James McCosh had a penchant for analogies and looked to nature itself for the many metaphors that enliven his philosophical prose. Thus he described the origins and progress of German idealism. "The icy and rigid Rationalism of [the] last age has dissolved in the heat of a warmer season, and of late we have had a time of wading deep in melted matter. . . . In [the] last age, certain of our 'excelsior' youths were like to be starved in cold; in this age, they are in greater danger of having the seeds of a wasting disease fostered by lukewarm damps and gilded vapours."[6] The philosophical background here is familiar. Kant had sought to settle the long-standing argument between intuitionists and empiricists by defining the limits of human knowledge. But when he refused to attribute to the human powers any ultimate knowledge of reality, any access to a noumenal world behind the phenomenal knowledge formed of sense experience and the categorical regulations contributed by the mind, he left a legacy of impatience and uncertainty. A romantic age quickly sought some means by which the mind might penetrate this higher realm, this transcendent abode of the moral and spiritual. Under the inspiration of Fichte and Schelling, German metaphysicians made a systematic and progressive effort to weld the worlds of nature and spirit. Physical nature was described as the objective form of absolute spirit; the universe consisted of an absolute ego of which all individual consciousness partakes. England received German idealism through the translations of Coleridge and Carlyle, and it now assumed the balder form of an aggressive intuitionism. The two English romantics reinforced the already extended anti-

[5] Ibid., pp. 171-72, 434.
[6] James McCosh, "The Limits of Religious Thought Examined," *North British Review*, 30 (1859), 137.

rationalism of Kant and linked philosophical success and the whole joy of living to an intuitional vision of life. The reason, defeated and discredited, became associated with the outdated analogy of a mechanical universe, unredeemed by spiritual power, cold and unreligious in its attributes. In Reason, not in the Understanding, lay the dignity of man, the marks of his unlimited spiritual potential, and the lines that led outward to unity with God.[7]

McCosh conceded many merits to the idealistic influence, even among the recent philosophers, like Ferrier, who were probably too greatly infected by it. To distill from the multiplicity of the universe a pervasive universality, and especially to discern an integrating spiritual power, marked a favorable quality, and was a worthy mark of any philosophy. In showing the connection and interdependence of all parts of nature, and the kinship of all with God, the new idealism, McCosh believed, prepared the way for a religious understanding of evolution. The German school and its followers had surely given a renewed sense of spiritual and moral power at work in the soul of each believer and in the world at large, answering the mechanical rationalism and moderatism of the earlier period. The transcendentalists had also placed needed curbs on the claims of the intellect and more thoroughly used all dimensions of the human personality in describing the religious life. Feelings, the inward uplifting of the heart, belief, and inspiration, once again became legitimate. All these factors, in McCosh's mind, were positive achievements of the romantic movement.[8] And evangelicalism, with its stress on the inward experience and with its obsession with spiritual power, was not too far removed from that movement and the age it described.

No system, McCosh believed, should be judged by its worst effects. Ultimately, though, he was quite prepared to measure by results. Practically and intellectually, idealistic philosophy and tran-

---

[7] Hamilton precisely described the transformation of philosophy in Germany: "Kant had annihilated the older metaphysic, but the germ of a more visionary doctrine of the absolute, than any of those refuted, was contained in the bosom of his own philosophy. He had slain the body, but had not exorcised the spectre of the absolute; and the spectre has continued to haunt the schools of Germany even to the present day. The philosophers were not content to abandon their metaphysic; to limit philosophy to an observation of phaenomena, and to the generalisation of these phaenomena into laws." *Discussions on Philosophy and Literature, Education and University Reform* . . . (London, 1852), p. 18. One needs of course to bear in mind here the distinction between "reason" as rationality or logic, and "Reason" as a superrational intuition.

[8] McCosh, *Intuitions*, p. 397; idem, "Limits of Religious Thought," 137.

scendental religion were inadequate and fundamentally wrong. The movement throughout was marked by the excessive recoil from science and reason. McCosh, who encountered many students excited by the romantic mood, was well versed in their claims for its superiority. He had heard their praise for the higher vision of poets and artists, their defense of religious ecstasy untroubled by intellectual analysis, of the quiet voices that speak in moments of mystical rhapsody. Here was a special kind of religious excitement or enthusiasm, and McCosh was, to be sure, sympathetic to much of it.[9]

To this apology McCosh could only reply that no such easy path to true inspiration exists. He for one was skeptical of all such facile claims, and those who gloried in such thrills failed to understand the workings of human nature. For the best and most useful gains of intuition spring invariably from learning and experience. "Almost everywhere there is involved in [great visions] the gathered wisdom of long, and varied, and ripened experience." From Archimedes to Franklin to the Abbe Hauy, great moments of insight are the end result and not the beginning of inquiry. Large original talents join to habits of scientific research and hours of careful observation to make possible the sudden insights that illuminate the world. McCosh, essentially, was too much the practical-minded Scot and too much the intellectual to believe otherwise. But he defended the same disciplined sources for the highest moments of religious awareness also. Those who have penetrated most deeply into the inner realities of life, who have discovered and described its inner harmony and moral unity, have toiled hard to unearth their treasure. "Profound reflection, long observation of human nature and of the ways of God, searching analyses, and a cultivated moral vision"—these, McCosh believed, are the ways of a Socrates, a Plato, a Leibniz.[10]

More seriously, however, the transcendentalist faiths suffered from their intellectual weaknesses, and these in turn emerged in the inadequate and essentially unchristian religion they fostered. McCosh answered his own criticism of this philosophy when he explicitly joined his intuitional realism to the knowledge of God, so

[9] McCosh: "At these times it looks as if a veil or cloud were removed, and we see—as it were by polarised light—the inward constitution of things which usually expose but their tame outside; and we gaze on naked truth without the robe which it commonly wears, but which conceals what is infinitely more lovely than itself. Our eye can then look on pure light without being blinded by it; and we stand face to face with truth and beauty and goodness, and, in a sense, with God Himself." "Limits of Religious Thought," 138.

[10] Ibid., pp. 138-39.

we need only summarize his case here. In many forms the "pantheistic" philosophies that emanated from Germany served largely to swell the pride of the individual. The effect on the religious life, no matter how effectively these philosophies generated a sense of God's reality, was to deliver the individual from a judging God. The sense of guilt and fear of punishment in the afterlife, so central to the evangelical credo, were comfortably suppressed under the easy spiritualism of the romantic theology. Moreover, McCosh remained true to his own philosophy in reminding his readers that consciousness itself discredits pantheism, for consciousness always carries the conviction of self and its concomitant personality, of the distinction of my being from others. So if there is a God he must be ontologically different from me, and a God who confronts me. A long tradition of Protestant thought, of course, lay behind this assertion, but for McCosh the point also demonstrated how a sound philosophy of mind illuminates a sound theology. To this extent, pantheism is also inconsistent with the intuitive knowledge that we have of mind and matter, a fact that demonstrates the impossibility of any system merging them. Moral good and evil also lose their distinct intuited identities under the amalgamating tendencies of pantheism. On these bases McCosh ruled against a German philosophy that too easily passed over the major tenets of evangelical Protestantism.[11]

But even before McCosh took up the Scottish defense against the German advance, Sir William Hamilton had doused cold water on its overheated ambitions. His controversial first essay on the philosophy of the unconditioned selected Cousin as its target, in part because Hamilton saw in Cousin's eclectic philosophy the first serious gains for German philosophy beyond its own borders. Hamilton described four possible positions with respect to our knowledge of the Absolute, each articulated by a significant thinker or school. By the unconditioned Hamilton meant, as we have observed, a principle of absolute existence, out of relation to everything else, dependent on nothing beyond it as a condition of its existence, simple, having no plurality within itself and not dependent therefore on any constituent of its being.[12] One position regarding the unconditioned believes that it is not only incognizable but es-

[11] McCosh, *Intuitions*, pp. 398-409.

[12] In these conditions one can use either the term "Absolute" or the term "Infinite" to illustrate the philosophical themes. Hamilton did, however, assign them different meanings. By the Infinite he meant the "unconditionally unlimited," and by the Absolute he meant "the unconditionally limited."

sentially inconceivable; it is a negative of the conditioned, which alone can be known positively or conceived positively. This position Hamilton defended. Another belief maintains that the unconditioned is not an object of knowledge, but does appear as a regulative principle of the mind itself and is more than a negation of the conditioned. This position Kant defended. From a third perspective, the unconditioned is cognizable but not conceivable; it is known by "a sinking back into identity with the absolute," but is not comprehensible by rational consciousness and reflection, for these are limited to the relative and different. This is the position of Schelling. The fourth belief insists that the unconditioned is cognizable and conceivable by consciousness, for relation and plurality give us the notion of an absolute. Cousin defended that proposition.[13]

Hamilton secured his reputation as the slayer of the German lion when he attacked with particular force the third propositon, on which, he believed, rested the possibility of transcending the realm of consciousness. But Hamilton stuck to his Scottish guns and with brilliant philosophical assaults pressed his quarry. The German's effort to reach the Absolute by a transcendence of consciousness altogether, and the complete obliteration of the self, ended, after Hamilton's critique, in hopeless contradictions. Kant, and Cousin for the French, fared no better in establishing a transcendental philosophy. Always for Hamilton, the elusive Absolute triumphed in escape.[14]

None who wrestled with Hamilton's philosophy of the unconditioned failed to perceive its important theological implications. Philosophy had long employed such terms as "the Absolute," "the Infinite," and "First Cause" as the counterparts of the theologian's "God." Hamilton was not the first, to be sure, to place God well beyond the realm of the knowable, a principle and being not within the definitional limits of the human intellect. And traditionally, such a course had been hailed as beneficial to religion, widening the realm of faith and belief and centering attention on the experience of grace and the subjectivity of the religious life instead. Nonetheless, Hamilton's remarks on God, faith, and belief have struck many as curious, if not confounding. The Scottish thinker dropped the first hint in the essay on Cousin. Summarizing the conclusions he was about to delineate with respect to the unknowableness of the unconditioned, Hamilton wrote: "We are thus taught the salu-

[13] Hamilton, *Discussions*, p. 12.   [14] Ibid., pp. 18-22.

tory lesson, that the capacity of thought is not to be constituted into the measure of existence; and we are warned from recognising the domain of our knowledge as necessarily co-extensive with the horizon of our faith. And by a wonderful revelation, we are thus, in the very consciousness of our inability to conceive aught above the relative and finite, inspired with the belief in the existence of something unconditioned beyond the sphere of all comprehensible reality." And in a footnote to these sentences, Hamilton further remarked, "True, therefore, are the declarations of a pious philosophy:—'A God understood would be no God at all.' " God is at once known and unknown.[15]

Within the circle of British theologians none seized the Hamilton philosophy with greater zeal than Henry Mansel (1820-1871). Every one of the eight Bampton lectures of 1858 bristles with Hamiltonian terminology and carries the philosophical points directly to their theological conclusions. Mansel had attained some distinction before the publication of the lectures the next year, but the work, entitled *The Limits of Religious Thought Examined*, won him immediate fame. Mansel came from Northamptonshire, England, where his father was rector at Cosgrove. He entered Oxford in 1839 and was ordained a deacon in 1844. He held the chair in logic at Oxford until his appointment to the Waynflete professorship of moral and metaphysical philosophy there in 1855. Having "a brilliant wit and memory" and holding a loyalty to "strong and high church principles," Mansel wrote with a vigorous but often difficult prose.[16] The encumbered style did not prevent the lectures from being an immediate sensation. They reached five editions by 1867 and were reprinted in America and on the Continent. They brought from Britain's leading theologian, H. D. Maurice, the rebuttal that appeared as *What is Revelation?* (1859), and they seemed to have affected John Stuart Mill as adversely as they influenced Herbert Spencer favorably. A major study of Mansel interprets the larger significance of the Bampton lectures as a reaction "to the slow but inexorable permeation of English religious thought by German ways of thinking."[17] Mansel wished to supply the antidote for the German virus by thoroughly discrediting the idealism of

---

[15] Ibid., p. 15n. See also Hamilton's letter to Henry Calderwood in the appendix of Sir William Hamilton, *Lectures on Metaphysics and Logic*, ed. H. L. Mansel and John Veitch, 2 vols. (Edinburgh, 1861), 2:530-35.

[16] *Dictionary of National Biography*, 12:966-68.

[17] Kenneth D. Freeman, *The Role of Reason in Religion: A Study of Henry Mansel* (The Hague, 1969), p. 1.

Fichte, Schelling, and Hegel, by demonstrating the irrelevance of the higher criticism, and by invalidating the accommodation of religion to culture. For this effort Mansel cast his net wide. The notes to the lectures show an immense reading of philosophy, and though his debt to Hamilton is writ large everywhere, he has many favorable references to McCosh and quotes him frequently. McCosh was quite willing to repay the compliment, but he could not let the new direction given to theology by Mansel go unquestioned.[18]

In essence, McCosh and Mansel divided because the latter wished to remove religion entirely from intellect. McCosh was by no means prepared to join the two, but he did believe Mansel went to an extreme in separating the laws of the mind from the province of faith and belief. Mansel began his lectures with a trenchant attack on rationalism and dogmatism, the prevailing religious styles, he believed, of the mid-nineteenth century. He perceived in religious rationalism all the pride and pretensions of human vanity. For reason feeds this vanity by creating a God in human form, a mere likeness of itself. In lowering the divine sovereign it unduly elevates human nature. But the errors of these ways did not justify the suspension of intellect. A rigid creedalism that affixes frozen forms to the articles of faith does equal violence to human nature and the religious life. So for Mansel, the theological challenge lay in steering a passage between these extremes, and for this endeavor only one course was available. Human reason might abandon its impossible dream if human reason fully understood its own limits. Thus Mansel asked the question: "If human philosophy is not a direct guide to the attainment of religious truth, . . . may it not serve as an indirect guide, by pointing out the limits of our faculties, and the conditions of their legitimate exercise?"[19]

Mansel took the Hamiltonian philosophy of the unconditioned and fortified it with prolific references to other philosophers. Using Hamilton's ideas on consciousness and causality especially, Mansel went on to speak of these problems in their religious outcome. By the time he was finished he had left nothing for human reason to do in the area of theology. Reason could only know its own limitations, and, all the wiser, judiciously avoid all claims of access to

---

[18] See Bernard M. G. Reardon, *Religious Thought in the Nineteenth Century, Illustrated from Writers of the Period* (Cambridge, 1966), p. 288 for another recent discussion of Mansel.

[19] Henry Longueville Mansel, *The Limits of Religious Thought Examined* (London, 1859), pp. 56–61. The quotation is on p. 61.

God. And like Hamilton, Mansel essentially relied on human analogy to postulate the attributes of the deity.[20]

On this basis Mansel made a special plea for Christianity by insisting that God intends to speak to us through the full range of the human faculties and that Christianity is the most genuine religion because it involves the entire personality. We know God, Mansel wrote, the more we know our human nature. On this point McCosh and Mansel quite concurred. For both the mental sciences in their fullest content were the most useful aspects of theology. Mansel even found McCosh a great asset in making this point, so often in his writings had McCosh made it himself. At one point Mansel quoted at length from McCosh's *Divine Government*.[21]

McCosh, in turn, had much to say about Mansel's book, for he considered it highly important. His lengthy review of the work for the *North British Review* clearly stated its place in modern philosophical and theological literature. "Every deep and influential system of philosophy," he wrote, "has its religious or irreligious applications by the founder of the system or his disciples.... We have now, in these lectures of Mr. Mansel, the philosophy of Hamilton in its supposed religious aspect." Moreover, McCosh stated that the work did for rational theology what Hamilton did for the theories of the Absolute.[22] And therein lay much of its merit. For although McCosh, unlike Mansel, did not dismiss the usefulness of rational philosophy, he could readily list its limitations. Rational theology, despite its appeals to human nature, in fact overlooked the facts of human nature—the sense of sin, the need for grace, the heroic dimensions of the human heart in its quest for love, purity, self-sacrifice, devotion. Scripture is far more effective than reason in rallying these inner springs of life.[23] Furthermore, McCosh appreciated the reaction that rose against a numbing rationalism in religion. The romantic movement was a natural consequence, and the intuitional philosophies expressed the longings of the undernourished heart. The intuitionists restored our oneness with God, and the transcendentalists gave him a home in nature. But no less than the rationalists did the later philosophers fail to speak to the realities of the human soul, and certainly their easy confidence and happy reconciliation of the divine and human betrayed the Evangelical's uneasy quest for grace. McCosh at least would look for a religious philosophy that answered those needs too. Mansel could be useful

---

[20] Ibid., pp. 74–80, 93–95, 99–100, 171–72.   [21] Ibid., p. 362.
[22] McCosh, "Limits of Religious Thought," 146–47.
[23] McCosh, *Intuitions*, pp. 429–30.

in deflating the claim of the optimistic philosophies. McCosh stated: "We have a work before us eminently fitted to lay an arrest on this speculative spirit, whether it founds on a formal rationalism or a loose intuitionism."[24]

But for all its merits, Mansel's theology was fraught with peril. It differed fundamentally from McCosh's approach to the knowledge of God through the positive intuitions, and the Scottish philosopher insisted that no good would come out of any theological system that divorced itself from these positive notions. The revolt against the speculative daring of the Germans was a rightful endeavor, but it prepared the way for a formidable skepticism. Philosophy, McCosh commented, had fallen into a quagmire through its recent loss of faith in reason and had succumbed to various forms of unearthly mysticism. "I have no toleration," he wrote, "for those who tell us with a sigh, too often of affectation, that they are very sorry that knowledge or reason yields to insoluble doubts and contradictions, from which they are longing to be delivered by some mysterious faith. . . . I do not believe that the understanding, or the reason, or any other power of the mind, lands us in scepticism."[25]

What struck McCosh particularly about Hamilton and Mansel was the propensity of both, having devastated the *notions* of the unconditioned, to go on to propound a *belief* in the same. Any theology, they believed, must begin in this extrarational domain, and not build upon the limited faculties of mind. But Hamilton and Mansel stopped short at just this point, McCosh believed, and failed to carry further the implications of their thought. We do indeed have deep inner inclinations that lead outward toward some absolute. But what are these exactly? McCosh would endeavor to show that they are the very intuitions of the mind that any sound philosophy establishes as the habit of our understanding the real world. If Hamilton and Mansel had tried to state precisely the nature of this belief, they might have recognized its intuitional basis and recognized its relation to the cognitive faculties. McCosh would further endeavor to show that this belief centers in no merely vague feelings, that it must, as all intuitions must, have an object. McCosh feared that Hamilton and Mansel were compounding an error of Kant, and with similarly dangerous consequences. For Kant, he said, saved himself from the nihilism of the speculative reason by an appeal to the practical reason; so the Hamiltonian school, lest the cognitive powers land us in nescience, calls in faith.

[24] McCosh, "Limits of Religious Thought," 144.
[25] McCosh, *Intuitions*, p. 173.

But these foundations of faith are too unstable. Connected to nothing, they will either fall quickly in the onslaught of the skeptic, or amorphous and vague emotions will surround them and constitute the whole of the religious life.[26]

And already the worst abuses were appearing. In 1862 Herbert Spencer published *First Principles*, the first volume of a "synthetic philosophy." In an effort to clear the air for his scientific and philosophical speculations, Spencer attempted a "reconciliation of science and religion" by a careful and adroit effort to delineate the boundaries of each. Part I of *First Principles*, entitled "The Unknowable," furnished his famous description of God, and the entire realm of religious thought, under that designation. Moreover, Spencer acknowledged his debt to Hamilton and Mansel: "Here I cannot do better than avail myself of the demonstration which Mr. Mansel, carrying out in detail the doctrine of Sir William Hamilton, has given in his 'Limits of Religious Thought.' And I gladly do this, . . . because his mode of presentation cannot be improved." Spencer followed Mansel carefully to this conclusion: "If Religion and Science are to be reconciled, the basis of reconciliation must be this deepest, widest, and most certain of all facts—that the Power which the Universe manifests to us is utterly inscrutable."[27] McCosh quoted from several passages of Spencer in a lengthy footnote in *Intuitions of the Mind*. He demonstrated the parallelism of language in Hamilton and Spencer and placed Spencer "quite in the spirit of the German speculatists."[28] Finding the British metaphysician a bold and highly suggestive thinker, McCosh nonetheless dismissed him: "The attempt by this giant mind to reach an unapproachable height, by heaping Ossa on Pelion, must turn out a lamentable failure."[29] McCosh and Spencer would clash again. For now, though, there was nothing in Spencer's fanciful projections that a realistic philosophy of the mind could not correct.

MCCOSH never believed or tried to demonstrate that human knowledge is coextensive with divine reality, that the attributes of

---

[26] McCosh, "Limits of Religious Thought," 150-51; idem, *Intuitions*, pp. 173n-174n. McCosh, in short, was charging Hamilton with the same inconsistency with which Hamilton charged the cosmothetic idealists.

[27] Herbert Spencer, *First Principles* (1862; New York, 1890), pp. 39, 46.

[28] McCosh should have named Kant, rather than his German successors. The third edition, revised, of McCosh's *Intuitions* appeared in 1874, several years after Spencer's *First Principles* of 1862. Into it McCosh incorporated remarks on Spencer's work; the original of *Intuitions* appeared in 1860.

[29] McCosh, *Intuitions*, pp. 348n-350n; idem, *The Supernatural in Relation to the Natural* (Cambridge, 1862), pp. 357-58.

the deity or even the awareness of his existence rested on some facile connection of the human powers with a higher spiritual realm. McCosh had inherited too much of the neo-Calvinism of the Scottish Evangelicals to boast such potential for a fallen human nature. Nonetheless, his effort to build directly from the Scottish philosophy, and more particularly from his own intuitional realism, toward an intellectual apprehension of God, constituted the essence of his effort to merge the two traditions that he represented. Specifically, McCosh tried to build upward from the facts of the intelligence, which described his mental philosophy, to show that we have an imperfect, or incomplete notion of God, but one that is real and not fanciful in the measure it takes of him. Our notion of God, in other words, is positive, building on the laws of the mind itself and their apprehension of real things, and it approximates a true understanding of God by virtue of its restriction to real things.

We can describe McCosh's position in the philosophical disputes we have examined so far, by noting first that he, like Hamilton and Mansel, wished to draw back from the Germans and their quest for the divine through a pure intuitionism.[30] But was it necessary in this recoil to remove divine knowledge wholly from human consciousness? McCosh thought not. So, having asserted that "I am not convinced that we are obliged to call in a separate intuition to discover and guarantee the Divine existence," he hastened to add that we need not despair of ever grounding such knowledge in the human faculties. The feelings, the imagination, the moral sense, all move our perspective beyond ourselves and rest in some ultimate ground of existence. But so also do the laws of the mind itself, in a careful and methodical manner. We need invoke no special "God-consciousness" to describe this process or account for its origin. It is the culmination of the natural unfolding of the mental powers and not some superrational leap beyond them.[31] While McCosh tried to illustrate this fact in several ways, the appeal again to causation and to an intuition of the infinite most forcefully demonstrated the theological aspects of his intuitional realism.

Recent philosophical speculation about causality, McCosh believed, well illustrated how genius, even when assuming a friendly posture toward theism, could do much harm to that position. Brown, Hamilton, and Mansel, each in the spirit of Kant, secured

[30] By this I mean an intuitionism not founded on experience with the world, one unmediated by the empirical senses. Pure intuitionism is thereby differentiated from McCosh's intuitional realism.
[31] McCosh, *Intuitions*, pp. 380–82.

a degree of certainty for the causative principle as a law of the mind, only by restricting it as such and forswearing any claims to its ultimate status as a fact of the real world. We have already seen McCosh's effort to demonstrate causality as a mental law that operates only via the media of substances and necessarily therefore carries with it the attribute of power in those substances. For that law, beginning with primitive cognition of material changes, is soon compelled to extend its sphere of activity as it embraces an expanding realm of natural phenomena. The greater the sphere the more forcefully are illustrated the corresponding cognitions and judgments. By this procedure alone we are led back to a first cause, by a simple reductive process. But McCosh did not wish to rest the case on a simple reductive process. An intuitional realism could strengthen itself by demonstrating the precise coincidence of the laws of mind and the laws of nature. Modern science, he felt, and particularly those biological studies that used an evolutionary theory to illustrate the interconnected elements of all varieties of life, supplied the most useful content for the causational law in its wonderful wholeness. For not only does the law require a cause for every effect, it is also "an essential part of the internal law that it requires the cause to be adequate to produce the effect." Further, if the effect be real, so also must the cause be real. "Hence the importance of adhering to the doctrine of natural realism as opposed to idealism." And finally, the law of causality further clarifies modern science by establishing not only substance, but substance with power, as necessary to the changes involved.[32]

On this point McCosh clashed directly with Hamilton, who believed that causality, as a negative law of the mind only, was not impelled to probe infinitely backward, even for a cause of the "First Cause"; he believed we could extricate ourselves from this phenomenological impossibility, and this embarrassment to theism, only by abjuring any extension of the mental law to ultimate reality. But McCosh insisted that the mind pursues no such limitless regression. Causality is satisfied only when power adequate to an effect is provided. The restless mind moves back only until it reposes in a power adequate to the whole effect (the sum of creation itself) and bears no marks of being itself an effect. Because the causal intuition works only amid substances, it rests in a God whose signs and power are manifest, but whose phenomenological attributes lie beyond us. To this extent, we do not have a primitive

[32] Ibid., pp. 384–86.

notion of the uncaused, but we reach the notion of a first cause as the summary of our positive cognitions in the experimental realm in which they operate.[33]

Finally, we confront the question, Do we have a positive intuition of the infinite (here, as in infinite space)? McCosh belabored this question, for on this point the ghost of Hamilton haunted him most. We have seen that McCosh wished at least to close the wide opening to skepticism that Hamilton and Mansel had prepared by their divorcing human intellectual powers from the object of divine knowledge. Mansel, echoing Hamilton, proclaimed for faith a large and legitimate exercise. Belief was larger than knowledge, and in fact flourished amid the humbling of the rational powers. McCosh, however, wanted none of this. He wanted to establish a relation between belief and knowledge, not by equating the two, but by demonstrating that belief follows automatically from the boundaries, from the ultimate extensions, of our positive knowledge. It comes, in short, on the heels of our intuitions and their necessary connection with the world of real experience. Religious faith is not the leap of mind that springs from its own ash heap; it is that toward which all the powers of the intelligence build with relentless logic and force. It is the ultimate resting place of these powers. All things build to God, and this juncture of divine and human summarizes the whole life of the mind in the growth and expansion of its powers.[34]

It was no easy task for McCosh to demonstrate this fact, and he labored over it several times and in several different ways. Having rejected any immediate, superrational intuition of God, and having determined not to overleap the world of experience, McCosh could only extend the intuitions to their furthest point and suggest that they bring us to the realms of the infinite. One illustration that McCosh urged sought to demonstrate that, the intellectual contortions of Hamilton and Mansel notwithstanding, we have a positive and live sense of the infinite, one that we cannot shake. The sailor at sea, McCosh noted, is not led by any native instinct to believe that the ocean has no bottom simply because his anchor has not sounded its depths. The astronomer can see no end to the array of stars reaching further into the universe, but he projects no extension of these into the indefinite limits beyond. "Man is constrained to believe that whatever be the point of space and time to which his eye or his thoughts may reach, there must be a space and time be-

[33] Ibid.   [34] Ibid., p. 195n.

yond." We can place ourselves in our imaginations at any point in space, no matter how far away, and we are still compelled to believe that space extends further. We may do the same for any moment of past time and still pursue its elusive beginnings. The analogy was simplistic, to be sure. McCosh, though, merely wanted to confirm an "intuitive belief, accompanied as it is with a stringent necessity of feeling." It would be important to account for the strength of this intellectual imperative.[35]

McCosh also examined Hamilton's statement wherein he alleged that we are wholly unable either to conceive of space as bounded, as finite, as a whole beyond which there is no farther space, or to conceive the possibility of the contradictory. But McCosh charged that Hamilton employed the verb "conceive" in a double and misleading sense. For in the second usage, the word designates an imaging, or representing in consciousness. In this sense we cannot have an idea of the infinite. But the imaging power of the mind is not to be equated with the thinking, judging, or believing power. In Hamilton's first proposition, the word "conceive" is taken to mean think, determine, or be convinced. "We picture space as bounded," McCosh wrote, "but we cannot think, judge, or believe it to be bounded." Here disappear the contradictions cherished by the Kantians and Hamiltonians. For both propositions, when rightly understood, are true. McCosh summarized: "We cannot imagine space as without bounds; we cannot think that it has bounds or believe that it has bounds." The former fact describes a mental impotency, the latter a mental potency, "one of the most elevated and elevating convictions of which the mind is possessed—and . . . a conviction of which it can never be shorn."[36]

---

[35] Ibid., pp. 190-91. Mansel replied directly to McCosh's argument. He insisted that the mental projection to any point beyond our imagined location in space or time is a necessary act of a consciousness that can think only in relation. "Whatever we conceive must be related to something else which we do not conceive." Further, we do not think of space and time as having no boundary; we simply refrain from thinking of them as having a boundary. They are thus presented to us as "indefinite," not as "infinite." And finally, we cannot think of space and time beyond our imagined point as infinite, because then we would have an infinity *plus* the space or time embraced by the extension projected by our imagination. The result would then be something greater than infinity, an absurd proposition. Mansel, on the other hand, did observe that he and Hamilton and McCosh all shared a disdain for an immediate mental grasp of the infinite. *Limits of Religious Thought*, pp. 290-91.

[36] James McCosh, "Sir William Hamilton's Metaphysics," *Dublin University Magazine*, 54 (1859), 164-65; idem, *Intuitions*, p. 196n; idem, *The Scottish Philosophy, Biographical, Expository, Critical, from Hutcheson to Hamilton* (New York, 1875), p.

Now McCosh began to work toward the point at which he rested his statements about the intuition of the infinite. He thought it sufficient, even while concurring with Hamilton and Mansel that the mind can hold no pure grasp of the infinite as such, to establish its existence as an intuition. For even stating so simply the fact that we cannot be made to believe that at any given time space should cease or that at any given instant time should begin, much is implied. For we know from all that a philosophy of intuitional realism has taught that space and time are not mere regulative habits of the mind, affixed by it onto the data of experience. Space and time are the conditions of real experience, or "conditions of the possibility of the existence of other objects." By this operation of the mind, therefore, we know the infinity of space and time to imply the possibility of infinite being to dwell in them. Moreover, McCosh urged, although we could not deny that space and time have independent existence apart from our minds' embracing them, the mind itself finds it a nearly impossible act so to conceive them. We simply cannot cognate pure space and time, know them as independent or separate entities. That difficulty has induced many philosophers to assign them only a mental existence, as forms given to objects by the mind. But space and time are no less real; we simply do not know space and time without a substantial existence in them. But here was an important clue. We never know without knowing substances, and we know substances only in space and time. Space and time are then, in a real sense, attributes of substances that we know. And if we have a positive intuition of the infinite, derived from extended space and time, we arrive as nearly as the mind can to the attribute of an infinite Being. Philosophers had been misled, McCosh believed, in their quest for the elusive infinite. For, he said, "the infinite [that is, as that grasped by the mind's intuition] is not to be viewed as having an independent being, is not to be regarded

---

447. Hamilton, in fact, admitted that we have a "belief" in the infinite, and said that the sphere of the belief is much larger than the sphere of knowledge. *Lectures,* 2:530. McCosh responded to this admission with skepticism. He observed that Hamilton had claimed a belief in something that Hamilton himself insisted is not and cannot be in consciousness. He therefore exposed himself to the same charges he leveled against Schelling, that he endorsed a belief founded "on the annihilation of consciousness." That is, McCosh detected that Hamilton had written that "knowledge and belief are both contained under consciousness," and correctly cited his *Lectures* 1:191. If so, then the consciousness that can conceive no absolutes and no infinites leaves us with a belief in "Zero." The only recourse for McCosh was to demonstrate the positive nature of our intuition of the infinite. *Intuitions,* pp. 195n-196n.

as a substance or a separate entity." Like space and time, which are the conditions of possible substantial existence, the infinite as intuited only suggests the conditions of infinite being; it must be considered an attribute of an object.[37]

McCosh here was testing the fullest possible extension of a philosophy of intuitional realism. That philosophy stood on the correspondence of the laws of the mind to the laws and realities of the external world and permitted the exercise of the mind's intuitions only under experience of the external world. But McCosh's extension of his intuitional realism to the knowledge of God was inferential only. He admitted as much. It was inferential because whereas the philosopher had shown that laws of the mind coincide in their operations with experienced things, with substantial reality, he was now inferring, with respect to the intuition of the infinite, and its existence, that they *must* somehow coincide with some substantial being. For the mind's intuitions, which are satisfied, indeed even realized, only when propelled into functioning by contact with experience, require a similar power with respect to the intuition of the infinite. "Our intuition," McCosh said, "is satisfied only by the contemplation of an infinite God." That intuition of the infinite lies vacuous, lethargic, barely cognizable, until awakened by the reality of an infinite power. "The mind feels as if there were something wanting, till it learns of One to occupy the vacuum; but it is met and gratified in every one of its intellectual and moral intuitions when it is brought to know Him who inhabiteth eternity and immensity, and filleth them with living and life-giving fullness."[38]

McCosh made no ultimate claims for his ideas here. He offered no intellectual "proof" of the existence of God. He did believe, however, that this approximate knowledge of God is the furthest extension of a sound philosophy of the mind and that it approaches the borders of faith and establishes its validity. He insisted that man's approach to God is carried along throughout by the expansion of the mental powers, that their unfolding through renewed and enlarged contact with the furthest limits of the real, the experienced world, was the certain path toward the God in whose image he is made. And despite his affinity with Hamilton, and despite the fact that McCosh's own evangelical character delighted to know that man's intellectual powers are both exalted and humbled in their quest for God, McCosh remained horrified by those philoso-

[37] McCosh, *Intuitions*, pp. 199, 197.   [38] Ibid., p. 200.

phies that found God in the negation of the human intellect. The fullest extension of a philosophy of natural realism, its acknowledged limitations notwithstanding, stood ready to enhance a Christian understanding of reality.[39]

IN DESCRIBING the theological possibilities of his intuitional realism McCosh believed he had demonstrated the cardinal value of philosophical thinking. But even to stop at this point was to fall short; philosophy could do even more in securing a Christian understanding of man and life by embracing their moral foundations and giving these a high measure of intellectual certainty. On this question McCosh intended to be consistent with the larger outline of his philosophy. His intuitional realism functioned as another kind of middle road in modern philosophy, for here too there were rival schools of thought that he judged both inadequate and incomplete. And McCosh's moral philosophy, like his intellectual philosophy, claimed to build on an inductive path of thought that eventually merged with the larger road of Christian theism to form a still larger pathway of faith.

In late 1867, less than a year before McCosh departed Ireland for Princeton, he delivered before a meeting of the Evangelical Alliance in Amsterdam an extensive paper on contemporary ethical philosophy. The essay, entitled "Moral Philosophy in Great Britain in Relation to Theology," reached an American audience with its publication in the *American Presbyterian and Theological Review* early the next year. McCosh described his moral philosophy in his larger treatises and used this occasion to discuss some general points related to this philosophy. He stated at the outset that "of all the de-

---

[39] Ibid., p. 202. To this extent, McCosh, perhaps more than he realized, took part in one of the major quests of the nineteenth-century romantic movement, what Franklin L. Baumer calls the "yearning for the Infinite." A restless generation pursued, in a variety of ways, the limitless reaching out of the human faculties, especially of all the faculties of the mind. As a religious thinker McCosh welcomed that search, for nearly any successful establishment of a principle of infinitude had theistic possibilities. But McCosh's choice of means, at least, clearly sets him apart from the typical romantic. As Baumer says, romantics burst the bounds of normal human consciousness—"If the romantics did not invent the unconscious, they were the first to talk about it freely and at length"—and invented extraordinary faculties of human powers as the means of realizing the infinite. Furthermore, the romantics tended to merge the natural and the supernatural. The singularity of McCosh's achievement is that he legitimized the notion of the infinite as a positive fact of normal human consciousness, and he provided access to the infinite at the limits of human experience; but he did so without any pantheisticlike joining of the natural and supernatural realms. See Franklin L. Baumer, *Modern European Thought: Continuity and Change in Ideas, 1600-1950* (New York, 1977), pp. 271, 284.

partments of natural knowledge the science of the human mind comes nearest to religion; and of all the mental sciences Moral Philosophy stands in closest relation to Christian Theology."[40] For it is the purpose of the latter science to unfold the moral and motive powers of human nature, and it is to these especially, McCosh believed, that the Christian religion addresses itself. Furthermore, a sense of God's power and justice is always consistent with a strong philosophical exposition of a universal moral law in which all human beings partake or under whose canons they stand judged. The Christian religion especially required this philosophy for, as McCosh tried to show, the whole meaning of atonement and redemption was formulated around it.

Most of McCosh's audience probably needed no reminder of the moral debates that had engaged philosophers in Europe and America over the past decades. McCosh's address followed by three years the publication in 1863 of John Stuart Mill's *Utilitarianism*, the most eloquent statement of an empirical ethics linked to the happiness principle. Mill, in his earlier *System of Logic*, also extended Thomas Brown's attempts to unite the moral sentiments with the emotions. McCosh labeled this school the "Sensational or Experimental" and listed Hobbes, Locke, Hume, Hartley, and James Mill as its leading exponents. Opposed to this group stood the "*a priori* or Rational" school of ethics, represented by Descartes, Ralph Cudworth, Clarke, Butler, Kant, Coleridge, Cousin, and the Scottish membership of Reid, Stewart, and Hamilton. Unquestionably McCosh was sympathetic to the latter, depreciative of the first. The rationalists had clearly established morality on a firm foundation by admitting a moral faculty in the human constitution and assigning it an independent authority relative to the other faculties. The empirical school had generally dissolved the moral faculty by joining it to the will and the sensibility. Deprived of an independent location in the mind, ethical truth roamed aimlessly amid the flux of experience, and that in turn furnished only the quantitative laws of pleasure and pain as standards of measure. McCosh spent no little time in seeking to discredit these measures, but we shall see also that shortcomings of the other school were nearly as mischievous. In his efforts to take from the school of experience and from the school of intuition, McCosh further elaborated the central theme of his philosophical system.[41]

The philosophical issue of morality was critical for McCosh, be-

[40] James McCosh, "Moral Philosophy in Great Britain in Relation to Theology," *American Presbyterian and Theological Review*, 6, n.s. (1868), 5.

[41] Ibid., 6–7.

cause in contrast to some Christian thinkers he contended for a morality independent of Scripture. The Bible, he said, does not furnish us a moral philosophy as such, though it does supply us with definite moral imperatives. As the Scriptures do not profess to prove the existence of God, but merely assume it, so neither do they demonstrate the foundations of moral right, but instead address all human beings as capable of discerning moral facts. Morality is then prior to and independent of the Word of God, or at least we must presume this fact at the outset. Any Christian, furthermore, must understand that the Bible exists as a means of salvation. But it is a salvation from our sin and to that extent depends upon the demonstration of sin as a fact of human life. Here for McCosh lay the crucial importance of an adequate moral philosophy. "We believe that this morality, shown on independent evidence to have a foundation in the existence of things, points to the need of a Redeemer, and thus furnishes valuable internal proof in favor of the Divine origin of Christianity." It thus also assures us that this independent morality joins with the Word of God itself. McCosh would try to show that an intuitional moral realism more faithfully described these facts than either of the two prevailing schools of thought.[42]

In siding with those who defended the existence of a moral faculty McCosh joined what had been a major tradition in Western thinking since the late seventeenth century. To this extent too he accepted probably the most important idea underlying the age of Moderatism in Scotland and its efforts to make the moral life do service for the outmoded ideas of grace as the essence of religious experience. But McCosh, we shall see, wanted to maintain the idea of a moral faculty while dissociating it from the comfortable, self-congratulatory, and smug age that first celebrated it. So McCosh immediately insisted that when he spoke of the moral faculty he intended no device by which morality is fashioned and then affixed to elements outside it. Conscience does not create moral truths. Human nature is not the source of good. The Scottish evangelist here again preserved enough of the Calvinistic perspective of the Evangelicals to disavow any anthrocentric morality. "I lay down this position in order to guard against the idea that moral excellence is something depending on the peculiar nature of man." On the other hand, McCosh and his party never severed man wholly from the source of all good. His own philosophy had done away with a wholly remote God, the inscrutable deity of early Reformed theology. All things lead to God, and the intellectual powers, as we

[42] Ibid., 10.

have seen, progress and perfect themselves as they move toward this understanding. So likewise does the moral faculty. Its role also enhanced our grasp of divine knowledge.[43]

If the moral faculty did not invent and dispense moral ideas, what precisely was its function? McCosh answered that its role was strictly similar to all other parts of our intuitive knowledge. The conscience makes known certain qualities of experienced things. It comes into operation only when it has experience from the world outside and then discerns the moral character of that experience, thereby selecting for our attention that particular moral quality of being presented to it. For in the same manner that causation is pronounced a reality not independent from experienced things, so also is moral judgment an a posteriori action. Like causation, moral judgment is an interaction with substance. It makes known no new substance or any independent existence. Moral reality "is not a colour thrown over the object by the mental eye which perceives it, but is a real quality of the object, is there prior to its being perceived, and is in the object whether it is perceived or not."[44]

McCosh, perhaps, could not escape the long reach of an Edwardsian Calvinist influence on his thinking. All that God ordains as good is good; we seek no higher ground or reason for its goodness and merely follow an obligation to cherish those things whose qualities inform us of their moral goodness.

Moral and intellectual ideas are similar in their origins, McCosh said, but are afterward distinguished by the fact that moral ideas carry with them an obligation of duty. Here again the analogy to the intellectual powers persists. "In this respect it is like some of our intellectual intuitions, which impel us to look around for something which they do not themselves reveal." So the moral faculty forsakes ultimate infallibility and "looks up for sanction and guidance." Indeed the moral qualities of things, no less than all the qualities of visible objects, come to us often obscured. We might say then that moral qualities extracted from the world of experience initiate the exercise of a moral faculty in us, but that faculty, in its

[43] McCosh, *Intuitions*, p. 256.

[44] Ibid., pp. 255-56. In defending this position McCosh mentioned one danger that he perceived in the counterproposition that the moral faculty is the inventor of moral truths. That possibility allowed that another race of beings, perhaps one indigenous to another world, might have a different kind of moral faculty with opposing moral truths. What our faculty pronounces good might be labeled evil by another. In that manner a moral philosophy designed to provide a measure of universality, or absoluteness, to ethical science, by certifying a moral intuition, might ironically involve itself in a dangerous relativism. Ibid.

sense of duty and obligation, seeks out an ultimate source of moral truth, some more absolute and certain foundation of moral law.[45]

McCosh, in outlining his theory, was not offering any "proof" of God's existence in the Thomistic sense. But the example served to illustrate the further uses of an intuitional realism. For the sense of obligation that rises with the moral will does not rest until it finds ample room for its reposing. Thus McCosh wrote: "Our moral convictions do not, so it seems to me, of themselves compel us to believe in the existence of God. I am persuaded, however, that like most of our deeper intuitions . . . they point upwards toward God." In this way the moral faculty traces itself not only upward but backward to its own source. Moral good may precede human existence, but in its ultimate operation it is never divorced from it. The faculty of conscience finds its way as best it can through the wide gamut of human experience, and, McCosh believed, the moral life is possible only in minds high enough in the scale of life to perceive the good. It is the evolutionary advancement of the human race, the progressive perfection of its intellectual and moral powers, that effectively extracts moral content from experience. So McCosh could believe, therefore, that however independent of human nature might be the origin and existence of moral law, its exercise coincided exactly with God's extension of himself into the human constitution.[46]

But it was clear to McCosh, as well as to rationalists and other intuitionists, that the possibility of an independent morality stood discredited by recent currents in philosophy. There was little new here, only a renewed and higher prestige for sensationalism and materialism in general. John Stuart Mill, the most renowned and eloquent defender of these views, tied the sensational basis of the moral feelings to his own associationist philosophy. Moral sentiments, he believed, arise from our personal experiences, and they recur in interrelated patterns of association with their attendant impressions and sensations. The analogy to physical causation was appropriate, therefore, and Mill likened the moral sentiments to all other ideas by suggesting "a process of a similar kind to chemical combination."[47] The moral life then can claim no more than a sub-

---

[45] Ibid., pp. 257-58. One notices the precise parallel between McCosh's moral theory and intuitional realism. As McCosh established the sense of the infinite as an extension of knowledge formed in experience, but entering where experience went no further, so does the ultimate ground of moral law enter to complete our moral experience.

[46] Ibid., p. 258. The next chapter elaborates the point about evolution.

[47] Quoted by McCosh in *An Examination of Mr. J. S. Mill's Philosophy; Being a Defence of Fundamental Truth* (New York, 1866), p. 198.

jective sanction for the individual, even though Mill's utilitarianism extended the happiness principle to the sum total of its realization in the largest possible realm of people. Even those who claim a "higher principle" as the basis of morality cannot escape the subjective confinements of their moral experience. We first perceive the evil or injustice of arbitrary punishment, Mill believed, because it has a potential reference to our own well-being, and therefore the feeling attending that experience is a painful one for us. Moreover, efforts to link moral imperatives to an objective duty, such as duty to God, reveal their emotional and subjective basis. For the belief in God urges a moral behavior that corresponds directly to the subjective, religious feelings, and is the exact measure of that feeling. "The sanction, so far as it is disinterested, is always in the mind itself." Virtue, therefore, is invariably grounded in the feelings. "These who desire virtue for its own sake desire it either because the consciousness of it is a pleasure, or because the consciousness of being without it is a pain, or for both reasons united."[48]

McCosh thought Mill's moral theory wrong and dangerous. He did not deny that association described a large part of our mental activity, but he did oppose Mill's efforts to substitute it for judgment. For judgment was critical to the mind's understanding of experience and necessary for an intuitional realism that would establish an objective basis for morality. Mill's sensationalism was at once fortuitous and deterministic. McCosh of course simply echoed the agony of many previous philosophers who despaired to see the moral sentiments deprived of any basis higher than the individual experience and tied to its emotional flux. Morality, they were convinced, either derived from within by some agent differentiated from the feelings, or expressed a universal character by virtue of its origin in a being or power transcending human experience. McCosh, we have seen, combined both these views. Judgments arose in response to experience, but that was much different from saying that they express only accumulated and associated experiences. Our higher laws of the mind, our primitive cognitions and judgments, are dissimilar in quality to simple ideas furnished through the senses. Here, McCosh believed, Mill's analogy of chemical and mental science collapsed. Associated ideas cannot generate anything different from themselves. We can mix the colors blue and yellow by hand to produce green, but the independent thought of these two hues does not produce the image of green in our minds. Nor do the ideas of time, space, or causality

[48] John Stuart Mill, *Utilitarianism*, ed. Oskar Piest (1861; Indianapolis, 1977), pp. 37, 48.

derive from associations; rather they emerge, like moral perceptions, as fundamental ideas drawn from the mind in its contact with real things.[49]

In McCosh's view, the sensationalist school, by trying to trace all moral sentiments back to associated experiences, deprived morality of its status as a judgment of the mind, one reflecting an external reality. It makes us the slaves of circumstances, McCosh added, the pawns "of blind chance or dead mechanism." It is a deterrent to individual responsibility, depriving morality of any useful external standard and reference. Should the associationist theories ever gain wide credence, their consequences would be as "fatal as those which flowed in the end of [the] last century in France, from the prevalence of the Sensational Philosophy." The only sure path of avoidance is to maintain that man is so constituted as to know originally something of the reality of things. One can, to be sure, induce good conduct by inculcating good associations, in the family and the community and the schools. By this means we might pass on the accumulated wisdom and good sense of the past, the sound moral experience available to our use. "But," McCosh urged, "it is a still higher end of the highest education to raise us above all hereditary and casual association of times or circumstances, and to constrain us to base our beliefs on an inspection of realities and actualities." To this extent philosophy, more than history, was the certain foundation of right action.[50]

Unquestionably, McCosh wanted to ground moral theory in evangelical understanding. Therefore, morality must incorporate emotion. The moral faculties must bring us to a sense of absolute right that we feel compellingly as the measure of our existence. To that extent, McCosh felt, philosophers from Hume to Mill had terribly confused the moral and the sensible. Mill's recent effort to summarize the moral life by locating it in the "social feelings" dissolved the good into a hedonistic utilitarianism that simply added up the sum total of individual happiness. But where is the sanctioning "ought" for the happiness principle, McCosh asked. "Why should I seek the happiness of any other being than myself?" McCosh posed this question by way of inquiring on what basis a utilitarian moral theory is possible. And is there no higher good than happiness?[51]

For McCosh, a correct moral philosophy cannot begin with the individual in this manner and build upward. Not only McCosh's

[49] McCosh, *Examination of Mill*, pp. 185-99.
[50] Ibid., pp. 229-30.
[51] McCosh, *Intuitions*, p. 265.

theistic biases, but their particular evangelical character led him to base moral truth in some higher objective good. His own intuitionism established as much, but he went further. For our very embracing of that good not only brings us into relation with the source of moral truth, it also secures the emotional foundations of moral experience. Here again he felt Mill had confused this issue. He lay the moral feelings in the ego of the subject, making the unselfish part of our nature stand on a selfish basis. But this misplaced the true source of moral feelings, which derive from the fitness of our inner experience to the moral structure of the external world. "I hold," McCosh wrote, "that we are led to love our fellow-creatures independently of its being pleasant to ourselves; and that it is when we love them that the affection is found to be pleasant, by the appointment of the Author of our constitution, who thus prompts us to benevolence, and rewards us for cherising it." Here for McCosh was a superior foundation for right. This one furnished a better reply to the skeptic who claimed no obligation to do good to others. The sensationalist could appeal to the feelings, but he could not extract the necessary element of obligation that constitutes a moral imperative. McCosh believed that his account did give a utilitarian basis or connection to moral experience, but it did not constitute utilitarianism. "For when it is shown that man has convictions as to moral good and evil, and that these require him to do certain acts and abstain from others, we may be the better prepared to admit, as to certain of these acts, that they do not contemplate the promotion of happiness." To love God; to deny any person due affection and gratitude—these are acts of moral right and wrong that have that status regardless of personal interest or any measure of accumulated happiness.[52]

McCosh thus arrived at a position that accepted neither a utilitarian ethical system nor a rational or formally intuitive one. His final judgment shows the persistence of McCosh's evangelicalism. Mill's system, he complained, was as "self-righteous" as Hutcheson's before him. It suited perfectly certain members of the comfortable and worldly middle classes that honored it, and it induced in them an easy sense of pride and gratification. McCosh believed the popularity of the Moderate Hutcheson and the utilitarian Mill lay in the facile escape they forged from the older and more severe demands of a religious age. For the rationalist and utilitarian moral philosophies both erased from the modern vocabulary the "archaic" con-

[52] Ibid., pp. 266n-267n.

cern for "penitence, meekness, and humility." But no moral philosophy is sufficient without these concerns, McCosh believed. So in fortifying an objective moral absolute, discernible through intuition and experience, McCosh defended not only moral realities; he insisted that by virtue of these realities we stand under judgment. Moral philosophy struggles in vain to locate moral truth if it does not also describe the means of our fulfilling it. And only the most optimistic philosopher attributes to the human soul the means of that fulfillment. Moral philosophy above all strongly suggests our need and dependence, the necessity of redemptory assistance from without.[53]

McCosh's own brand of Protestant scholasticism therefore reflects the cultural warfare of his day and his effort to reconcile the factions. He remained well within the Scottish position by emphasizing intuitional philosophy, the superiority of the moral sense over the passions and will, and the verity of ethical absolutes discernible by consciousness. And he would rely on these as far as he could. But ultimately they fell short of human needs. They neither described all of man's basic spiritual wants, nor the eternal war of good and evil in the human breast. And although a true philosophy can spell out these realities, their ultimate resolution is a matter of religion. McCosh, the academic metaphysician, delivered philosophy to the doorstep of the evangelical preacher.

THROUGHOUT McCosh's Belfast years, the academic philosopher and the evangelical preacher were interwined. For when McCosh left Brechin he put on academic robes but did not wholly shed clerical vestments. McCosh's philosophical writings, in fact, take on added meaning when considered within the entire institutional and social structure of northern Ireland. Many details document his activities here, though not all of them need to concern us. We note, however, that McCosh pursued with immense energy a double program of social and cultural reform. Like many other expanding industrial societies, Belfast exhibited in its midst all the signs of poverty and human depression that coexisted with the impressive prosperity and new wealth. McCosh could not remain indifferent to the spiritual needs of the "Lepper's Row" section of Belfast and conducted public worship and Bible classes in the local schoolhouse there. With Lowry E. Berkeley he helped to found the Bible and Colportage Society of Ireland, an agency that sparked the evangel-

[53] McCosh, *Examination of Mill*, pp. 412-13; idem, "Scottish Metaphysicians," *North British Review*, 27 (1857), 413.

ical movement in the country. McCosh was an active member of the Belfast Town Mission, an elder of the Rosemary Street Church, and a representative to the Presbyterian General Assembly in Ireland. Nor did McCosh the professor abandon his ministry on horseback. He not only preached in many of the local churches, including some Methodist ones, but traveled into the outlying countryside as well. When he delivered a farewell address in 1868 McCosh thanked the country residents for providing a bed for him in their manses and homes "from Saturday night to Sunday morning." And as in Scotland, McCosh impressed his friends and colleagues by his extraordinary organizational talents. He drew up an extensive scheme for the sustentation of the ministry, recruited for the local Presbyterian churches, and served on the national committee of the General Assembly for the support and supply of ministers.[54]

McCosh found in Ireland a people and culture congenial to his tastes and a challenge worthy of his aspirations. But he was still the Scotsman at heart and longed to return to "my native country." Shortly after his arrival in Belfast he began a long correspondence that pursued whatever details he could unearth about the philosophers, great and little, of Scotland. Out of this effort, together with his historical researches and philosophical work, emerged many years later the remarkable compendium, *The Scottish Philosophy*. McCosh was disappointed, however, to be twice defeated in efforts to win philosophy appointments at the University of Edinburgh, in spite of support from Hamilton, Hugh Miller, William Hanna, Thomas McCrie, Thomas Guthrie, and others. McCosh did have offers from other institutions, including the new Free Church University in Glasgow. But these positions were theological appointments, and McCosh, insisting that he was a philosopher, respectfully declined. But he had little time to weigh disappointments. His work was demanding enough, and the responsibilities of father-

---

[54] James McCosh, "Incidents of My Life in Three Countries," unpublished typescript in the Princeton University Archives, 118-22; *Northern Whig*, November 19, 1894; James McCosh, "Farewell to the Presbyterian Church of Ireland," *New York Times*, June 26, 1868; idem, *The Duty of Irish Presbyterians to Their Church at the Present Crisis in the Sustentation of the Gospel Ministry* (Belfast, 1868); *General Assembly Proceedings of the Presbyterian Church in Ireland* (July 1856), 461-62. McCosh was also heavily involved in public school issues and served prominently in a national campaign for a state-financed system of intermediate education, necessary, he felt, to supply the universities with qualified students. See James McCosh, *The Necessity for an Intermediate System of Education Between the National Schools and Colleges of Ireland* (Belfast, 1854).

hood grew. A second daughter, Margaret Sarah, was born in June 1852, and another son, Andrew James, in March 1858. McCosh did return many times to Scotland, often to see his mother. She died in January 1859, and, McCosh wrote to a friend, "I was with her when she breathed her last."[55]

Then in 1859 came the Ulster Revival. An event that paralleled the last great waves of religious revivals in the United States, it was denoted, one historian says, by "extravagant enthusiasm, often rising to hysteria," but also by "a striking, if not always durable, improvement in public morality." This kind of emotionalism was not new to northern Ireland, for an evangelical party led most recently by Henry Cooke had been active since the late eighteenth century. Its spirit and theology were more emphatically Calvinistic than its Scottish counterpart, also more bitterly and rudely anti-Catholic. McCosh had many reservations about this wing of Irish Protestantism. It was too rigid in its theology, and in its frequent alliances with the Orangemen, too lacking in Christian charity. But the religious revival did raise anew some critical issues, and McCosh could not ignore them. Like similar movements before it, it met both skepticism and ridicule. McCosh, now the scholar-academic, might have been expected to keep his distance. He chose not to, and remained true to his past and to his principles. Speaking to a meeting of the Evangelical Alliance in September, McCosh threw the weight of his prestige behind the revival. He believed the Ulster movement *was* the work of God, and though he acknowledged that the emotional excesses accompanying it did not prove its religious character, he was adamant that the divine presence within the individual could produce such effects. Almost point for point, McCosh's address recalled Jonathan Edward's famous defense of the earlier Great Awakening in America, described in his *A Faithful Narrative of the Surprising Work of God* (1737). McCosh, like Edwards, wrote from the vantage point of one who directly witnessed the revival and offered true testimonials of its remarkable results. But McCosh hastened to say that, much less than the external drama, it was the quiet spiritual and moral transformations that mattered.[56]

---

[55] *Applications from the Reverend James McCosh, LL.D., Professor of Logic and Metaphysics, Queens College, Belfast* . . . (n.p., n.d.); "Moral Philosophy Chair. Dr. McCosh's Testimonials. First Series," in *Pamphlets Biographical* (n.p., n.d.); McCosh to Robert Carter, February 8, 1868, in the "Correspondence of James McCosh," Department of Rare Books and Special Collections, Princeton University Library; Hew Scott, ed., *Fasti Ecclesiae Scotinae: The Succession of Ministers in the Church of Scotland from the Reformation* (Edinburgh, 1925).

[56] J. C. Beckett, "Ulster Protestantism," in *Ulster since 1800: A Political and Eco-*

In Great Britain, McCosh's philosophical efforts did not go unappreciated. Naturally, he received most attention in the periodicals that were sympathetic to religion, and to the evangelical emphasis in particular. But in an age in which religion in general was on the defensive we note McCosh's generally wide appeal to all professors of the Christian faith. A reviewer in the staunchly Roman Catholic *Dublin Review* introduced an essay on McCosh's *Intuitions of the Mind* by saying that "there are few writers, in England or in Scotland, whose names are in any way on a par with that of [McCosh]."[57] And although it is undoubtedly true that McCosh, threading his way precariously through two major philosophical schools and suffering the indifference that is the reward of most mediators, made only a slight impact in strictly philosophical circles, his works attained a wide general readership. Nearly every review of his treatises points to their lively and graphic prose. The same reviewer said of the *Intuitions*: "Since the days of Plato, perhaps, a more 'readable' book upon so abstruse a subject . . . has not issued from the pen of man. Throughout the language flows on so smoothly that the reader finds himself mastering page after page without any consciousness of fatigue or *ennui*, and yet its dignity never fails of being truly philosophic."[58] But another reviewer wrote: "We miss the gigantic intellectual energy, the immense learning, the mighty momentum [of Hamilton]," as well as "the pre-eminent scholarly culture, the choice philosophical learning, the severely classical style, and the dialectical keenness of Mansel." This person also insisted, however, that McCosh had compensating merits. He praised the Scotsman for "a quick discernment of truth and error, good and evil . . . a facile and felicitous exposure of the fallacies and sophistries [of speculative philosophy]; a sound, sensible, judicial quality of mind."[59]

---

nomic Survey, ed. T. W. Moody and J. C. Beckett (London, 1954), pp. 162-65; James McCosh, *The Ulster Revival and Its Physiological Accidents* (Belfast, 1859), pp. 5-11; idem, "My Life," 129. Further testimony to McCosh's evangelicalism was his commitment to a cause highly unpopular among many Irish Protestants, that of the disestablishment of the Church of Ireland. McCosh was more convinced than ever that state support of religion was a manifest evil and the great enemy of the evangelical spirit. For these views McCosh was vilified in a pamphlet by William MacAllistar, *Voluntaryism Unmasked: Dr. McCosh's Pamphlet Reviewed, and Protestant Establishments Defended from the Present Unholy Crusade* (Dublin, 1868). McCosh referred to this question throughout his *Duty of Irish Presbyterians*.

[57] [R. E. Guy], "Dr. McCosh's 'Intuitions of the Mind' and 'Examination of Mill's Philosophy,' " *Dublin Review*, 8 n.s. (1867), 172-91.

[58] Ibid., 184.

[59] "Reason and Faith," *British and Foreign Evangelical Review*, 10 (1861), 266.

Finally, McCosh found a small but vocal audience for the intuitional realism he defended. John Mackensie, in the *North British Review*, praised McCosh. He felt the same ill winds in the philosophical air that chilled McCosh. "So that if we are threatened on the one hand with the atheism of the positive school, we are threatened on the other by the pantheism of the Transcendental." One encourages a too objective and the other a too subjective measure of the world. McCosh's system was a necessary balance of both.[60] In the *British and Foreign Evangelical Review* an anonymous essayist concurred that McCosh had furnished the sanest reply to the fictions of the imagination unleashed by the German philosophy. McCosh's contention that the intuitions deal with real things, "we deem of the first importance. . . . It closes the crevasse opened by Kant, through which transcendentalism breaks out, leveling all embankments, burying common sense, and pure religion under its devastating flood."[61] Henry Calderwood, on the other hand, perceived a greater challenge from the empirical philosophies, made so popular by the rising prestige of the physical sciences. Modern philosophy, and mental science especially, could not ignore that challenge, and McCosh, he believed, had rendered an invaluable service by showing that a realistic philosophy could in fact support fundamental truths. "Philosophy," he said in assessing McCosh, "is, beyond doubt, a gainer. According to our thinking, the intuitional philosophy, even with serious odds against it, is more secure of its sway than at any previous time."[62]

ONE DAY in the spring of 1868 McCosh returned home from his classes to discover that a telegram awaited him on his doorstep. The brief message contained a question: Would James McCosh accept the invitation from the board of trustees of the College of New Jersey in the United States to become its new president? McCosh, in fact, was not unaware that such an invitation might reach him, but that story is a rather intriguing one that must await a later telling. At that moment, at least, there was no doubt that McCosh would accept. Professors are seldom modest people, and so far as this was true, McCosh was a genuine professor. He had long quietly believed that he was worthy of an institution of greater renown than

---

[60] [John Mackensie], "The Method of the Divine Government," *North British Review*, 13 (1850), 510.

[61] "Reason and Faith," 270.

[62] Henry Calderwood, "The Sensational Philosophy," *British and Foreign Evangelical Review*, 14 (1866), 396–412.

the small Belfast college. And on McCosh's behalf, the two historians of that institution concur. McCosh, they write, was "an inspiring teacher, a leader of opinion, an educationist, above all a fluent and powerful writer. . . . [He became] known to a wider public than probably any of his colleagues." They add: "There had been little scope in Queen's College Belfast, for the academic statesman in McCosh" and hence the suitableness of the Princeton appointment.[63]

McCosh completed the 1867-1868 academic year at Queen's and in early September prepared to depart for America. In his last week he was the honored guest at a large breakfast. Attending were Rev. Pooley Shuldham Henry, president of the college, Henry Cooke, Mayor McCausland of Belfast, the bishop of Down and Connor, and more than one hundred other people. McCosh was presented a handsome service of silver and eulogized in a statement signed by the guests. He was praised for his "catholicity of disposition" and for his efforts for "civil and religious liberty." The address also included a note of thanks. "You have laid this whole province under the deepest obligation," it said, "by your efforts for the social improvements of the working classes."[64] These efforts had spread McCosh's name in the area, and his philosophical writings had carried it abroad.

[63] Theodore William Moody and James Camlin Beckett, *Queen's Belfast: 1845-1949*, 2 vols. (London, 1959), 1:172.

[64] *New York Times*, September 10, 1868.

Chapter Six

NATURE AND NATURE'S GOD

The dividing religious factions in Scotland went their separate ways in 1843. But the next year there emerged a challenge to both that soon dwarfed in seriousness any of the troubles between the church groups. For in that year an anonymous amateur scientist published a work that startled his fellow Scotsmen and brought forth protestations of shock from all over Great Britain. The *Vestiges of the Natural History of Creation*, by Robert Chambers (1802-1871), was only a ripple compared to Chales Darwin's classic of fifteen years later, but it was a major signpost along the road to the *Origin of Species*. It was less ambitiously naturalistic than Darwin's interpretation, but it did ominously signal a new and sharp division between religion and science. The idea of evolution had already received many varied statements, and religious thinkers reviewed them with interest. Scientists debated the age of the earth. They questioned whether it was by cataclysmic change or by minute and gradual alterations that the earth had arrived at its present state. But it can be fairly said that Chambers was the first to induce a reaction of outrage and dissent from almost the entire religious community of Great Britain. After him, reconciliation between science and religion would become increasingly difficult, and Darwin of course was to leave permanent scars.[1]

Robert Chambers was a splendid example of the democratic intellect in Scotland. Largely self-educated, a dabbler in science, a popularizer, he made his impact when many still pursued and contributed to science as an avocation. And those conditions give an interesting character to the play of ideas in Chambers's period. For

[1] Charles Coulston Gillispie's *Genesis and Geology: A Study in the Relations of Scientific Thought, and Social Opinion in Great Britain, 1790-1850* (New York, 1951), is an excellent review of the scientific literature of evolution in the pre-Darwin period. And, as Gillispie notes in his preface, "during the seven decades between the birth of modern geology and the publication of *On the Origin of Species*, the difficulty [between science and Protestant Christianity] as reflected in scientific literature appears to be one of religion (in a crude sense) *in* science rather than one of religion *versus* science." Ibid., p. ix.

with him, and with Hugh Miller, James McCosh, and others, ideas exercised noticeable social influences. Even scientific discussions were entwined with the contending factions in church and society. Thus McCosh's ideas on evolution directly reflected his position in the contests of Moderatism and evangelicalism in Scotland. And in Ireland and the United States his extensive writings on this subject elaborated his continued efforts to locate a middle position between the two cultural forces. We shall examine here the full range of McCosh's writings on science. Although McCosh modified his opinions between the time of his first publications in Scotland and his later writings in America, they do form a progressive unity. Furthermore, they constitute an important background to his academic career at Princeton and, indeed, to the embroilments that marked his career at the college. McCosh's theories, like those of every writer before Darwin, would not outlive the nineteenth century. McCosh adjusted and reconciled his thinking to the Darwinian world far more than most religious thinkers of his day, but in science, and in philosophy, the universe of final causes that he upheld to the end yielded to the open universe of a purposeless cosmos. McCosh, then, interests us most as one line in the complex chart of nineteenth-century ideas about science and religion and as one illustration of the social history of intellect in that period.[2]

After 1844 the course of these ideas reflected the sensational impact of Chambers. Born in the Peebles region south of Edinburgh, Robert Chambers and his brother William were both hexadactyls, having six fingers on each hand and six toes on each foot. The operation to remove the disorder left Robert an awkward lad who forsook sports and games to find his pleasure in books. The unhappy commercial ventures of the father soon rendered him pen-

---

[2] As we proceed in this chapter, it is useful to be reminded of the remarks of A. Hunter Dupree, historian of science. In his biography of the American scientist Asa Gray, Dupree commented on the persistent tendency of the nineteenth-century mind to link the structure of nature with the structure of divine intelligence. The tendency was widely evident among scientists, and most notably Louis Agassiz. Dupree writes: "The twentieth-century mind finds this system of thought so foreign that it can only with difficulty reconcile it with the immense reputation Agassiz enjoyed in his prime. . . . Yet a general phenomenon in the biology of the middle years of the nineteenth century was the amazing amount of precise and brilliant research being done by those under the spell of *Naturphilosophie*, catastrophism, and idealism in general. [Von Baer, Owen, Agassiz, Sedgwick, and Murchison] had their share of authority in the scientific world of 1850, and they backed their positions no less with their grand generalizations than with their impressive research accomplishments." *Asa Gray, 1810-1888* (Cambridge, Mass., 1959), pp. 227-28.

Robert Chambers

urious, and he removed with his family to Edinburgh, where Robert and William entered the publishing business. Robert had developed a love for Latin poetry and an enthusiasm for philosophy, but he was enamored above all with his native country—its history, legends, and lore. At first that interest centered in the capital city itself, and the two brothers inaugurated a serial entitled *Traditions of Edinburgh,* full of local anecdotes. Robert then extended his publishing interests to include new works on Scotland—*Popular Rhymes of Scotland, Scottish Ballads and Songs, Scottish Jests and Anec-*

dotes, and other works. Increasingly, Chambers addressed his efforts to a particular clientele, the rising number of intelligent readers among the working classes. Here a yen for learning, nourished to a great extent by the Mechanics' Institutes in Edinburgh, gave new opportunities to writers in Scotland's age of improvement. And *Chambers' Edinburgh Journal* was one of the remarkable and popular products of that age. Its articles, most of them written by the two brothers, covered science, industry, politics, biography, and morality. There was nothing on religion. The *Journal* became a kind of popular and secular counterpart to the *Edinburgh Review*, the outlet of the new Whig intellectual elite. And now Chambers thought his audience, too, was ready for some new and bold ideas.[3]

Chambers vacated Edinburgh while he prepared the *Vestiges*. Hidden away in St. Andrews, he told only four persons of the authorship of his book. *Vestiges* won the approval of no eminent scientist of the day, but it did have popular appeal. "Development," the term that Chambers and McCosh also used for "evolution," explained the origin of life from a "single event." It suggested the derivation of all living forms from a common stock. Life, Chambers claimed, was a clear progression, with each higher form emerging out of lower ones. Chambers appealed to the familiar phenomenon of ontogeny, the embryonic growth of organisms, and its evident recapitulation of phylogeny, the history of life forms antedating the species in question. And Chambers included man within this process. Homo sapiens is the highest form of life, "the type of all types of the animal kingdom." Chambers did more than this, however, to alter man's station. Rejecting the dualistic account of man, he united all the human "higher faculties" to the emerging sensory powers of lower forms. But there is nothing degrading to man here, Chambers assured his readers. Each human has, in a sense, passed through these forms in embryonic development. As for the place of God, Chambers's view of life was emphatically a deism with progression. Nature was anticipatory according to divine foresight. Each stage of life unveiled another idea of God's mind. Chambers did not abandon teleology, and he did not deprive the universe of law and orderly behavior. A social churchgoer only, Chambers admired God above all for his masterful and designing intelligence. God created by an act of mind, and all held true to form thereafter. Indeed, Chambers's universe was a perfect uni-

---

[3] Milton Milhauser, *Just Before Darwin: Robert Chambers and "Vestiges"* (Middletown, Conn., 1959), pp. 11, 14-16, 19-24.

verse. It required no intervening force to correct and improve it, no miracle, nothing supernatural to steady its path or right its course. More perfect even than Newton's great watchmaker, Chambers's deity built more than a great machine; he designed a system whose every change was contained within the original construction. Chambers, at least, could worship such a God as this: "When all is seen to be the result of law, the idea of an Almighty Author becomes irresistible, for the creation of a law for an endless series of phenomena—an act of intelligence above all else that we can conceive—could have no other imaginable source."[4]

Chambers's little book inspired a fashionable posture of shock among some of the upper classes and a genuine following among the "dour materialists" of the Mechanics' Institutes.[5] McCosh's first references to the work labeled it "plausible, yet withal exceedingly superficial," indicating at least his openness to the idea of development.[6] But the person who came clad in armor to battle with Chambers was another Scotsman, the talented and fascinating Hugh Miller (1802-1856). He was a product of the far north country, the shire of Ross and Cromarty. And there are few more lively and graphic depictions of that rugged land and its people than Miller's own autobiographical account, *My Schools and Schoolmasters*. Miller was born the same year as his rival, but acquired an education that was more emphatically religious than Chambers's. His imagination first awoke to Bible stories and the heroic narrative in *Pilgrim's Progress*. His formal education, though, was unimpressive, and Miller, like Chambers, pioneered on his own. He found a local community of learning among the intelligent mechanics and tradespeople and discovered books of poetry in the home library of a literary cabinetmaker in the neighborhood. But Miller's school

---

[4] Ibid., pp. 29-30, 91, 100-102, 110-11; Gillispie, *Genesis and Geology*, pp. 153-59. The quotations are in Gillispie, pp. 156 and 159. Chambers, of course, was very much in the Scottish tradition of the two famous Scottish "uniformitarian" scientists of the late eighteenth and early nineteenth centuries, James Hutton and John Playfair, Hutton's "bulldog" at the University of Edinburgh. Hutton's *Theory of the Earth* (1795) was the first study greatly to extend the assumed age of the earth and to break from the catastrophic school of Abraham Werner of Freiburg. Hutton pointed not to vast upheavals denoting the stages of earth's history, but to an unbroken, uniform process of change over countless years. The other view, with its plausible corroboration of biblical floods, won the overwhelming support of religious opinion. Hutton's theory, on the other hand, registers the mark of the Scottish Enlightenment and the moderate and rational deity it described. Gillispie, pp. 40-49.

[5] Milhauser, *Just Before Darwin*, pp. 121-22.

[6] James McCosh, "Typical Forms," *North British Review*, 15 (1851), 407.

Hugh Miller

of science was the rugged rock terrain of the north and the hundreds of water inlets of the North Sea and the Moray Firth. Here, among the "wild cliffs and caverns" young Miller made "excursions of discovery on every side." The granite gneiss, the red sandstone, and the chlorite-schist lay all around the Hill of Cromarty, and "it was always with great delight that I used to pick my way among them, hammer in hand, and fill my pockets with specimens."[7]

But Miller did not pursue a career in science and was furthermore always detached from university life. He became a mason, a genuine member of the working classes. And for this curious and perceptive craftsman, masonry was itself an education. Miller worked among the red sandstone quarries of the north and became a student of rock formation and patterns. "It was the necessity which made me a quarrier," he wrote, "that taught me to be a geologist." Amid the beautiful Eathic Lias Miller discovered fossils that increasingly excited his quest for clues to the pattern of creation.[8] But Miller's conclusions about scientific evidence bore heavily the stamp of his social and religious outlooks. His autobiography recounts his early horror at some of the barbarisms of his age. He recoiled with disgust at the crude popular practice of cockfighting among the highland people. He remembered with extreme distaste the universal ceremonial practice of drinking among his fellow workers, a habit into which he once fell and then renounced with resolution. His outlook, in short, became moralistic, and when the religious struggle of the 1830s became decisive, Miller cast his lot with the Evangelicals. When his publications in science gained popularity and prestige, Miller became one of the luminaries of the evangelical intellectual circle, with Chalmers, Welsh, and McCosh. He assumed a major position in its ranks when he became editor of the new journalistic voice of the Free Church, *The Witness*.[9]

With both Miller and Chambers we can see how scientific opinion was entwined with the religious factions of Scotland. McCosh also will illustrate this theme. Miller fretted over Chambers's influence and feared the spread of his development ideas among the working classes. Materialism, among this class especially, was the path to social turbulence and the decay of authority, both spiritual and worldly. Miller thus alerted the "evangelistic churches" to the growth of this menace in the Mechanics' Institutes and urged ec-

[7] Hugh Miller, *My Schools and Schoolmasters, or, The Story of My Education* (Edinburgh, 1858), pp. 20, 28-29, 51, 58-59 (the quotations).
[8] Ibid., pp. 155, 163.
[9] Ibid., pp. 50, 158, 549, 554.

clesiastical efforts against this "consummately dangerous" doctrine.[10]

For Miller, then, scientific thought had a necessary relation to the prevailing temper in society. But Miller's excessive alarm in this matter did not really detract from his achievements in paleontology. His work was respected, even though his conclusions seem to have been overdrawn and somewhat forced. *Foot-Prints of the Creator* promises much in its title, but its subtitle, *Or, The Asterolepis of Stromness*, indicated that it is merely the study of a fish. That this quite technical little work should have won such a large readership is remarkable, and surely testifies to the extensive popular interest in science in mid-century Scotland. In its American edition, it contained a lengthy introduction by Louis Agassiz (1807-1873), who we shall see was a fellow fighter with Miller against the development theory. Agassiz praised Miller for combining scientific fact and Christian understanding.[11] Miller had no desire to vindicate stubborn biblical literalists and urged them to listen to the scientific evidence of the earth's great antiquity.[12] He generally accepted development but wished to show that life did not illustrate only smooth upward progression. The little fish of Stromness demonstrated in its antiquity a complexity of construction greater than later forms. If anything, here was a "regression" in development. Miller agreed with Chambers that final causes operated in the history of life forms, but the path to man was not an unbroken one. Like Agassiz, Miller believed emphatically in separate creations, each new form denoting a divine "fiat." Miller even accepted the recapitulation theory, but believed it gave no support to the development hypothesis. The emergence of man must be seen as a final and unique dispensation of God. Nothing in the record indicates post-Adamic creation; God had realized his own image in man.[13]

Miller spoke from the Free Chruch at about the time McCosh was leaving it for Ireland and then America. He had long followed Miller's life and work, and they had become personally acquainted, shortly before McCosh's departure, through the friendship of each with Thomas Guthrie.[14] McCosh enjoyed discussing religion and

---

[10] Hugh Miller, *Foot-Prints of the Creator: or, the Asterolepis of Stromness* (1850; Boston, 1864), pp. vi, 43.
[11] Ibid., p. xi.   [12] Miller, *My Schools and Schoolmasters*, p. 462.
[13] Miller, *Foot-Prints of the Creator*, pp. 181-204.
[14] Peter Bayne, *The Life and Times of Hugh Miller*, 2 vols. (Boston, 1871), 2:445-50.

science with Miller and endeavored later to bring him to Queen's College as one of its professors. But McCosh was by no means a disciple of Miller and used his ideas only to illustrate points of his own. McCosh, as we shall see, eventually conceded far more to Chambers and Darwin than Miller was prepared to do. But like Miller, it was always his major intention to illustrate how science enhanced a religious understanding of the world.

And McCosh, too, personified the amateur scientist. He brought to his writings a superb power of observation and a literary flare that gave lyrical and poetical qualities to much of his work. McCosh also read very widely among the British naturalists and interspersed their observations and ideas among his own. In fact, McCosh rarely entered upon causal explanations of any but the most general kind. For the most part he wished only to show that order, unity, and plan prevail in God's world, that the world in turn reflects divine intelligence. His elucidations of natural phenomena are observational therefore rather than analytical. McCosh rarely quarreled with the evidence as presented by those advancing science in his day. He did demand the right to show how religion might interpret the facts in a philosophical manner.

McCosh's great interest was morphology, study of the biological structure and forms of organisms. Morphology had won popular interest in the nineteenth century after Goethe's familiar efforts in the field, and it was one division in which the keenly observant amateur could work with profit. McCosh presented a paper on plant morphology to the Botanical Society of Edinburgh shortly before he undertook the Queen's College assignment, and then extended his studies in a long manuscript a few years later. The paper effectively outlined the approach of the larger work. By use of several pictorial illustrations, McCosh tried to show that a recognizable unity of form prevails in the different components of botanical organisms. In its best illustration, the essay demonstrated that the patterns of leaves peculiar to any special type of plant or tree are, with respect to several features, representative of the structure of the whole organism. Those features, McCosh showed, involve the patterns of the leaf venation, particularly the relation of the minor veins to the central stem (including their angulation to the central stem). The problem was simple. McCosh showed that a clearly similar outline is evident when one compares the venation of the leaves with the naked outline of the mature tree that bore them. Employing some twenty examples of tree types with their corresponding leaf structures, McCosh demonstrated their parallel features. The central vein of the leaf, similar to the trunk of the tree, sends out its smaller stems ("branches") at angles similar to those of the larger structure. So also do trees with a larger bare trunk issue leaves with a larger stem stalk, the continuity of design prevailing again. McCosh also found that trees whose branch-to-trunk angulation decreases from bottom to top also produce leaves whose venation shows a corresponding arrangement to the central stem. This was noticeably the case in the poplar and the beech, and it gave the leaves and coma of those trees a rounded and pyramidal form. McCosh included a table summarizing these patterns for the different types he had studied.[15]

When McCosh went to Belfast he probably entertained no large plans to extend his work, but it was his good fortune to make the acquaintance there of Professor George Dickie (1812-1882), in whom he found a similar fascination with morphology. Dickie was a fellow Scotsman, born in Aberdeen and educated at Marischal College. He pursued studies in medicine at Aberdeen University and the University of Edinburgh, then lectured for ten years on material medica at Aberdeen. In 1849 Dickie assumed the professorship of natural history at Queen's College. His many published articles and papers before the Royal Society gave him a respected name, especially in the fields of vegetable morphology and marine algae.[16]

Shortly after McCosh arrived, he and Dickie launched a lengthy collaborative effort, a 532-page volume published in 1855 and entitled *Typical Forms and Special Ends in Creation*. The exact nature of their collaboration is not known; McCosh mentions it only briefly in his memoir. Probably most of the detailed illustrations in the work came from Dickie. Most of the writing reflects McCosh's familiar style, some of it unmistakably. The American edition contains sections of a published review by Hugh Miller that refers only to McCosh. The chapter titles provide an accurate clue to the comprehensive scope of this work and its ambitious reach, and include: "The Minute Structure of Plants and Animals"; "The Forms of Plants"; "The Colours of Plants"; "The Vertebrate Skeleton"; "Teeth"; "Mollusca"; "Articulata"; "Radiata"; "Nervous, Vascular, and Muscular Systems"; "Geology"; "Inorganic Objects

---

[15] James McCosh, "Some Remarks on the Plant Morphologically Considered," *Transactions of the [Edinburgh] Botanical Society*, 4 (1853), 127-30. For an expanded discussion, see James McCosh and George Dickie, *Typical Forms and Special Ends in Creation* (1855; New York, 1856), pp. 104-19.

[16] *Dictionary of National Biography*, 5:937.

of the Earth's Surface"; "The Heavens"; and "Typical Systems of Nature and Revelation."

As McCosh had done for leaf and tree formations, so did these authors for the structures of a vast variety of natural formations. And this architectural portrait of the cosmos supplied much appealing narrative and illustration. It was more attractive certainly for its graphic aesthetic qualities than for its scientific, for in many places the narrative becomes ponderous and tedious. The authors discovered and described not only "typical forms," but "special ends" as well. The main subject of the work is the variation on forms that appear in nature, and the particular function of the variations, their specific serviceability to their organisms. To this extent the work belonged to a prolific genre of scientific and religious writing, most popularized by William Paley, who formulated the theological argument from "design" in its familiar analogous form. McCosh, however, considered Paley's famous watch analogy shallow and simplistic, "a mere truism." To make the bridge from nature to nature's God required a more compelling illustration of ingenuity in the operation of the universe and the interrelated functioning of its several parts.[17] Furthermore, as McCosh would rediscover in the years ahead, the mechanical model of the universe was simply inadequate to nineteenth-century science's understanding of the world. Evolution described a dynamic world and demanded new explanations of God's governance of it.

In exploring this subject *Typical Forms* elaborated ideas that McCosh had discussed earlier in his *Method of Divine Government*. The authors now employed the term "collocation" to demonstrate how evidence of design in nature significantly transcends the mere appropriateness of individual organisms, or the separate parts of organisms in relation to the whole. Collocation more widely embraced the coordinated interrelationships of separated phenomena. Forces essentially blind or indifferent to each other are made to combine in such a way as to assure the well-being of each, and even the well-being of other organisms. The pollenation of plants by bees, for example, illustrates collocation. Neither the seed-producing plant nor the nectar-drawing insect knows anything of the needs of the other, but the perpetuation of both species establishes a precise mutuality of interest in their separate functions. On a much larger scale we see collocation in the play of gravitational and centripetal forces in the solar system. The slightest alteration in

[17] McCosh and Dickie, *Typical Forms*, pp. 39-40.

these forces would draw the earth into the sun or propel it outward into the colder regions of the universe. But the precarious balance maintains and sustains the entire range of organic existence in the earth's environment. These and other cases describe the difference between "natural laws," most often simple mathematical formulas by which we can understand physical and chemical behavior, and "derivative laws," which illustrate a far greater, even unknown ingenuity. But it is clear nonetheless, the authors believed, that these "mutual adaptations of different and independent powers" cannot proceed from chance. Far more than Paley's analogy they demonstrate a comprehensive pattern of design.[18]

McCosh believed that the principle of collocation helped break the mechanical analogy of the universe inherited from Paley and generally out of vogue in the era of romanticism and evolution. We are no longer content to see a simple arrangment of means and ends here; rather we see a perpetuating and changing system of adjustments. Collocation, to be sure, can function in species over long periods. But we see continual adaptation and change along the way. McCosh at this point was quite willing to allow that new forms come into being as the environment changes. The seas retreat, and new forms of terrestrial life appear. New structures demonstrate their suitability to their situation. In the interplay of collocated forces ends become means to new ends. Life patterns then take on a dynamic quality, and the universe is in movement. *Typical Forms* in this way outlined a model that was evolutionary in form, though clearly non-Darwinian in its causal nature. For although collocation incorporated change, it did not describe an open-ended universe that precluded teleology; final causes, we shall see, prevailed throughout.[19]

One of the interesting subjects in *Typical Forms* was the phenomenon of homologies. McCosh and Dickie were intrigued not only by the continuity of forms among like organisms, but by the appearance of similar forms in quite different organisms. Here the authors most frequently cited the works of the British naturalist Richard Owen (1804-1892), later a combative opponent of Darwin. McCosh had earlier commented on Owen's *On the Archetype and Homologies of the Vertebrate Skeleton* (1848) in a lengthy review essay, using also Owen's *Lecture on Limbs* (1849). Owen studied the progressive appearance of the same organ in different animals. He cast his analogies broadly—forelimbs became fins in fishes, wings

---

[18] Ibid., pp. 33-40.   [19] Ibid., pp. 52-53.

in birds, claws in reptiles—but also narrowly—the five-part division of the whale's fin is akin to the pendactyl hands of man. Owen examined these variations and then referred to them in terms of the different functions that each exercised. Owen's perspective was theistic, and he believed that continuity of structure showed the single intelligence of a creator. But his system was somewhat static nonetheless. He believed that each species was created perfect "in relation to the circumstances and sphere in which it was destined to exist."[20]

But McCosh could not go all the way with Owen on this point. He was struck especially by the persistence of form across different species and wanted to raise the question, Is it possible that the priorities of that continuity actually outweigh the particular uses and functions of the structure in question? Owen's emphasis on the perfect adaptability of each structure to its circumstances was in the tradition of Paley's narrow utilitarianism. But with respect to the example of the whale's five-division fin, McCosh wrote, "It is a curious circumstance that every segment, and almost every bone present in the human hand and arm, exist also in the fin of the whale, though they do not seem required for the support and movements of that undivided and inflexible paddle." In short, there appeared to be a clear irrelevance to the details of the whale's fin, an absence of a strict relation of design to function. But just that fact led McCosh to speculate that something higher was at stake in this design. Nature, he suggested, is anticipatory. Whereas Owen was reluctant to move from a specific to a general teleology, McCosh was not. The appearance of the division in the whale's fin, though of no consequence to that organism itself, was nonetheless crucial to the later emergence of man, and to the distinguishing functional features of the pendactyl homo sapiens. The example here, along with many others, indicated "a general scheme of final causes to accomplish a higher end than the special adaptation." There is, then, a manifest progression in nature that looks to the ultimate end of creation. For McCosh, as for Owen, the evidence confirmed that the idea of man existed before the appearance of man. All parts of man have been sketched out in the inferior animals. Wrote McCosh: "The Supreme could foresee that which was to come, and which He had pre-ordained. . . . Man appears as the final and foreseen product of the one mighty plan."[21]

Of course this conclusion sounds very similar to Chambers's.

[20] McCosh quoted Owen in ibid., p. 325.
[21] Ibid., p. 331; McCosh, "Typical Forms," 405, 408, 411, 417.

But McCosh denied that the higher forms were drawn out of the lower; they merely reflect these. "It is not that one species has run into a higher by physical laws, but it is that the higher species is constructed after the same type as the lower." The only principle at stake here was the comprehensiveness of design, illustrating the unity of God's intelligence. "The prevalence of model forms shews that all things are after a predetermined pattern." This view gives "a more profound view of the intelligence displayed in creation."[22] But in fact, it requires no great effort to see that McCosh had all the evidence for "development" right before him. He had moved closer to an acceptance of that hypothesis than he realized at this time, and later, when evidence mounted for the theory of natural selection, McCosh would find it irresistible.

Typical Forms was published only four years before Darwin (1809-1882) offered his monumental work in 1859. Because that work later caused McCosh to modify his views somewhat, while he still preserved many of the ideas we have considered here, it will be useful to clarify more precisely how McCosh's ideas stood in his pre-Darwin period. McCosh borrowed extensively from others, but his heavy reliance on the phenomenon of collocation was the distinguishing feature in his natural philosophy. But this preoccupation also obscured McCosh's vision a bit. Collocation usually meant for McCosh two or more patterns of behavior that knew nothing of the other's purposes, but were compelled to their interrelationship by some external arrangement or higher cause. In this way McCosh could study terrestrial history and the organic history of the species without seeing any kind of adaptation of the one to the other. Thus McCosh argued that by collocation the earth was prepared for man. Formation of coal deposits, for example, located near the surface of the earth, grew to a point where humans could use them to maintain their lives on earth. The beautiful array of colors in flowers seems to have no functional purpose, but emerges just when a creature endowed with an aesthetic sense appears to appreciate them. Collocation, as even John Stuart Mill recognized, was an important principle, and a necessary one. But when carried too far, as McCosh's examples show, it became somewhat forced. Certainly it seems that in these instances it prevented McCosh from seeing how creatures emerge by means of a particular adjustment to a changing environment and that one form may be transformed into another in the process. Collocation, for now at

---

[22] McCosh, "Typical Forms," 407, 411.

least, obscured the evidence for development and natural selection.[23]

In addition to relying on Owen, McCosh fortified his explanations by use of Louis Agassiz, the Swiss naturalist who had become a professor at Harvard in 1848, and Hugh Miller. Agassiz has won an enduring reputation as the stalwart and unyielding opponent of Darwin, so much so that today it obscures the fact that he was probably the most renowned and prestigious figure in his field. He fought bitterly against evolution, insisting to the end of his life that each species was unique, each a separate "thought" of God's intelligence.[24] McCosh followed Agassiz in describing a scale of life that was idealistic and not naturalistic. Form runs throughout, but it reflects a higher conceptualization and not the interconnection of species by development of one from another. For now Agassiz's word was sufficient for McCosh, and he quoted him: "There is nothing like parental descent connecting [chronological appearance of new forms]. The fishes of the Palaeozoic age are in no respect the ancestors of the reptiles of the secondary age, nor does man descend from the mammals which preceded him in the tertiary age. The link by which they are connected is of a higher and immaterial nature; and their connection is to be sought in the view of the Creator Himself, whose aim in forming the earth . . . was to introduce man upon its surface."[25] After Darwin, Agassiz's views slowly lost ground. His theory could not adequately account for extinct species. And neither did *Typical Forms*, which simply ignored the problem. McCosh never claimed to see an unbroken upward progression in nature. He found his friend Miller's investigations sufficient to show some advanced forms of life existent in the very early paleontological stages.[26]

Finally, there is a marked difference of perspective between McCosh's sense of evolution at this point and Darwin's later one. McCosh's is emphatically teleological, and becomes fully known and comprehensible from the perspective of man's emergence as its end product. It is characterized throughout by design, and it almost seems as though the final product "explains" the earlier one. How different is this from Darwin's world of blind forces, where neither collocation nor design of any kind exists. With Darwin we enter a world of chance and spontaneity where man is but an ac-

[23] McCosh and Dickie, *Typical Forms*, pp. 346-50.
[24] Edward Lurie, *Louis Agassiz: A Life in Science* (Chicago, 1960), pp. 283-86.
[25] McCosh and Dickie, *Typical Forms*, pp. 332-33, quoted from Agassiz and Augustus Addison Gould's *Comparative Anatomy*.
[26] McCosh and Dickie, *Typical Forms*, p. 320.

cidental midproduct in an uncertain and open system. At no point on the Darwinian path can we look back and read an inevitable moving plan of things. And much less can we look chronologically forward to prognosticate or ascertain the appearance of known higher forms. McCosh had shifted with the nineteenth century into a moving and dynamic universe, but it was still an orderly and purposeful one. It also illustrated final causes.

THE QUESTION of final causes in nature raised for McCosh a problem that was essentially philosophical in character. In fact, McCosh was anxious to discuss the question of development in terms of several philosophical problems and believed that rash and emboldened scientific theorists might profit by closer familiarity with philosophy.[27] But his inclination embroiled him also with other philosophers, Herbert Spencer especially. For this phase of McCosh's discussions of evolution we need to include the works of his American period. The ideas of Darwin had become familiar by the time of McCosh's arrival in the United States in 1868, but the controversy deepened there and elsewhere in the ensuing years. McCosh wrote many articles and gave many public addresses on the subject while he was president of Princeton. In fact, this involvement was no small portion of the events surrounding the struggles of his presidency. It is well to clarify now, therefore, precisely what was at stake in McCosh's views. We will see that while McCosh adhered to a clearly religious understanding of evolution, he was, in the views of some, far too accommodating to science.

For a defense of final causes McCosh was content to go to its first elaboration in Aristotle's *Physics* and *Metaphysics*. But modern science itself would give the best illustration of the principle. In discussing causality, Aristotle presented four kinds—material, efficient, formal, and final.[28] Material merely referred to the nature or composition of substances, their "chemical" makeup. Efficient cause referred to interacting powers. We say that a plant was killed

---

[27] McCosh: "It is a notable circumstance that a number of the eminent scientists of the present day have not been trained at colleges or universities. They have betaken themselves to their favorite pursuits from their love to them, and made valuable discoveries because they have approached them by a new road. But they have not enjoyed the advantage of comprehensive instruction in philosophy and in the science of the human mind, such as it is required in our higher universities." "Final Cause, M. Janet and Professor Newcomb," *Princeton Review*, 3 (1879), 369.

[28] See Aristotle, *The Physics*, II, 3.

by frost, but in fact the true cause was not the mere frost or cold, but the state of the plant and the state of the temperature combined. Formal cause orders the multiplicity of forces that combine to give form, type, pattern, and conformity to general norms in nature. They are seen in the mathematically exact forms and harmonious colors of the shell, or in heredity. Final cause goes one step further to combine formal causes for beneficent ends. Formal cause unites all functions to one purpose, but final cause joins separate and distinct functions, each acting independently of and indifferent to the other. "Final cause," according to McCosh, ". . . implies a combination of physical causes, which are blind in themselves, but which are led by a prearranging power to combine to accomplish an end." Collocation is merely the illustration of the principle of final causes. And it implies nothing "miraculous." McCosh noticed that objections to final causes centered on the charge that they invoked intervention or interference in the chain of normal events. But final cause did not usurp or remove efficient cause. There was no violation of normal behavior or familiar and predictable patterns of interaction among things. "There is no interference with the machine in a factory," McCosh illustrated, "when it lets off its cotton, or its linen thread, or its paper; it was planned and adjusted for this very purpose."[29]

In dealing with the philosophical dimensions of evolution, McCosh gave a large portion of his attention to the writings of Herbert Spencer. He had watched the progress of this British philosopher and social theorist after he had published *Social Statics* in 1850. Then in his *First Principles* (1862) Spencer issued his troublesome doctrine of the Unknown and linked it with a comprehensive scheme of evolution. Spencer gained immense popularity in America. His system established a course of inevitable progress in nature and endorsed individualism and the survival of the fittest as the means of its advance. Some years after McCosh's arrival in America, Spencer's visit here in 1882 highlighted the public fascination with his ideas. American readers took a keen interest in the application of Spencer's ideas to life and social practice, but McCosh cared less for these than for the nature of Spencer's intellectual system itself.

---

[29] McCosh, "Final Cause," 372-83. The quotation is on p. 383. To state the case in another simple way, McCosh pointed out that final cause does not account for the producing of an event; efficient cause does that. But efficient causes do not show how causes or forces can combine to produce obviously intended beneficial results. Ibid., 380.

It must be noted that Spencer was something of a transitional figure. With the early nineteenth century he shared an obsession for system in nature and for system building in his philosophy. Certainly he moved with the leading thinkers in describing the cosmos as a progressive entity, a process struggling to realize its own foreordained and foreseen ends. Spencer was clearly a teleological thinker. But there is much of the new in his emphasis. He wanted philosophy to reconcile religion and science, and his recourse to the Unknown was his means of blowing the whistle on a debate he judged a "mere war of words."[30] There was no real concession to religion here, however. Spencer merely laid the problem of God aside and then embarked on a thoroughly naturalistic description of nature. He carried naturalism into his physiological psychology and his ethical theories also, and became one of many thinkers to prepare the triumph of realism in the late nineteenth century. But as McCosh showed, many perils beset his effort to straddle an older and newer view of the world.[31]

The ghostly nemesis of Hamilton lingered yet. McCosh still saw it in Spencer's unknown God, and later in the 1880s when he organized two volumes of essays entitled *Realistic Philosophy*, he included a long critique of Spencer. Spencer, in describing a dynamic evolutionary course in nature, had employed the language of Hamilton. "We are irresistibly compelled by the relativity of our thought," Spencer wrote, "to vaguely conceive some unknown force as the correlative of the known force."[32] Thus we have a cause of all that is known. It is the one permanent thing, this unknown reality. McCosh agreed that effects are known by their causes and appealed to Aristotle for endorsement. But if the effects are known,

---

[30] Herbert Spencer, *First Principles* (1862; New York, 1890), pt. 1.

[31] Spencer tried to avoid extreme philosophical positions—either idealistic or materialistic—and always took shelter under the Unknown when he was in danger of doing so. Thus, he refused to discuss the notion of "the real" apart from the "persistence of consciousness" by which it is known, and veered toward subjectivism. On the other hand, he insisted that "Force" is the "ultimate of ultimates," and out of it consciousness itself is also derived and filled. Here he veered toward materialism. Spencer saw no dilemma, however, for he labeled the two elements of experience the objective and subjective manifestations of the Unknown. We cannot know the ultimate nature of force or consciousness, therefore, only that they "coexist." Ibid., p. 171. These turns gave Spencer's philosophy a slippery quality. It clashes directly with McCosh's intuitional realism, and with the whole Scottish school in general (except Hamilton, of course), and it is instructive to see this debate carried into the subject of evolution.

[32] Ibid., p. 170.

then the causes of known effects are to that extent also known. But Spencer, in line with Hume and others, further urged that these effects are not known as things; they are phenomena only, appearances of an unknowable substance. We know power, force, motion, too, but not the nature of these, which emanates from the Unknown. McCosh then charged that Spencer had no basis for asserting that the Unknown exists and has reality: "We can from the known rise to the unknown, and thus make it so far known; thus we can discover the unknown cause of a known effect." But, he asked, can we logically rise from an unknown thing, or unknown things such as matter and force, motion, space, and time (that is, from these effects that we know but do not know as things) and reach a reality, and this the only reality? Spencer could have avoided the contradiction had he simply acknowledged that we do not know phenomena without knowing substance. But he took the skeptical approach of his unfortunate predecessors and landed in absurdity. He was left to say that the known is no reality—we do not know it as thing, with existence, real—and the unknown is the only reality. "We have here," McCosh wrote, ". . . the most confused and baseless metaphysics to be found in the history of speculation." And the confusion extended right into Spencer's theory of evolution.[33]

Because Spencer's Absolute in fact was devoid of substance and quality, and was epistemologically unknowable, the only contents of the evolutionary process he described were space, time, matter, motion, and force. All change is the particular combining of these contents to create higher and more complex and diversified forms of life. McCosh insisted that Spencer's one great omission was mind. Not only did it confound his psychology, as we shall see, but it caused Spencer to be negligent in an elementary philosophical problem. Here again the matter of causation entered. We must recognize, McCosh said, that in any causal arrangement, the constituent elements of the effect must reflect the transformed constituent elements of the causes. Or, there lies in the causes the powers to develop and produce the effects, and the causes can give to effects only their own powers combined or transformed in their contents. (This point also illustrated McCosh's remarks that the causes of known effects are also known.) The principle here is most usefully applied to the phenomenon of evolution. The inanimate

---

[33] James McCosh, *Herbert Spencer's Philosophy as Culminated in His Ethics* (New York, 1885), pp. 14-15, 21-22.

cannot produce the animate. The unconscious cannot produce the conscious. These products can derive only from the transformation of some substances having latent similar powers or by the addition to them of some substance with exactly similar powers manifest. So in the evolution of man we need to account for the emergence of some powers not anticipated by the lower forms of life. Self-consciousness and abstract thinking, logical deduction, aesthetic and moral judgment—from whence do they come? McCosh wrote: "Those who would account for the rise of the lower natures into the higher, say the ascidians into the fish, of the fish into the monkey, and the monkey into man, are shut between the horns of a dilemma if they follow the acknowledged principles of causation." For the power to rise from the original organic substance of life to the higher self-conscious forms was either in the first substance or it was not. If it was present there it clearly was imparted by some power of like quality. Evolution might easily be understood as the progressive manifestation of a latent mental or spiritual force breathed into the primordial elements of inanimate matter. Or, if we insist on purely material substance as the composition of evolving life, we are compelled to look for some intercessory act by a power capable of infusing its own nonmaterial being from which man derived his higher faculties. The same laws of causation must apply; powers in the effects must have commensurate qualitative counterparts in their causes.[34]

Clearly implied in McCosh's critique was a dualistic philosophy of human nature that extended directly from the Scottish school of philosophy that included McCosh. The dilemma he described was indeed a genuine one, if we are correct in saying that man has both a physical and spiritual nature and that the two are radically different in quality. But McCosh did not press this point strongly. He took a great interest in physiological psychology and awaited the judgment of experimental psychologists on the nature of nerves and brain-cell behavior in affecting conditions and character of thought. But open as he was to this approach, he nonetheless saw problems in it. Spencer was an important exponent of the new methods and disavowed the introspective psychology of McCosh's

---

[34] Ibid., pp. 18-20. It would seem that if we relate this question to Spencer's Unknown, we would find that Spencer does establish a kind of causal relationship between the Unknown and its manifestations. Thus the "higher qualities" might in fact derive from an original infusion from the source of all things, that of which they are phenomena, or appearances. But such a linking would immediately establish the character of the Unknown as such.

school. As Spencer tried to see physical nature in terms of forces, he also tried to see mental nature in terms of feelings. The interplay of feelings constitutes the forms of consciousness and all its ramifications, as the interplay of forces governs natural phenomena. But feelings are only the subjective correlates of changes in nerve vescicles. Spencer generated mental behavior from "an integrated series of nervous shocks."[35] These may very well be the genesis of mental sensitivity, McCosh believed, but they do not establish the existence of self-consciousness. By that term McCosh meant the knowledge that the mind has of self in its present state. For the mind can be to itself both subject and object, and therein lies its essential difference from material being. And, McCosh said, "taken in this sense, there is surely a difficulty which every wise man will acknowledge, in showing how it can have been developed from nerve force or from any material force."[36] Spencer wanted to generate self-consciousness from the continued unbroken series of impressions affixed to a central focus of the nervous complex.[37] But this speculation is, if not inadequate, incomplete in its description, McCosh contended. For the mind not only generates and exhibits forms of thought—imaginative projections, abstract moral good—that show no causal connection to outside forces, but, more important, thought of any kind shows no qualitative relationship to the nerve structure and the impressions acting upon it. There is no power in these commensurate with their product, nor can the product be dissolved back into its supposed components. In this way also Spencer's efforts to generate intelligence from feelings[38] recall the same problem of causation. The genesis of self-consciousness, and intelligence, was for now, McCosh believed, a mystery. But his argument clearly implied the fashioning of the higher human faculties by a power or being capable of endowing man with those faculties and a being in whose likeness he was fashioned.[39]

Finally, Spencer wanted to connect his theory of evolution with moral philosophy. So did McCosh, and once again they clashed. In ethics, Spencer wrote extensively but not uncritically in the tradition of the utilitarians. With respect to sentient life, the good, he said, is what brings "a surplus of agreeable feelings," the bad

---

[35] Herbert Spencer, *The Principles of Psychology*, 2 vols. (1855; New York, 1902), 2:270.
[36] McCosh, *Spencer's Philosophy*, p. 32.
[37] Spencer, *Principles of Psychology*, 1:403.
[38] See ibid., 1:403-6.
[39] McCosh, *Spencer's Philosophy*, pp. 30-35.

having contrary effects.[40] Spencer thought that the whole evolutionary process conspired to produce conditions of ethical good as so defined. For evolution placed all forms of life in greater suitability with their environments. Higher forms of life were qualitatively superior in all respects, including even their greater sensory capacity for experiencing pleasure. Life becomes increasingly "complete in fullness and duration."[41] McCosh also generally shared this view, but his analysis differed greatly from Spencer's.

The happiness principle, a virtual corollary of evolution for Spencer, was for McCosh another revelation of the known attributes of the Creator. For as in any other aspect of evolution the design and contrivance evident reflected their genesis in a causal intelligence. "These arrangements toward an end point to an arranging and therefore an intelligent cause. Not only so, but as the end is happiness, they give evidence of a benevolent cause." The effects are realities and so must be the cause. Spencer's continued recourse to a phantom Unknown made his ideas increasingly unserviceable to clear thinking about nature and its arrangements.[42]

But this was not the main point. Spencer linked evolution and benevolence as coincidental processes. The perfection of the species through the agency of adaptation enhanced the surplus of pleasures that constitute a utilitarian ethical standard. McCosh, however, believed that evolution could not be so easily summarized. We have seen already his case against the utilitarian measure of value. He wished to couple this case with a moral factor in evolution. Nature pursues a course of happiness, but, he insisted, the mere pleasure principle is eventually subordinated to a moral one. For with the arrival of man there is introduced to the evolutionary scheme a creature who knows not mere pleasure and pain, but right and wrong. He knows and discerns the moral principles that are the foundation of happiness, the laws of love, justice, and equity that promote well-being. For had nature not evolved such a creature, one whose moral apparatus secures its access to substantive moral truth, it would have failed to provide the motivation by which the general well-being of all humanity is assured. For once again, McCosh asked, "*Why* am I compelled to promote my neighbor's well-being?" Nature can pursue a principle of happiness through evolution only by the agency of a self-denying moral creature. McCosh did not deny the benevolence of evolution, then; he did

[40] Herbert Spencer, *The Data of Ethics* (1879; Boston, n.d.), pp. 29-30.
[41] Ibid., p. 27.
[42] McCosh, *Spencer's Philosophy*, pp. 47-48.

carefully link that principle to the larger structure of his Protestant scholasticism.[43]

Once again, McCosh found a remarkable coordination and design in the reinforcing roles of these two ends of nature—happiness and morality. The moral principle is a critical and distinguishing feature of the evolution of humanity. As nature, even as Spencer described, perfects itself in happiness, the moral law emerges at a useful juncture to secure that perfection. McCosh even noticed the delicate adjustment that occurred in human feelings, for, although he did not follow Spencer's single-minded attention to feelings in moral consciousness, he did not dismiss or overlook them. There is a marked adaptability of our sentient to our moral nature. Deeds of altruism and benevolence induce good feelings. Spencer, like Mill, of course counted these as so much more addition to the sums of pleasure and related them to the general adaptability of mind to action in evolution. McCosh conceded that this kind of self-interest can indeed generate altruism. But he did not believe it could generate love. A far-sighted selfishness does not constitute virtue, and it does not create it. Those qualities derive from a deeper law within us. By a special collocation it joins to human happiness, and evolution again illustrates an instructive adjustment of ends and means in nature.[44]

WHILE MCCOSH explored the various philosophical facets of causation and final ends in nature, he kept an even closer eye on the testimony of scientists. By the time of his arrival in the United States evolution had become the most engaging matter of the day in the intellectual community. There is no doubt that McCosh judged himself first and foremost a defender of theism, ready to state the claims of religion on any issue of scientific discussion. Undoubtedly his pronouncements therefore were biased and contrived, the theistic stance being a kind of a priori frame of judgment. Yet too much can be made of this. McCosh had no a priori system

[43] Ibid., p. 52.

[44] Ibid., pp. 54–56. McCosh also applied to the moral question the earlier dilemma he outlined regarding the origin of the higher faculties in human beings. For man illustrates the same gap here between simple reflex feelings and higher moral consciousness. Was the moral consciousness latent in the original organic substance of life? There is no evidence that it was, though it might share some characteristics with certain animal instincts, particularly the parental. And if we rule out this consideration, we must look to some intervening force that gives of its own. Evolution suggests either an all-providing designer or an active power entering and shaping life's progression at various critical points. Ibid., pp. 49–50.

as such to defend. He did not look to science to confirm a preconceived outline describing how God had fashioned the world or the means of his dealing with it, now or henceforth. Scripture no doubt furnished a large and useful account of history, spiritual and mundane, and the necessary prescriptions for the conduct of life. But it was never the sum of Christianity, and a literal adherence to the Word forced a foolish and wrongheaded consistency on Christian believers. McCosh therefore chastised fellow believers who resisted the geologists' evidence respecting the age of the earth. When expert study of fossil remains continued to increase the age of the world, even into the "millions of ages," it was useless to be calculating the generations from Adam as a reliable guide to this essentially scientific question. Religion would surely be the loser in such an unnecessary contest.[45]

McCosh himself saw the need to be flexible about evolution. *Typical Forms* had incorporated an outline of evolutionary change, but not the kind that people meant when they used the term "development." McCosh and others employed this to mean an account of evolutionary change in which one form of life actually evolves out of another. The authors of *Typical Forms* had seen no reason to confirm this kind of change, nor can it be said that the scientific community itself was at all prepared to confirm it. Chambers raised the possibility and was dismissed. But this was no longer the case after 1859 when Charles Darwin published *The Origin of Species*. Darwin was so critically important not because he affirmed evolution, but because he furnished a convincing explanation of its causes. Natural selection now focused attention on the means by which species adapt to their circumstances and what kinds of physiological changes occur through that process. On some questions, such as those dealing with the extinction of species, Darwin seemed to have a more plausible answer than others. He cited the struggle for existence among different species and of species against nature itself, and he could illustrate with numerous examples how nature provided the key biological transformation that perpetuated the existing forms of life. Furthermore, Darwin introduced a startling reversal of older explanations. His emphasis shifted away from the designing activity of a creator to stress the undirected and sporadic play of natural forces. Increasingly Darwin rejected teleology and final cause. The life history of the species was essentially an acci-

---

[45] James McCosh, *The Supernatural in Relation to the Natural* (Cambridge and London, 1862), pp. 20-21.

dental one, and man too was the unordained product of ageless and uncontrolled natural forces.[46] This perspective above all agitated the religious community.

Increasingly and under the pull of mounting evidence, McCosh moved away from the separate creation argument of *Typical Forms*. To be sure, he had never defended it unequivocally, and when many scientists confirmed Darwin's hypothesis he moved with the tide. And as he relinquished even his general support of creationism, he warned fellow religionists not to be dogmatic in defiance of scientific evidence: "I am not sure that religion has any interest in holding absolutely by the one side or other of this question, which it is for scientific men to settle. I am not sure that religion is entitled to insist that every species of insect has been created by a special fiat of God, with no secondary agent employed."[47]

McCosh's writings reveal his progressive accommodation to the theory of natural selection as expounded by Darwin. His Boston lectures of 1871 show his first emphatic statements, and they were outlined fully in his first book published after his assumption of the Princeton presidency. Here he gave a summary of Darwin's views and urged that "it is for naturalists to determine the points which have been stated by Mr. Darwin." McCosh then referred to adaptations in nature, but he did not appeal to the kind of design that is the causal framework of the "special ends" illustrated in his Belfast book. "Depend upon it," McCosh wrote, "when the process is explored, there will be found an immense number and variety of adaptations to secure that the peculiarity of the individual, found to be useful, will not perish with the individual, but go down to future ages."[48] Four years later McCosh admitted "a tendency in

[46] This subject has been a controversial one, in part because Darwin's ideas seem to lend themselves to different readings. Many people did detect a teleology in Darwin, and some even chastised him for asserting there existed the "greatest possible adaptability to prevailing conditions," as though even he too were crediting a romantic *Naturphilosophie* and designing nature. The more religious were pleased to see Darwin at least confirming final cause in nature, not in the older sense of all signs pointing to man as a terminal point, but as demonstrating the clear presence of design in the universe. Even Thomas Huxley saw similarities between Darwin and Paley, and the *Origin* itself suggests such a perspective in some places. But we know also that Darwin came, privately, to entertain severe reservations about any benevolent purposes in nature. "There seems to me too much misery in the world," says one of his letters. See Gertrude Himmelfarb, *Darwin and the Darwinian Revolution* (New York, 1969), p. 667.

[47] James McCosh, "On Evolution," in *Wood's Bible Animals*, ed., T. G. Wood (San Francisco, 1875), p. 667.

[48] James McCosh, *Christianity and Positivism* (New York, 1871), p. 41.

the very organism itself to rise to higher states . . . by a succession of immeasurably small additions." He was now giving wide credence to the very likely possibility that forms of life do succeed each other in unbroken progression. And Darwin's accounting for these was also convincing. "As new and trying circumstances arise there is a struggle for existence; the unfit disappear and the fit survive, and there is progress upon the whole through the long ages."[49] A year later McCosh reviewed some of the writings and speeches of Darwin's famous defender Thomas Huxley and on several points admitted the superiority of his position over that of Richard Owen. The cases illustrated by Huxley, McCosh remarked, "indicate a tendency on the part of the reptile to rise to the bird, and of the bird to retain properties of the reptile; and natural selection and development can alone explain this."[50]

More and more, McCosh was coming to see the development hypothesis as a positive enhancement to the religious understanding of life. Darwin's ideas were plausible, although not all of them had won full scientific endorsement, and certain obvious questions remained. But could one accept natural selection under Darwin's terms and necessarily conclude with him that evolution was a blind and undirected system, that chance loomed so large in evolution as to preclude design, intelligence, and final cause? Here was a case where the religious thinker might demand the right to interpret the evidence along with the scientist. McCosh intended to let the scientific community establish the empirical authority for development, but he would try to understand its ultimate significance.

When we examined McCosh and Dickie's study of patterns in nature as they illustrated them in *Typical Forms*, we noticed how a plausible case for development was latent in their own evidence. Agassiz, too, really had all the evidence he needed for the theory, yet he held tenaciously to a dogmatic, idealistic interpretation of species. But McCosh relied just as much on collocation and final cause when he accepted the development hypothesis as he had when he wrote *Typical Forms*. For evolution that described the development of one species from another gave a wider and even more complex illustration of contrivance and combination of purposes in nature: "I discover adaptation not only in the products," as his older work emphasized, "but in the very process of development."

[49] McCosh, "On Evolution," p. 652.
[50] James McCosh, "Is the Development Hypothesis Sufficient?" *Popular Science Monthly*, 10 (1876), 88.

For in the case of any species assumed to be unchanging, it was possible to describe the coordination of any organ with the entire complex of the organism. But in development, in one species changing into another, there was a far greater intricacy, one that could hardly be explained by anything like a mechanical integration of parts. Development, especially in Darwin's description of the organism within the vast milieu of its environment and the manifold changes occurring therein, greatly extended the interplay of natural forces. The development processes "imply the concurrence of an immense number of agents, mechanical, chemical, electric, galvanic." We see collocation on a grand scale, merging blind and indifferent forces to make the most careful and minute transformation of the forms of life themselves. It was certainly as appealing to the imagination and intelligence to cite "proof of purpose" in such arrangements as to resort with Darwin to blind chance.[51] Development did not mitigate the case for teleology. For McCosh "the union and conspiracy of forces involved in Evolution furnish new proof, as it certainly supplies new illustrations, of purpose and ends."[52]

Development also demonstrated the unity of all creation. Older naturalists might marvel at the features and forms that made each species distinct, each specially designed to function in the manner that it did. But once again evolution, by the progressive and integrated creation of forms, showed the work of a single mind. The world reflected the style and impression of an artist, as a composer gives thematic unity to all the diverse parts of a symphony. Now McCosh's discovery of homologies assumed a more forceful meaning. Nature is shown to be anticipatory not by a segmented in-

---

[51] Ibid., 97.

[52] James McCosh, *The Religious Aspect of Evolution* (1888; New York, 1890), p. 70; idem, "Development Hypothesis," 96. McCosh took a position here quite similar to that of Asa Gray, Agassiz's famous scientific rival at Harvard. On the subject of interpreting the data of science, Gray simply pointed out that *any* natural phenomenon may be interpreted from an atheistic point of view, and development, or evolution, was no more inherently atheistic than, for example, the theory of gravitation, or the separate creation of individual species. Moreover, natural selection demonstrated everywhere for Gray design, purpose, and teleology, and his writings amount to a brilliant scientific case for a religious interpretation of evolution. "To us," Gray wrote, "a fortuitous Cosmos is simply inconceivable." Asa Gray, *Darwiniana*, ed. A Hunter Dupree (1876; Cambridge, Mass., 1963), pp. 44, 120-21, 126 (the quotation). See especially Article III, "Natural Selection Not Inconsistent with Natural Theology," and Article XIII, "Evolutionary Teleology." McCosh had some correspondence with Gray, but the extant materials concern business matters only, and it is uncertain whether or not they ever shared their ideas on evolution.

stallation of forms, but by final ends that run the whole gamut of the species. McCosh thus came to a position not far from Chambers's, although he could not endorse Chambers's theory that all the higher faculties lay somehow embodied in the original material of life. He could accept Chambers's development, but not the inactive God that the deistic Chambers established as its source. The nagging question of the origins of these higher human powers led McCosh to a God who intervenes at critical junctures along the path of development. But the intervention is imperceptible, and the appearance of order and continuity is everywhere.[53]

McCosh, of course, examined the evolution question from the perspective of a theist, but a Christian theist in particular. Did evolution at all conform to a Christian understanding of the world? Did it in any way elucidate Christian doctrines? We note first that McCosh did not accept all of Darwin's data, as indeed few scientists did. Persuasive even as the natural selection hypothesis was, McCosh stated that it was anything but final; in the three or four thousand years of human history we find no record of a new species of plant or animal appearing. We have not yet put natural selection under human observation.[54] More important, the place of man in the scheme of evolution was still unclear, and most difficult to assess. McCosh said neither man nor God was disserved in the development of homo sapiens out of lower species, but there clearly existed no evidence that such was the fact. McCosh cited the authority of Alfred Russell Wallace on the comparative brain sizes of human beings and the highest form of simians. Even the relative brain sizes of human savages were distinctly greater than those of apes. Wallace's prestige as a naturalist greatly discredited the theory of a direct and continual descent of man. "Natural selection," Wallace wrote, "could only have endowed the savage with a brain a little superior to that of an ape, whereas he actually possesses one but little inferior to that of the average member of our learned societies."[55] McCosh concluded nothing final from Wallace's observations, but he never abandoned the conviction, on the other hand, that man was clearly a product at least partly fashioned in

---

[53] James McCosh, "Religious Aspects of the Doctrine of Development," *Report of the Proceedings of the First Presbyterian Council* . . . (Edinburgh, 1877), p. 267; see also idem, "On Causation and Development," *Princeton Review*, 7 (1881), 383-86.

[54] McCosh, "On Evolution," 654.

[55] Quoted by Loren Eisely, in *Darwin's Century: Evolution and the Men Who Discovered It* (Garden City, N. Y., 1961), p. 311; see also McCosh, *Christianity and Positivism*, pp. 46-47.

the image of a creator not contained within the limitations of natural forces.

McCosh, finally, applied some specific Christian categories to evolution. What science says about man in evolution enables us to separate him at least partly from naturalistic forces there. In fact, the appearance of man marks a new "dispensation" in the evolutionary process, even if it is not admitted that it demonstrates a spiritual intervention. For as Darwin showed, what we see in evolution before man is the play of strength and brute force, or the skillful arrangement of physiological forms as the determinants of a bitter struggle for survival. The first dispensation in evolution gives all to speed and power, and those that lack these assets disappear from the struggle. Under these terms, man, by every external indication, should have lost out long ago. Wallace had said as much, pointing to the thin, hairless skin that distinguished man from even the apes below him. But the complete absence of the tough, protective, and hairy skin on primitive homo sapiens further strains our acceptance of natural selection.[56] At this point, McCosh believed, a new dispensation was operating. The hairless and weakly structured new species adapts remarkably to the world. He alone can inhabit all parts of it, successfully endure all climates and conditions. Now it is demonstrated that intellect has superseded strength as the agency of upward progression. "The giants disappear and the civilized people take their place." Out of forbidding terrain and forests, cities emerge; the earth yields new means of sustenance as intellect takes over from natural forces and itself changes the environment. Skill, ingenuity, imagination give new dimensions to the struggle for existence. Technology, it seems, is the crowning glory of that species who inherits and exercises these grand intellectual faculties.[57]

But the dispensation of intellect does not lead to the perfection of the species. Intellect hardly soothes the savage drives of lower forms of life, and beastly passions reign in the breast of humanity. Technology builds bridges and monuments but finds more ingenious and cruel means of killing as well. Herbert Spencer might rejoice at this manner of nature's purging itself of its weaker elements, but the Christian, McCosh said, could not. If evolution worked by this means only, all the arguments for a benevolent design would be worthless. But there is, we are happy to discover, a third dispensation. With reference to history, McCosh said that

[56] McCosh, *Christianity and Positivism*, p. 48.
[57] Ibid., p. 55.

the strictly intellectual dispensation culminated in Greece. The dispensation of morality begins with Christ. But morality enters as a force because it is joined to spiritual grace as represented and dispensed by Christ. The moral era introduces the possibilities for the new community of love and justice. Grace triumphs over strength (Christ even pronounces now that the meek shall inherit the earth), and it gives new direction to intelligence, science, and enterprise also. With Christ a new level of the evolutionary plane is possible, one barely anticipated in the earlier stages. Now the evidence of a moral governor, a beneficent deity, and the clearest signs of a progression in nature are manifest.[58]

It is important that we understand McCosh's position carefully here. For when he elaborated on the meaning of moral and spiritual dispensation he intended something quite different from what the major new groups of religious thinkers dealing with evolution and trying to reconcile it with theism were concluding. For that effort produced in the late nineteenth and early twentieth centuries what Sydney Ahlstrom has called the Golden Age of Liberal Theology in America. At the most prestigious seminaries of America there emerged a group of thinkers who wished to assume a rational view of religion, accommodating it to science. In brief outline, what the new liberals wished was a spiritual reading of evolution. One could accept the evolutionary hypothesis, but one should view it as a progressive manifestation of God in his creation. "Immanence" became a critical term in the liberals' theological vocabulary. The growth of the human race in intellect, reason, and spiritual understanding was ultimately the process by which God merged with the collective mind of humanity and by which social and moral perfection grew in the world community. God was being rejoined to his creation. Reason replaced original sin as a preoccupation of the liberals; progress was a greater concern than divine judgment. "The dominant tendency was in the direction of a benign naturalism," Ahlstrom says. What was taking place was the progressive and certain redemption of the world.[59]

But McCosh could not read the record in such blatantly optimistic terms. In fact McCosh's Christian interpretation of evolution demonstrates continuity with his whole career in the ministry and

---

[58] Ibid., pp. 56-57, 67.

[59] Sydney E. Ahlstrom, *A Religious History of the American People* (New Haven, 1972), p. 780. Among this group of liberals were Henry Ward Beecher, Lyman Abbott, John Bascom, and Shailer Matthews. Liberalism, of course, had many varieties and representatives.

his service to evangelicalism. The power of Christ makes possible the moral era of human history, but it does not assure it. Not even the period of the third dispensation has obliterated the awful record of wars and destruction, racial hatred and tyranny, from the pages of history. Great gains have been made, but sporadically and with vigilant struggle. They established no law of progressive amelioration, however. Our world, McCosh said, "is not what the rationalist would have it—a peaceful landscape, with nothing but order and beauty." Nor was a rational world automatically emerging from the rubble.[60] "The champions of Natural Religion," McCosh also remarked, " . . . have drawn far too fair a picture of the state of our world." They too easily glance over pain and suffering. Our world knows evil aplenty, and even final ends seem incomplete in a comprehensive view of the world's situation.[61]

McCosh believed that if Christian understanding coincided with evolution it did so in terms that the evangelical Christian knew best. Thus, McCosh linked the period of moral dispensation to the experience of grace, and linked them necessarily. Grace is the existential foundation of the moral life, the internal transformation that propels a true benevolence. Here, of course, McCosh perpetuated the old clash between Evangelical and Moderate. He appealed not to the intellectual apprehension of moral law, but to the conversion of heart. In the new group of liberal theists McCosh might have seen a direct link to the Moderates of his former country. Certainly the religious emphasis was similar, for Moderatism rejoiced in the rational and intellectual progress of the world and subsumed the moral life under it. But for McCosh the last dispensation in evolution signified yet a new mode of struggle—the struggle of the spiritual against the natural and not, as the liberals would describe it, the mergence of the two. "We now see clearly," McCosh wrote, "the nature of the dispensation under which we live—the dispensation of the spirit. There is, as there has been, in our earth, a struggle. But the contest is not between element and element, between the brutes and the elements, or between animal and animal. It is first a contest between man and nature, but it has also become a contest between the spiritual and the natural. It is specially a contest between sin and holiness." In short, the episodic history of creation has now come to center on the war of evil and grace that rages in the human breast.[62] If there be any message for

[60] McCosh, "Religious Aspects of Development," 269.
[61] McCosh, *Christianity and Positivism*, p. 70.
[62] Ibid., p. 76.

religion and the churches here, it is simply what the evangelical preachers had been advocating all along. McCosh had so construed the Christian interpretation of evolution as to endorse the efforts of the gospel ministry in the conversion of the world.

But McCosh's writings on this subject clearly do reflect both the Scottish Enlightenment and evangelicalism, the cultural forces that had shaped his career in the church and in philosophy. An adherent of Darwin or any committed naturalist would have found much that was unsatisfactory in McCosh, especially his view of final ends. In America, his stance was soon to come under heavy assault, especially in the writings of John Dewey, who, by translating Darwin's open-ended system into a philosophical statement of the open universe, represented the culmination of the whole Darwinian impact on American thought.[63] McCosh also used evolution to elaborate his form of Scottish philosophy and to enhance Christian theism. And he had moved noticeably, in some respects, from the early essay on typical forms to his last writings in the United States. He had accommodated his ideas to the new researches of science in the middle and late nineteenth century, far more, in fact, than most in the religious camp were willing to do or willing to tolerate. McCosh's accommodation would embroil him in controversy in his new country, and even as he crossed the Atlantic he pondered the merits of introducing his ideas into the classrooms at Princeton. He resolved that he would do so.

[63] The title essay in Dewey's *The Influence of Darwin on Philosophy and Other Essays in Contemporary Thought* (New York, 1910) may be said to signal the full triumph of the Darwinian revolution in American thought and the ultimate rejection of a teleological universe. The view was more completely summarized in Dewey's *Reconstruction in Philosophy* (New York, 1920).

Part III

AMERICA

Chapter Seven

ACADEMIC REFORMER

🌣 THE INVITATION that reached James McCosh from across the Atlantic has, in retrospect, much historical logic. But the affairs that immediately surrounded the appointment to Princeton demonstrate that fortuitous circumstances often dominate the events that transform individual lives and institutions. The Princeton years, although marked by bitter animosities and unrelenting warfare against forces that threatened to undo him, produced significant triumphs for McCosh. He who had sought to merge in his own career two cultural forces that had shaped his own life and outlook, now inherited a singular opportunity to give them institutional expression. It may seem ironic, but the impulse of the Scottish Enlightenment, denoted by the peculiar academic characteristics of the Scottish university in the age of Moderatism, and the Scottish evangelical movement that gave birth to the Free Church of Scotland, would find their most complete and happy reconciliation in a college of the new world. McCosh's long acquaintance with the universities of his native country formed the background of a long program of academic reform at Princeton. But his was not a headlong rush into the future. Indeed, Princeton during McCosh's tenure evidenced to the outside a pronounced religious character, one that reflected the energy and commitment of nineteenth-century revivalism. McCosh, in fact, always marched confidently into the era of modern learning, but his confidence derived from the security that Princeton rested on a solid base of religiosity. McCosh quickly learned that academic reform was not easy. The modern academic leader was a politician, too, and in his program of reform McCosh had to forge new alliances, with the further ironic result that his own success laid the foundation for a later Princeton much different from that he envisioned.

Although the larger theme of these next chapters is the perpetuation of McCosh's Scottish inheritance in the United States, naturally the success of his efforts depended on his adaptation to a new environment. Princeton College, which still bore the official title of the College of New Jersey, had been shaped by historical forces that very often proved to be difficult obstacles to McCosh's reform efforts. But at its inception, Princeton sprang from a movement akin to that which brought McCosh into the Free Church. Like all the other colonial colleges of America, Princeton was the child of religion. But more important Princeton was the first institution born of the Great Awakening, the sustained movement of emotional religion that swept the colonies for about twenty years after 1730. Established in 1746 Princeton represented a mildly Calvinistic pietism that had broken from narrow denominational lines to join in a religious movement that looked for the conversion of the continent. And to the spirit of religion it added broad classical and scientific learning. Early leaders of Princeton cherished the collegiate tricolors of learning, piety, and virtue.[1]

Princeton was not entirely a product of native Americanism. From its earliest years it had a Scottish connection that was fortified anew with McCosh's appointment. Indirectly that influence came from the dissenting academies of England where Presbyterians and others influenced by Scottish academics broke from the deadening scholasticism of Oxford and Cambridge and introduced the mathematics and natural and experimental philosophy familiar to the Scottish universities. Princeton's founders had a direct acquaintance with these studies, and as a result Princeton probably had a fresher curriculum than its colonial sisters. At least there existed in this period a quiet confidence that the study of the physical universe could only illuminate the ways of God to man and surely could not harm true piety and theism. It was left to the next century to make bitter enemies of science and religion, and to the extent that Princeton preserved the peace it reflected a mode of the Enlightenment that was peculiar to Scotland and the American colonies.[2] But the fullest and most direct impact of the Scottish culture came from John Witherspoon.

With his arrival in Princeton in 1768 John Witherspoon antedated McCosh by a hundred years. A striking similarity characterizes the careers of the two Scottish presidents of Princeton, for Witherspoon first gained notice as an evangelical minister whose *Ecclesiastical Characteristics* ridiculed the smugness and polite decorum of the

[1] Thomas Jefferson Wertenbaker, *Princeton: 1746-1896* (Princeton, 1946), p. 19; Howard Miller, *The Revolutionary College: American Presbyterian Higher Education, 1707-1837* (New York, 1976), pp. 81-83.

[2] Douglas Sloan, *The Scottish Enlightenment and the American College Ideal* (New York, 1971), pp. 36-72; Wertenbaker, *Princeton*, pp. 81-82.

Moderate ministers and furnished delightful satirical fare for McCosh and the later Evangelicals. Witherspoon's first serious works, *Essay on Justification* (1756) and *Treatise on Regeneration* (1764), stressed the authority of Scripture and held up against Moderatism the theological standards of God's absolute sovereignty and the depravity of human nature. But there emerged at Princeton another major influence on Witherspoon. For like McCosh, he stood very much in both streams of Scottish culture. A product of Glasgow and Edinburgh universities he had been a student of John Stevenson and a classmate of William Robertson, Alexander Carlyle, Hugh Blair, and John Home, all of them prominent illuminati of the Moderate church leadership. Witherspoon came to Princeton well fortified with the reigning philosophy of those leaders and soon had the occasion to employ it. When Witherspoon discovered that several of the Princeton tutors had become enamored of the idealistic metaphysics of George Berkeley, he provoked a famous incident in which he argued that philosophy right out of the college. Princeton under Witherspoon thereby became the first American center of the Scottish realism of Reid and Stewart. But in fact, Witherspoon had the same reservations about some aspects of the Scottish system that McCosh had. Hutcheson's easy equation of the moral and the aesthetic rubbed against the Evangelical's fears that Christian virtue was merely high and decorous living. Too much of that polite and formal age took comfort in such a doctrine. So Witherspoon instead described the moral sense as God's will implanted on man's heart. Like McCosh he sought an extrahuman source of the ethical, one separated from the rational conscience of man. All legitimate moral laws, he said, are rooted in the divine will.[3] In this and other ways Witherspoon joined Scottish intellectual and religious life to Princeton. He borrowed directly from the reform curriculum of the Scottish schools, and cited as the sources of his academic reforms his own "constant intercourse and great intimacy with the members of the university of Glasgow."[4]

Samuel Stanhope Smith (1751-1819) was a graduate of Witherspoon's first class in 1769, later his son-in-law, and his successor in the presidency. And it was he who brought Princeton into the fullness of its early liberal era. Smith had followed the philosophy tutors into idealism, but Witherspoon thoroughly broke the spell.

---

[3] Sloan, *Scottish Enlightenment*, pp. 105-7, 114-15, 124-25.
[4] Ibid., pp. 112-13.

Smith won the president's approval and appointment to the chair of moral philosophy in 1779, and from that position further secured the dominance of the Scottish philosophy at the College of New Jersey. But in the field of science Smith innovated. Fascinated with recent theories of evolution and the origin of the races, he pointed to the impact of environment and social conditions on the diversification of the human species. He saw no challenge to religious orthodoxy here, for these factors merely made for changes on an original, unitary human nature acceptable to the Genesis account. In fact, Smith believed that science wonderfully amplified the truths of Scripture. His *Essay on the Causes of Variety of Complexion and Figure in the Human Species* (1787) proclaimed that "the most accurate investigations into the power of nature ever serve to confirm the facts vouchsafed by the authority of revelation." Smith's plan for an expanded scientific curriculum at Princeton testified to that faith, and his latitudinarian spirit extended also into the welcome he gave to modern languages and his intention to modify the standard four-year program of studies.[5]

But the Princeton president was not his own master, a fact that McCosh too would learn. By the end of the century a reaction to academic liberalism and a resentment of the gains of science had set in among the trustees of the college. Students whom Smith permitted to take a special program of scientific studies were denied a full degree and handed a certificate instead. Complaints circulated that divinity students reared on Scottish philosophy became "velvet-mouthed" preachers and that the doctrine of ultimate depravity lost support. Now the trustees scanned the writings of the faculty for signs of unorthodoxy, and soon Smith was out.[6] But the course of reaction here, it must be noted, derived from events that took place well beyond the walls of the college. Because they set the whole course of Princeton's relation with the outside world, and because they created realities that affected the whole of McCosh's career at Princeton, they merit some examination.

When McCosh arrived at Princeton he only vaguely hinted that he wished eventually to preside over a college with national influence. But gradually he came to believe that Princeton must become more than a collegiate expression of the Presbyterian denomination. In fact, those same objectives had struck the imagination of Princeton's founders. Early Presbyterianism in America was marked by factional quarrels that climaxed in the subscriptionist controversy

[5] Wertenbaker, *Princeton*, pp. 119-20; Sloan, *Scottish Enlightenment*, pp. 147-55.
[6] Wertenbaker, *Princeton*, pp. 121-22.

that raged during the Great Awakening. Partisans of a strict confessional loyalty wished to impose on all initiates into the Presbyterian ministry a sworn allegiance to the Westminster Confession. This Old Side group, dominated by a Scotch-Irish element, met the opposition of New Side Presbyterians, most of them of New England extraction, who held up the standards of piety and grace as more critical than creedal loyalty. The latter group, furthermore, was inclined to look beyond the institutional church for an enlarged arena of religious and moral activity. This party became strong partisans of the Awakening and joined in the several efforts of that movement to spread social and moral reformation. Not surprisingly, some of the first expressions of an American religious nationalism sprang from the Great Awakening, a thoroughly intercolonial movement, and millennial expectations, such as those of Jonathan Edwards, gave an unlimited scope to the goals of Evangelicals. And among these goals education had high priority. The creation of Princeton by the New Side Presbyterians was wholly consistent with the logic of revivalistic and evangelical Protestantism. Moreover, the quest for an institution of national influence was also consistent. Princeton barred no student for reasons of doctrine, and its first board of trustees was interdenominational. The school, furthermore, was legally independent of any denominational body. Like the other colonial schools, it existed to train ministers, but it trained other professionals as well. Piety would spread throughout the land and moral reform attend it when religion and learning shaped the lives of Princeton graduates. Princeton, as Howard Miller has indicated, was "a broadly conceived intercolonial instrument of social integration and reformation."[7]

Witherspoon clearly reflected this spirit. He symbolized the transatlantic character of the institution and had probably been familiar with the party of Princetonian emissaries, Samuel Davies and Gilbert Tennent, who toured England and Scotland in a fund-raising effort for the college in 1753 and 1754. Princeton contacts with the old world had been widened by Jonathan Edwards, who, despite his death shortly after his appointment to the presidency of Princeton, enjoyed a solid reputation among the Scottish Calvinists. Edwards corresponded with Scottish contacts and solicited their support for the traveling Princetonians. Witherspoon himself had national ambitions for the College of New Jersey and went often before the American public. His tours up and down the Atlantic

[7] Miller, *Revolutionary College*, pp. 53-55, 63, 67-68, 71. The quotation is on p. 67.

seaboard were missionary efforts for the school that gave it connections with a wide Presbyterian and non-Presbyterian element. Princeton formed a close friendship with the southern population, which endured until the Civil War. Moreover, Witherspoon's energetic and outspoken involvement in the Revolution placed Princeton in the heat of great events. James Madison, Henry Lee, Charles Lee, and Luther Martin merely highlight the names that won for the college the nickname "school of statesmen." More than 16 percent of the representatives to the Constitutional Convention were Princeton graduates.[8]

We need to remember that the spirit that carried Princeton into national events was as much a religious as a political one. Especially among those remaining partisans of the Great Awakening and evangelical religion, the American Revolution was something more than those secular principles that governed fair taxation and the laws of representative or republican government. Among this contingent the Revolution embodied millennial hopes. Republicanism had particular new world connotations that were emphatically moral. Fleeing old world tyranny, aristocratic dissipation, and the corrosion of luxury, the progressive forces of history worked to establish a new spirit of liberty, equality, and moral health in the new world. The Kingdom of God on earth might now realize its fulfillment in this final revolutionary break with the past. None better expressed this nationalistic spirit than the two youthful Princetonians, Philip Freneau (1752-1832) and Hugh Brackenridge (1748-1816). Their commencement oration in 1771, *A Poem on the Rising Glory of America*, hailed the "morning of the world" now dawning in America. Like Edwards before them, the college poets described millennial America in neither narrow political or religious terms, but believed that the flourishing of the sciences and arts and the progress of intellect were also certain signs of history's course in the new world. These ingredients were judged perfectly compatible with a moral fervor that was synonymous with republican virtues. Witherspoon could look upon his new country, then, and describe America as a land "growing every year in beauty and fertility . . . in numbers and wealth, arts, and sciences." Republican and religious America seemed even to be transforming human nature, a daring speculation for such a Calvinist as he.[9]

[8] Wertenbaker, *Princeton*, pp. 32-35, 115-16; Miller, *Revolutionary College*, p. 73.
[9] Miller, *Revolutionary College*, pp. 110-19; Kenneth Silverman, *A Cultural History of the American Revolution* (New York, 1976), pp. 232-34. The quotation is in Miller, p. 111.

And that was just the point. For this easy confidence and optimism did not sit well with much of the Presbyterian leadership. This element, strictly Calvinistic in its theology, had always been distrustful of the emotional extremism of revivalism and the Arminian tendencies of such leaders as George Whitefield and others. Jonathan Edwards, whose neo-Calvinism flourished within a revivalistic style, had probably done as well as anyone could in keeping the two Presbyterian factions together, but after the Revolution, tensions renewed. The element that spoke for a broad Presbyterianism with large national alliances had forged a Plan of Union in 1801 with like-minded Congregationalists and in a cooperative spirit worked to extend evangelical religion to the new areas of settlement. To this extent too these "New Light" Presbyterians bespoke the spirit of the great renewal of revivalistic religion best symbolized by the Cane Ridge revival of the same year. It was soon clear, however, that forces conspired against the Calvinism embraced by Edwards and the earlier Puritans. Evangelical Protestantism merged with the democratic spirit of the frontier; its message was voluntarism and the responsibility of individual choice in accepting Christ and winning salvation. The old tenents of arbitrary damnation and personal helplessness found barren soil amid the buoyancy and self-congratulatory mood of a free people. But it was not these problems alone that induced the reaction that followed.

For the most part the liberal academic spirit of Princeton was the work of those who were also allied with evangelical religion, although Smith was aloof from that spirit in a way that Witherspoon was not. Regardless, by the middle of the 1790s resentment against Smith, against the extension of science in the curriculum, and against the decay of Calvinism at Princeton had set in. Many, like Archibald Alexander and Samuel Miller, soon judged the college unfit for the education of ministers and called for a theological seminary under direct control of the Presbyterian General Assembly. Those who shared that viewpoint led a successful effort to organize Princeton Theological Seminary in 1812. It would be for many decades thereafter the most illustrious and venerated voice of Calvinism in America. The seminary had no legal connection with the college; in fact it was to be preserved uncontaminated by that wayward institution. This development might in turn have taken the pressure off of Princeton College, but as Thomas Wertenbaker has described, no such liberation arrived. For in the year of the seminary's establishment the same forces that created it succeeded in placing Ashbel Green, an early and outspoken critic of Smith, in the presidency of the college. Reaction had triumphed, and Princeton College for years to come breathed not a breath of reform or change. It now entered what its historian has labeled the nadir of its history.[10]

What was occurring at Princeton was denominational retrenchment. But that retrenchment was also a recoil from the major cultural force shaping America in the early nineteenth century— evangelical Protestantism. That movement was characterized by a broad interdenominational spirit that used such organizations as the American Bible Society, the American Home Mission Society, and the Society for the Promotion of Collegiate and Theological Education in the West as the means for the spiritual and moral redemption of the nation. Furthermore, the movement brought the cooperative spirit into the campaign for specific social causes— temperance, Sabbatarianism, antislavery, and others. The agency of national redemption was the revival, the means by which individual souls were prepared to receive the spiritual grace that could recharge a nation foundering in materialism and religious indifference.[11] Often intolerant and inflexible, the Evangelicals nonetheless evidenced an immense religious energy. In them the quest for the Kingdom of God in America had its most direct continuation from the early inspiration of the New England Puritans.

Presbyterian conservatives never warmed to the revival. Samuel Miller heard only loud clamor and noise drowning out the "still small voice of God" at the frontier camp meetings. In 1804 the General Assembly saw fit to condemn the "antic gestures, ridiculous contortions . . . and apparent levity" that marked revivalism. Calvinists also denounced the theology of the revival, its preaching of "universalism" and "self-sufficiency." Again in 1807 the General Assembly reproached free will exponents for the "increasing dereliction of truth" that "pervades all classes of society." Increasingly such projects as the Plan of Union came under suspicion, subverted, it was believed, by new liberal strands of New England theology. Many Presbyterians withdrew from the great interdenominational agencies as new ones of strict Presbyterian affiliation appeared. So also did denominational magazines that spoke to the narrower interests. Amid the homogenizing and integrating effects of evan-

[10] Wertenbaker, *Princeton*, pp. 146-50, 153.

[11] Perry Miller, *The Life of the Mind in America: From the Revolution to the Civil War* (New York, 1965), pp. 36-42, 47, 83; see also Timothy L. Smith, *Revivalism and Reform: American Protestantism on the Eve of the Civil War* (New York, 1957).

gelicalism, and amid the heresies that beset a world straying far from the faith of the fathers, Old School Presbyterians would see to it that at least they would protect the purity of their denomination and doctrine.[12]

But Presbyterianism would not survive the ensuing years without bitter interdenominational conflict. The disputes centered around three major issues, which we need only list here. First was the issue of broad and narrow denominationalism, and it centered on the question of the extent to which the Calvinistic Westminster Confession was the essence of Presbyterianism. Second was the matter of the revivals. Old School followers never denounced revivals as such, but warned against their perversion by fanaticism and the delusions of unconverted sinners. Third, slavery increasingly became a matter of contention. Evangelical Presbyterians helped fill the ranks of a Protestant clerical force that wished no accommodation with slavery. But Old School voices like Charles Hodge were noncommittal and believed that this "political" issue was not the affair of the churches.[13] In a fiery showdown in which all of these issues played a part, Presbyterian schism occurred in 1837. For thirty-two years a formal division prevailed with yet another break occurring when the southern churches, which had flocked to the Old School at first, went their own way when it would not issue a positive sanction of slavery.

Throughout the years of clash and division Princeton Seminary and Princeton College remained major strongholds of Old School Presbyterianism. At the college academic progress was slow. The school had men of scholarly eminence, to be sure, and certainly the achievements of Joseph Henry in the field of electromagnetic physics made him the most renowned name in American science. But for the most part Old School Presbyterianism was far more suspicious of science than the New School. The latter's spokesmen believed at least that science should stand on its own merits and speak the truth as it perceived it. Christians should not strain too hard for a direct reconciliation with religion. Thus the first issue of the *Presbyterian Quarterly Review*, the periodical voice of the New School, asked "Is the Science of Geology True?" The writer warned Christian intellectuals not to look at Genesis for the answer to scientific questions; one might as well seek there the correct method

[12] Howard Miller, *Revolutionary College*, pp. 201-3, 227.

[13] For detailed discussion of these issues, see George M. Marsden, *The Evangelical Mind and the New School Presbyterian Experience: A Case Study of Thought and Theology in Nineteenth-Century America* (New Haven, 1970).

of navigation. Christian intellectuals should surrender their prejudices against geology and admit that science has in fact proven irrevocably that the earth has existed for millions of years and that creation was not accomplished in a week, but over many ages. Theists should ask only for the right to interpret the evidence of science along with the scientist himself, confident that no ultimate contradiction of science and religion would prevail.[14] To be sure, the liberal attitude here did not speak for all New School exponents, but it was clearly more generous than opinion among the Old Side. Princeton under John Maclean, McCosh's predecessor, was academically reactionary. The faculty he inherited was not wholly undistinguished, "but all were Calvinists, of the old school of orthodoxy." When he retired, seven of the ten faculty members were ministers, and "all were ardent Calvinists."[15] Maclean wanted Princeton professors to prove that astrology and geology in no way discounted the literal interpretation of the Bible, and he worried that Professor Charles Woodruff Shields, appointed to reconcile science and Scripture, had, in his opening lecture, conceded too much. For at Princeton the curriculum existed to defend religion, to which "every other part of education" was to be subordinated.[16]

SUCH, then, was the situation with American Presbyterianism and Princeton College. But events were moving toward a decisive turn for both. The experience of the Civil War had brought a quiet rapprochement between the northern Presbyterian churches. Many believed at the war's end that it was time to bury the creedal hatchets and work toward reunion. The opportunity for such a reunion arose in 1866, for both groups had selected St. Louis for their annual meetings, and both would gather at the same time for that purpose. And at Princeton, as President Maclean anticipated the imminent termination of his service, the board of trustees pondered the selection of his successor. By a curious and unexpected twist of events, the career of James McCosh now meshed with each of these institutional developments.

The United States had always held a certain fascination for McCosh. This "land of the future" as he called it had impressed him by its political achievements and by its strenuous Protestantism of the evangelical variety. Like many other Evangelicals, especially his friend Thomas Guthrie, McCosh had been an outspoken op-

---

[14] Ibid., pp. 143–44.   [15] Wertenbaker, *Princeton*, pp. 259, 287.
[16] Ibid., pp. 258–59, 284–85, 287.

ponent of slavery and vigorously supported the Union cause in speeches and addresses in Ireland. He was relieved to see American democracy survive the ordeal of the Civil War.[17] McCosh, moreover, had been gladdened but rather surprised that his philosophical works had found their largest market in the United States. Furthermore, he had maintained an active correspondence with many among his American audience. Francis Bowen, professor of moral philosophy at Harvard, for example, was among his supporters and once wrote McCosh a letter of encouragement in his contest with the "daring speculator" Mill.[18] Francis Landy Patton, later McCosh's successor at Princeton, recalled that his copy of the *Method of Divine Government* was thick with red and blue marginal notations, so absorbing was the work; he believed that many owed their first philosophical impulse to its reading.[19] These factors were enticing enough to excite McCosh's interest in a trip to the United States. He was interested especially in seeing the American colleges. He had traveled to Germany for a similar purpose a few years before and now wished to see what he might learn from the American schools.

In early 1866 McCosh began to plan for his voyage to America. He arranged the details of the trip through his American publisher, the former Scottish immigrant Robert Carter of New York City. McCosh arrived in that city on May 13, remaining two days before boarding a train that took him up the Hudson River to Niagara Falls (he had heard so much about that place that he could not deny himself the indulgence of a brief visit), through parts of Canada, to Detroit, and then to Chicago. He had anticipated that this would be the western terminus of his trip and that he would return east to visit the colleges. But along the way he heard news of the forthcoming Presbyterian meetings in St. Louis and received urgent invitations to attend. McCosh at first declined, but then succumbed to the pleas. On May 22 he arrived in St. Louis where about twelve hundred people had gathered for the events.

McCosh quickly discovered that he was a figure of wide recognition at St. Louis. When New School officials heard of his

[17] James McCosh, "Incidents of My Life in Three Countries," unpublished typescript in the Princeton University Archives, 126; *New York Observer*, February 19, 1868.

[18] April 20, 1868, in the "Correspondence of James McCosh," Department of Rare Books and Special Collections, Princeton University Library.

[19] F. L. Patton, Review of *First and Fundamental Truths*, by James McCosh, *Presbyterian Review*, 10 (1889), 341.

presence they secured resolutions from their body offering him a welcome and inviting him to a special seat on the auditorium platform. McCosh returned salutations, offered greetings from the Scottish and Irish churches, and further expressed hope that British and American Presbyterians would contemplate means of closer affiliation and cooperation. The Old School people were equally receptive. At their meeting the next day they also voted McCosh a "place at his pleasure" beside the Moderator and invited him to address the convention. McCosh acknowledged their greeting and elaborated more fully on British-American cooperation. He called for a large American role in the Evangelical Alliance, for cooperative missionary work, and for an exchange of British and American college professors. And he spoke openly on other matters. He hoped that the victorious northern states would use their victory in the war to secure positive liberation for the black population. He feared the rising ideologies of race and encouraged the churches to unite in preventing racial warfare. McCosh circulated widely among the St. Louis conventioneers and was surely a source of the emerging goodwill between the factions. His visit, in addition, did much to enhance his name among the Americans.[20]

McCosh now decided to expand his tour even more. He traveled up the Mississippi to St. Paul, then by train out into the Minnesota and Iowa prairies. Stops at Cincinnati and Pittsburgh marked his trip back east. In Virginia he sought out schools and churches of the former slaves, engaged vehement secessionists in discussion, and spoke for the need of an extensive program of schooling for blacks. In New Jersey he made a special short stop at Princeton to see the "famous University and Theological Seminary," as he described them on his return home. He was quite impressed, too, as a letter back to Carter suggests: "Princeton is a remarkable place—we have nothing precisely like it in our own country. It is astonishing to find such a company of eminent professors centered in a small village."[21] By now the trip had become an extended tour. At Philadelphia McCosh joined in the celebration of the nation's ninetieth birthday. Then he went back to New York. Here some of the Presbyterian churches had arranged for him to give an ad-

[20] James McCosh, "The Religious and Social Condition of the United States as Gathered in a Summer Tour; with the Formation of an American Branch of the Evangelical Alliance," *Proceedings of the Evangelical Alliance* (1866), 15; *New York Observer*, May 24, 1866, May 31, 1866, June 7, 1866.

[21] McCosh, "Religious and Social Condition of the United States," 15-16; McCosh to Carter, June 25, 1866, in the McCosh Correspondence.

dress, following which the Presbyterian *New York Observer* reported that "Dr. McCosh might, if judged by his readers, be accounted an American teacher. He fights our battles with Mill, Comte, Spencer, and the Pantheists."[22]

Several of those attending the St. Louis meetings of the Presbyterians had traveled there from Princeton Seminary and Princeton College. And having confronted one problem, they knew they must soon face another. At the end of the next year President Maclean submitted his resignation, and the choice of a successor fell to the trustees. Several questions were pressing. Was Princeton ready for academic change? Was it ready to open itself up to the new studies that had been locked out of its program by a rigorous required curriculum? Might it still maintain its loyalty to religion yet exercise a friendlier attitude to the sciences? Those who looked for liberalization should not have been too optimistic. Some at Princeton were cool to the idea of a Presbyterian reunion and wanted no compromises or renewed affiliation with the liberals. Opponents included Lyman Atwater, professor of moral philosophy at the college, and, more important, Charles Hodge and his son A. A. Hodge. The elder Hodge (1797-1878) was clearly the most brilliant and resolute voice of Princeton Calvinism and the leading spokesman for the Old School.[23] Furthermore, Hodge happened to be the senior member of the board of trustees of the college and the presiding officer of the group that sat to choose a successor. And when the trustees nominated William Henry Green (1825-1900) for the position, they answered all the questions about a possible new direction for the college.

Green was the forty-three-year-old professor of oriental and Old Testament literature at Princeton Theological Seminary. For many reasons his nomination made sense. The college and seminary were institutional affiliates, the legal separation notwithstanding. Green, furthermore, was the nephew of Chancellor Henry Woodhull Green, a powerful figure in New Jersey politics, and John C. Green, Princeton's largest benefactor. Furthermore, there was no doubt that Green was doctrinally sound. He was a leading defender of biblical literalness in the warfare over the higher criticism. "By temperament, training, and conviction he was unable to accept in any measure [any hypothesis] that questioned the historical truth,

---

[22] *New York Observer*, July 12, 1866.
[23] Marsden, *Evangelical Mind*, pp. 213-16; *Minutes of the General Assembly of the Presbyterian Church, 1862-1869*, May 28, 1868. These records indicate that Archibald Alexander Hodge, a son of Charles Hodge, also opposed the union.

the unity, or the Mosaic authorship of the Pentateuch." He was also "generally recognized as the scholarly leader in America of the ultraconservative school of Biblical criticism."[24] What might have been Princeton's future under Green it is perhaps useless to conjecture. He politely turned down the offer.

There are indications that from the beginning of the deliberations over the new president, McCosh's name circulated and had definite support. It seems clear too that one or more persons had apprised him of their support. In January 1868, three months before the offer went out to Green, McCosh wrote to Robert Carter saying that he had heard about his possible candidacy for the Princeton position. He also added that he was not seeking it, but would "favorably consider it" were it offered.[25] And just after the nomination of Green one Princetonian wrote to McCosh conveying his disappointment. "I was in hopes," he said, "and all the alumni I have seen have expressed the idea, of seeing a new element introduced into the dear old Institution and place. . . . Instead of this they have cut a plug out of the bow to stop a leak in the stern of the ship." He personally regretted that the offer had not gone to McCosh.[26]

After Green's rejection of the offer, the trustees had no obvious choice for the position. Legend says that someone then remembered that it was exactly one hundred years ago that Princeton had turned to Scotland and John Witherspoon for new leadership; history might bless the school again in a similar way.[27] McCosh said later that he had learned that this suggestion came from Irenaeus Prime, the editor of the *New York Observer*, the leading Presbyterian newspaper and one that had recounted McCosh's earlier trip to the United States in full detail. In fact, it is more likely that the main supporter was John A. Stewart, the New York financier.[28] When McCosh was suggested, there seems to have been no dissent. He could appeal to all Princeton factions if only because he had not been a party to their former quarrels. Clearly a residue of goodwill lingered from the visit of two years ago also. But more positively, McCosh could offer himself as a solid religious thinker in an age of waxing skepticism. The *Observer* called McCosh "the leading thinker and champion of sound philosophy in the United King-

---

[24] *National Cyclopaedia of American Biography*, 6:128-29, hereafter *NCAB*; *Dictionary of American Biography*, 7:560-61, hereafter *DAB*.

[25] January 22, 1868 in the McCosh Correspondence.

[26] Letter signed "F. B. H.," April 10, 1868, in the McCosh Correspondence.

[27] Wertenbaker, *Princeton*, p. 290. [28] See Chapter 8.

Academic Reformer 229

dom." So the invitation went out by telegram to McCosh in early May. Undoubtedly he had no reluctance in accepting, although word did not reach America until late May. But that week was significant for another reason. The Old School and the New School were holding separate annual meetings again, but the main business was to be the approval by each of the reunion of the two divisions. On the same day that Presbyterian reunification was at last secured, both sessions paused in the middle of their transactions to hear their Moderators read telegrams informing them of McCosh's acceptance of the Princeton offer and to pass resolutions welcoming "the good news." Probably few college presidents in America have inherited such immense goodwill as surrounded McCosh's appointment to Princeton in 1868.[29]

THE INAUGURATION of James McCosh was one of the great gala events in the history of Princeton. McCosh and his family departed Liverpool in late September. Their ship, the *Tripoli*, arrived at New York on October 20, and they went by train to Princeton. On the campus, great expectation surrounded their arrival. As four o'clock approached, the students moved en masse behind the faculty to the railroad station, and with wild cheering welcomed the arriving party. The buoyant group then escorted the McCoshes to the president's home, now thoroughly renovated for them. There Professor Atwater introduced the new president to the assembled crowd. "He stepped forth, [and] was received with loudest hurrahing."[30]

The community in which McCosh thus arrived in 1868 physically reflected the process of transition through which the new president would try to lead the small college that sat off of Nassau Street. Streetlights had been introduced but were still in a primitive state, with feeble gaslights widely spaced. Handicrafts—builders, wheelwrights, blacksmiths, saddlers, harnessmakers, shoemakers—still dominated the economy. Princeton also contained some of the finest old colonial homes in America, and these reminders of the past seemed to tell the visitors that here was a place where the age of steam and iron must make its way slowly. Princeton was "a country college," as some called it, and among its several stone buildings the oft-restored Nassau Hall stood most prominently.[31]

[29] *New York Observer*, June 4, 1868.
[30] George R. Wallace, *Princeton Sketches: The Story of Nassau Hall* (New York, 1893), p. 109.
[31] William Berryman Scott, *Some Memories of a Palaeontologist* (Princeton, 1939), pp. 14-18.

But beneath these quiet niceties a real crisis lurked. Princeton's strong contingent of southern students had been virtually depleted during the Civil War, and they simply were not coming back. Enrollment had fallen, and as the college now drew almost entirely from the states of New York, Pennsylvania, New Jersey, and Maryland, it clearly had lost its stature as a national institution. Its financial situation was acute. The cheers that welcomed McCosh therefore were anxious ones. In the eyes of many he was the institution's last hope.[32]

A large crowd gathered for McCosh's inauguration at Princeton. Alumni, faculty, students, and noted academic officials from other colleges, including Professors Noah Porter and Daniel Coit Gilman from Yale, attended, and the event received wide coverage in the national press. Thus fresh from Ireland did McCosh walk into Princeton's history. Indeed, it was an act of innocence. McCosh composed his inaugural address before he departed Queen's College, and, selecting his title, "Academic Teaching in Europe," he organized his reflections on higher education as formulated from his own experience of two Scottish universities, his years at Belfast, and his extensive travels to universities abroad. He had to this point virtually no experience with Princeton and probably very little familiarity with its history. In outlining his academic philosophy to this large assemblage, McCosh therefore presented a model of the future Princeton to which the realities of the past and the contentious forces of the present must somehow be made to fit. And there were persons present who wanted McCosh to know what those realities were. Charles Hodge from the seminary delivered the address of welcome, and, lest anyone doubt, his message was emphatic: "We desire that the spirit of true religion should be dominant in this College, that a pure gospel should live here." "Unsanctified learning is a curse," he said. "Nothing is more evident than that knowledge uncontrolled by religion becomes Satanic." Hodge had no doubt that science and religion were compatible, but the priorities were clear. "The religion of Jesus should form the basis of all instruction in this institution." So Hodge had the first words. Then it was McCosh's turn.[33]

---

[32] Wertenbaker, *Princeton*, p. 288. Other observers were manifestly optimistic, however. A writer for the *New York Times* commented: "This is destined to be a memorable date in the history of 'old Princeton,' for it marks the day on which this venerable institution takes a new lease on life and prepares for a more vigorous career." October 28, 1868. The *Times* writer made these remarks after listening to McCosh's inaugural address.

[33] *New York Observer*, November 5, 1868.

In fact, McCosh's address was moderate; liberals and conservatives could each take heart from several sections of the two-hour discourse. McCosh said that he had no desire to "revolutionize" the American college by transplanting European methods onto it. But whereas Europeans might learn profitably from American success in fine primary school systems, Americans in turn would gain by adopting carefully from university models in Europe. For in its schools of higher learning, McCosh believed, the United States was tenaciously conservative. In his own Scotland the revolt against the dry, dull method of teaching the classics had been accomplished long ago. This literature still formed the best of humane learning, he felt, but it must be made to enliven and excite the mind. In fact, McCosh spoke of education in the manner of the evangelical preacher. As the gospel must ignite the emotions and imagination of the convert, so must education inspire. Properly taught, the ancient letters would do just that, but so also would the best of the modern learning. McCosh, who as a student in Glasgow devoured the works of Scott and scoured the local libraries for the newest novels, urged that English literature generally take its place with the classics in the modern university.[34]

McCosh's emphasis here, however, stayed well within the framework of traditional American pedagogy. When McCosh pronounced that a university exists to "educate," to draw out and improve the mental faculties given by God, he invoked the language that had been employed for years by academic conservatives and enshrined by Yale College's famous defense of the traditional ways in 1828. Indeed, the Scottish philosophy that McCosh himself represented had undergirded the whole edifice of the "faculty psychology" that he here defended. "Education," he said, "ought to be a gymnastic to all our powers. . . . It should seek especially to stimulate and strengthen by exercising the intellectual powers." But McCosh now went further to ask whether those noble goals of mental training could not find room for new and liberal content. We need no longer adhere rigidly to the rote mastery of old languages to discipline the mental muscles, he believed. These, in fact, deserve better, and hard mental work should have the rewards of excitement. Furthermore, whole mines of new learning were waiting to be tapped and used. The modern sciences especially could serve the needs of mental training, and they were profitable and

[34] James McCosh, "Academic Teaching in Europe," in *Inauguration of James McCosh, D.D., LL.D., as President of the College of New Jersey* (New York, 1868), pp. 37-39, 42, 60.

exciting as well. McCosh even opined that suspicion against the sciences bordered on "superstition." Here the address reverberated with the refrain of utility. McCosh would not yield to those who clamored for vocationalism or invoked the standards of a narrow practicality to justify education. But education must bear fruits. "I hold that in study," McCosh said, "while the true end is the elevation of the faculties, they never will be improved by what is in itself useless, or found to be profitless in the future of life." If the meaning of this statement was not wholly clear, it nonetheless signaled that McCosh held to no hard and fast commitments. He had some general guidelines, but the future would provide the details.[35]

On the question of professional education McCosh was likewise noncommittal. He acknowledged a place for it, not an "unworthy place," but an inferior place. A university (already McCosh was using that word instead of "college") should not try to make its students merchants or manufacturers, but that fact should not preclude opportunities to select courses with a particular career objective in view. McCosh's stand echoed that taken by Sir William Hamilton several years before. The university should lay the broad philosophical and intellectual basis that underlies the governing rules and standards of the professions. A prospective lawyer may choose to study political theory, and a prospective minister should acquire a strong foundation of metaphysics and moral science. "All this," McCosh urged, "is in harmony with the idea of a university, whose office it is to train the powers, but which may do so by anything which is fitted to elevate and refine the mind."[36]

Anything? Surely McCosh must have caught the attention of his listeners with that statement. For it was a wide door he was opening. Then McCosh became specific. If the university were to accommodate different tastes and needs, then it was time to liberalize the hard and fast curriculum that governed the undergraduate's four years. New knowledge was begging for admission to the university, and it deserved a place. Surely then a policy that permitted limited choice was warranted. McCosh made it clear that he did not want to go the way of the German universities, which, he feared, produced either narrow professionals or scholars with a love of the abstract and the recondite. Clearly the biases of McCosh's Scottish realism and its suspicion of German idealism informed his mistrust of that university system, which saw as its

[35] Ibid., pp. 40-41, 45, 47-48, 63-64.   [36] Ibid., pp. 48-49.

main end the indefinite creation of new knowledge. Can we not still uphold the standard of the universal scholar without invoking either the pure German ideal or the inflexible older ways, McCosh asked. A rigid stand with the past would in this day produce "a pedant as dull as a dictionary," he feared. McCosh then called for a standard broad program of some required courses in the freshman and sophomore years, followed by several elective courses in the last two years.[37] He remained loyal to this idea in the years ahead, and its achievement marked a major accomplishment of his administration.

Finally, McCosh asked his fellow Princetonians to take confidence in themselves and look to a renewed influence in their nation. In an era of "such devotedness to practical and money-making pursuits" Princeton's sons should go forth to spread "a civilizing and humanizing influence" in the land. Like Athens and Alexandria in ancient times, Princeton should be "an intellectual metropolis where a refining influence goes to the provinces."[38]

McCosh outlined such a promising future at a time when American higher education was alive with the excitement of change. He was one of a new generation of academic leaders that came into influence within a brief span of years. It was a diverse but powerful group. Andrew Dickson White assumed the presidency of Cornell the same year that McCosh arrived at Princeton. At Harvard, the remarkable tenure of Charles William Eliot began the next year. Two years later Noah Porter acceded to Yale's leadership and ensured that the older ways still received an intelligent defense. James B. Angell, arriving at Michigan at the same time, and John Bascom at Wisconsin in 1874, gave a new high stature to the midwestern state universities. And then in 1876, the establishment of the Johns Hopkins University in Baltimore symbolized the triumph of the long-sought goal that research and scholarship be recognized as the quintessential purposes of higher learning. American institutions were moving in different directions, each groping for its own style, each articulating its own philosophy. A veritable revolution seemed to be taking place.[39]

McCosh spent much of his career at Princeton looking at Harvard, where the revolution was most thoroughgoing. Harvard symbolized in an awesome way all that he admired, envied, and deplored in modern education. At different times he was the bitter

---

[37] Ibid., pp. 49-50, 73-74.   [38] Ibid., pp. 51-52
[39] For a complete account of these developments, see Laurence Veysey, *The Emergence of the American University* (Chicago, 1965).

antagonist of Eliot and a valued ally. The elective system had actually been in operation at Harvard for some time when Eliot (1834-1926) assumed leadership there in 1869. His famous inaugural address announced that Harvard would rise above the late clamor over what kind of education, what fields of study must prevail in the university. Harvard would have them all, and at their best. Eliot won just renown for the liberal sentiments here expressed and later practiced. But Eliot's views in certain respects were not radically different from those of McCosh, who had come fresh to America from a long acquaintance with the European systems the year before. Eliot too deplored the neglect of the English language by American colleges. He too wanted an elective system, one broader than McCosh's plan, to be sure, but one denoted "by very rigid limits." "There is a certain framework that must be filled," he said, "and about half the material of the filling is prescribed. ... All the studies which are open to [the Harvard student] are liberal and disciplinary, not narrow or special."[40] But in the years ahead the implicit libertarianism of Eliot became more pronounced. He called the elective system "liberty in Education" and used a large public forum for its wide defense. Increasingly he appealed to the "unique" character and personality of the individual student, the only reliable guide for a useful educational program. He called for diversity not uniformity in education, and that at "the earliest possible moment." By 1885 Harvard had so extended the elective principle that only an English writing course, elementary French or German, and a few lectures on chemistry and physics remained of the old standard curriculum. Nor was any structured program or arrangement of studies forced on Harvard's unique students. Eliot's admitted educational agnosticism said that no standards exist by which to determine whether any body of knowledge is essential for the educated man. So fast was new knowledge accumulated in the modern age, none could now say what constitutes the "accumulated wisdom of the race."[41]

Actually, Eliot was less the radical than he appeared; in a sense, he was quite within the tradition of the institution he headed. From the days of the Wigglesworths in the eighteenth century, when Harvard began to train a rational-minded New England ministry that broke the mold of Calvinism, to the Unitarian takeover of Harvard at the end of the century, Harvard sifted for the country

[40] In Richard Hofstadter and Wilson Smith, eds., *American Higher Education: A Documentary History*, 2 vols. (Chicago, 1961), 2:602, 609.
[41] Ibid., 2:705-6, 708, 711.

the liberal currents of thought and culture. Eliot, then, was as much fruition as beginning. Yale, on the other hand, had virtually defined itself in reaction to liberalism. And now, with the election of Noah Porter (1811-1892) to its presidency, Yale continued to do what it had always done well; it gave a refined and eloquent defense of the older ways. Porter had begun that defense in 1869 with his article "The American Colleges and the American Public," later a book. Now, in his inaugural address, Porter took an emphatically skeptical view of the elective system. The stern Porter would have nothing to do with Eliot's romantic faith in the seventeen-year-old student. He has "neither the maturity nor the data" with which to determine his best course of studies. Porter had no truck with the utilitarian ideal and remarkably echoed the spirit of the old Yale Report of 1828. "The more urgent is this noisy tumult of life without," he warned, and the stronger its pressure against the doors of the college, "the greater need is there that certain studies which have little relation to this life should be attended to." Liberal culture, denoted by intellectual training, alone was acceptable in the American college.[42] Actually, in 1876 Yale did inaugurate an elective system. But when closely examined, the Yale version of the elective system meant essentially that students would now have more choices in the ancient languages![43] Yale, it turned out, would have to be dragged screaming into the twentieth century.

That Princeton endured these rites of passage with greater ease owed much to the dexterity of McCosh. He had to work painstakingly for reforms at Princeton, and often against entrenched opposition. But he eased the way for change partly by presenting to the outside world an image of conservatism. To a degree, that placated those in his own backyard who feared his innovations. By addresses to the public, letters to newspapers, and, most dramatically, in two celebrated debates with Eliot, McCosh exuded a style of cautiousness and safe adherence to the tried and true. But he made it clear at the same time that he was not defending the reactionism embraced by Yale. This message surely emerged forcefully before the assemblage that gathered in New York in 1885 to hear Eliot and McCosh debate the academic issues of the day. The encounter, under the auspices of the Nineteenth Century Club, was intended as a three-cornered affair, but Noah Porter, who lacked

---

[42] Ibid., 2:699-700; Brooks Mather Kelley, *Yale: A History* (New Haven, 1974), p. 240.

[43] Kelley, *Yale*, p. 266; George Wilson Pierson, *Yale College: An Educational History* (New Haven, 1952), p. 44.

both McCosh's and Eliot's flair for public controversy, bowed out. McCosh then stood alone to attack "the new departure" at Harvard.

McCosh wanted to expose this new departure to the American public. Eliot's system had all the rhetorical glitter to make it attractive—freedom, liberty, equality; who could disparage these great American ideals? "But O Liberty! what crimes and cruelties have been perpetuated in thy name!" McCosh, for one, was not fooled. "I can prick the bubble so that all may know how little matter is inside."[44] But dissent from the Harvard ways did not necessarily signify reaction: "I will not allow anyone (without protest) to charge me with being antiquated or old-fashioned, or behind the age—I may be an old man but I cherish a youthful spirit." Further, McCosh said he would admit to the university every branch of knowledge that constitutes "true learning." Here McCosh did reinvoke the faculty psychology and the standards of mental discipline. And like Porter, he charged that Eliot had an all too optimistic view of human nature. The elective system was the pathway of self-indulgence, the course of least resistance for the average college student. Few youths entering college, furthermore, are yet fully aware of their own powers; they may atrophy by a misguided emphasis on one division of learning, and the result is a product that is "narrow, partial, malformed." McCosh had seen enough of that type in Germany.[45]

For the most part these were familiar points that had always marked this debate among educationists. Many, in fact, probably missed the one issue of importance in this particular exchange. Criticism of the elective system had invariably been levied in the name of academic conservatism and adherence to tradition. But in a significant and telling sense, it was McCosh who emerged as the greater "liberal." For McCosh exposed Eliot at his weakest flank. The greatest flaw in the elective program at Harvard, McCosh proclaimed, was the very fact that it permitted students to avoid the new and necessary elements of learning that Eliot claimed to cherish. For the same freedom that enabled the modern student to circumvent the ancient languages, also permitted him to avoid the modern sciences. And these especially, McCosh believed, must underlie any contemporary program of collegiate education. Biology, geology, psychology, and also some of the new social sciences such as economics and political science "should be judiciously spread over the years of school and college training." Eliot's de-

[44] In Hofstadter and Smith, *American Higher Education*, 2:716.
[45] Ibid., 2:720-21, 716, 726.

fense, said McCosh, was replete with contradictions, for the same Eliot who hailed knowledge of the mother tongue as the true basis of culture would also allow his students to graduate with no serious study of its literature.[46] McCosh elaborated his case. He believed that the Harvard curriculum was full of "dilettanti" courses—like "French Novels and Plays." He constructed for his audience an imaginary but not implausible four-year course of study at Harvard. The package was a mongrel assortment—"Watercoloring," "Counterpoint (in music)," "Greek Art," "Free Thematic Music." Such a lopsided and lightweight smorgasbord was, to McCosh's eyes, an academic scandal. And it was condemned by what it omitted as well as by what it included. For where is religion? Harvard no longer teaches religion! Here was the greatest exposé of all. "Let parents know it, let the churches know it, let all America know it, let scholars in Europe know it—for what is done in Harvard has influence over the world. . . . I wish my voice could reach them all—that in a distinguished college in America a graduate need no longer take what the ages have esteemed the highest department of learning." The issue of religion in college, McCosh felt, was itself worthy of a whole new debate between him and Eliot. One year later they were at each other again.[47]

MCCOSH relished large public spectacles such as the debate with Eliot, but the real business of his life now was something a little less exciting but far more necessary. How exactly was he to give reality to the broad educational ideals he presented to the American public? How was Princeton to stand out as a national example of these lofty objectives? From the time of his inaugural address, presented one week after his arrival in America at the end of October, McCosh had almost two months in which to prepare his first report to the Princeton trustees. During that period he brought every aspect of the college under his close scrutiny. And what he found appalled him. How much now did his opinion differ from the superficial impression of two years ago. And how much work needed to be done to bring this institution to its full potential. McCosh resolved to lay all the facts before the trustees at the mid-December meeting. He still believed that Princeton had some eminent scholars, but there were many weaknesses. Salaries were clearly too low, and money must be found to raise them and to endow new chairs. This matter, he believed, required immediate

[46] Ibid., 2:719, 722.   [47] Ibid., 2:721-22, 729-30.

action, "lest we be outstripped by other colleges." Campus buildings, furthermore, were in deplorable shape, conducive to disorder and, some of them, "positively unhealthy." The museum and scientific apparatus of the college, he judged, "are in a very defective state." The library, he was astounded to discover, was open only one hour a week—an institutional outrage. These were the "critical" matters. There were others. Princeton must have more fellowships, "to promote high scholarship" among its best students. And there was the matter of the curriculum.[48]

McCosh had already appointed a trustee committee to examine the curriculum. Working closely with McCosh, that group produced a report that had his handwriting all over it. It listed seven areas of study that it judged "worthy of a fuller development." They were: modern continental languages and literature; natural history; English language and literature; political science; the science of languages; history of philosophy; special branches of natural philosophy or astronomy. These subjects were all necessary ingredients of a sound modern educational program. But, as McCosh pointed out more and more in the years ahead, there were other compelling reasons why Princeton must "keep up with the times." Harvard could offer all this new learning and more, but students who go there will acquire knowledge without sound religion. Princeton will have both, but to no purpose will it uphold sound religion if it loses students to other places by virtue of their more attractive and modern curriculums. This in essence was the grand strategy that characterized much of the philosophy and practice of education that McCosh now worked to perfect.[49]

The execution of that strategy depended very heavily on the faculty that McCosh developed at Princeton. Here another fact disturbed McCosh when he arrived in 1868. Princeton was excessively inbred. Irrespective of what that might say of the quality of the faculty, McCosh believed that Princeton must acquire much greater diversity to win national recognition. More than 60 percent of the Princeton professors had earned degrees either from the college or the seminary. Its intellectual temperament was of a distinctive Old School cast, and at least a few of the staff were stalwarts of that persuasion. John Thomas Duffield (1823-1901), the most dogmatic of these on the faculty, was a Princeton graduate of 1834

---

[48] "Minutes of the College of New Jersey," December 16, 1868. This document is the Board of Trustees' Reports, and will hereafter be cited as TM, for trustees' minutes.

[49] TM, December 16, 1868, December 2, 1875.

who had entered the seminary in 1844. He had been a tutor in Greek, and, since 1854 professor of mathematics. Very active in the Presbyterian Church, he had been Moderator of the Synod of New Jersey and, we shall see later, a staunch opponent of any deviation from orthodoxy. Second, Lyman Atwater (1813-1883), though a Yale graduate, had joined the Princeton faculty in 1854 as professor of moral and mental science. He did part-time lecturing at the seminary also. He was a visible defender of the Old School position, as best witnessed by his 1863 article, "The Doctrinal Attitude of Old School Presbyterians," in *Bibliotheca Sacra*. More moderate was Charles Woodruff Shields (1825-1904), a graduate of both the college and the seminary, who had inherited a chair in the harmony of science and revealed religion.[50] McCosh had no intention deliberately to break the alliance of college and seminary. That he did so to a great degree was the consequence of his effort to secure diversity. That effort led him to appoint professors who had undertaken advanced study at European universities. If he could appoint Presbyterians with this experience, so much the better. But even as late as 1876 he observed that only two professors were not Presbyterians, and that, he thought, was probably not good. Nonetheless, an emphatic change did occur under McCosh. In the first twelve years of his administration McCosh brought seventeen new professors to Princeton; thirteen of these had had no affiliation with the college or the seminary before their appointments.[51]

McCosh had to be careful in how he went about this. Suspicious eyes skeptically viewed the breaking of the mold. McCosh reported to the trustees, in a manner that was technically true but less than straightforward, that his criteria for appointments gave first preference to an alumni candidate, "if his qualifications are equal to others"; next he looked for signs of teaching ability, an imperative for the job; third, he would appoint no man who "is not known to be a decided Christian"; and finally, from these he would try to select a Presbyterian. Aside from the fact that McCosh moved away from alumni appointments and in at least two cases did not appoint "decided Christians," he adhered fairly closely to these guidelines. Above all, he insisted on first-rate teachers. McCosh often listened to glowing academic reports about a prospective professor, only to exclaim afterward, "but mon, is he *alive*?" He

[50] *The Princeton Book* . . . (Boston, 1879), pp. 145, 147, 150-51.
[51] This fact is derived from information about Princeton faculty members listed in the *General Catalogue of Princeton University, 1746-1906* (Princeton, 1908); see also TM, November 9, 1876.

once asked for a reference for a candidate from Daniel Coit Gilman at Yale. "He is said to be a man of ability," McCosh wrote, "and a high scholar. I am anxious to know whether he is also *a lively teacher.*" He clarified his position to the trustees. Princeton must have sound Christian scholars, but "nothing would injure our College so much as the appointment to any chair, of a respectable, dull, lifeless man, merely because he is orthodox."[52] McCosh's words surely recalled all the old wars of the Evangelicals and their efforts to rout Moderatism in the pulpit.

As he promised, McCosh took definite steps to improve English instruction at Princeton, although he had no immediate success. With the arrival of Theodore Whitefield Hunt (1844-1930) in 1873, McCosh secured a man who effected lasting gains. A genuine specialist in the science of languages, he had been a tutor in the college, and with McCosh's encouragement went abroad for study at the University of Berlin. Hunt tried ambitiously to integrate literature, philosophy, philology, and history, and was one of the prominent faculty members who gave McCosh's Princeton its decidedly philosophical atmosphere. He outlined his approach to the subject in an article entitled "The Philosophical Method in the Study and Teaching of English," in the *Presbyterian Quarterly and Princeton Review* in 1876.[53] Second, James Ormsbee Murray (1827-1899) was a graduate of Brown and Andover Theological Seminary and had served as minister at the Brick Presbyterian Church in New York City. He was a highly popular teacher and productive scholar, whose efforts were characterized by religious earnestness. He fought the new realism and naturalism in American and European letters and laid the basis for Princeton's long defense of the genteel tradition, strongly fortified by his successor, Henry Van Dyke.[54] But overall, the gains were not spectacular, and a graduate of the 1877 class recalled that English instruction was "decidedly elementary."[55]

[52] TM, February 8, 1877, December 16, 1874; letter of December 11, 1876, in the "Gilman Correspondence," The Johns Hopkins University Library, Manuscripts Room; Charles G. Osgood, *Lights in Nassau Hall; A Book of the Bicentennial: Princeton, 1746-1946* (Princeton, 1946), p. 27.

[53] Darrel Likens Guder, "The History of Belles Lettres at Princeton; An Investigation of the Expansion and Secularization of the Curriculum at the College of New Jersey with Special Reference to the Curriculum of Language and Letters" (Ph.D. dissertation, University of Hamburg, 1965), 530-31, 546-47.

[54] Ibid., 158; *NCAB*, 10:298.

[55] Henry Fairchild Osborn, ed. *Fifty Years of Princeton '77: A Fifty-Four Year Record of Princeton College and University* (Princeton, 1927), p. 50, hereafter, *Princeton '77*.

In the languages, also, McCosh fared only moderately well. He brought William Alfred Packard, with degrees from Dartmouth and Bowdoin and recent study at Göttingen, to supplement the work in the classics handled by Henry Clay Cameron. Cameron (1827-1906) though he was said to have "an almost encyclopedic knowledge of the Greek language," nonetheless was leading students through a "dry and lifeless" program of study. His tests asked students merely to translate the underlined words of a Greek passage, with the result that the "divine poetry of the Greeks" was lost along the way. Packard (1830-1909), however, was credited with giving students a graphic and revealing account of ancient life and culture, but he used a German edition of Cicero's "Letters" that scrambled the letters out of any schematic order and made their location in an English edition "nye impossible." Students used to easier ways resented this obstacle. Then with the appointment of S. Stanhope Orris (1838-1905) to teach Greek literature, Princeton received a genuine scholar with an academic background from Berlin and Heidelberg.[56] Finally, McCosh acquired in Joseph Kargé (1815-1892) a man who was "alive," but perhaps not in the way McCosh intended. The "General" had combined a scholarly training at the University of Breslau and the University of Berlin with an impassioned military service in the cause of Polish revolution in 1848 and then with the Union forces in the Civil War. A man of expansive liberal sympathies, his head and heart were half in the Continental languages he taught at Princeton and half in the great social and political movements of the day, about which he expostulated with zest in his classroom. He was a sympathetic man and would ask a student who failed an examination to have tea with him; if he failed again the General would give him ice cream and cake with the tea. Better yet, the students found that they could easily distract their teacher from the dreary translations by asking him a question about some war. For a whole semester, it was said, the class read only the first chapter of a light German novel.[57]

In history and political science McCosh made some significant gains and one egregious error. Both areas of study were new to the Princeton curriculum, but they constituted two aspects of the "new learning" that Princeton must foster if it were to step to the front ranks. William Milligan Sloane (1850-1928) was Princeton's first genuine historian, although, typical of the emerging scholarly

[56] Ibid., pp. 52, 77, 163; *Princeton Book*, p. 152.
[57] *Princeton Book*, pp. 153-54; James Mark Baldwin, *Between Two Wars, 1861-1921* . . . , 2 vols. (Boston, 1926), 1:36-37; *Princeton Alumni Weekly*, November 11, 1934.

profession of the day, he had an eclectic academic background. A Columbia graduate, he taught school briefly before studying philology at the University of Berlin. He was private secretary and researcher for George Bancroft, the noted historian, then pursued further studies in the classics and semitic languages at Leipzig. McCosh found him intellectually impressive and simply wanted him at Princeton. What he taught was secondary. So he began as a Latin instructor in 1879 and did not assume a history professorship until four years later. But in that field he made noteworthy and popular contributions, with books on the French Revolution and Napoleon and on contemporary American history. He stayed at Princeton throughout the McCosh years, then retured to Columbia. He became president of the National Institute of Arts and Letters in 1910 and president of the American Historical Association in 1911. The urbane Sloane, who "resembled the diplomat and man of affairs rather than the typical professor," soon came to typify the "new Princeton."[58] He would emerge as one of McCosh's strongest allies on the faculty and later would edit his autobiography.

McCosh perceived an able man in Sloane, who came from outside, but he wholly missed a chance to use one from his own ranks. John Bach McMaster (1852-1932) was teaching engineering at the college, and, quite unknown to almost everyone there, was writing a lengthy history of the United States. When *A History of the American People* appeared in 1883 it won immediate high recognition by the fledgling historical profession that McMaster was helping to bring into being. Sloane wanted a chair for McMaster in history, but when he proposed the idea to the trustees he met only "density and obtuseness." Nor was McCosh's reaction any more pardonable. McCosh's institutional ego got the better of him, and when he saw no recognition of Princeton in the book he asked McMaster about the oversight. McMaster simply replied that Princeton had given no recognition to him.[59] McCosh did, however, perceive a man of talent in Alexander Johnson (1849-1889). A Rutgers product, he wrote sound studies of New England politics and history, commented extensively on contemporary political events through his contributions to *Century* magazine, and more than any other professor helped put the Princeton curriculum in

[58] *Princeton Book*, p. 166; *NCAB*, B:292; *DAB*, 17:214.
[59] Scott, *Some Memories*, p. 12; *Daily Princetonian*, June 9, 1885; see also Eric F. Goldman, "The Princeton Period of John Bach McMaster," *Proceedings of the New Jersey Historical Society*, 57 (October 1939), 214–30.

touch with the modern world. James Mark Baldwin later recalled of Johnson: "He opened to us the question of public interest and social welfare. Gaunt, unkempt, vocally insufficient, he was still the man from whom we got most of what was to make us good and well-informed citizens."[60]

Finally, an evangelical minister like McCosh could not be indifferent to oratory. And with the appointment of George Lansing Raymond (1839-1929), he gave renewed emphasis to that art and also laid the foundations for some later spectacular achievements in the study of art at Princeton. Raymond was a Williams graduate who had further study at Princeton Theological Seminary. He studied abroad for three years at the University of Tübingen, returned to the ministry for a while, then taught at Williams. McCosh in 1880 made him professor of oratory and aesthetic criticism at Princeton. He was the author of many books, not all of them of serious scholarship, and was described as "one of the most just and pregnant critics as well as one of the most genuine poets that America has produced." That judgment overstated his merits a bit, but Raymond's *Orator's Manual* and his *Comparative Aesthetics* became standard college textbooks. He significantly enriched the humanities under McCosh.[61]

But even before he strengthened the humanities, McCosh had taken steps to improve the program in science. Not only did his main fund-raising efforts concentrate on this field, but his messages to the trustees made it clear that it was a critical area of competition with other schools. He wanted higher prizes for student achievements in the sciences and much more equipment. Heretofore scientific work at Princeton was largely executed by the lecture or older recitation method. But "lectures without experiments performed by the students may widen the mind, but they will not make chemists or give accurate scientific knowledge." Here was one example of the old mental discipline merging with the solid content of new knowledge. Princeton must train professional scientists, and McCosh now called for a separate school of science to achieve this end.[62]

Joseph Henry (1797-1878) had departed Princeton for the Smithsonian Institution in Washington before McCosh's arrival, but he still preserved ties to Princeton through his service on the board

---

[60] *NCAB*, 24:369-70; Baldwin, *Between Two Wars*, 1:24-25.
[61] *NCAB*, 8:457-58; *DAB*, 15:407-8.
[62] TM, December 21, 1870, December 20, 1871, December 22, 1875, June 18, 1877.

of trustees. In the field of geology, however, Princeton had an estimable scientist, Arnold Henry Guyot (1807-1884). A very close friend of Louis Agassiz at Harvard, Guyot also was a Swiss. He came to America in 1848 bringing a high reputation from his studies of glaciers. In 1854 he became professor of geology and physical geography at Princeton. Less orthodox than his Harvard friend on matters of religion, Guyot did, however, take a great interest in the religious questions raised by modern science and spoke frequently on these matters to such organizations as the Evangelical Alliance. With Guyot, McCosh, and some significant scholars who came later, Princeton was as alive with the questions of science and religion as any institution in America.[63]

McCosh's own additions to the science program included two of Princeton's major names—Cyrus Fogg Brackett (1833-1915) and Charles Augustus Young (1834-1908). Both were a credit to McCosh because they show that, his reports to the trustees notwithstanding, he was willing to bring professors of professional accomplishment to Princeton even when they had no commitment to religion.[64] Brackett had graduated from Bowdoin in 1849 and had imbibed many modern scientific ideas. He wrote some articles on evolution that had caught McCosh's attention and interested him in bringing Brackett to Princeton even before the school of science opened. Brackett's scholarly interests were the latest theories of energy, heat, and electromagnetism, and as the Henry Professor of Physics at Princeton he contributed, albeit modestly, to the current discussions. But Brackett excelled far more as a teacher and did much to generate student enthusiasm for his subject. He was a close friend of Thomas Edison and conducted several experiments for him. His classroom at Princeton, it has been said, was the first electrically lighted classroom in the United States, and "with the cordial approval of McCosh," he planned the first American academic course in electrical engineering.[65]

In Charles Augustus Young Princeton could claim a scientist of

[63] *Princeton Book*, pp. 142-43.

[64] In fact, though, McCosh's record on this policy was not consistent. David Starr Jordan, a noted scientist at Indiana University and later president of Stanford University, reported, after applying without success for a position at Princeton, that McCosh construed evolution in narrow religious terms and did not take kindly to Jordan's naturalistic variety. See David Starr Jordan, *The Days of a Man*, 2 vols. (New York, 1922), 1:150-51.

[65] *Princeton Book*, p. 155; *Princeton Alumni Weekly*, April 15, 1908; Fred B. Rogus, "Cyrus Fogg Brackett: 1833-1915: Physicist and Physician," *Journal of the Medical Society of New Jersey* (September 1855), 4.

large national reputation. He too was a New Englander and had graduated first in his class from Dartmouth, where his father was professor of natural philosophy and astronomy. McCosh induced him to come to Princeton in 1877, and there his classroom and observatory brought the study of science at Princeton into the vanguard of discovery. Young wrote major articles on solar spectroscopy, designed an automatic spectroscope used throughout the world, and devised a method for calculating the velocity of the sun's rotation. His several books included the highly popular *The Sun*. His professional stature won him the presidency of the American Association for the Advancement of Science in 1883, but his dedication embraced his work with the Princeton undergraduates too. He helped organize several scientific expeditions such as the one in 1878 that took a Princeton party of professors and students to Denver to study the solar eclipse. The western scientific expeditions became biennial traditions at Princeton. The *National Cyclopaedia of Biography* wrote of Young: "Under his able leadership the [new] Princeton astronomical observatory gained the reputation of being the best in the country." And another source asserted that "there would be almost unanimous agreement that Young's books were among the best textbooks in astronomy ever written."[66] Young was every bit the scholar. He stayed aloof from faculty politics and quietly dedicated himself to his work. McCosh assured him every possible support in that preference, although Young and Brackett were held in suspicion by some of the strong-minded religious interests at Princeton. Brackett had a home next to Young, and their street became known as the "atheists' corner."[67]

McCosh's hopes for the improvement of scientific instruction at Princeton were symbolized by the creation of the John C. Green School of Science in 1873. Here Princeton followed the patterns of Yale and Harvard. The Sheffield and Lawrence schools at these institutions had originated as a kind of compromise between those who demanded a break with the older curriculum and those who opposed the new subjects. McCosh, however, wanted no radical divorcing of scientific and literary-humanistic studies. Students in the Scientific Department faced requirements almost the same as those in the Academic Department. Their training, McCosh asserted, would not become "exclusively physical or materialistic." Moreover, scientific studies were not to be tucked away in the school of science. If anything truly distinguished the program and

[66] *NCAB*, 6:325; *DAB*, 20:623-24.
[67] Rogus, "Cyrus Fogg Brackett," 4.

philosophy of Princeton's McCosh from Harvard's Eliot, it was the fact that no student could go through the Princeton program without taking required courses in natural history, physics, chemistry and astronomy, and geology or psychology.[68] The school of science was launched with a hefty financial gift, an impressive ceremony, and an inaugural address by Joseph Henry. But it was an uphill struggle nonetheless. While such acquisitions as the observatory aided some fields, other subjects, like chemistry and zoology, sorely needed better equipment, and even the students recalled the rather meager fare they received in those courses. But the groundwork was laid, and McCosh would live to see the sciences flourish at a later date, and for reasons he could not in 1873 wholly anticipate.[69]

And in his efforts to enliven and reinvigorate academic life at Princeton, McCosh must be accounted the hero of his own story. Like all college presidents before him in America McCosh was a teacher also. Only with Eliot's inauguration at Harvard did the day of the president as administrator dawn on American higher education. Yet McCosh inherited that burden also, as well as the tasks of scholarly writing and publication, which he was determined to continue. The old wars of ideas that he had waged in Scotland and Ireland he renewed with vigor in his new country, and here McCosh would die the last defender of a great philosophical tradition. But even into the years of his retirement McCosh made the Princeton classrooms resound with intuitional realism. Sometimes seeking accommodation with new ways, at other times lashing out at modern heresies, McCosh preserved almost to the twentieth century the school of thought that first won wide renown with the writings of Francis Hutcheson in the third decade of the eighteenth. We shall review McCosh's literary efforts later. As far as the students of Princeton were concerned, it was McCosh the teacher who made the intellectual life of their undergraduate years so memorable.

In his course on mental science (later called psychology) and especially in his history of philosophy class,[70] McCosh championed

[68] *Princeton Book*, p. 134; James McCosh, "The Course of Study in Princeton College," *Education*, 5 (1884-1885), 358.

[69] *New York Observer*, July 3, 1873; *Princeton '77*, p. 57.

[70] McCosh did not teach the traditional course in moral philosophy, probably because Atwater still did. But many genuine Evangelicals like McCosh slightly distrusted this subject, for they perceived in all its elaborated lists of "duties" an implicit doctrine of good works. The tradition, furthermore, actually orginated with Hutcheson and the Scottish Enlightenment, which gave this venerable colle-

the ideas already elaborated in several tomes. McCosh believed that much was at stake in his instruction. He once wrote to a former student, James Mark Baldwin, that "the rooting of good principles in students depends much on the philosophy they are taught."[71] That may explain why students found the classes so animated and engaging. Testimonials of that experience abound. After two years of dull, required courses, Henry Fairchild Osborn recalled, "we burst into the new thought and vision of our junior year, under James McCosh in philosophy and Cyrus F. Brackett in physics." He recalls of McCosh: "The lectures were delivered with utmost clearness and were illuminated year by year with beautiful illustrations; the whole history of the science of the soul was told, from its beginnings under the Greeks, and by the end of the year McCosh was securely enthroned as the master-mind of the College."[72] Many others experienced an intellectual awakening under McCosh's instruction, and of these several became the nucleus of a new generation of Princeton scholars. Academic reform at Princeton came first from the recruits that McCosh brought from outside; later it came from within.

This survey of Princeton academic life takes the McCosh period to about 1880, which, we shall see, was something of a watershed in McCosh's presidential career. The years were a minor triumph, denoted first by the extensive expansion and modernization of the curriculum and second by the improvement in the faculty. Compared to Harvard's offerings, Princeton's were few; but the program at Princeton was much better balanced, without being restrictive. McCosh's reports to the trustees revealed that students made chemistry, political science, modern languages, geography, and the history of philosophy their most frequent elective choices.[73] McCosh did try vigilantly to determine whether real learning was taking place at the college, and to this end he could be an active, even a meddling president. To one professor he sent a note saying that the professor's grades were too high; he suspected that others' exams were too easy. This was one price he had to pay for the

---

giate subject its first post-Calvinist content. For a thorough treatment of the moral philosophy tradition in the nineteenth century, see D. H. Meyer, *The Instructed Conscience: The Shaping of the American National Ethic* (Philadelphia, 1972).

[71] Quoted by Baldwin, *Between Two Wars*, 2:201.

[72] *Princeton '77*, pp. 39-40. A useful source on McCosh's treatment of the history of philosophy is Andrew F. West, "History of Philosophy from Notes Taken in the Lecture Room of James McCosh," Princeton University Archives.

[73] TM, November 9, 1882, November 8, 1883.

elective system, for, as he reported to the trustees, "idle and lazy students" fairly effectively sniff out the easy courses and flock to them. Consequently he held several discussions with the faculty to discuss the problem and to work for common standards.[74] McCosh furthermore knew that the life of the classroom must be engaging and interesting to the young scholars. He encouraged his faculty to employ the lecture method in combination with the recitation system. Again he outlined to the trustees that he and the faculty were trying to encourage solid thought and not mere "spouting." But these gains came slowly. He admitted in 1873 that "I am not satisfied with the results we have reached. The spirit of the College is far from being as literary or as scientific as it ought to be." Princeton in this respect clearly lagged behind European universities and behind other American institutions as well. But patience and perseverence seemed to bring rewards. Shortly thereafter he reported that "an inquiring and independent spirit of thought" was now taking hold among the upperclassmen.[75]

McCosh himself knew one reason for this change. The elective system might have been a friend to lazy students, but it was also a boon to the brightest. It enabled faculty members to branch out into their areas of interest and competence, and the excitement was evident in their instruction. With McCosh's full encouragement the best students now even worked with the professors on their research. Even if Princeton in 1880 had a faculty that could clearly be labeled good without being called outstanding, the improvements for the best students were electrifying. Osborn clearly spoke the mind of his classmates when he summarized the first two years of the curriculum; it was deliberately constructed, it seemed, "to smother any love of learning or any enthusiasm for the classics." It was drill, drill, drill in a relentless daily routine. Then came the electives. "Only in the beginning of the Junior year did we start to breathe the fresh air of modern science under Brackett and Guyot, of Philosophy under McCosh, of contemporary thought and politics under Atwater."[76] The more liberal atmosphere in other fields also produced rewards. Henry Van Dyke later described literary discovery at Princeton. "I can't remember just when I read 'Henry Esmond,' " he wrote; "perhaps it was about the beginning of the sophomore year." But at all events, "it was then that I ceased to love books as a boy and to love them as a man."[77] Woodrow Wilson

[74] TM, June 26, 1871, December 20, 1871.
[75] TM, December 17, 1873, June 22, 1874.   [76] *Princeton '77*, pp. 39, v.
[77] Tertius Van Dyke, *Henry Van Dyke: A Biography* (New York, 1935), p. 31.

discovered the thrill of history and commented in his journal after a long engagement with Macaulay: "If all history were written thus I would read little else."[78] But as several students remembered, it was McCosh himself who set the tone and intellectual atmosphere at Princeton. One recalled that because of McCosh's force as a teacher and power as a personality, the distinctive characteristic of Princeton college life was "the particular habit of philosophical inquiry . . . so apparent that it colors discussions over beer and even in tobacco smoke." Winthrop Daniels, reflecting, perhaps with an excess of stereotype on "Princeton Traditions," believed that whereas the Harvard man is likely to measure things by literary standards, at Princeton the philosophical temper was "pervasive and universal." "This," he added, "is one of our many inheritances from Dr. McCosh. So habituated to this habit of mind is the Princeton teacher, that he scarcely realizes the strength of this prevailing tendency."[79]

WHAT WAS OCCURRING at Princeton under McCosh in the 1870s also took place at many other American colleges. Indeed, the "emergence" of the American university in these years is a story told many times over, each time with a particular institutional color, but withal in a similar pattern. The breaking of the old rigid curriculum, the appearance of new, modern subjects, the rise of professional academics specialized in their training and dedicated to the advancement of knowledge through research, and the transformation of an institution reared under religious auspices into one denoted by a more distinctly secular character—all these signs marked this great period of transition in American higher learning. And with these changes there occurred a distinct change in academic leadership. Gradually there disappeared a major symbol of the old ways, the clerical president, who yielded, not yet to the businessman, but to the new academic statesman, who was very likely a leader in the new fields of learning. Charles William Eliot at Harvard, Andrew Dickson White at Cornell, Daniel Coit Gilman at Johns Hopkins, Arthur T. Hadley at Yale, Charles Van Hise at Wisconsin—these and others presided over institutions where discipline and piety gave way to all the various purposes that redefined the American college and university. To be sure, there were in-

---

[78] Arthur S. Link, ed., *The Papers of Woodrow Wilson* (Princeton, 1966-), 1:133, hereafter, *WWP*.

[79] Winthrop Daniels, "Princeton Traditions and Tendencies," *Critic*, October 24, 1896.

congruities and exceptions. William Rainey Harper, professor of Old Testament studies at Yale, moved west at the end of the century to preside over the gigantic educational enterprise that was the University of Chicago, a major symbol of the new ways. And what also are we to make of Princeton, where a man who began his career preaching the gospel in tent and barn in the Scottish Highlands took a venerable American college through the difficult path of modernization?

But perhaps this poses the question in the wrong terms. For only in a restricted sense did McCosh consider himself a modernizer. He believed that American colleges could learn much by the European example, and his own Scottish experience guided McCosh's curricular reforms at Princeton. But McCosh's memory was long, and he never forgot the worst abuses of Scottish university life. He remembered early friends who came with him to Glasgow, to cope by themselves amid the evils of the big industrial center. Their quick path into delinquency and dissipation was smoothed by the total neglect of the university's officials. McCosh, haunted by those memories, exercised a moral, *in loco parentis* vigilance at Princeton that recalled his life in the gospel ministry. But more than this, none can mistake the fact that something about McCosh clearly separated him from the new academic leadership. Essentially, that distinguishing factor is religion, and without some attention to McCosh's ideas and practices respecting it the whole meaning of his Princeton career is lost. For if on the one hand, the liberalization of Princeton reflects the long reach of the Scottish Enlightenment and the age of the Moderates, then the moral fervor, the prominent place of religion in the Princeton curriculum, and the energetic revivalistic and evangelical atmosphere of the campus, demonstrate the spirit of the Free Church of Scotland. Unquestionably, the latter emphasis is continuous with Princeton's own past, but the strange and often paradoxical combination of the old and new at Princeton really reflects the large thematic structure of McCosh's life and career. For once again we see McCosh trying to weave together the two major cultural forces in his life. As his version of the Scottish philosophy was shaped by the spirit of evangelical Protestantism, so would the Princeton he reformed perpetuate that influence. And much of Princeton's distinctive character derived from these peculiar ingredients.

Within the Princeton community McCosh clearly had the image of a liberal and reformer; to the American public he was the eloquent defender of the older ways. Well before the first debate with Eliot,

McCosh had become familiar as a spokesman for cautious change. But his views on religion in the colleges tempered even that image. Of course he was no reactionary on that matter. As he told a meeting of the Presbyterian Alliance, he assigned no specific role to churches in managing the institutional life of American colleges—in formulating criteria either for hiring teachers or for determining the intellectual life of the institutions. If religious leaders think they can preserve a Christian America by allowing only pious men to teach their children, they will as quickly undermine that ideal as any atheist. Students will quickly notice the mediocre quality of instruction and will go elsewhere for their education. The main task for American colleges, then, is the training of Christian men who are full scholars in their professional disciplines. In the face of new secular state universities, McCosh said, the worst defense is the already overused American habit of setting up rival denominational colleges. "I tell you," he said, "unless they get teachers in these [colleges] equal in ability and scholarship to those in our great Universities, our eager, able, and ambitious young men will . . . flock to the Secular Colleges." Here precisely McCosh broke from the European models he was otherwise anxious to emulate. State education was, in its moral and religious aspects, disastrous. McCosh held a prejudiced and exaggerated view of the new state schools, scarcely a threat to religion if one observed them closely in the 1870s, and feared that America might go the way of Europe should her sectarian schools lose out in the race for academic achievement. Intellectual distinction, then, was the sine qua non for a school such as Princeton that would safeguard its own religious past.[80] Such a view of the matter enabled McCosh to work energetically for both traditions of his own Scottish inheritance.

On behalf of a definite place for religion in the college McCosh was willing to make a large public plea. McCosh had concluded his first debate with Eliot by issuing a challenge to another; this one would confront the great issue of religion. And Eliot again was the logical and strategic choice. He had been outspoken on this

---

[80] James McCosh, "The Place of Religion in Colleges," *Minutes and Proceedings of the Third General Council of the Alliance of the Reformed Churches Holding the Presbyterian System* (Belfast, 1884), 466-69. McCosh had also pointed out emphatically to the Princeton trustees: "Everyone who has studied the subject is aware that it is intellectual life in the instructor which is the main source of drawing students to a college. When we have thus gathered students to our College, we must seek to bring them under religious and moral influences, and pray for the blessings of God upon them." TM, November 9, 1876.

subject and highly critical of religious influences in education, remarking at one point that a "really learned minister is almost as rare as a logical sermon."[81] Eliot, though, was not unfriendly toward religion and somewhat ambivalent about its place in colleges. A Unitarian, he held latitudinarian religious views that incorporated modern science in an enlarged spiritual sense of God. He could even agree with McCosh that no real conflict exists between science and religion, that the bitter warfare between them was injurious to the best interests of both. Eliot, further, as much interested in morality as McCosh, frankly admitted that he did not know how one could teach morality apart from religion.[82] But, as in all academic matters, the issue must be decided by the "system of liberty." Consequently, Eliot ended required religious instruction and compulsory chapel attendance at Harvard. McCosh, on hearing that news, was outraged. Here, he exclaimed, began the new "battle of the age," and to the Princeton trustees he reported: "I mean not only to defend, but to fight, for what I believe to be a fundamental principle with this College, that religion is not to be abolished in College teaching."[83] So he engaged Eliot once more. The Nineteenth Century Club again played host, and on a cold February night in 1886 the two combatants went to New York City and locked horns once more.

McCosh used the New York City forum to speak to the larger purposes of college education. Essentially, he said, the colleges exist to secure learning, both the old and the new. McCosh then spoke of the role of Christianity in shaping the Western tradition, of those who drew directly and indirectly from Scripture—Dante, Shakespeare, Milton, and great moral philosophers. Religion had been the great promoter of the arts; it was, he believed, the sense of personal responsibility to God and the awareness of an immortal soul that generated artistic inspiration over the many centuries. Western civilization, McCosh said, was the fruit and gift of a people that had been Christianized.[84] With these views Eliot could concur, but McCosh insisted that the passing on of these acquisitions could not be effected apart from the religion that nourished them. For McCosh, the two must be preserved intact. "Withdraw Christi-

---

[81] Hugh Hawkins, *Between Harvard and America: The Educational Leadership of Charles W. Eliot* (New York, 1972), p. 123.

[82] Ibid., p. 125.

[83] TM. February 12, 1885.

[84] James McCosh, *Religion in a College: What Place It Should Have: Being An Examination of President Eliot's Paper* . . . (New York, 1886), pp. 9-12.

anity from our colleges," he warned, "and we have taken away one of the vital forces which have given life and body to our higher education."[85] Furthermore, he added, the new physical and social sciences, which have a legitimate place in the colleges, insufficiently answer the needs of young men. Colleges must assist students in the quest for life's meaning and for moral imperatives. They can do the most good if they speak to the needs of the heart as well as the mind. And religion alone can sound the depths of the heart.[86]

McCosh did not supply elaborate details about religion in college in his debate with Eliot, but his work at Princeton wholly clarified his intentions. Students at Princeton were required to attend chapel twice daily (although McCosh himself later induced the faculty to suspend the evening prayers), to attend campus or town religious services on Sunday morning, and to take biblical instruction Sunday afternoon. The last requirement McCosh initiated his first year at Princeton when he found students napping through Sunday afternoon Bible reading sessions. He himself would now institute a series of lectures on the life of Christ, and students would face examinations on their content. Furthermore, McCosh taught formal classes on the Bible to Princeton students for eight years, begging to be relieved of the assignment in 1876 because of the other overwhelming burdens of his office.[87] But it was an assignment that he gladly bore while he could, and one facet of his administration marked by a distinctly envangelical emphasis. For McCosh demanded no simple courses in theology or religious philosophy. These courses did not meet the needs of the true religious purpose of the institution. "I speak of *Biblical instruction*," he told the trustees, "for I believe that what the students require are not courses of theological lectures, or general religious teaching, but instruction that brings them into immediate contact with the living Word." Here was one note of style reminiscent of the Free Church gospel minister. McCosh indicated another when he boasted unashamedly that "no student passes through our College without his being addressed from time to time, in the most loving manner, as to the state of his soul."[88]

To a very large degree, then, it was a difference of style that distinguished the evangelical McCosh from the new generation of academic leadership. Style mostly, but in some cases ideology too.

[85] Ibid., p. 12.
[86] Ibid., pp. 15-16.
[87] TM, December 17, 1868; McCosh, "The Place of Religion," 468.
[88] TM, June 26, 1876; McCosh, "The Place of Religion," 468.

At Harvard, for example, the "system of liberty" registered Eliot's faith in a kind of Spencerian laissez-faire that allowed students to learn from their mistakes. If, as once happened, a student chose to spend the semester sunning himself in Jamaica, thus availing himself of Harvard's abandoning of required attendance, then so much the worse for him. He would regret the indiscretion sooner or later and profit by it eventually. But McCosh could exercise no such indifference. He watched the moral life of his students with a preacher's vigilance. He would even bring detected evils to the attention of the trustees. There was too much "idling" among the students, he found. And thus he reported, with due exaggeration, that "our greatest evil lies in bands of students collecting in each other's rooms and idling their time."[89] We shall see presently McCosh's extensive crusade to rid the campus of such evils, but in fact the struggle with the forces of darkness off the campus was nearly as troublesome.

For as long as he could remember McCosh had seen life as a righteous struggle against the menacing nemesis of moral evils. That struggle had propelled McCosh into the gospel ministry, but he kept up the good fight during his academic years in Belfast also. And surely McCosh, this man with so strong a sense of human sin, could not have been surprised to find the presence of saloons even here in "country" Princeton. He was not surprised, but vexed and troubled nonetheless. He reported as early as 1870 that he had unearthed several cases of Princeton students drinking in town. His initial action was to rally student moral sentiment behind him, first by having each student sign a pledge not to take intoxicating beverages during his college years, then, a few years later, by organizing a mass meeting of the students. Here McCosh formed student groups that would seek out the local sellers and bring legal action against them.[90] This legal campaign, indeed, was one of McCosh's great efforts. First by letters to local papers, then by personal visits to the state legislature and the governor, McCosh succeeded in securing a tougher antiliquor law in New Jersey. He then addressed the problem of enforcing it, and apparently induced some of his faculty members to run in the local elections for this purpose, though they failed to win.[91]

But McCosh saw at least partial success in this and other efforts. An ominous sign in Princeton was the appearance of "some loose

[89] TM, June 24, 1872.
[90] TM, June 27, 1870, December 17, 1873.
[91] See TM, December 17, 1874, June 28, 1875, December 16, 1874.

young women" running around town and "waylaying our young men."[92] And when McCosh learned that young Princetonians had discovered the delights of a billiard hall recently licensed by the town, he decided to fight fire with fire. He went to a wealthy benefactor of the college and persuaded him to purchase three billiard tables and place them in the gymnasium for the students to use there.[93] Life may be a righteous struggle against evil, but compromise is no small virtue.

In these activities McCosh revealed an important aspect of the evangelical mind, both in Scotland and the United States. But another ingredient needed to be added. For the great reforming medium of the Evangelicals was the revival. With the emphasis on personal conversion through voluntary acceptance of Christ, the revival could be either a massive frontier camp meeting with thousands of people assembled, or a quiet gathering of students in a college dormitory. The revival was an energizing event, designed to convert the stubborn heart of the sinner or renew the spiritual life of the saved. At any rate, McCosh put a lot of stock in it. No one who patiently reads his reports to the trustees can fail to detect that fact. Thus, in 1870 he proclaimed that "by far the most important occurrence that has taken place in our College . . . is a blessed revival of religion among the students." Or three years later: "Every few weeks we hear of this student or that student publicly consecrating himself to Christ." McCosh added that he tried to provide the spark for revivals by inviting "popular preachers" to the campus. And the surest sign that things were not going well on campus was a decline of religious fervor. It did not suffice that most of the students described themselves as "professors of religion," for McCosh wanted signs of genuine religious quality.[94] Nor can it be said that McCosh's words were mere pap for a religious minded board of trustees. One increasingly perceives that McCosh was dedicated to the evangelical style and encouraged it openly. In a private letter of 1880 he wrote to a student studying in Europe: "Thank God there is a deep religious thought and feeling in the College at this moment. Fully one half of the students are praying earnestly."[95]

Princeton had several revivals during the McCosh years, as it had had many times before. They occurred about once every two or three years. But probably in all of Princeton's history there was

[92] TM, June 26, 1871.
[93] TM, December 16, 1874.
[94] TM, June 27, 1870, June 23, 1873, June 28, 1875.

nothing quite like the revival of 1876. It took place over a period of about three weeks in February. McCosh was not quite certain how exactly it began, but an outside source attributed it to the defeat of the secret societies after an exhausting campaign by McCosh that had rallied many students to his side. It emerged quietly and was mostly so throughout. Meetings of the campus Philadelphian Society swelled; student religious leaders worked earnestly to win personal conversions; prayer sessions in the students' rooms went on into the late night and early morning. The aura of these events was unmistakably evangelical. "What can I do to be saved?" several students asked, and heard the refrain, "Come to Jesus." McCosh gave his personal blessings to the revival in two ways. First, he brought to the Princeton campus none other than Dwight Lyman Moody and Ira Sankey, certainly the most famous revivalist team in the world. The two held services in the Second Presbyterian Church in Princeton on a Saturday evening and Sunday afternoon. Moody was electrifying, preaching a sermon on regeneration before the many students in the church. Several of them made professions of religion, and, the *Observer* reported, "the impression was so decisive that one hundred arose to ask for prayers." Further, McCosh himself presided at a large ceremony of the Lord's Supper, offering the sacrament to any professing Protestant. He even made special arrangements with the First Presbyterian Church for confirmation of those not heretofore members of a church, among them a Japanese student whom McCosh baptized. About 260 students, McCosh reported, communicated. (The fact that Episcopal students abstained further indicates the intensely evangelical character of the revival.) For McCosh it was a significant, most memorable event. "The scene of that Sabbath," he testified, "was one of the most solemn, tender, and impressive scenes I have ever witnessed."[96]

The evangelical ways carried over into another habit of the president. For McCosh dealt with delinquent students in the same manner he dealt with the wayward souls of his old congregations in Arbroath and Brechin—by personal examination. "Cross-examine him and endeavor to make him tell the truth," McCosh described it. In this way he renewed the old method of sounding the depths of the sinner's heart, exploring the inward state of his spiritual condition. Sometimes McCosh made the event a personal

[95] To William Berryman Scott, March 15, 1883, in the McCosh Correspondence.
[96] *New York Observer*, February 10, 1876; *Princeton Book*, pp. 222-23; TM, June 26, 1876 (the McCosh quotation).

Academic Reformer 257

challenge. He knew that a guilty party sat before him, and he would make him confess. He recounted this case of a student he suspected of drinking: "I catechized him for two or three hours, and he parried me off. But I persevered and at last he broke down." Only once, as of 1882, had he encountered a student who proved unassailable.[97]

As Princeton moved in the two directions of academic reform and religious rekindling under McCosh, it emerged as the institutional leader of the collegiate religious movement of the late nineteenth century. The agency of this movement was the Philadelphian Society, a Princeton organization since 1814. It had languished by mid-century, began to recover after a revival in 1870, and blossomed during the revival of 1876. During that event emissaries from Princeton went out to other eastern colleges and endeavored to ignite religious fires there by prayer meetings and discussion sessions. At the same time the Philadelphian Society joined directly with the Young Men's Christian Association of America just when the latter was beginning to look at the nation's campuses as a new arena of activity. Luther Wishard, a member of the Princeton class of 1877 and president of the Philadelphian, also founded the student department of the YMCA, a department he supervised for many years. He immediately sent out letters to two hundred colleges and by 1891 had organized more than three hundred campus organizations with twenty-two thousand members. McCosh encouraged the effort and secured from Hamilton Murray, of the class of 1872, a gift of $20,000 for a new building for the Philadelphian Society, Murray Hall. Of the college movement sparked by the Princetonians, Dwight Lyman Moody is said to have remarked that it was "the greatest Christian movement of the century." Whatever validity that statement may have, it is surely no wonder that a Columbia University student newspaper referred to Princeton in 1881 as a country college "run on the muscular Christianity plan."[98]

McCosh, in fact, would have run much of the country on that plan. But he was little inclined to speak out on the major political

---

[97] TM, June 19, 1882.
[98] *Princeton Book*, pp. 213-14, 220-24; C. Howard Hopkins, *History of the Y.M.C.A. in North America* (New York, 1951), pp. 275-82; *Daily Princetonian*, April 8, 1881 (quoting the *Columbiad*). Probably it is no wonder too that Princeton, despite a decline in the portion of its graduates who entered the ministry during the McCosh years, had, nonetheless, a higher proportion than both the older eastern schools and the new state universities. See Baily B. Burritt, "Professional Distribution of College and University Graduates," *U. S. Bureau of Education Bulletin*, 19 (1912).

and social issues of the day. The Bible, he believed, was not a blueprint for the political reconstruction of this world and its social arrangements, and ministers should guard their words in trying to deal with these. On the other hand, McCosh was not entirely reticent, and when he addressed public matters his evangelical background again became evident. That background had involved McCosh and the Free Church party in Scotland in a campaign against the religious and social character of affluence. Their main allies were the middle and lower middle classes of the country, and their great hopes were the uplifting of the poor and destitute. Ultimately they looked to a great national church that would unite all classes. And McCosh, when he began his American tour in 1866, expected democratic America to furnish an example of such social amalgamation in its various churches. But, as McCosh once explained, many times on his tour he visited American churches incognito and discovered the most segregated institutions he had seen anywhere. For the nation that had broken down class barriers in its political system had reinstituted them in its religious life. "It is certain," McCosh wrote, "that as a rule the working classes [here] do not join the Churches so heartily as in Great Britain and Ireland, with the middle and upper classes in public worship." He wanted no return to the state church model, but did believe that in old and aristocratic Europe those churches were more socially democratic than in the United States.[99] On another occasion, McCosh was invited with other well known American religious leaders to contribute to a volume of essays on the labor problem. Here too McCosh abstained from economic and political analysis. He did believe, however, that the churches could be mediators in the struggle between capital and labor. The churches had a special mission to serve the working classes, and McCosh urged renewal of pastoral visitation of the kind he had perfected in rural Scotland and industrial Belfast. "You who sit in these cushioned pews put money in the plate to send the gospel to Timbuctoo. Do you send it to that man who sits next door to you and combs your horse and works your garden?"[100]

McCosh resolved to take some positive measures on this problem within the Presbyterian Church in the United States. A few years' experience in America led him to the distressing conclusion that

---

[99] McCosh, "Religious and Social Condition of the United States," 148; idem, "Relation of the Church to the Capital and Labor Question," in *Problems of American Civilization* (New York, 1888), p. 114.

[100] McCosh, "Capital and Labor," pp. 115-16.

Academic Reformer

inequality of wealth among the various Presbyterian congregations was a dangerous situation. Poor churches could barely support their ministers in a decent manner, while the wealthier ones supported theirs in regal splendor. McCosh first presented the problem at a large meeting of Presbyterian officials in New York City, using, as he did in his campaign against drink in Brechin, a vast array of statistics. Many well educated Presbyterian ministers, he showed, were forced, for want of an adequate salary, to take on extra jobs to support their families. So here, and formally at the national meeting of the General Assembly, McCosh introduced his Sustentation Plan to distribute wealth among the Presbyterian churches. The plan, interestingly, built directly on the model of Thomas Chalmers in the Free Church. Its objective was a minimum salary of $1,000 for each minister, with each poor congregation paying at least a minimum and the rest drawn from a pool of funds contributed by the wealthier churches. Year after year McCosh campaigned for this proposal, writing letters and speaking wherever he thought it would do good. But even though the Sustentation Plan had the approval of the General Assembly, it suffered from private indifference. It simply did not get off the ground.[101]

How did these ideas affect the kind of Princeton McCosh wanted to build? Clearly McCosh desired an institution serving the national interest and all classes in the nation. In fact, it is no exaggeration to say that he lived in fear that Princeton might become a "rich boys' school," or even be known as such. Thus, in his second year, he reported with great pleasure on the students in the first class of his administration, that "they belong to all classes of society, rich and poor."[102] But by the middle of his years at Princeton he could not be so sanguine. He reported to the trustees in 1879 that fully one-third of the new students were Episcopalian, worried not so much that Princeton was losing its Presbyterian identity as that the Episcopalian element represented a large sample of wealthy students.[103] McCosh, in fact, had been watching the trend for several years. He was further disturbed that the poorer students had a rough time at Princeton. There was insufficient campus housing, and many went into cheap boardinghouses in town, living, McCosh himself discovered, in near squalor. In 1877 he therefore organized among the trustees a Special Committee on Indigent Students to examine the needs of that group and determine how

---

[101] *New York Observer*, January 11, 1872, March 28, 1872.
[102] TM, December 22, 1869.   [103] TM, November 13, 1879.

Princeton might better serve them. McCosh's own idea called for a "new and plain" dormitory for "our struggling students." It would provide modest, but adequate and inexpensive rooms for the poorer students. That was a genuine obligation of the school, McCosh believed, but he was not indifferent to its indirect benefits. He considered it the best public advertisement to deter the growing image of Princeton as a college for the sons of the well-to-do. By 1880 the new edifice was under construction. McCosh was immensely pleased by the event, and further heartened that it was to be named Jonathan Edwards Hall. Edwards, McCosh believed, was "the greatest intellect that America has produced," and he expressed his desire to be buried next to the great revivalist theologian.[104]

FINALLY, in this chapter, let us have a look at the "Princeton family." What was life at Princeton like during the McCosh years? And what kind of a person was the man who headed the college for twenty years? How did students and others remember him? How did he help give Princeton its particular institutional identity?

McCosh, like nearly all of his counterparts in American higher education, encountered a host of problems, and not the least of these was student disorder. In fact, it is quite clear that Princeton had as large a share of that evil as any other college in America. Jonathan Baldwin Turner of Illinois, one of the leaders of the state university movement, once envisioned a newspaper whose first issue would ask its readers to imagine that during the last week a certain number of fires, murders, epidemics, and other such events had taken place. His paper would ignore all these routine affairs and concentrate on the real news of the period, the spiritual progress of the human race. Certainly anyone who has read even a half-dozen college and university histories would wish that all the recurring facts that document student rebellion could be similarly dismissed. They are always there; merely ask the reader to "imagine" them and then get on to more important items. So it is with McCosh's reports at Princeton and, even more so, with the minutes of the faculty meetings. That group in fact met about three times

---

[104] TM, November 8, 1877, February 13, 1879, February 12, 1880, June 16, 1879; McCosh, "The Place of Religion," 470. McCosh's concern was further reflected in a letter he wrote to Robert Bonner. He thanked him for a $1,000 gift to aid poor students, and commented: "Several of them I learned had been obliged to leave their boarding clubs as not able to pay, and were trying to sustain themselves on wretched food in their rooms." September 27, 1870, in the McCosh Correspondence.

a week in the McCosh years, and the business it confronted was almost entirely dedicated to student misdemeanors. Constantly McCosh recounted to the trustees cases of students gambling, drinking, fomenting evil through the secret societies, or sneaking off campus over to Trenton, the "graveyard of purity," as he called it.[105] McCosh, we have seen, fought these evils with every ounce of his energy. He demanded that the faculty be watchdogs of student behavior, and Professor Scott, for one, became "utterly disgusted" with the assignment, "the dirty work," of taking attendance at chapel.[106] McCosh participated in an intercollegiate network of communication, by which one college would inform another whether a transfer student had participated in a campus rebellion.[107] He even tried to influence the issue by calculating a student's academic rank in combination with his moral record; offenders would lose points.[108]

A few things need to be said about McCosh's handling of these unpleasant facts. First, he did worry, and with good reason, about Princeton's reputation. The fact is, Princeton had a bad press. The New York papers habitually described in detail every incident of campus violence or disorder. Reports on hazing appeared in all their very gory details. These were Princeton realities, although McCosh believed, with some truth, that they were overplayed by the press. But reports of a shooting in 1877 clearly did the college no good. McCosh tried to rally the alumni to use their influence in local places to discount the "wild tales" that circulated about Princeton, but when he read that one account even reached the London *Times* he was thoroughly discouraged. The worst student offenders were handed directly over to him, and, apparently, what he said to each person had a distinct pattern: "You've disgraced yourself, sir; you've disgraced your family; you've disgraced your college; and tomorrow it will be in all the New York papers and the next day in the Philadelphia papers."[109]

The roots of college disorder in late nineteenth-century America

---

[105] TM, June 28, 1869, and nearly any other date in the trustees' minutes; Henry Wilkinson Bragdon, *Woodrow Wilson: The Academic Years* (Cambridge, Mass., 1967), pp. 16-17. On Turner, see Winton U. Solberg, *The University of Illinois, 1867-1894: An Intellectual and Cultural History* (Urbana, 1968), p. 41.

[106] Scott, *Some Memories*, p. 136.

[107] "Faculty Minutes" (of the College of New Jersey), Princeton University Archives, April 15, 1884.

[108] Faculty Minutes, December 17, 1884.

[109] TM, June 18, 1878; *Princeton '77*, pp. 32-33 (the quotation).

still defy analysis. Clearly the disorders declined when college athletics rose and provided a new outlet for student energy. And so also did revivals wane then. In fact, the key to the periodization of campus rebellion until this later period is probably the pattern of revivals. At any rate, McCosh confidently believed that religious revivals were the only guarantee against outbreaks of disorder. Almost invariably, when McCosh reported major disorder, he regretted to say that he could not cite any incidents of revivals on the campus. But McCosh seriously misjudged the whole phenomenon of student disorder, despite his genuine encouragement of athletic programs. For it seems clear that rebellion flourished as a by-product of student boredom, especially with the dull academic routine. This, of course, is not a complete explanation; much of the behavior was quite thoroughly institutionalized in the form of class rivalry. But it is significant that in 1879, when McCosh reported on new course introductions, new scientific equipment in use, and improvements in the library, he also reported on the "quietest" year he had yet seen at Princeton. Perhaps the solution to the biggest headache of his tenure at Princeton was staring him in the face all along.[110]

From some students' point of view one of the big headaches at Princeton was the program in religion. McCosh swept many into the evangelical tide, but even the most enthusiastic agreed that the routine was just too heavy. "Religion was drilled into us," they recalled, and the whole week culminated in the dreaded three o'clock chapel session with McCosh on Sunday afternoon, "the drowsiest hour of the week." Students often stamped their feet, snickered, and snored. Some employed whatever ingenious device they could conceive to exempt themselves from morning chapel. And the most clever even used their "conversions" during a revival to claim they had no interest in the "ordinary means of grace" and begged to be excused from chapel on those grounds. McCosh observed this ploy apparently without detecting the deception.[111]

But this issue was a mere ripple compared to that involving the secret societies. McCosh hated them. These organizations were on the campus when he arrived, but grew in the next few years. They had tentacles that reached down into the high schools from which Princeton drew students and out into the alumni. Sons of wealthy benefactors and trustees were members of them. So when McCosh

[110] TM, June 16, 1879.
[111] *Princeton '77*, pp. v, 15-16; TM, June 18, 1877.

took an uncompromising stand against them he made enemies. Opposition became so bitter, and at one point seemed so insurmountable that, McCosh said, he nearly resigned in the face of it. But, resolving not to be undone, he "bore from within." He used every means he could to find out about the societies. He wrung confessions of membership from the students; he used the religious course he taught to moralize against the societies and to wean students away from them; he circulated the worst reports about them, and one can hardly tell fact from fiction in the accounts. One of the societies, he contended, met secretly to read Tom Paine and "other atheistical works"; others brought in playing cards and drinks. One society was known as the SLP—the Society of Love and Pleasure, a name guaranteed to scare any Evangelical. Gradually, McCosh involved the faculty in his campaign. Over the summer of 1875 it worked to get all the information it could about the groups, then pooled its data, and in the fall brought the exposed student members by groups before the faculty meetings. They were formally dismissed from the college, but allowed to petition for readmittance on an individual basis. Then, that same fall, McCosh levied his notorious anti-secret-society pledge. This unequivocal pledge, exempting only membership in the Whig and Clio literary societies, which McCosh also induced to expel members of the underground groups, was now forced on every member of the college and would be required for years to come of every student entering Princeton.[112]

In the end McCosh won. He won because his heavy-handed methods took their toll, but also because he did win the respect and moral support of the students. He could not have succeeded without that, and the victory was in part a personal triumph. By the 1880s the secret societies had virtually gone, and a new social Princeton, marked by the beginnings of the eating clubs, was emerging. McCosh claimed that the secret societies fostered habits of concealment and deceit, and he believed them unchristian in character. But he also insisted that they did much damage to the academic life of Princeton. He mentioned cases of students showing much scholarly promise who fell into decline after joining the organizations. And indeed this is important to bear in mind. McCosh won a reputation for belligerence as a result of the well-publicized campaign, but he had a point. The faculty minutes list the names

---

[112] TM, December 22, 1875; Faculty Minutes, November 15, 1875; *New York Observer*, December 2, 1875.

of students suspended for their secret society membership, and a glance at the academic standing of the 1876 seniors shows that the highest ranking of this element was no higher than seventy-first in a class of one hundred students. The remaining nine further testify that the apprehended delinquents represented the poorest stratum of academic achievement at Princeton.[113]

McCosh's hopes always lay with a more mature and more serious element of the student body. That he was able to enlarge this group over the years was also important for it was related to his best hopes for a renewed Princeton. One problem with Princeton students was familiar to McCosh from his own experience as an entering scholar in Glasgow; the boys were simply too young, many entering at fifteen. William Berryman Scott reflected on this fact later and said that his fellow students "brought to college a schoolboy habit of mind." They made suspicion and distrust of their teacher a matter of honor and wreaked vengeance on anyone who cultivated close relationships with the hated faculty.[114] That attitude carried to McCosh also and was compounded by the fact that many students were "desperately afraid" of him.[115] But feelings were mixed. To the more self-confident student, and to the more serious and ambitious, McCosh was an inspiring, even a lovable figure. He endeared himself both by his leadership and his idiosyncracies. Woodrow Wilson, a member of the illustrious class of 1879, said of McCosh, "He was a man you could laugh at every day, and yet never for a moment despise." Wilson, in fact, spoke for a group of students who wholly identified with the college and joined their own personal hopes for the future to its success and improved reputation. They followed closely and applauded vigorously McCosh's efforts to give it national renown. At home, they saluted McCosh's campaign against the students who threatened those efforts. Wilson was editor of the *Princetonian* and editorialized zealously to this end. He blasted the "ignorant rowdies and puerile idiots" responsible for the "wounded honor of the College" and believed that McCosh and the faculty had actually been too lenient with them. Wilson was an apostle of earnest endeavor, and like McCosh, inveighed against the levity and horseplay on campus. He condemned his own classmates for "disgraceful conduct" in Professor Guyot's classroom; their behavior was "ungentlemanly and unworthy of men." Princetonians should be serious, mature, and dedicated to work. Of all the college types, Wilson editorial-

[113] Faculty Minutes, June 15, 1876.
[114] *Princeton '77*, pp. 15-16.
[115] Ibid., pp. 21-22.

ized, "the most despicable is the habitual loafer."[116] And this kind of campaigning gradually achieved its purpose. By the end of McCosh's administration a more mature student body was evident, a group that took academic life seriously. To most of the Princeton students, all the conflicts notwithstanding, McCosh was something of a hero. When in 1888 McCosh was about to retire, the senior class petitioned the trustees to extend that date to the date of their graduation so that McCosh's signature might appear on their diplomas.[117]

When the Princeton class of 1877 held its fiftieth reunion it had a contest to see who could tell the best stories about McCosh. Memories of the old man, it seemed, lingered that long. Many of those stories, no doubt, recalled life in the classroom with the president-professor. McCosh was well over six feet tall and had long white sideburns that extended down half his face. Although badly bent at the shoulders, commentators kindly attributed the "scholarly stoop" to his academic habits and judged it all the more imposing for this reason. To friends, professors, and students he was a Scotsman through and through. Wilson recalled that McCosh's speech was "redolent with the flavor of the Scottish accent, that gave piquancy to everything he said. There was always some phrase or turn that seemed wholly his own."[118] And McCosh loved to recount incidents from his Scottish years. "I've drunk whiskey wi' men who've drunk whiskey wi' Bur-r-ns," he told. When the students feigned shock at such a revelation from this man of temperance, McCosh quickly disclaimed any real imbibing of the stuff. It was only a matter of passing the cup, just "here's to you and here's to you."[119]

Among themselves the students referred to McCosh as Old Jimmie, a term of affection for the most part, but it did not signify that all was always well between them. McCosh endured many a classroom ordeal with the students. One member of the class of 1872 recalled that "our class was unmanageable and Dr. McCosh could not preserve order to save his life." "The president would rave and shout, hammer the desk, until his knuckles were black and blue." Matters improved, however, and this commentator said that McCosh eventually had the best order on campus.[120] But he

---

[116] *WWP*, 1:336, 365; Bragdon, *Woodrow Wilson*, pp. 20, 37.
[117] *Princetonian*, March 16, 1888.
[118] Princeton '66, p. 309; *Brechin Almanac*, (1894), n. pag.; *WWP*, 17:330.
[119] Princeton '77, p. 34.
[120] Karl Kase, *History of the Class of '72 at Princeton* (Princeton, 1872), pp. 32-33.

was in fact impatient with the dullards in the class. Once in a religion course he asked a student, "What was the object of the Tower of Babel, sir?" To which the student replied, "To get out of the way of the flood." Small wonder he preferred the lecture system! At another time McCosh tried to catch a robin that had flown into the classroom, all the while lecturing the students on the prevailing sinful levity. "The divil is among ye," was a favorite expression. But the students learned to see through what Scott called the "big bow-wow" manner of McCosh. Andrew West remembered him as "a man of granite with a heart of a child."[121]

McCosh had a terrible time remembering names. Sometimes in class he would pick on someone whose name he could not recall or had even confused. Thus: "Mr. Libbey, I distinctly saw you laughing Sir!" When the real Libbey rose to defend himself McCosh interrupted his plea with the rejoinder, "Your apology is accepted, sir, sit down." When he met students outside of class, his memory failed him even more. But he would exclaim, "I know you, I know you. You belong to me College" (as if he could have belonged to Yale). Then he would ask, "What's your name?" or, possibly, "How's your father?" One story says that McCosh went through this routine with a graduate student, who replied, "My father's dead, sir." The president then gave an apology and condolences. But later in the same day he encountered the student again and once more asked, "How's your father?" To which the student replied, "My father is still dead, Dr. McCosh."[122]

McCosh's difficulty in adjusting to a new culture tripped him up on occasion and provoked considerable mirth. Apparently he was just not attuned to the new vocabulary of women's fashions when in a chapel talk he described the difference in temperament between Martha and Mary. He put great stress on his climactic remarks: "While Mary sat at the feet of our Lord," he said, "Martha walked around with a great bustle." The students immediately roared with laughter. McCosh, though, was oblivious to the why or wherefore of it, so repeated with a louder voice, "I say, Martha walked around with a great bustle." This time the laughter was louder than the first, and the bewildered McCosh terminated his talk in despair.[123]

McCosh was an impatient man, and anyone who tested him on this count met rough treatment. John Maclean, his predecessor, was still around Princeton and often led prayers in chapel services.

[121] *Princetonian*, November 10, 1882; Bragdon, *Woodrow Wilson*, p. 20.
[122] *Princeton '77*, p. 38. [123] Ibid.

But they were known to be tediously long. One day, however, he outdid himself by invoking divine blessing on the whole gamut of American authority, beginning with the president, and moving down to the Senate, the House, the governor, and the state legislature, then to the new president of Princeton, and the faculty. But he did not stop here. He went on to pray first for the seniors, then the juniors, finally the sophomores, and at last the freshmen. McCosh endured the ordeal as best he could, but was heard to say after the doxology, "Surely Dr. Maclean is in his dotage; he ought to have more sense than to pray for the Freshmen."[124] On another occasion, a library session to which special individuals and students were invited, McCosh became irritated at remarks made by two persons, one of them wrong, the other uninformed. To the first person he blurted out, "Silence! ye're na better than an atheist." And then to the other, "But that's better than a fule."[125] To one old professor, McCosh, caught in a mood of irritation, once said: "Ah, Dr. Miller, ye have a fine woman for a wife. She is a much better woman than ye are a mon." When these remarks came twice in the same day, Miller retorted that he could reply in kind.[126] And finally, there is posted in the Woodrow Wilson home in Washington, D.C., a letter from McCosh to young Wilson in 1877. The latter had written to the president asking for an autograph for his growing collection. McCosh's reply reads: "Life is too earnest a thing to be spent in gathering autographs from supposed eminent men, whom I have found to be no better than others, or from mediocre men like myself who should be allowed to do their duty without being troubled by foolish requests from persons who should be doing something better."[127]

The above disclaimer notwithstanding, McCosh had a notoriously large ego. He referred constantly to Princeton as "me College," and delighted to show visitors the campus, pointing to the new buildings and saying "I built that. It's mine." Students detected the obvious pride he took in the college: "Look at old Jimmy saying to himself, 'This is the great Babylon which I have builded.' "[128] McCosh, who won support from the students from his first day when he noted in his inaugural address the need for a new gymnasium, had worked to build up the athletic program at Princeton.

[124] Ibid. [125] Osgood, *Lights in Nassau Hall*, p. 25.
[126] Frederick N. Wilson, "Reminiscences," clipping from *News-Letter* (June 1929).
[127] The letter is in the room to the left of the entrance to the home and is dated April 8, 1877.
[128] *Newark Daily Advertiser*, November 19, 1894; *Princeton '77*, pp. 31-32.

The new gymnasium that he secured, and also the beginnings of intercollegiate athletics, had his blessings, though he lived to see abuses and fight against them. McCosh, who attended America's first intercollegiate football game between Princeton and Rutgers in 1869, delighted at Princeton's victories and grieved over its defeats. Indeed, it was a sad day when the Princetonians met defeat at the hands of Yale.[129]

McCosh's pride could be injured in other ways, too. Harvard was celebrating its 250th anniversary in 1886 and had invited academic dignitaries, including McCosh, to attend the festivities. Eliot handed out honorary degrees from Harvard to members of the schools represented, but bestowed no such honor on Princeton. Matters worsened when the aged Oliver Wendell Holmes read a poem containing a reference to Calvinistic Princeton. McCosh may have resented the reference to religious Princeton, or he may have concluded that he had tried for nearly two decades to give Princeton a progressive image only to find the ghost of Calvinism once more yoked with its name. Whatever the reason, he abruptly bolted the meeting, remembering only later that Harvard had been the first to recognize him with an honorary degree when he accepted the Princeton nomination.[130]

On another occasion, McCosh and Seth Low, president of Columbia, were attending the inaugural banquet for Ethelbert D. Warfield, a Princeton graduate, recently appointed president of Lafayette College. The two sat on either side of Warfield, who first called on McCosh for a speech. McCosh, true to form, used the occasion to sing the praises of Princeton and its progress under his direction. Low followed in a similar vein on behalf of Columbia, remarking at one point that Princeton sent its best students to Columbia for graduate degrees. At this point, McCosh leaned over to Warfield, whispered something in his ear, and departed. Later Warfield spoke and said on McCosh's behalf that he had had to catch a train but requested that Warfield confirm that what Low had said was true—Princeton made heads and occasionally sent them to Columbia to be fitted with hats.[131]

---

[129] McCosh even boasted that he had done as much for athletics as any college president, except President Stearns of Amherst; but at the end of his administration he was working closely with Eliot of Harvard to curb abuses. See "Eliot Papers," Harvard University Archives, letters from McCosh, December 7, 1886, January 12, 1887, January 15, 1887, and another, n.d.

[130] *New York Sun*, November 17, 1894.

[131] Wilson, "Reminiscences."

Most people remember McCosh for the colorful incidents that characterized his quick temper, immense pride and vanity, and occasional arrogance. But there was, as students knew, a gentle and tender side of the man, less memorable than its opposite, but which had a larger public display. One account refers to William Thaddeus Elsing. He was working in a type foundry in Chicago when he was caught up in the Moody revival movement there and vowed to become a minister. It took him four years to save money for college and to prepare for the Princeton entrance examinations. He arrived in Princeton one day with $15.25 in his pocket and went directly to McCosh's office to beg admittance. McCosh told him sympathetically that he had several "conditions" on his exams and did not qualify for entrance. But the young man replied: "I came to Princeton to go to College and I will sit on the doorstep here until you let me in." McCosh, moved by such resolution, melted. He took up the case himself and convoked a special meeting of some faculty members. Within the hour Elsing was fully registered. He became an outstanding student, was class orator, and won several academic prizes. Later he headed a missionary church in New York City.[132]

McCosh may have perpetuated stern puritanical habits from his Scottish preaching days, but Princeton flourished socially during his years there. The McCoshes annually entertained each of the undergraduate classes in turn, and a host of visitors, such as Matthew Arnold, as well. On these occasions McCosh survived while Isabella shone. The president yielded to his wife on all matters of social arrangements and decorum. He would greet the students at the door saying, "Glad to see you, sir; hope you're well, sir. There's Mrs. McCosh." The McCoshes provided lavishly for their guests, and McCosh kept busy at the entertainments by making sure that everyone had his fill to eat. Whenever he noticed someone unengaged he would direct him to the service table. One poor student, too shy to say that he had eaten already, was ushered seven times to the plates by the overcautious McCosh.[133] At least some of the students, however, had the pleasure of courting the youngest McCosh girl, Margaret, while "me son Andrew" was a prominent athlete at Princeton and an outstanding scholar. He went on to a highly distinguished medical career as a surgeon at the Presbyterian

---

[132] *Princeton '77*, pp. 19-20.
[133] William G. Sutpen, *History of the Class of '82 of Princeton College* (Princeton, n.d.).

Hospital and Columbia University Medical Center in New York City. He died in an accident in 1908 when he was thrown from a runaway carriage.[134] Tragedy continued to beset the family. The other son, Alexander Guthrie McCosh, had become a successful merchant but died at age thirty-one in 1881.

But through the good times and the bad it was the fiery and energetic Isabella McCosh who made things go, for the family and the college as well. No student went through four years of Princeton, it seemed, without the benefit of her kindness and professional care. Discovering that Princeton in 1868 had no infirmary or any formal means of medical service she became a one-woman nursing association, bringing to Princeton the skills learned under her illustrious father-physician. Each morning she received from the proctor's office a list of the sick or injured students, and then began the day's round of visits. Several students testified that she saved them from serious affliction or even death. The gentle knock on the door and the kindly "May I come in?" were always welcomed, and sometimes with a sense of relief, for there was also the chance that it might be the president coming to pray with the infirm student; and somehow that only compounded the infirmity. Surely the Isabella McCosh Infirmary at Princeton, with the striking picture of the tireless bearer of its name in the waiting room, is a fitting monument.[135]

And further on her behalf, it must be said that Isabella was the only one at Princeton who could handle McCosh. She would not be fooled. When McCosh stubbornly saw his way to a course of action, he fended off all compelling reasons against it by claiming, "It's the will of God." To which she replied, "Indeed, I'll be thinking it's the will of James McCosh." She knew his vanity and made sure it did not run away with him. Once, when McCosh was late in his years, the two were invited to a private viewing of a recently completed portrait of him. McCosh scoffed at the picture, saying "It makes me look as though I had no teeth." To this Isabella replied, "James, you hae non an' it's a fine picture."[136] But Mrs. McCosh played no favorites, and many others came to know her peppery tongue and quick wit. One story says that she and McCosh went to Princeton Junction to meet the train bringing Andrew Carnegie to the campus. Carnegie greeted the president, saying,

---

[134] *Princeton '77*, pp. 113-19.

[135] *Isabella Guthrie McCosh* (a pamphlet); Baldin, *Between Two Wars*, 1:21-22.

[136] Philip Ashton Rollins, "Reminiscences of Mrs. McCosh," an informal address, delivered in 1935, Princeton University Archives.

"Dr. McCosh, for a long time I've been much interested in Princeton." Isabella saved her husband the words. "Indeed, Mr. Carnegie, thus far we have seen no financial evidence of it." The noted philanthropist admitted it was a fair exchange, a case of Scot against Scot.[137]

And so it went. Princeton was indeed a lively place during the McCosh years. And for about the first decade of his administration McCosh enjoyed immense goodwill; indeed, he had almost everything his own way. The school prospered; new money came in; buildings rose annually; the academic life revived; and, it seemed, the old Presbyterian wars had been forgotten. But all the while ominous clouds were gathering. Year by year resentment was swelling against McCosh, and by the end of the 1870s he was about to face the severest challenge of his life. It would test all his sagacity and skill to survive it, but the effort probably showed McCosh at his very best. For he was now to learn, as many college presidents have learned, that to be an academic reformer he would also have to be an academic politician.

[137] The incident is related in the *Isabella Guthrie McCosh* pamphlet.

Chapter 8

ACADEMIC POLITICIAN

THE MAKING of the modern university was done neither by mirrors nor by the ideas of its visionary leaders. The university is an institution and is integrally related to the society in which it lives, defines its goals, and seeks to realize them. To be sure, the university has, and must have, its autonomous purposes, and it functions best when it enjoys the greatest liberty in using its own assets and resources. Yet it must be said that the United States' universities have had no easy time in defining their objectives and purposes. A certain "vagueness," to recall Daniel Boorstin's word, surrounds the great era of university building in late nineteenth-century America. Our universities were born of millionaires' money, the collected fortunes of men with no university training themselves. They were shaped by the aspirations of local communities, by young men's dreams of success, by the loyalties of alumni, by the moral, civic, and patriotic sentiments of a host of individuals. Somehow these resources had to be forged into a larger purpose, the business of advancing learning and training intellects. But collectively, as Boorstin notes, they gave "a peculiarly mercurial character to the problem of institutional self-definition."[1] And for any given institution, exactly how it interacted with these forces became a critical factor in its own quest for identity. This quest is the focus of this chapter. McCosh was able to realize many of his hopes for Princeton College because, by a program of skillful and energetic efforts, he was able to ally the college to several communities of interest that lay outside it. Princeton, in the McCosh years, involved itself with the external world to a degree unprecedented in its history. And by such involvement the parochial little school of the Presbyterians progressed almost year by year toward

[1] See Daniel J. Boorstin's essay, "Universities in the Republic of Letters," *Perspectives in American History*, 1 (1967), 369-79. I have made similar observations with respect to the midwestern state universities. See "Higher Education in the Midwest: Community and Culture," *History of Education Quarterly*, 14 (1974), 391-402. For a different emphasis, see Laurence Veysey, "Toward a New Direction in Educational History: Prospect and Retrospect," *History of Education Quarterly*, 9 (1969), 343-59.

an institution of national dimensions. Princeton's history then merged with that of other institutions and interests—business and financial groups, new elements in the Presbyterian community, high schools and preparatory schools, alumni, the publishing world, and new geographical interests related to all of these. James McCosh was the governing force in Princeton's new departure.

What occurred was a product of good planning, necessity, and serendipity. The basic theme was simple in outline: McCosh discovered, sometime around the beginning of his second decade at Princeton, that he could not achieve the educational reforms he envisioned by relying on forces within the Princeton community. With these he could go so far, and no further. Furthermore, McCosh was finding that substantial opposition had surfaced against him and threatened to undo the mild reforms he had effected. If he were not to abandon the path on which he had embarked, McCosh would need new political alliances, both within the college and without. And as he forged these new alliances, Princeton gradually acquired a new character, one that McCosh could never wholly have anticipated, and one that he did not wholly endorse. But the changes were emphatic, and they endured far beyond his lifetime.

In speaking of the several communities of interest that affected Princeton's history in the McCosh years, we must begin with the most immediate, the intellectual community. Princeton College, it was pointed out, had for most of the nineteenth century enjoyed a peculiar relationship to the Princeton Theological Seminary. That institution had been the major voice of Old School Presbyterianism and of the Reformed, or Calvinistic theology, for which it was known. Many members of the college faculty at the time of McCosh's arrival were graduates of the seminary, and at least four representatives of the seminary sat on the college's board of trustees, including the president of that body, Charles Hodge. McCosh, as we saw, had quickly broken the seminary's hold on the faculty by bringing in graduates of other institutions, and especially men with European training. But the forces that defended Old School Presbyterianism and clung to the standards of the old theology remained very powerful in the college. How long could they live in peace with McCosh, who, it became apparent, departed from their views on two critical matters? One, to be discussed later, was the issue of modifying the Westminster Confession, Calvinistic standard of Old School Presbyterianism. The other issue was evolution, and this was often a bitter dispute.

It is not certain to what extent McCosh's views on evolution were known in this country at the time of his appointment at Princeton. But he continued to elaborate them during his American years. He did so both in his religion and philosophy classes at Princeton, and in important lecture engagements around the country. McCosh urgently pursued a reconciliation of the evolutionary hypothesis with Christian theism and became known as the first prominent Protestant spokesman in America to do so.[2] He was also open and honest with the Princeton authorities about his intentions. "We cannot keep our students from reading the works of such men as Herbert Spencer, Darwin, Huxley, and Tyndall," he told the trustees. Let students read these authors under the corrective influence of Christian apologists rather than force the ideas out of the school where students will discover them on their own without that influence. McCosh reported that some students had been "shaken" by the new ideas, but he was always able to persuade them of a proper theistic interpretation. Many, as a result, became "more decided Christians than ever." So Princeton's policy would be clear: "We give to science the things that belong to science, to God the things that are God's." And McCosh's stance did become something of a cause célèbre at the college. Even the students knew that McCosh and several members of the faculty divided seriously on the issue, and one remembered his admonition to his rivals: "Ye'll not teach the young men that evolution is false; tomorrow ye may wake up and find that it is true."[3]

But while the Princeton community had a leading evolutionist in McCosh, it also had in Charles Hodge the most outspoken theological conservative. In the seventh year of McCosh's administration Hodge published his *What Is Darwinism?* To be sure, Hodge did not demand a literal reading of Genesis, and McCosh wholly shared his objections to evolutionary ideas in their manifestly naturalistic emphasis. To that extent, both were anti-Darwinians. But Hodge differed from McCosh in his refusal to accept the evidence of science, to which McCosh wholly deferred. Hodge

[2] McCosh's leadership in the reconciliation of Christianity and evolution is generally recognized by intellectual historians. See for example Paul F. Boller, Jr., *American Thought in Transition: The Impact of Evolutionary Naturalism, 1865-1900* (Chicago, 1969), pp. 29-31, and Cynthia Eagle Russett, *Darwin in America: The Intellectual Response, 1865-1912* (San Francisco, 1976), pp. 27-32.

[3] "Minutes of the College of New Jersey," June 22, 1874, hereafter, TM; McCosh baccalaureate, reported in the *New York Times*, June 18, 1888; Charles G. Osgood, *Lights in Nassau Hall: A Book of the Bicentennial: Princeton, 1746-1946* (Princeton, 1946), p. 29.

could believe that man might be as old as eight or ten thousand years, whereas biblicists calculated the generations from Adam back six thousand years. But incredible to Hodge was the speculation that the earth might be millions of years old. Genesis simply could not be stretched that much, even allowing for some liberal readings. Because the evolutionary theory pointed to minute changes that nonetheless effected great transformations of species, the extension of time, allowing patient nature to perform this work, had become a necessary proposition. Hodge blasted the whole notion: "Here is another demand on our credulity. . . . We have no faith in the chronology of science." To this Christian, in fact, the evolutionary case was damned on its "prima facie incredibility." "Who can believe that all the plants and animals that have ever existed upon the face of the earth, have evolved from one (little) germ?" But to Hodge the case was ultimately incredible because it refuted Scripture.[4]

Even among the Princeton seminarians, however, a moderate trend emerged. Archibald Alexander Hodge (1823-1886), son of Charles, had fewer difficulties in accepting the scientific evidence for evolution and used Hugh Miller to allow for a large symbolic reading of Genesis. Like McCosh, he believed that development was quite compatible with theistic design. But A. A. Hodge would not go to McCosh's length in allowing that man himself might be part of the scheme of organic evolution, a speculation he dismissed as a "mere dream of unsanctified reason, utterly unsupported by facts." Nonetheless, a liberal trend is apparent in the younger Hodge, and it assumes larger significance because of the possibility that McCosh himself was partly responsible for it.[5] Also, Benjamin B. Warfield, who entered Princeton with the first class under McCosh, later remembered McCosh as "distinctly the most inspiring force which came into my life during my college days." Warfield never wholly shared McCosh's ideas on evolution, later judging them to be too liberal, but he was clearly persuaded to an accommodationist stance by his teacher. And one study of the Princeton Seminary group indicates an important trend. Those

[4] Charles Hodge, *What Is Darwinism?* (New York, 1875), pp. 142-44; Daryl Freeman Johnson, "The Attitudes of the Princeton Theologians toward Darwinism and Evolution from 1859-1929" (Ph.D. dissertation, University of Iowa, Iowa City, 1969), 73-75, 92-95, 101. Hodge's book presents the Princeton Seminary position in its most extreme form. For a comprehensive view of science in Princeton theology, see Theodore Dwight Bozeman, *Protestants in an Age of Science: The Baconian Ideal and Antebellum Religious Thought* (Chapel Hill, 1977).

[5] Johnson, "Attitudes of Theologians," 128-30, 150, 169.

seminarians who came after Charles Hodge, "though loyal to his basic theological position, followed the lead of James McCosh."[6] Again Princeton College was creating a liberalizing influence in American Presbyterianism.

It is difficult to state exactly how this trend affected matters at the college. McCosh's views undoubtedly caused anxiety among creationists, but resentment might also have arisen over the liberalizing influence that McCosh was having among Presbyterians graduating from the college. On the Princeton faculty the leading McCosh critic was Thomas Duffield, hardened champion of the Old School ways. He too took painstaking efforts to spell out the case against evolution, a concept that he traced back to the "old Greek atheists." For Christians, he said, only one question counts: "Is evolution, as it respects man, consistent with the Bible?" Duffield believed that it was not. When God breathed into the dust and created the soul of man, he acted in a way that was wholly supernatural, and no germ theory of evolution could coexist with that fact. Duffield used other biblical "facts" for his case, but what one eventually senses in the Duffields and Hodges on the one hand, and McCosh on the other, is a difference of spirit. None could fault McCosh on his loyalty to Scripture, for which no amount of theological education could, in his view, substitute in Princeton's religious education program. But when Duffield warned that any questioning of the essential truth of Genesis would open up a whole Pandora's box of skepticism on other "truths" of religion, he revealed a fear that never troubled McCosh. Let science tell us what it knows, McCosh said, and surely Scripture will assist in a spiritual understanding of it.[7]

On his home grounds McCosh met the opposition of those who disavowed his liberalism, and whose mistrust brought all of McCosh's reforms under closest scrutiny. On both the faculty and the trustees, William Berryman Scott recalled, there were "extreme conservatives," whose watchword was "change is not reform." Moses Taylor Pyne remembered that some of the trustees "spent most of their time fighting Doctor McCosh," and another recalled that "they were so conservative that they wouldn't do anything in the way of innovation."[8] Both the faculty's and trustees' records

---

[6] Ibid., 189, 198, 248, 291.

[7] John T. Duffield, "Evolution Respecting Man and the Bible," *Princeton Review*, 1 (1878), 150-51, 160-61; see also Henry Fairchild Osborn, ed., *Fifty Years of Princeton '77: A Fifty-Four Year Record of Princeton College and University* (Princeton, 1927), p. 238, hereafter, *Princeton '77*.

[8] *Princeton '77*, pp. 26, 237-38, 328.

are disappointingly polite, and it is difficult to find the precise points of conflict. Much of it seemed to take the form of generalized grumbling or mere resentment at McCosh's alleged liberties respecting scriptural truth. That was the case, as Caspar Wistar Hodge explained in a letter to his brother Archibald Alexander Hodge, when he encountered George W. Musgrave, a clerical member of the trustees who was the last to serve as Moderator of the Old School General Assembly. "I met him in the street," Hodge wrote, "and he entered upon a vociferous denunciation of McCosh as an evolutionist—a sneaking heretic, whom he was ready to impeach and rejoicing at your coming to herd the lion in his den."[9] McCosh, though, was unswayed by these attacks; he persevered both at Princeton and around the country. The *Pittsburgh Commercial Gazette* reported on one of McCosh's many talks on this subject and quoted McCosh's messages to the American public:

Religious people are frightened unnecessarily at the idea of development, for the reason that radical evolutionists leave out God in accounting for evolution. . . . The idea exists that evolution is destined to overthrow religion. . . . I say, do not be captivated by theories, but accept the truths of science.

My first position is the certainty of evolution. Evolution is but the continuing of one thing out of another. No scientific man under 30 years of age in any country denies it, to my knowledge. To oppose it is to injure young men. I am at the head of a college where to declare against it would perplex my best students. They would ask me which to give up, science or the Bible.

Let me warn you, the defenders of religion should be cautious in assailing evolution. . . . The legitimate evolution supports Christianity.

But from outside of Princeton as well as from within, McCosh inspired wrathful reaction to his views. The Chicago *Inter-Ocean* accused McCosh of "galvinizing" around the country and making money from his evolutionary talk and defending ideas that are "false to all metaphysics and to all spiritualism [and to] all theism."[10]

---

[9] August 9, 1877 in the "Hodge Letters and Papers," Department of Rare Books and Special Collections, Princeton University Library. Hodge says, though, that after Musgrave actually read one of McCosh's papers on evolution he retracted some of his statements.

[10] The Chicago *Inter-Ocean* quotes the *Pittsburgh Commercial Gazette*, December 19, 1883.

But McCosh had his defenders as well as his detractors. At home, his brightest students, young men who themselves were soon to play significant roles in the college, found inspiration in his views. James Mark Baldwin (1861-1934), who added important interpretations to evolutionary thought, recalled his education under McCosh. "The principle of organic evolution . . . was welcomed by him and assimilated to the body of his thought at a time when American biologists themselves were divided into two camps. . . . This attitude of McCosh was the more remarkable, since Princeton was the citadel, in the Theological Seminary across the street, of a very intolerant dogmatic theology."[11] Henry Van Dyke, a member of the class of 1872 and later a major voice in the liberal Presbyterian movement, took heart from McCosh's philosophy and saw that a new apologetic might arise from the kind of reconciliation of evolution and theism received from McCosh.[12] Woodrow Wilson also followed the issue, first in McCosh's classroom, and then a few years later when his uncle, Rev. James Woodrow of Columbia Theological Seminary, met vehement opposition for his acceptance of evolution. Wilson wrote to his future wife: "If uncle J. is to be read out of the Seminary, Dr. McCosh ought to be driven out of the church, and all private members like myself ought to withdraw without waiting for the expulsion which should follow belief in evolution."[13] Furthermore, other noted persons had definite thanks to offer McCosh for his efforts. E. T. Williams, the missionary, described his own intellectual history, denoted by an early reaction against evolution: "It was some time before I could bring myself to entertain the possibility of its truth. That came in time, however, especially after Dr. McCosh, President of Princeton, accepted the theory and gave it a Christian interpretation."[14] And from the perspective of one who viewed the ages-long conflict of science and theology, Andrew Dickson White hailed McCosh as a "deus ex machina" who saved religion from a tragic alliance with antiscience hostility. "Whatever may be thought of his general system of philosophy," White wrote, "no one can deny his great service in neutralizing the teachings of his [Princeton] predecessors and colleagues—so dangerous to all that is essential in Christianity."

[11] James Mark Baldwin, *Between Two Wars, 1861-1921* . . . , 2 vols. (Boston, 1926), 1:21.

[12] Tertius Van Dyke, *Henry Van Dyke: A Biography* (New York, 1935), p. 37.

[13] Arthur S. Link, ed., *The Papers of Woodrow Wilson* (Princeton, 1966-), 3:217, hereafter, *WWP*.

[14] E. T. Williams, "Recollections," (Unpublished autobiography, E. T. Williams Papers, Bancroft Library, University of California, Berkeley), 50.

White agreed with McCosh that the most certain means of turning college men into unbelievers was to rail against the conclusions of science.[15]

The evolution controversy was important for the intellectual life of Princeton, but it had other consequences also. Although McCosh's relations with the seminary and its spokesmen were never so strained as some of the extreme remarks might suggest, it did become clear to McCosh, very soon in his administration, that the college, if it were to progress and attain a wider respect among the academic community in America, would need new support from without. Its long close intimacy with the seminary had now clearly become disadvantageous. And even though McCosh remained a loyal Presbyterian, active in the church and solicitous of its interests, he would not bind the college to its traditional Presbyterian ties. And in the late nineteenth century there was emerging in the United States a different kind of Presbyterian group, a new community of interest, that would serve McCosh's purposes very well indeed.

WHEN MCCOSH won the nomination of the trustees to the presidency of Princeton in 1868, he presented as credentials his background and experience with British universities and his scholarly efforts on behalf of a sound religious metaphysics. But probably few of the trustees recognized another asset that McCosh brought to Princeton. During his years in the pastoral ministry in Scotland, and in Ireland too, McCosh had learned and even perfected the skills of an organizer. The struggles of the Free Church of Scotland had tested these to the full, for McCosh had to be fund raiser, church builder, ambassador of goodwill, and politician all at once. It would require precisely the same talents to rebuild the institution he was now called upon to lead. McCosh proved to be one of the most energetic leaders in Princeton's history. Constantly he was on the road, to meet with New York businessmen, to visit Princeton alumni in Cincinnati, to plan for local examinations for Princeton applicants in Chicago. These new assignments he discharged at an exhausting pace, one that he began at Princeton when he came at the age of fifty-seven, and one that he maintained until he retired at the age of seventy-seven. The first positive results of these efforts came when McCosh turned to the world of American business.

The wealth of America was joined in a remarkable and significant

[15] Andrew Dickson White, *A History of the Warfare of Science with Theology in Christendom*, 2 vols. (New York, 1898), 1:80, 320.

way in the late nineteenth century to American higher education. Many of the new barons of American industry and finance gave their money and their names to the large educational enterprises born in the new era of the university. Thus Leland Stanford, Cornelius Vanderbilt, Benjamin Newton Duke, Jonas Clark, Johns Hopkins, Paul Tulane, and others translated their financial profits into the permanent legacies of libraries and classrooms. Curiously, these great benefactors were not themselves graduates of a college or university, and they articulated no grand philosophy of education to be enshrined by their munificence.[16] To be sure, higher education also advanced in these years in a more traditional manner—by the help of local communities. American boosterism had always been a factor in the proliferation of American colleges, and now it assumed a grander scale. In Chicago, commercial and financial leaders rallied to save John D. Rockefeller's designs for a great new university amid the failure of the American Baptist community to meet his goals; in Baltimore, businessmen saved the Johns Hopkins enterprise when the Baltimore and Ohio Railroad stock went sour; and at Harvard Charles Eliot struck important alliances with Boston's commercial leaders.[17] But how was Princeton to fit into these patterns? The college bore the name of no great benefactor. It had no great local supporters whose sentiments of affection could also mean dollars for construction. McCosh, it was clear, would have to build Princeton's own community of interest

Of course McCosh did not have to begin afresh with this enterprise. Princeton had always drawn upon loyal friends, connected both to the churches and to business, and upon loyal alumni as well. Nonetheless, the McCosh years do witness the beginning of a significant change in the pattern of Princeton's endowments. McCosh did not so much change this pattern as exploit it. As a general rule, although exceptions existed, Princeton's benefactors were successful businessmen. But they were businessmen who had some kind of church, and specifically Presbyterian, connections, and almost invariably a Scottish or Scotch-Irish background. In an earlier era, these individuals would have been men of prominent local stature, pillars of the community, so to speak, noted by their large influence and most likely by their contributions to the local church. But the benefactors of the later period headed enterprises of national and international dimension. They undoubtedly main-

[16] Merle Curti and Roderick Nash, *Philanthropy in the Shaping of American Higher Education* (New Brunswick, N.J., 1965), pp. 113-15.

[17] Ibid., pp. 118, 138.

tained local interests, but their immediate communities were the extensive networks of trade and marketing that tied them to the entire national economy. To that extent their careers extended their perspective beyond the local area, and their stewardship changed accordingly. These were men who thought in terms of a large national scale of activity and sought to make their influence work at that level. But they also wished to preserve traditional ties, to maintain communities of interest that had been important to their own families and history in America. Further, because many of these individuals were not themselves graduates of Princeton and were very much models of the revered self-made man in America, they looked for a general means of using their money on behalf of the enterprising young of the country. Such a combination of factors as these, it seems, turned the attention of these individuals to Princeton. Their support now went beyond the local Presbyterian church to a Presbyterian institution that aspired to national stature for itself. Both the college and the seminary, but the college increasingly, became the focal points of a new informal community of interest, the new caste of American wealth that shared a particular national heritage and a particular Protestant denominational affiliation. Princeton could fulfill this role because this body of businessmen had no institutional center; they were geographically diffuse. McCosh made contacts with them by trips to New York City, Philadelphia, and beyond, to places where he might spend a Friday afternoon at the office of a banker, Saturday night with an alumni club, and Sunday morning at a wealthy Presbyterian church. At each place the same appeal could elicit support for Princeton College.

Princeton received extensive new financial gifts from the very moment that McCosh's selection was made public. Exactly why this was so is not entirely clear, but a large portion of that money came from John Aikman Stewart (1822-1926). Stewart joined the board the very day that McCosh was chosen, and in fact the strongest support, probably even the suggestion to select McCosh, came from him. Stewart was a remarkable person. Born into a family of Scottish stock, Stewart at the age of nineteen outlined to John J. Astor, Peter Cooper, and other prominent New York businessmen his plans for a novel banking institution to deal in fiduciary capital. The organization became the United States Trust Company, a landmark in American financial history. Stewart was secretary of the organization until 1864, and its president from then until his retirement in 1902. He was also a renowned financial wizard, an adviser to American presidents from Lincoln to Coolidge. But he was a religious man also, "one of the oldest and most zealous promoters of the American Bible Society." He gave extensively to educational and religious organizations, and Princeton, where Stewart for twenty years was McCosh's financial confidant, received much of his generosity. Stewart died in 1926 at the age of 104.[18]

Another associate of the United States Trust Company was William Libbey, who had begun his association with Stewart in 1859 after much success in the international wool and silk trade. Libbey, whose son figured largely in McCosh's academic reforms at Princeton, was a member of the Fifth Avenue Presbyterian Church in New York and had been active in forming the YMCA. He too provided generously for Princeton College.[19]

John Cleve Green (1800-1875), Princeton's greatest benefactor, was another businessman who had only informal connections with the school. He was a descendant of Jonathan Dickinson, the first president of the College of New Jersey, and was born in Lawrenceville, New Jersey. He had an academic but no collegiate education, and at an early age entered a countinghouse in New York. Gradually he became involved in commercial ventures in South America and China. He rose to prominence in the firm of Russell and Company, "the most powerful house in the American China trade," and in 1839 returned from China with a very large fortune. Green was a devoted Presbyterian, and his nephew was William Henry Green, first selected, as was noted, to succeed Maclean. Green gave money to both the seminary and the college, and most important, provided the funds for the John C. Green School of Science. Both Princeton institutions were vehicles for Green's interest in religion joined to a national educational enterprise. Furthermore, the creation of the school of science at Princeton attested to the liberalizing effects of Green's kind of benefaction. He was prepared to let the president of the college handle the building of the college and was content simply to be a financial contributor to the cause. Thus as Jonathan Dickinson Hall, bearing the name of his ancestor, was under construction, Green wrote to McCosh: "I am desirous that the building should be completely furnished and equipped, that nothing should be omitted on economic grounds. . . . The expenses of every kind, on the building, the

---

[18] *New York Observer*, July 30, 1868; "Trustees Folders," Princeton University Archives; *Dictionary of American Biography*, 18:10-11, hereafter, *DAB*.

[19] Trustees Folders.

furniture and the equipment, and the regulation and the ornamentation of the ground, I am prepared to pay."[20]

Two important benefactors who came to Princeton after McCosh's arrival were Robert L. Stuart and Robert Bonner. Neither was an alumnus, and both demonstrated the Scotch-Irish connection from which the college benefited. Robert Stuart (1806-1882) was the eldest son of Kimloch Stuart, a native of Edinburgh who emigrated to the United States. He succeeded in the candy business, which was inherited by Robert and his brother Alexander. The R. L. & A. Stuart Company became known as the first successful refiner of sugar by steam and was immensely profitable. Robert Stuart was a staunch Presbyterian who helped erect the Fifth Avenue Presbyterian Church in New York, where he and his brother also contributed heavily to the Presbyterian Hospital. He acquired a considerable art collection and was president of the Museum of Natural History. His wife, who inherited his wealth, was also deeply religious. She refused to give money to the Metropolitan Museum of Art because it stayed open on Sunday. Then in 1880 she deeded $100,000 to Princeton College, with the proviso that the instruction at the college shall at no time "be at variance with the principles of the Christian religion or antagonistic to the leading doctrines and general beliefs of the Presbyterian Church of the United States." Neither the trustees nor McCosh batted an eye at accepting those terms.[21]

Robert Bonner (1824-1899), born near Londonderry, Ireland, emigrated to Hartford at fifteen and entered the printing office of the *Courant*. From a mastery of the typesetting art, he moved into reporting and was correspondent for several eastern papers. Eventually he became the publisher of the New York *Ledger*, a paper that spared no expense to mix sensationalism with quality contributions from such writers as Henry Ward Beecher, Charles Dickens, Horace Greeley, and others. He was president of the Scotch-Irish Society of New York City, and sensitive enough about his religious dedication to take the trouble to deny in his newspaper allegations that he had raced one of his beloved horses on the Sabbath.[22]

One could easily extend this list, but the details are unnecessary.

---

[20] *National Cyclopaedia of American Biography*, 11:336, hereafter, *NCAB*; *DAB*, 7:551; Green to McCosh, June 25, 1870, in the "Correspondence of James McCosh," Department of Rare Books and Special Collections, Princeton University Library.
[21] *NCAB*, 10:24; Curti and Nash, *Philanthropy*, p. 151; TM, November 11, 1880.
[22] *NCAB*, 10:298-99.

McCosh was significantly enlarging the Princeton family in ways that were most important to his program. In the first four years of his administration alone, Princeton received more than a million dollars in financial gifts. Within the next years McCosh had attracted a million and a half more. And in the process Princeton outwardly lost its provincial character. McCosh cultivated people with national financial connections and political connections, too. Increasingly, Princeton loomed larger in the public eye, and the *New York Observer* commented on the presence, at the 1871 Princeton commencement exercises, of the president of the United States, the secretary of war, the two New Jersey senators, and the governor of the state. At the trustees' dinner afterward McCosh and Grant were conspicuous, and the newspaper described the event as "a brilliant affair."[23] The Princeton campus, furthermore, was greatly transformed. A new gymnasium, new classrooms, a new chapel, and new dormitories appeared, and progress under McCosh, the *Observer* stated in 1875, was "almost incredible."[24] But McCosh also received some criticism for these developments. Too much, it was said, was going for bricks and mortar, and not enough for the strictly educational work of the college. McCosh himself acknowleged the general truth of these charges, although each year he had been able to report new scholarship grants from alumni groups, most of them earmarked for the new academic subjects McCosh was introducing into the curriculum. Nonetheless, in 1875 McCosh proposed to the trustees that all new money now be dedicated to academic prizes, scholarships, and encouragement for original research.[25] But there was more to this proposal than met the eye. McCosh was preparing to take the college in a major new direction, and he was playing academic politics to do so.

McCosh's desires to undo the provincial character of Princeton had led to his extensive efforts at faculty recruitment and the appearance at Princeton of a new faculty without prior ties to the college or seminary. McCosh had not broken the Presbyterian identity of the faculty, nor would he do so in the years ahead. But he did bring to Princeton academicians who had won advanced degrees at European universities and who introduced a measure of

---

[23] *New York Observer*, July 3, 1873, November 24, 1882, July 6, 1871.
[24] Ibid., June 25, 1875; Thomas Jefferson Wertenbaker, *Princeton, 1746-1896* (Princeton, 1946), pp. 294-98.
[25] *New York Observer*, September 30, 1875; James McCosh, "Dedication Address: The New Gymnasium," *Presbyterian*, January 22, 1870; TM, June 28, 1875.

professionalism to the Princeton staff. Now, however, at precisely the time when McCosh's honeymoon at Princeton came to an end, and the reaction against evolution and other liberal tendencies at the college set in against him, McCosh did an about-face. He executed a master stroke that was at once a reaction against his own earlier course and at the same time a measure that proved absolutely critical for his educational scheme. For McCosh was resolved to modernize Princeton, although he would modernize on his own terms. And the ends would legitimize the means. So a curious new pattern begins to appear at Princeton in 1881. For if we look at the appointments to the faculty that McCosh made at this time and in the years following, we notice a distinct return to a provincial faculty. Precisely ten of the nineteen new faculty members at the college from this year until the end of McCosh's administration were Princeton graduates. They were McCosh's own students. To McCosh, in fact, these were "me bright young men," of whom it is said McCosh boasted endlessly. On this group rested his hopes for the future of Princeton, the new academic Princeton that would win recognition from its scholarly achievements. But the academic dimensions blended with the political. McCosh could no longer count on the goodwill and automatic support of the trustees and the old faculty. In short, he needed new political allies, and he would pluck them directly from the ranks of his own students.[26]

McCosh marched along this new course in a cautious but deliberate manner. At the very beginning of his administration he had called for new funds for academic prizes and scholarships. Princeton did receive many new gifts of this kind, but, as we have seen, the building program gathered most of the new money. And from the beginning also McCosh called for scholarships to support postgraduate study. As approved by the faculty the new program required that recipients either remain at Princeton for one year after graduation for study in the department of their specialty, or go abroad for a year to study at a foreign university.[27] McCosh still believed that European universities surpassed American in their production of first-rate scholars and "profound scientific men," though he looked forward to the day when the best American students would no longer need to go abroad for this training. The United States was making progress in its efforts to equal the Eu-

[26] Data on the new Princeton faculty come from the *General Catalogue of Princeton University: 1746-1906* (Princeton, 1908).

[27] "Faculty Minutes" (of the College of New Jersey), Princeton University Archives, October 25, 1869.

ropean achievement, and McCosh hoped that Princeton would be among the leaders. But America still awaited its day of excellence, and until its arrival Princeton could do no better than to send its own best abroad, from there to return and work for the scholarly improvement of their alma mater.[28] All these objectives McCosh could defend on sound educational grounds. But the program he outlined became urgent only when a definite faction in opposition to McCosh became articulate at the end of the 1870s. McCosh now had both political and academic reasons for accelerating this scheme.

Graduate study at Princeton was an adjunct of this plan. McCosh had already introduced graduate work into the college and had followed Scottish and English examples in providing the student scholarships for it. In the winter of 1876-1877 he took seventeen of the most promising members of the senior class and organized special periods of work for them with interested faculty members. These first faculty members were Brackett, Guyot, and Sloane, but the number grew quickly. McCosh believed the new efforts to be of "historic" importance for Princeton, but, significantly, he did not speak of a new German university model emerging at Princeton. Rather, he upheld the graduate studies for their beneficial impact on undergraduate teaching and the extension of the curriculum. The gradual expansion of graduate study would help keep Princeton abreast of the new knowledge without jeopardizing the core of the undergraduate curriculum. An organic relationship would exist between both levels of study, and as truly advanced and specialized work developed the graduate program would absorb the new learning into its own curriculum. In fact, the following year the Princeton catalogue announced formal graduate courses in philology, philosophy, and science, and the college granted its first master's degrees. John Franklin Williamson received Princeton's first Ph.D. degree in 1879.[29]

Who were the bright young men around whom McCosh helped build the new Princeton? Any measure of McCosh's importance to Princeton, and any assessment of his life as an educator and leader, must consider his highly successful implementation of the

[28] James McCosh, "What an American University Should Be," *Education*, 6 (1885-1886), 35-45.

[29] Willard Thorp, "The Founding of the Princeton Graduate School: An Academic Agon," *Princeton University Library Chronicle*, 32 (1970), 1-2; "Henry Fairchild Osborn: A Man of Parts," *Princeton Alumni Weekly*, October 12, 1928; TM, June 18, 1877, June 20, 1887, November 14, 1878; *General Catalogue of Princeton University*, p. 373.

scholarship program and the benefits that accrued to the college from the Princeton scholars who returned from study abroad and assumed positions of highest rank in their academic fields. Through these persons, above all, Princeton's metamorphosis, its emergence into the full light of the university era, took place.

The transition is illustrated by the case of William Berryman Scott (1858-1947). He was a grandson of Charles Hodge, and son of a Presbyterian clergyman and professor at Centre College in Kentucky. At Princeton Scott graduated first in the class of 1877, among whose members he helped organize Princeton's first scientific expedition to the western states. Scott won a scholarship for study abroad and went first to London, where he worked with Thomas Huxley. But he was also anticipating pursuit of a Ph.D. at Heidelberg and wrote to McCosh for his thoughts on the plan. McCosh endorsed the idea completely, underscoring "*You should by all means do so.*" He also urged Scott to keep Princeton in mind for a teaching position afterward, promising "to promote your interests in every way I can." McCosh did get Scott appointed as an assistant professor to Guyot when Scott returned with his doctorate from Heidelberg in 1880. In 1884 he became Blair Professor of Biology at the college and went on to a career of highest distinction in his field. He wrote numerous scientific articles and books on land mammals of the western hemisphere, and also contributed to evolutionary theory. A recipient of honorary degrees from Harvard and Oxford, Scott was in turn president of the American Society of Palaeontologists, the American Philosophical Society, and the Geological Society of North America. Scott was a Presbyterian and as much as any of McCosh's students embodied the mentor's ideals of religious dedication that flourished compatibly with the highest quality of work in academic science.[30]

Similar to Scott in many respects was Henry Fairchild Osborn (1857-1935). Also a member of the class of 1877, Osborn joined the Princeton expedition to the west and from it preserved a lifelong interest in fossils. He used his Princeton fellowship for an extra year of study at the college, then, like Scott, studied with Huxley at the Royal College of Sciences in London with another year at Cambridge University. He returned to Princeton in 1880 as its first fellow in biology and in 1883 became professor of comparative anatomy. In 1891, the year in which he served as president of the

---

[30] *Princeton '77*, p. 228; McCosh to Scott, December 12, 1879 and March 15, 1880, in the McCosh Correspondence; William Berryman Scott, *Some Memories of a Palaeontologist* (Princeton, 1939), pp. 127-28; *NCAB*, 36:426-27.

American Society of Naturalists, Osborn went to Columbia University. New York proved a better outlet for his talents than Princeton under Patton, and Osborn served both the university and the Natural History Museum in New York City. He immersed himself in scholarly work, but was also an energetic popularizer of evolution. He worked for its public acceptance by organizing impressive displays of mammals and reptiles in a manner that gave dramatic visibility to the theory. His books, *From the Greeks to Darwin* (1894), *Evolution of Mammalian Molar Teeth* (1907), and *Origin and Evolution of Life* (1917), presented detailed scientific evidence for the evolutionary hypothesis. But Osborn had none of Huxley's animosity toward religion and in fact saw no threat to theism in a proper scientific understanding of evolution. His 1923 work, *Evolution and Religion*, clarified that position, as did his signature on a petition, signed by thirty-five other scientists, affirming that science furnishes a sublime conception of God and one wholly consonant with the highest ideals of religion.[31] Osborn too was truly an intellectual descendant of McCosh.

One of McCosh's strongest supporters on the Princeton faculty was William Libbey (1855-1927), another product of the remarkable class of 1877. Libbey's father, the partner of John A. Stewart, was, as we have seen, an important Princeton benefactor. The younger Libbey won another of the science fellowships and did graduate work in terrestrial magnetism with Hermann von Helmholtz at the University of Berlin and with Emil Dubois-Raymond at the University of Paris. He became another assistant to Guyot when he returned to Princeton in 1880, then assumed the chair in physical geography, which he held until 1922. An energetic scientist, but less productive than Scott or Osborn, Libbey led several Princeton expeditions and participated in polar exploration parties in 1894 and 1898. He was a fellow of the Royal Society of London and vice-president of the American Society of Naturalists.[32]

Perhaps the most interesting of McCosh's students, and an example that shows the ebb and flow of intellectual history, was James Mark Baldwin. Baldwin, a product of Columbia, South Carolina, came to Princeton after attending a private school in Salem, New Jersey. He graduated second in the class of 1884 and won the fellowship in mental science. His work with McCosh, Baldwin said, had aroused his interest in philosophy, and he decided on further study. McCosh had been introducing the subject of psyiological

---

[31] *Princeton '77*, pp. 222-25; *NCAB*, C:26-28.
[32] *Princeton '77*, pp. 210-14; *NCAB*, 10:401-2.

psychology in his library meetings and Baldwin was fascinated by it. He used his Princeton fellowship to go to Germany. In three separate semesters, Baldwin studied with Wundt and Heize at Leipzig, Paulsen and Delitsch at Berlin, and Stumpf and Riehl at Freiburg. McCosh thought that Baldwin's dissertation, which he completed on returning to Princeton, did not sufficiently refute materialism and made him revise it. But McCosh respected Baldwin highly and urgently wanted him on the Princeton faculty. There was no immediate room in philosophy, so McCosh assigned him to teach, of all subjects, French. Here is a strong hint that McCosh's appointments were mixed with political motivations, for Baldwin readily admitted his inadequacy in the subject and even his intimidation when he learned that two French boys were in the class.[33] But in 1893 Baldwin did become professor of psychology at Princeton, and his career in that field justified McCosh's confidence. Baldwin was a prolific scholar, noted most for his *Dictionary of Psychology and Philosophy* (1900), a valuable anthology produced by sixty American and European scholars. He was a cofounder of the *Psychological Review*, and author of *Handbook of Psychology* (2 vols., 1889-1891). Other works included *Mental Development in the Child and the Race* (1896), *Development and Evolution* (1902), and *Genetic Theory of Reality* (1915).[34]

William Francis Magie and Henry Burchard Fine were the first-ranking scholars in the classes of 1879 and 1880. Magie (1858-1943) remained at Princeton a few years and then went to Germany where he earned a doctorate in physics at the University of Berlin. He published many articles on scientific subjects and became an important member of the new young faculty that began to exercise its strength around the time of McCosh's retirement.[35] Fine (1858-1928), the son of a Presbyterian minister, pursued the study of mathematics under Felix Klein at the University of Leipzig, where he earned a doctorate in 1885. He became Dod Professor of Mathematics at Princeton and later dean of the faculty and dean of the school of science. With a special interest in the logic of mathematics,

---

[33] Baldwin, *Between Two Wars*, 1:20; Faculty Minutes, June 14, 1884; *NCAB*, 25:89-90.

[34] Baldwin has been described as a "pioneer in experimental psychology" and actually effected an important continuation of McCosh's thought on evolution. He perpetuated the Scottish emphasis on the moral sense by locating it in the survival instincts of the race, thereby giving it a Darwinian, utilitarian basis, and by further positing a social principle in human nature. Baldwin, *Between Two Wars*, 1:32; Russett, *Darwin in America*, pp. 114-16; *WWP*, 12:78.

[35] *NCAB*, 12:425.

Fine wrote several textbooks and became president of the American Mathematical Society in 1911. He was to play an important role in the movement that brought Woodrow Wilson to the presidency of Princeton.[36]

Other McCosh students played an even more critical role in Princeton's history. Andrew Fleming West (1853-1943), a member of the class of 1874, was one of McCosh's favorite students. When he graduated from Princeton he went to a school in Ohio where he taught Latin for seven years. For a brief period he was president of Morris Academy in New Jersey, but McCosh brought him back to Princeton in 1883, and he became Giger Professor of Latin. At Princeton and throughout the United States, West was an eloquent and passionate defender of the classics. He militantly criticized the free elective system and pleaded for a gentlemanly tradition of learning with the English system as a usable model. West's most noted and controversial work derived from his efforts as dean of the graduate school at Princeton and his plan to segregate its buildings and programs from the rest of the college, a scheme bitterly denounced by President Woodrow Wilson.[37] John Grier Hibben (1861-1933), a midwesterner and son of a Presbyterian clergyman, ranked second in the class of 1882 and won the mathematics prize. He pursued graduate study at the University of Berlin and at Princeton Theological Seminary. He was ordained into the ministry in 1887 and served in St. Louis. He was the Stuart Professor of Logic at Princeton after 1894 and was elected president of the university shortly after Wilson's retirement.[38]

Princeton flourished with new courses and new scholarly endeavors under McCosh, including for the first time not just the embellishments of the fine arts, but serious scholarship in that area as well. This development owed much to the work of Allan Marquand (1853-1924), highest scholar in the class of 1874. His father was a leading Princeton benefactor and had amassed an impressive collection of art masterpieces in his New York City home. The younger Marquand's interests lay first in philosophy, especially logic and ethics, and he went abroad to the University of Berlin in 1877 and 1878, then returned for his doctorate in philosophy at the Johns Hopkins University. McCosh at that time wrote to Marquand and urged him to consider a Princeton appointment. After dividing his attention between logic, Greek, and art, Marquand

[36] *DAB*, 6:386-89.
[37] *DAB*, suppl. 3:809-11.
[38] *NCAB*, 33:45; *DAB*, suppl. 1:398-401.

began to narrow his efforts to the last subject. With rigorous dedication, Marquand pioneered in the scholarly study of art history, and, it was said, "shared with Charles Eliot Norton, of Harvard, the distinction of introducing the serious study of art history into the curriculum of the American colleges." Marquand virtually founded and supervised the growth of the department of art and archaeology at Princeton, and also planned and supervised the construction of McCormick Hall, which housed it. Described as "exquisitely the gentleman and the aristocrat," he was a most productive scholar. Marquand acquired rare books and art treasures for Princeton, and in thus endowing the college with many landmarks of high culture he helped to realize one of McCosh's fondest hopes for the institution.[39]

And most of his other hopes, too, McCosh entrusted to the work and success of these bright young men. There were others among this group of Princetonians, such as Arthur Lincoln Frothingham, Jr., Alexander T. Ormond, Samuel Ross Winans, and Moses Alan Starr. These young scholars were McCosh's pride and joy, and he was ready to hand them every needed assistance. One of them, Osborn, recalled: "No one can forget his kindly words of encouragement as he aided the early faltering steps of learning and of research. Original thinking among the advanced students was fostered by putting upon them as much responsibility as they could bear."[40] And as these individuals returned to the college, McCosh's spirit was buoyed. He announced to the trustees that he hoped "to be able to organize these gifted and eager youths so as to make them do important work for literature and science as well as for the College."[41] And McCosh, in fact, had already devised a useful means of this organization.

It was in the late 1870s, when the McCosh administration began to move in new directions, that another innovation, and one that became for many the most memorable of their Princeton experience, took root on the campus. At this time McCosh introduced his famous "library meetings." These were sessions held in Prospect, McCosh's home, and they gathered together, on an occasional but increasingly frequent basis, the best students from the undergraduate body, almost all of the graduate students, and the most

---

[39] McCosh to Marquand, June 30, 1881, in the McCosh Correspondence; *New York Times*, October 25, 1924; *NCAB*, 37:336-37; *DAB*, 12:291-92.

[40] Henry Fairchild Osborn, "Plain Living and High Thinking at Princeton Fifty Years Ago," *Princeton Alumni Weekly*, March 3, 1925.

[41] TM, June 20, 1881.

active scholars among the faculty. The library meetings had a clear academic and intellectual purpose. Always they featured a lecture by one of the professors, or, as the habit grew, a noted scholar from another institution. Discussion, almost always lively and sometimes heated, followed the presentation. McCosh invariably had his say, but so did other members of the faculty, and often students as well. The meetings served a variety of purposes. McCosh considered them an important means of encouraging and displaying the research work of his young intellectuals, for this group especially dominated the forums. The topics therefore were chosen to elaborate on special problems on which the faculty, whose members now provided a large critical audience, were engaged. McCosh also used the library meetings to confront what he considered the major intellectual problems of the day. Probably at least half of the sessions explored controversial themes in philosophy and psychology. Baldwin recalled that McCosh allowed much room for schools of thought that rivaled his own, but when the discussion period followed he made sure that proponents of materialism and pantheism did not pronounce with impunity. Often he pounded the table in front of him and shouted, "No, this table is real," a method surely as effective as Samuel Johnson's kicking the stone to refute George Berkeley.[42] With such lively engagements, the reputation of the library meetings spread. In 1876 about sixty to seventy people attended, but there were twice that number ten years later when the sessions had become a standard part of Princeton's intellectual life. In 1878 the *Princetonian* commented that McCosh had introduced "a new and powerful element" into the college and once, when some time had gone by without a meeting, it called for a quick renewal of the sessions.[43]

By all judgments the library meetings gave a new measure of intellectual excitement to Princeton. But the meetings had another function and another significant purpose, which is likely to be overlooked if we ignore the whole context of McCosh's administration at the end of the 1870s. For the meetings also elaborate McCosh's role as an academic politician. He read clearly the trouble signs of these years and recognized the weight of intellectual opposition to him. The evolution issue was only the main feature of this antagonism and to some extent a symbol of a larger clash of principles. For McCosh's liberalism on the evolution question be-

[42] *Princeton '77*, p. 26; Baldwin, *Between Two Wars*, 1:20.
[43] *Princetonian*, November 9, 1876, March 15, 1886, November 7, 1878, September 30, 1887.

trayed, in the eyes of some, his larger intention to change the whole character of Princeton. The latitudinarian spirit that had already destroyed the old required curriculum and had given a new, prominent place to the sciences, clearly did not sit well with many defenders of the old Princeton. To be sure, McCosh made avowed enemies of only a few individuals. His evangelical ideals, the obvious religious direction and traditions that he upheld in the college, purchased much goodwill from persons who would otherwise have vilified his educational reforms. Nonetheless, it is quite clear that McCosh perceived that the prevailing atmosphere in and around Princeton was such that he could not yet go as far as he wished in the program of educational change. In a sense what McCosh proceeded to do, therefore, was to build a university within the college. The library meetings became the vehicle for an intellectual extracurriculum. Amid the clamor against the new learning that echoed from outside, McCosh, in a quiet and unostentatious way, opened a path to new ideas and new scholarly explorations inside. Without the formal title and structure of a university (and McCosh remarked repeatedly that Princeton was not ready to assume such a title), Princeton nevertheless moved ahead steadily in the direction of advanced research and the creation of an atmosphere and clientele to support it. But above all the library meetings demonstrated McCosh's academic commitment to an open atmosphere of learning at Princeton. His determination was illustrated in two ways.

McCosh had given his approval to the evolutionary hypothesis by way of saying that the factual evidence deciding the case must come from scientists, and scientific opinion so far seemed to corroborate it. But he also believed that the issue would not have a conclusive resolution for some time, and much shifting of evidence would occur in the future. By the later years of his administration McCosh had attracted to Princeton an array of highly reputable scientific scholars, several of them his former students. These professors, we have seen, had also immersed themselves in investigations on evolution, and McCosh wished to use them in giving the matter a wide discussion at Princeton. The library meetings of course were precisely suited for that purpose. Certainly the most memorable of these occurred in November and December 1887, when Professor Scott presented a full scientific discussion of the subject. His presentation was an unqualified defense of the hypothesis and widely illustrated the serious deficiencies in the separate creation thesis.[44]

[44] Ibid., November 29, 1887, December 2, 1887.

But more closely tied to McCosh's own field of interest was the new field of physiological psychology, with its particularly important developments in Germany. McCosh of course perceived the larger implications of the new direction and the challenge it presented to the dualistic nature of his own system. But he also, it seems, recognized that physiological psychology might have useful implications for a philosophy of realism. Nevertheless, McCosh never fully articulated his motivations respecting the new studies. But one thing is clear; he made every possible effort to ensure that Princeton would be abreast of the developments and active in exploring the new field. He chose to launch Princeton's investigations on the subject through the library meetings where an inconspicuous and friendly intellectual environment prevailed. It is also interesting to note that the Princeton pioneers in these investigations were all from the ranks of McCosh's young academics. Professor Baldwin, fresh from his term of study in Berlin, asked McCosh if he might use one of the library sessions to explain the methods employed by Wilhelm Wundt in his experimental psychophysics laboratory at Leipzig. McCosh, Baldwin reported, responded "with the open-mindedness that characterized him" even though he saw the skeleton of materialism in the closet.[45] And McCosh did soon conclude that the studies should be a regular part of the Princeton curriculum. According to Osborn, McCosh had talked frequently of the idea in the winter of 1881-1882. In 1883 he gave an introductory lecture for the course, and Osborn followed with three lectures on the nervous system. Scott, whom McCosh also recruited for the new program, gave several more lectures. Laboratory work accompanied the lectures, and the course attracted a large number of students. Even before the course began, much excitement surrounded the new venture, and the nonscientific members of the faculty also took an interest. Thus Libbey, Scott, and Osborn, joined by Sloane and Marquand, began to meet Friday evenings in the zoological laboratory where, as the self-constituted Wundt Club, they discussed the new scientific literature. Scott and Osborn gave lecture demonstrations on the brain and nervous system. McCosh, it was said, "after courteously asking permission," attended several times and insisted that Scott and Osborn organize an undergraduate course on the subject. Baldwin, contributing new scholarship to the field, took over the course several years later. From these efforts, and after McCosh's retirement, the participating faculty and students published a series entitled *Princeton Contribu-*

---

[45] Baldwin, *Between Two Wars*, 1:20-21.

tions to Psychology. For McCosh these academic developments conformed to his model of an organic university, one that he felt should emerge from the gradual maturation and scholarly progress of the college. Surely those who grew to intellectual leadership, from the days when they first sat in McCosh's Bible classes at Princeton, testified to the good results of the president's patience and encouragement.[46]

But McCosh needed even greater patience for another of the political problems he confronted—the board of trustees. Consisting of a roughly equal number of clergymen and secular careerists in business, law, and politics, this group possessed considerable legal power at Princeton. Whereas it has been said that at Harvard the president leads, and at Yale the faculty, at Princeton the trustees were always a powerful, often immovable force. With this group McCosh dealt deftly, and by preserving an outward manner of religiosity at Princeton and a good measure of academic conservatism, he won a degree of freedom in areas critical to his program. Thus, even though the trustees held full authority for academic appointments, there is no evidence that they exercised that authority to interfere with McCosh's selections. That McCosh made significant improvements here owed much to the initiative left to him, even though McCosh and the trustees had a common stake in a faculty that could render effective support to the religious character of the college. McCosh, with the leeway granted, secured a faculty with these loyalties and a dedication to scholarship as well. Yet McCosh and the board did differ, and sometimes vehemently, on matters of academic philosophy. Again, the exceedingly polite trustees' records only hint at the dissension, but persons with vivid memories of the McCosh years at Princeton testify that animosities sometimes cut very deeply. They recalled McCosh's angry outbursts against the "old men" who ruled the college. "One-half me board are in their dotage," he would exclaim, and the seventy-year-old McCosh often felt like a youthful radical amid the stalwart resistance raised against his reforms.[47]

Only late in his administration did McCosh succeed in directly influencing the composition of the board of trustees. The selection of new members was the board's prerogative, and one jealously exercised. McCosh, as we shall see, first tried to gain some leverage

---

[46] Ibid., 1:21, 63-64 (Baldwin quotes a letter from Osborn); Scott, *Some Memories*, p. 146; *Princetonian*, April 6, 1883.

[47] "Some Notes on the Life of Moses Taylor Pyne," *Princeton Alumni Weekly*, 21 (1921), 662.

by creating alumni positions. But failing in that, he directly intervened and campaigned actively for a personal choice in 1885. McCosh had just been through the worst crisis of his administration[48] and was prepared to throw all caution to the wind to reverse the downward trend. By this point, in fact, McCosh was fighting for his legacy at Princeton. His retirement he knew must come within the next few years, and unless the ruling body of the college were invigorated by men who shared his spirit and educational philosophy, his greatest hopes for the college would go unrealized.

McCosh's first choice for the board was a leader from one of his favorite classes, Moses Taylor Pyne (1855-1921) of the class of 1879. Pyne was the son of a very successful New York financier who had emigrated from London and made his way to the presidency of the National City Bank and the directorships of many American railroads. After graduate work at Princeton and Columbia, Moses Taylor Pyne succeeded to many of these positions. Pyne symbolized the new man of wealth who formed so strong a part of McCosh's connections, but he was the first to come directly from McCosh's tutelage to a position of influence among the trustees. McCosh tagged Pyne early for this position, and Osborn remembered how emphatically the president urged his case: "Mr. Pyne is a fine young man. We must have a fine young man on our board. The Board is full of old dotards and sometimes they go to sleep. We want a young man." And McCosh and Princeton got more than that. For Pyne proved to be the most dedicated Princetonian of his time. For thirty-six years after his appointment in 1885, Pyne served as trustee without once missing a meeting. Princeton's welfare, it was said, "became almost the ruling passion of his life." For many years he remained to champion McCosh's causes: promotion of athletics, improvements in faculty salaries, the election of alumni trustees, and the campaign to add University to Princeton's name. He was also one of Princeton's largest benefactors, though his gifts almost always arrived anonymously. And it is also noteworthy that Pyne was an Episcopalian, the first non-Presbyterian trustee in many decades at Princeton, and another indication of the liberalizing influence of McCosh's policies.[49]

McCosh believed he could do good for Princeton by making use of the leadership of practical businessmen and loyal alumni like Pyne. But since at least twelve of the maximum of twenty-seven college officers had to be clergymen, McCosh needed to introduce

[48] See the next chapter.
[49] "Notes on Pyne," 662; *Princeton '77*, p. 59; *NCAB*, 19:178-89.

a liberal element among this group too. Naturally he looked to the ranks of the Presbyterian ministry that he himself had helped to educate. So at the same time that he pleaded for Pyne, McCosh worked for the nomination of Simon McPherson, an outstanding student in the class of 1874. McPherson was also a Princeton Theological Seminary student and after a time in the ministry would become director of McCormick Seminary, then headmaster of the Lawrenceville School. McCosh wrote directly to McPherson spelling out the need for his presence on the board. "We need someone in the Board who knows the new regime and can keep it up." The trustees as a whole, McCosh added, were competent to manage the secular affairs of the school, but "most of them know little about the education." McCosh looked to the future and told McPherson that "I am not willing that my work shall pass away."[50] McPherson was not available for the trustee spot in 1885, but did join the board in 1897. Increasingly after 1888, when McCosh retired from the presidency, former students became officers of the college. We shall later see the profound effects of that fact.

The elevation of Pyne to the board of trustees highlighted an important and critical aspect of McCosh's administration. McCosh's relations with the Princeton alumni had been excellent, and from the very beginning of his administration that group always figured in McCosh's plans for the reconstruction of the college. But in the second half of his administration the alumni alliance became even more important and compounded the political complications of the 1880s. In the earlier years the alumni were useful as benefactors. They played an indisputably significant role in providing McCosh the financial means to undertake his building program and endow the scholarships and academic prizes that he valued. In fact, precisely at the time when Princeton announced the appointment of McCosh to the presidency, Princeton alumni living in and around New York City organized themselves and undertook efforts to help their alma mater.[51] The constituting of alumni groups by geographical region was a significant addition to the arrangement by classes that already existed. These groups could more easily arrange annual meetings and coordinate their gifts and contributions to the school. Moreover, as McCosh quickly illustrated, the college president, with faculty members and trustees, could travel to the annual meetings to explain the progams and needs of

[50] McCosh to McPherson, May 20, 1885, in the McCosh Correspondence; *General Catalogue of Princeton University*, pp. 24-25; TM, June 18, 1877.
[51] *New York Observer*, May 7, 1868.

the college. These visits created for McCosh another complex of outside political support for his regime. That fact became increasingly apparent as the alumni organizations drew their ranks from the former students of McCosh. More and more the alumni represented a force that cherished the academic ideals of their former teacher and resolved to use their influence to fashion the college in conformity to those ideals.

This turn of events actually affected Princeton more after McCosh's retirement than it did before 1888, but the alumni groups did win important gains for him. When McCosh called for money to support academic scholarships and prizes, the class of 1859 responded by presenting Princeton with a gift of $2,000 to endow a prize for the best student in English literature. Other alumni organizations followed suit, and the money became valuable especially because it confirmed the alumni's interest in, and support of, the courses that McCosh was introducing into the curriculum.[52] The alumni's activity owed much to McCosh's energetic cultivation of that constituency and their respect for the president. But that involvement also derived from a changing social pattern in the nation at large. Princeton, in the post-Civil War years, sent a decreasing, though still comparatively large, portion of its graduates into the ministry. More and more the professional ranks of law and business received college graduates, and these elements often had special commitments to the alumni organizations they formed and joined.[53] Increasingly also these graduates came to judge their alma mater less for its strictly religious character or conformity to doctrinal truths, even though they themselves maintained church ties and promoted religious benefaction. With respect to education, they were voices of modernism. They wanted their institution to have a large public visibility and supported academic reforms that would enhance its stature as a leader in the new fields of learning. To a large degree, no doubt, they wanted the prestige of their colleges to enhance their own prestige, and here personal interest mixed with honest sentiments of pride. However it stood, these factors created a new force in the environment of American higher education in the late nineteenth century.

Alumni had served Princeton's interests in the years before McCosh's arrival.[54] But it was during the McCosh years that the

---

[52] Ibid., July 8, 1869.

[53] The next chapter will further illuminate the important role of this group in the post-McCosh years at Princeton.

[54] See Wertenbaker, *Princeton*, pp. 215-55.

alumni acquired formal organizational structures and a more definite standing within the entire college's community of interests. The formation of a Princeton Alumni Association of Philadelphia followed closely on that of the New York group. The Princeton Alumni Association of Maryland was organized in 1869 (admitting graduates from any southern state), and three years later there appeared an organization in the District of Columbia. By 1876 Princeton groups from Cincinnati, western Pennsylvania, and St. Louis, and a Princeton Alumni Association of the Northwest (centered in Chicago) increased the rolls.[55] McCosh welcomed these groups and repeatedly called for new ones. And he would travel hundreds of miles to meet with them. The effort, we will see, supported his plans to make Princeton a national university.

It was exactly at the time when McCosh's position at Princeton became precarious that he presented for the first time to the board of trustees his plan to augment that group by new members elected directly by the alumni. McCosh outlined the proposal largely as a device to enhance alumni interest in the school and gain larger financial support.[56] But McCosh, and the trustees too, knew that much more was at stake. McCosh's plan clearly would give a voice in the governance of the college and in the making of its policy to a group that certainly would ally itself with the growing reformist elements. And while McCosh promoted his idea, alumni groups petitioned the board to create the new positions. McCosh's original plea was for advisory status only; the alumni came increasingly to call for voting power, a concept that McCosh soon endorsed himself. By 1882 the issue could no longer be postponed. An alumni petition that called for the election of future trustees from their ranks, until they constituted one quarter of the membership, now met the board's review. A committee of three trustees took the idea under advisement. The committee consisted of John Thompson Nixon, a lawyer, politican, and judge, who had been an active layman in the Presbyterian Old School; William Charles Roberts, a college and seminary graduate, and a clergyman; and Samuel Bayard Dod, son of Albert B. Dod, a prominent faculty member at Princeton Theological Seminary, of which Samuel was a graduate. Their report was, to say the least, an honest statement of sentiments. But it was a rude and undiplomatic reply to the alumni. It stated forthrightly that the trustees must select persons whose interests in the college's goals coincided with those of the present

---

[55] *The Princeton Book* . . . (Boston, 1879), p. 235.
[56] TM, November 14, 1878.

body. This curious wording surely suggested that the ruling powers perceived the alumni as a force ready and waiting to take the college in a new and radical direction. A further hint at these fears came in the committee's suggestion that the broad body of American Presbyterians that formed the larger interests of the college was "a stable people" and not likely to "favor new and untried methods as long as old and tried methods work well." The report, drawing attention to the petition's reminder that Yale and Harvard had already instituted alumni representation, merely queried, "To what good results?"[57] McCosh's objections notwithstanding, the trustees sustained the report, and the alumni were shown a cold shoulder.

But it was the college that paid the price. Contributions fell immediately, although that fact also owed much to the deaths of some wealthy benefactors. A letter from an alumnus that appeared in the *Princetonian* the next year may well have spoken the sentiments of many in the larger group. This letter asked why the writer and other alumni should respond to the college's recent appeal for money when the alumni had no voice in the government of the college. This alumnus mentioned specifically the late rebuff and wondered why the college could be so indifferent in its time of need.[58] And this issue was not about to die. It soon reemerged in connection with McCosh's last grand scheme for the salvation of Princeton.

WE HAVE SEEN that McCosh's plans for the reconstruction of Princeton and his hopes that the school might attain a wider sphere of influence in the United States depended to a great degree on his establishing a series of interconnecting relationships between the college and different bodies external to it. At the heart of these alliances was Princeton's relation to lower schools. The problem had a practical dimension, for Princeton needed to ally itself with schools from which it could draw students. And it had an ideological dimension, for McCosh wanted students who were prepared to enter directly into Princeton's modernized program of studies. Eventually these needs would require of McCosh a calculated effort to expand Princeton's reputation beyond the Middle Atlantic area, where it was strongest, to the midwestern region of the country. McCosh did not realize great success in this effort, but he did succeed in securing new connections for Princeton, with results that proved to be somewhat ironic. And in this effort also the

[57] TM, November 9, 1882.
[58] *Princetonian*, October 5, 1883.

greatest impact of McCosh's success became apparent only in the years after his retirement. Altogether McCosh's efforts with the lower schools illustrate the political dimensions of academic change in this period and McCosh's particular skill in this area.

McCosh began modestly. He looked first mostly to the New Jersey area and the wider Middle Atlantic region for the college's students. Princeton, he hoped, might be a signficant force here in the way that Harvard and Yale were in New England. But these two schools, much larger than Princeton, enjoyed the special advantage of well-established preparatory schools that furnished a large portion of their student bodies. These feeder schools, as McCosh called them, were especially important to Harvard, to the point that Eliot could be quite indifferent to the fate of public high schools in New England, even though they were widely established by law. But McCosh did not wish to build a Princeton student body around upper-class schools, and neither could he immediately have done so, for the Middle Atlantic region lagged far behind New England in this category. McCosh at first was undisturbed by this fact. His Scottish and evangelical ideals looked to the broad middle classes as the source of his Princetonians, and he would do as much as possible to make it feasible for the sons of poor families to attend also. It quickly became apparent to McCosh, after his arrival in America, that Princeton's future would depend to some degree on the successful establishment of free public high schools in New Jersey and the Middle Atlantic. If Princeton could draw from these schools, it would make itself an important regional institution. McCosh soon learned, however, how difficult it would be to realize this ideal.

One day in March 1871 McCosh entered the assembly chamber of the New Jersey State Legislature to address a combined session of the Senate and House. He came to plead the cause of a new, extended system of public high schools in the state. Since his arrival in the United States, McCosh had discovered to his considerable disappointment, that New Jersey, like most of the United States, lacked such a system; and this was so despite worthy accomplishments in public primary schools. But overall the American way of education was confusion and chaos. No integrative system existed. McCosh reviewed for the gathered legislators the varieties of European approaches, spoke with Scottish pride of the organic relation that tied the secondary schools to the universities in his native country, and especially recommended the German gymnasiums and the foundations they laid for university study. McCosh, in fact, was fighting the same battle that he had waged in Ireland. It was time, here also, to "plug the great gap." He urged the legislators to undertake a bold educational effort, "to institute High Schools all over the State." These should be free schools admitting the "brightest boys" on examination. McCosh promised great benefits to the state.[59] Of course, Princeton too might profit by the arrangement.

In the short run, McCosh's efforts proved unavailing. Only slowly did the idea that he and others encouraged make headway. In the meantime, Princeton had a real problem. Too many applicants to the college lacked the skills necessary for successful college work. So the college itself had to do something. It addressed the matter in a way that other colleges had, by initiating its own preparatory school. It enabled promising candidates who needed sharpening to spend a year at Princeton before entering the regular freshman class. Once again McCosh received outside help, as Henry Marquand provided several thousand dollars for the undertaking. And it proved to be a sound idea. Forty-six students were attending the preparatory school in 1875, and by 1880 it had furnished about seventy-five students for the regular Princeton classes.[60] This kind of holding action at least helped assure the college of more qualified freshmen, though it did not meet McCosh's need for a secondary system that could supply new qualified students for Princeton.

McCosh needed some larger blueprint to tackle this problem. To be sure, enrollments at Princeton increased steadily during the first thirteen years of McCosh's administration. Only in the early eighties did they decline. But even before they declined McCosh had come to realize that he needed a different strategy for the growth and scholarly improvement of the student body. McCosh believed that New England's advantage in private preparatory schools hurt Princeton. A father anxious for his son to go to college, he explained to the trustees, will seek out a good preparatory school. Almost invariably the boy will attend one of the New England schools, where he is likely to hear only of Harvard as a

---

[59] McCosh, et al., *Addresses Delivered in Reference to Free High Schools Before the Legislature of New Jersey* . . . (Trenton, 1871), pp. 3-9. McCosh even believed that the creation of free public high schools was so imperative that it should be the responsibility of the federal government to assist. He recommended that money from the sale of federal lands be used by states in this endeavor and outlined his ideas in a lengthy letter to President Hayes. See McCosh to Hayes, December 7, 1880, "Garfield Papers," Library of Congress, Washington, D.C.

[60] TM, November 9, 1876, December 17, 1873; *Princetonian*, November 5, 1886.

college choice. Then he is lost not only to Princeton but to sound religion too. Making these remarks in 1880, McCosh said that he was not prepared to give up yet on state-supported schools from which Princeton might derive a socially democratic student body. But in fact, McCosh had suggested as early as 1872 that it would be very much in Princeton's interests to encourage private academies in the Middle Atlantic region. The trustees should individually use their influence in their own regions to this end. McCosh also wished that wealthy Americans would desist from their fruitless practice of endowing new colleges in proliferation throughout the country. The benefits to good education were meager, and much better results would come from private benefaction in the cause of secondary education.[61]

So Princeton prepared to enter the American boarding school movement of the nineteenth century. Doing so would involve the college in a series of events that later had profound consequences for its social character. It is true that the American boarding school has been associated with a kind of social elitism, and has had an image of privilege. But this identification has usually been overstated, and especially in its early period the American boarding school was associated with educational reform. Its early leaders were interested followers of the educational theories of Continental reformers, and some Americans, like George Ticknor, wanted to use the boarding school as a basis for the modernization of the university.[62] William Augustus Muhlenberg carried some of his quiet missionary spirit into the establishment of the Flushing Institute and was one of the first to give the American boarding school its Protestant and increasingly Episcopalian affiliation. That identification had important consequences, because in the nineteenth century the Episcopal Church emerged as the religious affiliation of an eastern and urban elite class in America. The Episcopalians' success in creating a broad community of interest, linking church and educational institutions, was a fact of which Presbyterian educators like McCosh needed to take cognizance. As James McLachlan noted: "Rather than depend on the instant conversion of the revival, Episcopalians typically founded institutions that drew individuals together in organic units which allowed for the

---

[61] TM, February 12, 1880, December 18, 1872; James McCosh, "The Importance of Harmonizing the Primary, Secondary, and Collegiate Systems of Education," National Education Association, *Addresses and Proceedings* (1880), 143-46.

[62] James McLachlan, *American Boarding Schools: A Historical Study* (New York, 1970), pp. 49-70, 95-96.

gradual Christian nurture of the child." Could McCosh rally Presbyterians into a similar and rival organic unit that could serve the needs of Princeton College?[63]

McCosh's search for feeder schools led to the revitalization of two academies in the Princeton area. The example of Blair Academy, reopened in 1875, illustrates the means by which Presbyterian affiliations worked to the advantage of the college. John Inslee Blair was descended from John Blair, of Scottish Presbyterian stock, and was nineteen when he entered business for himself in 1821. His keen business sense led to successful ventures in coal and iron and then to railroads to service these interests. He boasted that he never speculated and paid for every road with cash. He was an active Republican and loyal Presbyterian, who built some one hundred churches along his railroad lines. He endowed a professorship at Princeton and gave $6,000 to the Blair Presbyterian Academy in Blairstown, New Jersey. The school seems to have had a specially close relation to Princeton and helped to solve part of the problem that McCosh confronted.[64]

Even more important to Princeton's future, and to the later character of the school, was the revitalization of the Lawrenceville Classical and Commercial High School. Located a few miles down the road from Princeton, this school had been the recipient of native son John C. Green's benefaction. McCosh and others believed that the academy could be reconstructed in such a way that it would become an immediate link to Princeton College. Consequently, he worked closely with the trustees of the Green legacy, especially Caleb Green Smith, Jr., an 1837 graduate of Princeton College and since 1872 a trustee of the school, and Charles E. Green, a New York lawyer and nephew of the businessman. In 1879 they bought the property of the school and planned for a complete new building program and reorganization of the governing structure of the school. The link to the college was manifest in the fact that the new trustees of Lawrenceville were virtually an extension of the Princeton College board of trustees. All had some connection with the college, including William Milligan Sloane from the faculty, and all were connected to the Presbyterian church. McCosh tried to ensure that in every respect the Lawrenceville School would develop a program that was genuinely preparatory to Princeton College. To this end he also secured the appointment as headmaster of his personal choice, James Cameron Mackensie, a Scottish im-

[63] Ibid., pp. 100-19; 136-41. The quotation is on p. 141.
[64] *New York Observer*, September 23, 1875; *NCAB*, 7:21-22.

migrant before McCosh and an important collaborator in organizing the school. The new school opened in 1883 with 122 boys and had more than 200 at McCosh's retirement.[65] In fact, Lawrenceville, we shall see, reappeared just in time to save McCosh and the college from an enrollment crisis.

While these plans matured, McCosh pursued two other ideas for making the school more widely attactive. He believed that Princeton could be a successful rival to the New England colleges in winning students from the Midwest. With the advance of religious liberalism in the East, he believed that Princeton's evangelical commitments might lead parents from the hinterland to judge Princeton a "safe" college for their sons. Moreover, as McCosh's hopes for the school grew more ambitious in his later years, he was anxious to see Princeton attain a national stature through a student body that drew from all regions of the country. When McCosh sent a letter to the parents of all Princeton students in 1884 dealing with religious and moral oversight of students at the college, he was encouraged to note that the issue was taken up by several midwestern newspapers.[66] By this time, furthermore, McCosh had tried to form a midwestern connection in a tangible way. In 1877 Princeton arranged to have entrance examinations for the college administered in the midwestern cities themselves. These first took place that year in St. Louis, Cincinnati, and Louisville. Four years later McCosh, with typical energy, undertook an extensive midwestern tour to promote Princeton's name. He had gone as far as Colorado when news of his son's illness brought him home. By then the local Princeton entrance examinations were being given in Chicago and as far away as Salt Lake City. Cleveland and St. Paul were added in 1885.[67] But McCosh's efforts had only marginal success. The school, for the time being, still retained its Middle Atlantic geographic identity.

McCosh wished to establish ties with the high schools, in New Jersey and in the Midwest, because he knew that potential students often learned of colleges from teachers. That fact disturbed him, because when he examined the Princeton record he discovered that the school had no tradition of educating teachers. In fact, he believed

---

[65] Roland J. Mulford, *History of the Lawrenceville School: 1810-1935* (Princeton, 1935), pp. 87-90, 93-95; McLachlan, *American Boarding Schools*, pp. 197-203; McCosh to Mackensie, December 11, 1881 and June 5, 1882, in the "Mackensie Papers," Lawrenceville School Archives, Lawrenceville, N.J.

[66] TM, June 16, 1884.

[67] TM, June 18, 1877, November 10, 1881; Faculty Minutes, June 26, 1885.

that the Middle Atlantic area far lagged behind New England in producing teachers. Graduates of the New England colleges blanketed the country and worked vigorously to promote the interests of those colleges. McCosh therefore urged upon the trustees that Princeton concentrate on graduating teachers.[68] But he also tried to create an interest in Princeton among the teachers themselves. He achieved the unlikely feat of inducing the New England School Club, with representatives of Willostan, Andover, Exeter, and other boarding schools, to hold their 1886 meeting at Princeton. McCosh and other Princeton representatives addressed the group, and the Princeton Hotel gave the meeting a proper convention atmosphere.[69] Two months later McCosh and several members of the faculty constructed a weekend program for teachers from the growing number of preparatory schools in the Middle Atlantic region, where meetings and sessions discussed the whole gamut of educational problems.[70] The drive for new institutional contacts was now moving at full steam.

McCosh designed his administration at Princeton to coincide with his own intellectual career. His classroom teaching was one vehicle for the dissemination of his own variety of the Scottish philosophy, and it furnished McCosh the occasion to use that philosophy as a means of criticizing and assessing other historical and contemporary movements of ideas. McCosh also blended the liberal spirit of his eighteenth-century Scottish predecessors, and the receptivity of the earlier Scottish universities to the new learning, with Princeton's new commitment to an expanded and freer curriculum. But McCosh's leadership at Princeton also ensured that the liberal learning spirit thrived amid an evangelical commitment that was equally strong. That commitment, we have seen, is the essential element of uniqueness in McCosh's position in the Scottish philosophical school. It flourished even as McCosh merged Christianity with evolution, and even as he combined revivalism on the Princeton campus with the significant gains made in scientific studies under his presidency. The coincidence of McCosh's intellectual career and his administrative programs is further reflected in the relations that both he and the college maintained with the world of publishing. For that world too is clearly another part of the external relations of an institution. Its role determines how ideas

[68] TM, November 8, 1883.   [69] *Princetonian*, March 15, 1886.
[70] Ibid., May 26, 1886.

are disseminated and received. For McCosh, the reception of his philosophical system was critical to the larger success of his academic program. Or so he believed. If his precise combination of intellectual liberalism and religious conservatism could gain acceptance, then in turn Princeton's reputation as an academic institution reflecting those ideals might assure its growth. Ultimately, of course, success in this effort depended again on the interlocking arrangements that linked the university to a chain of external relationships.

We have seen that much of McCosh's success in the financial improvement of the college lay in his relations with a group of benefactors united by an informal Scotch and Scotch-Irish Presbyterian identity. McCosh's relations with that American group actually began before his arrival in Princeton, for probably his first American contact was the remarkable Robert Carter (1807-1889), the publisher. In a real sense, Carter played a crucial role in McCosh's career. He was a Scotsman, born in Earlstown, Berwickshire. Disciplined by hard work in the economic depression of the post-Waterloo years, Carter pursued a demanding course of self-education and business initiative. After migrating to New York City in 1831, Carter joined to his immensely successful adventures in publishing an active participation in the cause of evangelical religion. He served on the board of directors of the Princeton Theological Seminary and helped to found the New York Sabbath Committee. In 1856 he was elected a manager of the American Bible Society. Carter wished to make his publishing career serve the larger cause of Christian regeneration in America, and he kept an eye out for books that aided the intellectual means to that end. He first encountered McCosh's *The Method of the Divine Government* on one of his many European tours and very quickly printed an American edition. Eventually he printed four, so briskly did McCosh's work sell in the States. Carter and McCosh became good friends. Carter visited and stayed with the McCoshes in Belfast, and the publisher returned the favor in New York when McCosh launched his American tour of 1866. And through Carter, McCosh was introduced to several noted Americans, including Mark Hopkins and Harriet Beecher Stowe.[71]

Toward the end of his career McCosh published his books through another house, that of the famous Scribners. But in this

[71] Annie Cochran Carter, *Robert Carter: His Life and Work, 1807-1889* (New York, 1891), pp. 144-49, 175-76; *NCAB*, 8:41.

case too, personal contacts were important. Charles Scribner, Sr. (1821-1871), founder of the publishing firm, graduated from Princeton in 1840 and then established a publishing partnership, Baker and Scribner, in New York City. The firm had an eclectic list of works, but it excelled in high scholarly, and especially theological, works. These included books by Horace Bushnell, Henry B. Smith, Noah Porter, and others that especially illustrate the Princeton connection—Archibald and James Waddel Alexander, Charles Hodge, and then McCosh.[72] In 1879 the company reorganized, and Scribner's sons, Charles, Jr., and Arthur, became partners. Both were McCosh's students at Princeton. Charles, Jr. (1854-1930), a graduate of the class of 1875, took charge of the firm on the death of another brother, John Blair Scribner, and began to expand the firm into "probably the most comprehensive publishing business in the country." Charles was a dedicated alumnus and later gave generously of his time and money to organize the Princeton University Press. Arthur Hawley Scribner (1859-1932) was a distinguished student and athlete at Princeton, one of the founders and first presidents of the Ivy Club. He graduated in 1881 and joined his brother in publishing. He was equally active in Princeton's welfare afterward and served with the Mission and Tract Society of New York City, becoming its president in 1916. Arthur married Emma L. Blair, daughter of John Inslee Blair. The loyalty of both Scribners to Princeton extended also to their work with their former teacher.[73]

McCosh's dealings with his publishers show all the ferocity of his egoism, but demonstrate also that this business was for McCosh an important link in his whole program for America. McCosh lived and died with everything he wrote. He wanted maximum efforts made for his literary cause, and a sense of desperation about it breathes through his correspondence with his publishers. He was a perfectionist. Once he wrote to Carter asking to see samples of the paper to be used in his new book.[74] He was even more severe with the Scribners, perhaps because they were former students who might still be expected to do their master's bidding. Advertising of his books of course was imperative, and McCosh watched the efforts with urgency: "My books being philosophical they need *pushing* in order to accomplish their end, which is to do good."

---

[71] Annie Cochran Carter, *Robert Carter: His Life and Work, 1807-1889* (New York, 1891), pp. 144-49, 175-76; *NCAB,* 8:41.

[72] *NCAB,* 6:366. [73] *DAB,* 16:515-17; *NCAB,* 36:101.

[74] McCosh to Carter, September 28, 1861, in the McCosh Correspondence.

This reminder went to Arthur Scribner, and McCosh added to it, as if it were really necessary: "I am anxious to keep philosophy right in this country."[75] But other topics, he believed, might appeal to the public's immediate interests. He once told Scribner that the evolution topic was lively and his book on that subject "ought to have a larger sale than others." But when Scribner's published his *Religious Aspects of Evolution*, McCosh was furious at their tardiness in getting the book out. "You should have made it a *Christmas book*," he railed, "but this cannot be done now!" He then told them to wait until February to release the book, because people are too poor in January to buy it![76]

McCosh often visited the Scribners in New York, stopping off from alumni or business meetings to see how things were going. He would check the list of people to receive complimentary copies of his works. He made certain that all the appropriate denominational and philosophical journals received copies for review. He also wanted the educational and literary journals to know of his books. And McCosh kept a keen eye on the reviews. The *New York Times* and the *New York Tribune* had not reviewed one of his books, so McCosh wrote to both newspapers, and they promised to recognize it. But McCosh wanted to be certain about this, and wrote to the Scribners, "What step are you and I to take to get these promises fulfilled? How can we reach the *Evening Post?*" Those who favored McCosh's views instantly won the author's blessings. When his book was finally noticed, McCosh wrote back to the Scribners: "The critique in the *Tribune* is admirable. I must somehow or other write the author thanking him."[77] But in the end McCosh knew more disappointment than joy at the fate of his works. As the Scottish philosophy waned amid new and strong rivals at the end of the century, McCosh too lost prestige. He lamented to Scribner's once that a large stack of his *Philosophical Series* sat on his desk. Is no one asking for them, and could we not sell them at reduced rates? McCosh above all did not like to be ignored, and increasingly his constant complaint was, "They won't give me a hearing."[78]

---

[75] McCosh to Scribner, March 31, 1886 in the "Scribner Papers," Department of Rare Books and Special Collections, Princeton University Library.

[76] McCosh to Scribner (brother not designated), March 17, 1883 and December 12, 1889 in the Scribner Papers.

[77] McCosh to Scribner (brother not designated), December 3, 1884, March 3, 1885, January 26, 1883, and March 17, 1883, in the Scribner Papers.

[78] McCosh to Scribner (brother not designated), June 11, 1889, in the Scribner

One other venture in publishing was dear to McCosh's heart and particularly affected the interests of the college. Specifically, McCosh wanted a publication that reflected the new spirit of the school, a review that would have national circulation and interest. Such publications flourished in the nineteenth century as vehicles for denominational viewpoints on the religious, intellectual, and literary matters of the day. The Presbyterian churches were heavily engaged in these activities, but for definite reasons McCosh, toward the very end of his administration, wanted to change the relationships. His efforts involved a pronounced shift in political strategy and constituted another part of his effort to give Princeton College a new community of interests.

The *Biblical Repertory and Princeton Review* was the oldest and longest literary staple of the Presbyterian denomination in the nineteenth century. It was founded at Princeton Theological Seminary in 1825, edited then and for many years by Charles Hodge. It was the major voice of Calvinist theology in America, and received contributions from Hodge, Archibald Alexander, Samuel Miller, Samuel Dod, James Carnahan, John Maclean, and indeed from almost all the giants of the Old School. The second part of the title was added in 1830, and did not belie its true intellectual identity. Charles Hodge was the spirit and force behind the review, and he contributed over a hundred articles to it. In the meantime, the New School Presbyterians pressed their views through the *American Presbyterian Review*. After Hodge's retirement in 1872, the older journal became somewhat less theological in emphasis and removed to New York City, merging with its former rival amid the renewed goodwill of the Reunion. John M. Libbey, of that city, became the editor, and, with the title *Presbyterian Quarterly and Princeton Review*, the journal tried to emulate the *North American Review*. Lack of financial support, however, led to its suspension in 1884.[79]

McCosh intended to revive the review, but he wanted a new character and identity for it. He had been trying for many years, in an unostentatious manner, to liberate Princeton College from its affiliation in the public mind with the seminary. Hence McCosh emphasized the shift by selecting *New Princeton Review* as the title, and by printing its cover in the recently established orange and black of the college's colors. He also wanted a topical journal, one

---

Papers; *Memorial Book of the Sesquicentennial Celebration of . . . Princeton University* (Princeton, 1898), p. 433.

[79] Frank Luther Mott, *A History of American Magazine, 1741-1850* (New York, 1930), pp. 529-35.

that spoke to the interests of the day. McCosh felt that the *New Princeton Review* to this extent would directly supplement the work of the college. He wrote to an alumnus of the college, explaining the purpose of the new publication and urging his support. "It is intended by us," he said, "that the new Review may help you to keep up and carry on the knowledge, literary and scientific, acquired by you at the College." Furthermore, McCosh appointed William Milligan Sloane, a major force in the "New Princeton" movement, to edit the *Review*. With an article entitled "What an American Philosophy Should Be," McCosh launched the new effort in 1886. Among its contributors in the next three years were some notable individuals: Theodore Roosevelt, John Bach McMaster (bygones were bygones, one assumes), James Russell Lowell, George Bancroft, Charles Eliot Norton, E. L. Godkin, Washington Gladden, William Crary Brownell, Woodrow Wilson, and Henry Van Dyke. By no means was the journal daringly new. It was clearly more genteel than radical, but to that extent it spoke to a certain quality about Princeton that had set in at the end of McCosh's years. Nevertheless, the journal did reflect the somewhat secular and cosmopolitan tenor of Princeton. It did not survive beyond McCosh's administration and merged in 1888 with the new *Political Science Quarterly*.[80] McCosh had sought to supplant Princeton's primary affiliation with a religious denomination by bringing it into contact with the wider academic and public community in America. Others, we shall see, would try to secure that part of McCosh's legacy at Princeton.

[80] McCosh to "Banks," December 1, 1885, in the McCosh Correspondence; McCosh to Noah Porter, January 30, 1886, in the McCosh Correspondence.

Chapter Nine

THE NEW PRINCETON

MORE THAN ANYWHERE ELSE in the Western world, the nature and purpose of higher learning were joined in nineteenth-century America to the social and intellectual aims of the Protestant churches. Learning seldom presented itself to the American public as an end in its own right. The American college, from its seventeenth-century beginnings at Harvard, acquired a pronounced moral atmosphere that was meant to reflect and perpetuate the moral meaning of life and the intellectual foundations on which it thrived. To this extent moral and mental philosophy, the traditional courses taught by the college president to the senior class, represented a rounding out of the standard four-year program, a rite of passage for American collegians as they departed the sequestered confines of the campus and entered the arena of public life. Even as late as 1860, the Harvard Board of Overseers reviewed with concern the quality and effectiveness of philosophical instruction at the college. For without proper drill in moral philosophy, they said, Harvard graduates could easily fall away from the "fundamental principles of religion and ethics."[1] McCosh at Princeton did not place quite so much store on moral philosophy as such. But he never ceased to believe that there were great intellectual battles raging in the world and that the Princeton classrooms were one place they should be fought. And as in Scotland and Ireland, McCosh saw himself surrounded by enemies. Furthermore, these enemies had familiar faces.

McCosh arrived in America just when a revolution in ideas was beginning to take place. In the area of Boston, there was a great fermenting of ideas, which gradually found their way into Harvard College and made that institution one of the most important centers of philosophy in the world. It was this exciting and significant reconstruction of thought that signaled the full maturation of phi-

[1] Bruce Kuklick, *The Rise of American Philosophy: Cambridge, Massachusetts, 1860-1930* (New Haven, 1977), p. xv.

losophy in America and gave the United States its peculiar identity in the realm of philosophical ideas. Harvard indeed became the focus of most that was fresh and new in American thought, while Princeton under McCosh won, if not reinforced, its status as champion of the older ways. By no means did this fact mean that McCosh was unappreciated. There were elements all over America that looked to him as guardian against the new and dangerous directions of ideas. But it does seem clear that McCosh found his audience mostly among a religious-intellectual community and that the new professional class of academic philosophers in America lost interest in him. To be sure, McCosh's philosophy was never strictly "apologetic." Nor did McCosh close Princeton's doors to the new ways. Physiological psychology, we have seen, won admittance into the curriculum with McCosh's receptiveness to explorations in that new field. Nonetheless, Princeton and McCosh stood at the crossroads and championed the familiar ways. Harvard pioneered in new directions. We need to look briefly at the American philosophical scene and McCosh's place in it.

From the early nineteenth century Harvard philosophy had made itself the intellectual champion of the Unitarian establishment of the Boston area of New England. For Unitarianism had triumphed as the prevailing religious creed of the Boston gentry and their clergy, and Harvard College was the institutional focal point of that social order. Challenging their supremacy, however, was another intellectual group, lacking institutional cohesiveness and gaining an unsavory reputation among the Unitarians. The Transcendentalists had signaled their stand against the Unitarian order in Emerson's famous "Divinity School Address" of 1838. Social rivalry was apparent here, but the intellectual clash was more interesting and more profound. Harvard Unitarianism had been shaped by its earlier effort to defeat the skepticism of the French Enlightenment and the fashionable appeal it had among members of the Harvard collegiate set of the 1790s. Harvard Unitarians became the champions of a natural theology in America. They defended a dualistic account of human nature and confirmed the reality of a spiritual order in the universe. Even biblical miracles might win intellectual confirmation by this indirect defense of Christianity. In rearing this philosophical edifice, the Harvard Unitarians directly imported the Scottish thinkers. Thomas Reid and Dugald Stewart became the main props of a Harvard philosophical program designed to uphold the moral nature of man and the twin realities of physical and spiritual being.² For a long time it worked. From Witherspoon's Princeton and now to Unitarian Harvard, Scottish metaphysics began its conquest of academic philosophy in the United States.

For a growing number in America, and especially for the emerging Transcendentalist party, the efforts to employ a rationalist system to describe reality were neither intellectually adequate nor spiritually sufficient. And just this dissatisfaction helped prepare the way for the post-Kantian direction of American philosophy, much in the manner it had already done in Europe. For the problem from Hume still lingered—how to legitimate belief in the external world. Even McCosh had found Reid's and Stewart's defenses inadequate and tried to give realism a stronger defense. But Kant had shown that we can never get outside of our ideas, that the world we know is only the reality constructed for us by the categories of our mind. But what was for Kant an epistemological problem became for others a metaphysical one. For in Germany and then in England there began the challenge to break through to the unknown noumenal realm that lay hidden behind the world of phenomena. The post-Kantians could not rest content with a reality confined to individual consciousness and made increasingly bolder efforts to bring the ultimate structure of reality into conformity with a universal human consciousness that shapes it. They then not only constructed the world of experience from mind alone, but appealed more and more to a suprarational faculty in the human soul as our access to a higher reality, one joined to that within. Such possibilities received an English formulation from Coleridge and Carlyle, and they became available for ready use by the Americans. By the 1840s, idealism was making its way in American circles.³

At Harvard, the trustees of the Unitarian conscience now faced the challenge of an ungodly materialism on the one hand and the undisciplined and suspicious enthusiasm of idealism on the other. As Unitarianism looked skeptically at the overzealous religion of the heart as expressed in evangelical Protestantism, so also did it mistrust the easy religion of the expansive soul. Harvard at mid-century was fighting the philosophical extremes against which McCosh was setting himself in his own philosophical works, in

---

² Daniel Walker Howe, *The Unitarian Conscience: Harvard Moral Philosophy, 1805-1861* (Cambridge, Mass., 1970), pp. 13-14; Arthur W. Brown, *William Ellery Channing* (New York, 1961), pp. 24-25.

³ Kuklick, *Rise of American Philosophy*, pp. 14-15; Paul F. Boller, Jr., *American Transcendentalism, 1830-1860: An Intellectual Inquiry* (New York, 1974), pp. 36-42.

Scotland and Ireland. At this time, the Harvard defense had fallen largely to Francis Bowen (1811-1890), Alford Professor of History from 1853 to 1889. Born the same year as McCosh, Bowen matured amid the Unitarian-Transcendentalist rivalry around Harvard. His early essays for the *Christian Examiner* and the *North American Review* took on Emerson's challenge and upheld the Unitarian cause. Bowen tried to reverse the downward course of philosophy that had followed the Kantian revolution. Kant's ambitious successors were dangerously egotistical, he believed. Philosophy must be disciplined by empirical reasoning and grounded on the sure observations of the senses. Bowen, who had compiled an edition of Stewart's works for use by his Harvard students, then called upon Sir William Hamilton to save him from the Transcendentalists' threat. Bowen valued Hamilton because he discredited skepticism by an appeal to the authority of consciousness, but also because he threw cold water on the idealists. Confining all knowledge to the relativity of cognitive experience, Hamilton placed the inconceivable Absolute beyond the realm of intellectual conjecture. By thus upholding natural realism in the tradition of the other Scottish philosophers, and also by returning to the safer speculations of Kant, Hamilton supplied Bowen with Harvard's version of the middle way.[4] But the middle way, and the extremes also, soon met a new challenge.

Sir William Hamilton became no less powerful and controversial a force in the United States than he was in Great Britain. Beyond the mental philosophy classrooms of American colleges, Hamilton also received extensive attention in the religious periodicals. Until the last quarter of the century the religious periodicals served as the major focus for the serious discussion of the intellectual currents of the day. And they gave considerable quality to American intellectual life. Usually these journals had denominational affiliations—the *Princeton Review* (Presbyterian), the *Bibliotheca Sacra* (Congregational), the *Christian Examiner* (Unitarian), the *American Theological Review* (liberal Presbyterian), the *Methodist Quarterly Review*, the *Baptist Review*. In all of these reviews, one of the major centers of attention in the 1860s was the issue touched off by John Stuart Mill's *Examination of Sir William Hamilton's Philosophy* in 1865. McCosh and Henry Mansel also figured prominently in the Americans' discussions. Mill's devastating review of Hamilton was immediately perceived as a crucial challenge to the intellectual foun-

[4] Kuklick, *Rise of American Philosophy*, pp. 18-19, 28-34.

dations of Christian America. The Scottish philosophy had for a long time supported those foundations, so the religious-intellectual community in the United States reacted swiftly to Mill. To be sure, Hamilton was no universal friend of the religious thinkers, and his removal of the Absolute from the realm of thought was usually judged a position unfriendly to theism. Henry B. Smith, in the *American Theological Review*, had written a critical summary of Hamilton's *Lectures*, but was more friendly to the Scot when he reexamined him in the light of Mill's challenge.[5] For the Methodists, Rev. O. S. Munsell made perceptive critiques, first of Mansel's extension of Hamilton into a theological system in his Bampton lectures, then of Hamilton himself, in whom he found a multitude of contradictions. Munsell concluded that Hamilton's system, extended by the "ingenious but erratic" Mansel, made a poor ally for Christian thought.[6]

For the Unitarians, Bowen took on Mill directly and defended Hamilton. This was a thorough and painstaking review, a meticulous reexamination of the issues. Not only had Mill utterly misunderstood Hamilton, Bowen claimed, but his own theory of matter and mind was "an elaborate failure." Bowen ended with a brief notice of McCosh's book on Mill and spoke of its contribution to the defense of sound philosophy.[7]

Even before his arrival in America, McCosh had received much attention in the religious reviews. Hamilton had been the opening to a Kantian restatement of the Scottish philosophy, and for all Hamilton's alleged value in defending natural realism, he was nonetheless viewed with some suspicion here, as the aforementioned reviews suggest. McCosh was a friendly critic of Hamilton, and, as we have seen, he tried to demonstrate that our intuitive faculties do lead us from the realm of experience to an intellectual apprehension of divine reality. It was usually for this elaborate defense that McCosh was appreciated in the United States. A critic for the *American Theological Review* praised McCosh for defending "the

---

[5] "Hamilton's Theory of Knowledge," *American Theological Review*, 3 (1861), 124–61; "Mill's Examination of Hamilton's Philosophy," *American Theological Review*, 4, n.s. (1866), 126–62.

[6] Review of Mansel's *Limits of Religious Thought Examined*, in *Methodist Quarterly Review*, 42 (1860), 357–59; "Sir William Hamilton's Philosophy," *Methodist Quarterly Review*, 43 (1861), 447–49.

[7] "Mr. Mill and His Critics," *American Theological Review*, 1 (1859), 351–75, 427–48. But another Unitarian voice, an anonymous reviewer for the *Christian Examiner*, came to Mill's defense and defused the charges of irreligiosity made against him. See "Mill's Review of Hamilton," *Christian Examiner*, 79 (1865), 301–27.

positive nature of our idea of the Infinite" and credited him with some fresh and independent thinking on the subject.[8] Likewise, the *Methodist Quarterly Review* thought that McCosh had defended intuitionism on a realistic basis and thus provided the best defense against positivism. It blamed Hamilton and Mansel for preparing the way for Bain and Comte by relegating spiritual reality to the realm of the inconceivable.[9] Other reviewers made similar points, indicating a wide appreciation for McCosh as a philosopher doing much to promote a theistic understanding of reality.[10] McCosh further enhanced his stature by quickly joining the Hamilton-Mill controversy with his *Examination of Mr. J. S. Mill's Philosophy*. When one journal drew attention to McCosh's inauguration at Princeton two years later, it readily recalled that "he has measured a victorious sword with the mightiest anti-Christian thinker of his age, John Stuart Mill."[11] It was essentially for this usefulness to Christianity that the *Methodist Quarterly Review* said of McCosh that "we rejoice in the popularity of his works."[12]

But just at this time, however, the reorientation of American philosophy was beginning. Above all, the Unitarian position was most vulnerable. It had tied religion and philosophy to an ordered universe and rendered ordinary reason competent for religion and philosophy. Indeed, the Transcendentalist challenge had helped force the Unitarians into that position. But Darwinism, with its portrait of an undirected and purposeless cosmos, steadily eroded this point of view. With profound implications for metaphysics, ethical theory, and epistemology, Darwinism demanded a whole reordering of the basic propositions that had fortified philosophical views of life that had long been compatible with the main tenets of Christian America. At Harvard, a philosophy that had clung so tenaciously to dualism and to a rational theism quickly succumbed to Darwinism and the varieties of pragmatism that arose with it.

---

[8] Notice of McCosh's *Intuitions of the Mind*, in *American Theological Review*, 2 (1860), 375-76.

[9] Notice of McCosh's *Intuitions of the Mind*, in *Methodist Quarterly Review*, 42 (1860), 344.

[10] See for example, "McCosh on the Intuitions," *Bibliotheca Sacra and Biblical Repository*, 17 (1860), 661-64; Rev. J. Dempster, "McCosh on the Intuitions," *Methodist Quarterly Review* 43 (1861), 267-76; J. H. A[llen], Notice of McCosh's *Examination of Mr. J. S. Mill's Philosophy*, *Christian Examiner*, 82 (1867), 245-50.

[11] Notice of McCosh's *Inauguration of James McCosh* . . . , *Methodist Quarterly Review*, 51 (1869), 153.

[12] Review of McCosh's *The Supernatural in Relation to the Natural*, *Methodist Quarterly Review*, 44 (1862), 525-26.

The Scottish alliance would fade elsewhere as well in the midst of this challenge. But only at Harvard would the decay of the old yield so magnificently to fresh and exciting redefinitions of philosophical understanding in America.[13]

Chauncey Wright (1830-1875) was one of the first to come to terms with Darwin and to incorporate Darwin into philosophy. But this curious Cambridge thinker, so facile of tongue, so awkward of pen, reared himself first in the orthodoxies of his day. The enigmatic Wright attended Harvard College. Even though he had read Robert Chambers's *Vestiges* and had become immediately captivated by the evolutionary point of view in it, Wright discovered a philosophical hero in Hamilton. His devotion to Hamilton was legendary among the few who befriended Wright, and the young philosopher mastered the Scot's writings and defended the law of the unconditioned.[14] Then came Mill's critique. Wright tried to hold on to the Hamiltonian structure and even endeavored to show that Mill had unjustly charged Hamilton with contradictions in his thinking. But Mill made his way with Wright, and slowly the old edifice crumbled. When Wright reviewed Mill's critique for the *Nation*, he credited the empiricist with putting forth one of "the most important contributions to psychology which have been made in modern times"—the doctrine of substances as "permanent possibilities of sensations."[15]

But Wright was still somewhat ambivalent. Again for the *Nation*, he reviewed McCosh's *Intuitions of the Mind* and took a long look at the Scottish school. Wright credited McCosh with much independence but correctly placed him at the heart of the Scottish philosophy. And Wright had much praise for McCosh's own intuitional realism: "In ingenuity this theory appears to us to exceed anything which has come from the Scottish school, and in pliancy it exceeds, we think, any system which has ever been propounded. The extremes of philosophy are avoided by it with surprising agility."[16] Despite some qualifications, the review of McCosh's book was altogether friendly. How curious, then, is this letter from Wright to a friend: "I have on hand . . . a new installment of Scottish metaphysics which Mr. Godkin has sent me, viz., McCosh on the Intuitions of the Mind. I have gone through its four hundred

---

[13] Kuklick, *Rise of American Philosophy*, pp. xix, 24-25.

[14] Edward H. Madden, *Chauncey Wright and the Foundations of Pragmatism* (Seattle, 1963), pp. 3, 5, 7.

[15] [Chauncey Wright], "Mill on Hamilton," *Nation*, 1 (1866), 279-81.

[16] [Chauncey Wright], "McCosh on Intuitions," *Nation*, 1 (1866), 627-29.

pages of mistakes and 'dangerous errors,' and come out a confirmed sensationalist, idealist, utilitarian, positivist, sceptic—all in short, which the book condemns; and I intend to hold these positions or as many of them as I can until I have overthrown this presumptuous orthodoxy."[17]

Wright's influence grew in the Cambridge area. He became the master spirit of the little Metaphysical Club in that community and engineered lively discussions on philosophy, evolution, and other timely subjects. By his sparkling conversations, Wright was leading a quiet redirection of philosophy. William James, Oliver Wendell Holmes, John Fiske, Frank Abbott, and others all benefited by their encounters within the club.[18] The most important of Wright's literary efforts was his seminal essay, "The Evolution of Self-Consciousness." It is a landmark of the new directions both for its philosophical twists, and for its direct accommodation with evolutionary ideas. For Wright carried through the accommodation from where McCosh left off. McCosh, it will be remembered, believed that Darwinism ran into an insurmountable problem of causality. If effects must resemble in their constitutive substance the causes from which they emerge, then evolution cannot derive the higher mental faculties of man out of the precognitive faculties of lower animals. Either a spiritual quality derived from a superior being must lie latent in the original substance of life, or an intervention must take place along the evolutionary process.

Wright believed differently, however, and his essay was a genuine tour de force. Wright proposed to answer the question of how something new could occur in evolution by showing, first, that effects need not resemble their causes, and second, that causality is really a problem of dispositional intentions. Thus, even a measurable dissimilarity between two phenomena does not invalidate their causal connection; self-consciousness may then be the product of antecedent conditions that are not in fact similar to it. Just how this was possible in such a case as the evolution of self-consciousness, Wright explained by referring to the volitional characteristics of organisms. Wright traced progressive habitual dispositions in lower animals toward a consciousness of ends, "ulterior motive in volition." Such a progression, though, requires certain conditions, so that the ego, and its attendant self-consciousness, "emerge" in a manner that reflects a connection of higher human qualities with

---

[17] Madden, *Chauncey Wright*, p. 149.
[18] Ibid., pp. 21-22; Elizabeth Flower and Murray G. Murphey, *A History of American Philosophy*, 2 vols. (New York, 1977), 2:537.

their lower sources, but does not manifest any apparent resemblance of causes and effects.[19] It is some question whether Wright's ideas establish the origins of American pragmatism, but they do clearly signal the tendency to describe human mental habits in biological terms, a distinguishing mark of the whole pragmatic movement in the United States. From Wright's essay to William James's *Principles of Psychology* in 1890 there is a direct line and a major shift in philosophical discourse.

Wright had now traveled from Mill to Darwin. In doing so, he carried forth one line of thought that McCosh had made a major effort in Great Britain to discredit. Pragmatism in America would reproduce in Charles Sanders Peirce and William James a familiar American situation, in which philosophy stood as a reconciling medium between science and religion,[20] and even in Wright it could play that role. The complete Darwinization of philosophy was still several years off and awaited the enormous influence of John Dewey to secure its most naturalistic statement. For all of the pragmatists, though, the ground was shifting; for each of them the nature of the universe as an open, evolving structure was a reality that challenged nearly every important proposition with which philosophy must be engaged. For this new perspective the Scottish philosophy was too rigid and too rationalistic. McCosh had endeavored to bring intuitionism, dualism, and even a kind of ethical utilitarianism into an evolutionary framework. For that effort he rather stood out among the religious philosophers of America, and won some credit for his efforts. But within the philosophical community he lost ground. Darwin created a breach in American thought, and the older alliance of philosophy and religion would not survive the nineteenth century.

In Great Britain, McCosh fought the great philosophical battles of his day. In America, he became increasingly remote from them. None of his books published in America can be considered an important contribution to the ongoing philosophical arguments here. *Christianity and Positivism* derived from a series of lectures sponsored by the Ely Foundation, and it contained some useful commentary on evolution and its relation to theism. But most of the work was unexciting. McCosh did succeed, after years of work, in publishing his monumental *The Scottish Philosophy* in 1875. This lengthy book arrived too late to do much good for a fading school,

---

[19] Flower and Murphey, *History of American Philosophy*, 2:544–45.
[20] Ibid., 1:xvii.

but it makes up for that fact in its contribution to history. Its rich biographies, its recovery of thinkers theretofore overlooked, and its critical commentary make it to this day an invaluable piece of research. McCosh did turn to a problem he had not discussed at length before, and in 1880 issued his two-volume study, *The Emotions*. But this work was simplistic and tedious, and it showed that McCosh, amid a frantic administrative career at Princeton, was losing ground in the prolific philosophical literature of the day. McCosh in America never duplicated the quality of his greatest work, *The Intuitions of the Mind*, to this day a penetrating and suggestive book.

Nonetheless, McCosh was not to be written off the American philosophical scene. His best critical work came in smaller packages, and much of it spoke to the new directions in American thought. McCosh observed the Kantian and Hegelian revivals in America with interest. He had much to say on their behalf, but feared they were quite inappropriate to the American temper. He wrote several short essays on the subject and a long pamphlet of sixty pages, *A Criticism of the Critical Philosophy*, published in 1884. This is one of McCosh's best pieces of his later period. At the very least it confirms McCosh's position as the last great spokesman for the Scottish tradition in America, for the essay is a thorough critique of the idealistic movement from the realistic position of Scotland. McCosh wrote several lengthy essays such as this and published them collectively in his two-volume *Realistic Philosophy* (1887). The series contained two essays on evolution, including the very skillful attack on Herbert Spencer's philosophy. But McCosh did little more than this in meeting the new directions of philosophy and the evolutionary currents that were carrying it into pragmatism. His last large-scale effort, *First and Fundamental Truths* (1892) was a barren rehash of the *Intuitions* and indicates, sadly, how remote was McCosh from the engaging problems of American philosophy. He was losing influence, and he despaired to realize it. McCosh publicly said that he hoped America would find its own way in philosophy and strike an independent chord. But he failed to appreciate how William James and others were already doing that, and when, in 1886, he launched the *New Princeton Review* with the article "What an American Philosophy Should Be," his prescription had all the ingredients of the old Scottish philosophy.

Thus did McCosh preside over the waning days of a formative philosophical tradition in America. In the judgment of history, he earned the title, provided by Elizabeth Flower and Murray G. Murphey, August Overseer of the Realist Establishment.[21] Toward the end of his career McCosh surely knew that his enduring legacy would not lie in the realm of ideas. It would lie in his transformation of Princeton College. He fought hard for that legacy. And he secured it.

AT PRINCETON, things were falling apart. The years 1882 through 1885 were the nadir of McCosh's administration at the school. The nature of his crisis, his triumphant victory over it, and the transformation of Princeton through the work and influence of those who came after him and carried out his plans, are the remaining subjects of this last chapter. Together, they bring to fruition that precise skill that McCosh exercised in weaving ideas and institutions together. McCosh had articulated a model of the new Princeton with increasing precision over the two decades of his presidency, and he had reconstructed Princeton's relations with a variety of external groups. In the last years of the century those groups became increasingly integrated into the college. Then the war between the old forces and the new became an open battle. It culminated in an academic coup that expelled one president and inaugurated a new one. And in that final act, the whole force and legacy of McCosh's life at Princeton were evident. Ironically, however, McCosh would have called it an ambiguous triumph.

The most obvious sign of trouble in the early 1880s was declining enrollment. McCosh had always stressed expansion of the student body and did assign a quantitative measure to his success. Students had grown in number every year at Princeton until 1882; and then three successive years of decline began. McCosh could take some comfort in the fact that college enrollment in the nation was leveling off in this period, and the number of degrees awarded fell dramatically in 1884.[22] But he had expected better things of Princeton. He had hoped to make Princeton strong in the Middle Atlantic area, but reported that the college was losing badly in the big cities. Philadelphia, Baltimore, and New York were sending only a trickle of students, and McCosh concluded that the need to draw from the Middle West was more imperative than ever. McCosh drew some painful, tentative conclusions. Perhaps Princeton had set its admissions standards too high in its drive for improved academic quality. He suspected that some potential students, especially mid-

[21] Ibid., 1:205.
[22] *Standard Education Almanac, 1973-74* (Orange, N.J., 1974), p. 90.

westerners, might have suffered from inadequate preparation, particularly in the sciences. The president in fact now was in the unhappy position of discouraging the board from raising admission requirements even further.[23] This was practical medicine, but McCosh had to swallow his pride with it.

But the enrollment issue mattered less to McCosh than another one—the recurring nightmare of campus disorder. Indiscipline among students was the bane of his administration. For a while in 1877 and afterward, discipline was relatively good, the campus peaceful. Then in 1882 trouble broke out anew and assumed insidious forms. The faculty minutes for this year are a dismal and tedious chronicle of student misdemeanors brought before a faculty that should have been giving its time to more productive work. Ironically, McCosh had succeeded only too well in repressing the secret societies. But their elimination seemed only to encourage more resentment and disorder. Bitterness against the faculty was noticeably acute. One incident involved a student throwing a rock into a professor's home. The *Princetonian* printed scurrilous references to some of the more unpopular professors until finally the faculty determined that license of the press had gone far enough. The editor was "censored," and new controls applied.[24] There was also the issue of student athletics. By the 1880s McCosh had become more sensitive to the abuses than to the merits of the athletic program he had encouraged at Princeton. Gymnastics, disciplined exercise, and competitive sport were supposed to produce a certain kind of gentleman-scholar-athlete. Instead, McCosh reported, they were producing the athletic specialist, skilled in his sport and dedicated to it, but skilled in nothing else and uninterested in all else. McCosh checked the records, and his suspicions were confirmed. He reported to the trustees that Princeton's best athletes were no longer, as they had been earlier, the best students.[25]

McCosh confronted some genuine problems and some genuine abuses, but it is hard to avoid concluding that much of the problem was of his own making. Certainly one may wonder whether McCosh's kind of earnest, often strident moralism, born of his evangelical experience, was suitable to the Princeton of the late nineteenth century. Was it at all suitable to the kind of modernized, scholarly Princeton he himself was trying to build? To be sure,

---

[23] "Minutes of the College of New Jersey," February 14, 1884, hereafter, TM.
[24] "Faculty Minutes" (of the College of New Jersey), Princeton University Archives, May 29, 1882, and others; TM, February 9, 1882.
[25] TM, June 15, 1885.

most students were immature, many having no sense of academic purpose and indifferent to the educational aims of the college. These probably merited the heavy curbs that McCosh placed on them. Nonetheless, overreaction was often the rule. For example, McCosh was not one bit happy to learn what happened to Princeton students when they went to New York City for a football game. Students and players were invited to a theater, specially decorated with Yale and Princeton boxes. The actresses wore special orange and black outfits for Princeton and blue ones to honor Yale. Afterward, McCosh claimed, they lured the Princeton innocents into prostitution, and worse, as a result, they missed church the next morning. McCosh's report seems clearly exaggerated, but he resolved that Princetonians would travel to New York City no more.[26]

Even if McCosh did take the right action here, which is doubtful, his treatment of the faculty was clearly questionable. Somewhat to his chagrin, McCosh found that in organizing a faculty that would pursue research and scholarship, he had hired men who did just that. His professors were manifestly uninterested in the wearisome task of overseeing students and guarding their moral behavior. McCosh never appreciated this attitude, but he was almost resigned: it was the "spirit" of the age, this trend toward greater freedom. Teachers today want to teach and do research, he said; they are less concerned with the "spiritual" well-being of their students. That attitude had appeared at other American colleges, and now it was "creeping in" at Princeton. No longer do faculty members make it a point to attend chapel, McCosh reported. "Some never attend." He warned his delinquent staff that it set a bad example for the students. Also, although McCosh claimed that he "abhorred" the "spy system," he warned that each faculty member had a responsibility to "keep his eyes and ears open" for students' misdemeanors. No professor could excuse himself from this obligation. No doubt McCosh genuinely feared that American colleges were in danger of repeating the bad European examples in forsaking all moral oversight of students. He had not forgotten the sad experiences of his own collegiate days in Glasgow, the dissipation of his friends, and the indifference of the university's officials. But at Princeton, it was McCosh's own bright young men who complained most about the moral surveillance requested of them. There was clear irony in this fact, and McCosh perceived it. He had reared a generation of scholars committed to their dis-

[26] TM, February 12, 1885.

ciplines of learning. With their arrival in positions of influence at Princeton, the moral and evangelical style of their mentor-president simply lost force.[27]

Princeton's misfortunes in the early eighties hurt McCosh. His opponents now had more means to discredit him, perhaps even to get him out of office. The *Princetonian* in March 1882 reported on rumors that some of the trustees wanted McCosh out. Nonetheless, student editors of the *Princetonian*, however bitterly they treated some of the faculty, were fiercely loyal to McCosh. They absolved McCosh of responsibility for the recent troubles and announced that they would welcome no change in the presidency. But the pressure on McCosh remained heavy. William Berryman Scott once described the enmity between McCosh and the conservative trustees. He reconstructed this scene:

> Conservative: "Do you know what you will be remembered for in the history of Princeton?"
>
> McCosh [yielding once again to his massive egoism]: "I suppose you refer to the growth and development of the College under my administration."
>
> Conservative: "Not at all: you will be known as the President under whom evening prayers were discontinued."[28]

At the end of June 1883, McCosh decided he had had enough. To everyone's surprise he announced at the trustees' meeting that he was calling it quits. But the majority of the board, despite the noise of the conservatives, was not prepared for this event and not pleased with McCosh's intentions. It met the next day without McCosh and resolved to ask for his continued service. It promised some faculty reorganization along the lines of McCosh's requests, and it promised to appoint new executive officers to lighten the burden of his presidency. Professor Murray became dean of the faculty and assumed charge of the whole problem of discipline in the college. (A year and a half later Murray begged release from that unhappy assignment!) McCosh accepted the new arrangement and continued in the presidency.[29]

McCosh's support from the trustees in no way eased the real crisis he faced. He knew quite well that the spirit of the earlier

[27] TM, February 9, 1882, June 19, 1882; see also McCosh's essay on this subject, "Discipline in American Colleges," *North American Review*, 126 (1878), 428-41.

[28] *Princetonian*, March 24, 1882; *Princeton Alumni Weekly*, June 13, 1930.

[29] TM, June 18, 1883, June 19, 1883, November 12, 1885.

years had waned, and in spite of all the recent improvements, a new sense of purpose and dedication for the college was needed. Part of the problem was money. Princeton's large donors, McCosh said, had given all they could, and all they should. The defeat of the alumni representation issue had soured interest among that group. Princeton, McCosh said, was "in a rut." He had been racking his brains, he reported, to find a way out of it, and now, in 1886, he believed he had found it.[30]

McCosh thought he could turn a bad situation into a good one. More than that, he believed he could take advantage of the present crisis in a way that would benefit his larger objectives for Princeton. In June 1885 McCosh proposed to the trustees that the school's official name, the College of New Jersey, be changed to Princeton University. The immediate need was a pragmatic one. The college needed to create a new "interest," such as had existed after the Civil War at the time of his own arrival. Now the University Campaign, as he called it, could be an issue to rouse the interest and support of the alumni and other friends of Princeton. It would symbolize Princeton's great educational ambitions and intentions, announcing that the institution was joining the front ranks of American higher education.[31]

In fact, McCosh, who had heretofore believed that Princeton's proclamation of university status was premature, now had sound reasons for changing. The faculty had improved noticeably in the last seven years. Graduate programs were fairly well established, and a faculty dedicated to scholarship was enhancing the institution's academic reputation. The idea was superb strategy, besides. It would further signal Princeton's break from its older mold. It would again activate alumni, McCosh's most reliable supporters and forces of modernization. And it would also attract to Princeton the type of student-scholar McCosh had pursued. To this end McCosh also proposed a new program of university scholarships, to be awarded on a competitive basis to graduates of any college in America, not to Princetonians only. There was only one problem. The trustees understood exactly the implications of all these changes.[32]

---

[30] TM, February 11, 1886; see also the letter of McCosh to Robert Bonner, March 6, 1884, in the "Correspondence of James McCosh," Department of Rare Books and Special Collections, Princeton University Library. It shows the strained relations with this important benefactor.

[31] TM, June 15, 1885, February 11, 1886.

[32] Willard Thorp, "The Founding of the Princeton Graduate School: An Academic Agon," *Princeton University Library Chronicle*, 32 (1970), 2.

McCosh had already prepared the groundwork for his campaign, and once again the alumni were the main force behind it. In the face of the enrollment decline McCosh traveled widely to alumni meetings to explain the problem and ask for ideas in resolving it. But more and more the word "university" entered his talks. He presented to the alumni groups the vision of a Princeton worthy of their names, an institution of national renown and scholarly prestige. Then in the spring of 1884 he undertook yet another grand tour—to Columbus, Chicago, Omaha, St. Louis, Louisville, Lexington, and Dayton. The indefatigable man of seventy-three was fired again with the ambitions of his educational design. In 1887, when a new Princeton Alumni Association of North Eastern Pennsylvania was formed, McCosh was there for its first meeting. He spoke of the need for further liberal reforms in the Princeton curriculum and again pleaded the case for the change in Princeton's name.[33] And in this effort McCosh had the tireless help of his newest trustee ally, Moses Taylor Pyne. Pyne was greatly responsible for the creation of a half-dozen or so of the new alumni groups and McCosh's earnest supporter in the University Campaign.[34]

Despite this help, McCosh found the road rough going. He did all he could to assure the skeptics that the change to Princeton University promised no revolution in the school. The entire new Princeton had evolved slowly and carefully out of the undergraduate program. Everything good in a college, he said, can be retained in a university: "its good order, its discipline, its religion." McCosh knew that this campaign was to be his last one for Princeton. Increasingly he came to feel that all he stood for, the whole influence and legacy of his administration, were now being offered for endorsement in the proclamation of a Princeton University. To that extent the issue was at least partly a symbolic one. And so it was perceived by others. Hardened clerical interests especially sensed a threat to the religious character and identity of the college. Others probably resented any endorsing of the liberal academic changes of the past two decades. But McCosh was determined. He pressed the issue on the trustees in November 1886 and again in February 1887. Finally the vote came on June 20 that year. McCosh was the loser. The trustees decided that the change of title at that time was "inexpedient." A disappointed, but not embittered McCosh, voiced his dissent.[35]

[33] TM, June 16, 1884; *Princetonian*, January 12, 1887.
[34] *Princeton Alumni Weekly*, October 28, 1955; TM, February 11, 1886.
[35] TM, February 11, 1886, November 11, 1886, June 20, 1887; Henry Wilkinson Bragdon, *Woodrow Wilson: The Academic Years* (Cambridge, Mass., 1967), p. 214.

McCosh could not be too disheartened. He had set Princeton's course, and he knew that the university would continue to move in the direction he had given it. Moreover, the last years of his administration gave him much reason for happiness. Princeton's situation in 1886 took a marked turn for the better. A dramatic increase in enrollment occurred that year, and the largest freshman class in the history of the college entered in the fall. Princeton certainly profited from a national trend, but there were other factors at work in its case. First, as McCosh announced to the trustees, 20 students entered Princeton from the Lawrenceville School, and 10 others from other nearby boarding schools. Here was the first sign that McCosh's efforts to create feeder schools for Princeton had paid off. In fact, the closeness of Princeton and Lawrenceville became greater in the years ahead. By 1893, 335 students had graduated from Lawrenceville, and 190 of them had entered Princeton. By 1898, 366 of 682 graduates had entered. No wonder McCosh said that Lawrenceville had come to Princeton's rescue. He could rejoice not only at the numbers, but at the fact that Lawrenceville provided students who were well prepared for college work. Princeton's own preparatory school soon became a thing of the past.[36]

Two other trends were encouraging. First, no fewer than fifty-one students, according to McCosh, had arrived at Princeton after taking the local entrance examinations that McCosh had established around the country. McCosh had placed much hope in these examinations, "each of them conducted under my care hundreds of miles away," and was clearly proud of the results.[37] And second, McCosh announced that sixty students from the New England states were now attending Princeton. That was a noteworthy increase, for enrollment patterns heretofore had clearly confirmed Princeton's inability to compete with Harvard, Yale, and other New England colleges in their own backyard.[38] Why this turnabout? One can make no definite conclusions, but there are indications again that McCosh's strategy was bearing fruit. Thus, it is significant that Princeton's marked increase in students came the

---

[36] *Decennial Catalogue, Lawrenceville School, 1883-1893* (Boston, [1893]), p. 60; *Quindecennial Catalogue, The Lawrenceville School, 1883-1898* (Philadelphia, [1898]), p. 59; Roland J. Mulford, *History of the Lawrenceville School, 1810-1935* (Princeton, 1935), p. 90; TM, February 11, 1886.

[37] TM, November 11, 1886.

[38] Ibid. The trustees' minutes list the names of the graduates and their home residences.

year after the celebrated McCosh-Eliot debates. These had received extensive newspaper coverage and had greatly clarified the opposing academic philosophies of Princeton and Harvard. Furthermore, Harvard had recently undertaken a noticeable and highly controversial liberalization of its religious requirements, including the abolition of compulsory chapel. McCosh's debate with Eliot on that subject certainly drew attention to Princeton's religious conservatism and, it seems safe to conclude, won support from religious-minded parents seeking a "safe" place for their sons. Undoubtedly, the same factor prevailed in the Midwest and helps account for the new representation from that part of the country.[39] McCosh, at least, received much favorable reaction for his stance, including a letter from Austin Phelps of Andover Theological Seminary who mourned the "agnostic decline of Harvard."[40] But whatever the reasons, Princeton in the last three years of McCosh's administration enjoyed substantial growth in enrollment. Slightly more than six hundred students were attending when he retired.

McCosh's success in these last three years seemed clearly to demonstrate that his efforts to bring the college into a new series of external alliances were justified. In his twenty years at Princeton College, he had reduced its academic affiliation with Princeton Theological Seminary. But McCosh did want to preserve the religious character of the institution, and he maintained a strong allegiance to Presbyterianism. His work for the church had already in fact brought McCosh into leadership in the international Presbyterian community. The establishment of the World Alliance of Reformed Churches in 1877 derived from McCosh's initiative in ecumenical work for this element of Protestantism. Amid the challenges to evangelical religion, McCosh wished to give it a solid intellectual underpinning. His efforts began in Ireland when he organized a committee to discuss with leading evangelical theologians in Germany the means of an intellectual exchange in theological opinion. Eventually the effort joined Evangelicals from more than a dozen countries and led to the first international meeting of the Alliance in Edinburgh, where McCosh was the chief executive official.[41] The organization remains today the institutional center of world Presbyterianism.

[39] Hugh Hawkins, *Between Harvard and America: The Educational Leadership of Charles W. Eliot* (New York, 1972), pp. 132-37.
[40] Phelps to McCosh, March 20, 1885, in the McCosh Correspondence.
[41] I have provided a more complete narrative of the World Alliance and McCosh's ecumenical ideas in "Evangelical Ecumenism: James McCosh and the Intellectual

McCosh naturally took an interest in American Presbyterianism as well. Here, as at the college, the forces of the old and the new were steering toward a serious clash. The 1880s and the early 1890s saw the emergence of an outspoken liberal group within the Presbyterian churches and seminaries. Increasingly that group sought reform of the standards of Presbyterianism and general modernization of its entire theological premises. McCosh believed that Princeton College had a stake in these issues, and, although his most critical involvement occurred after his retirement, he gave a careful and qualified endorsement to the liberals. The issue was a delicate one, but quite important to Princeton's quest for a new identity, and to McCosh's reconstruction of the school's external alliances.

Many points of contention divided liberal and Presbyterian conservatives, but most of them found expression in the explosive heresy case of the late nineteenth century, the Briggs case. Charles Augustus Briggs (1841-1913) was born in New York City, graduated from the University of Virginia and Union Theological Seminary, and after three years' study in Germany became Union's professor of Hebrew and cognate languages. By 1876 Union Theological Seminary had attracted many Presbyterian leaders formerly identified with the New School branch of the Presbyterian church. Union had also received much of its liberal theological stamp from Henry Boynton Smith, who had combined some of the German higher critical thought with German evangelical theology. Union's identification with this direction in American theology became most evident in the writings of Briggs. Briggs became Union's voice in the *Presbyterian Quarterly and Princeton Review*, when, amid a lingering spirit of friendship after the Reunion, the two Presbyterian factions collaborated on a religious publication. Archibald Alexander Hodge, as coeditor, represented the Princeton Theological Seminary and assured conservative opinion of a voice in the publication. But Briggs's study in Germany had clearly induced a liberal bent. At Berlin he had studied with Isaac Dorner, whose work he disseminated in America. Briggs at least saw himself as an apostle of higher criticism and German evangelical theology. He became the self-appointed missionary to spread this perspective in America, convinced that here and in Great Britain, religious thought had too long been preoccupied with narrow dogmatic and doctrinal concerns. Briggs now used the *Quarterly* as the vehicle

Origins of the World Alliance of Reformed Churches," *Journal of Presbyterian History,* 55 (Spring 1977), 58-73.

for his views, and, when Princeton seminarians demanded a hearing for their views, the pages were opened to a lively but unfriendly warfare between the two sides.[42]

Briggs's position incorporated historical relativism, derived from his understanding of German theology. Each age has its own spiritual needs, and each age must translate anew, in its own language and to its own understanding, the eternal truth. To this end, both reason and the Church have a critical role, and necessarily supplement Scripture. In his early writings, Briggs presented these ideas in mild form, but a more daring position evolved. "By the summer of 1883, Briggs was the acknowledged leader of a group of liberal minded men." He was now speaking out against the doctrine of biblical inerrancy, and did so most forcefully in his inaugural address in the Robinson Chair in Biblical Theology at Union. By 1889, Briggs, changing from an earlier view, now called for a liberal revision of the Westminster Confession. And by this time too all of American Presbyterianism was embroiled in the conflict that surrounded him.[43]

Briggs had many opponents among Presbyterians, but the fight against him was engineered almost exclusively by Princeton Theological Seminary. In the *Quarterly* the issue was first taken up by A. A. Hodge, the coeditor, and Benjamin Warfield, later to succeed Hodge at the seminary. Hodge, shortly to become a Princeton College trustee in 1881, was a more moderate and flexible man than his father, though on this issue he and Warfield went the limits in defending the cherished doctrine of biblical inerrancy. Other Presbyterian journals now took up the issue, and it was everywhere debated. As the major study of this issue has found, personal allegiances on the matter were quite predictable. Former New School people sided with Briggs and Union, and Old School people with Princeton. And on Princeton Seminary's side, one man in particular led the defense.[44]

Francis Landy Patton (1843-1932) was a still young and brilliant polemic. Born in Warwick, Bermuda, he graduated from Knox College, and from Princeton Theological Seminary in 1865. He had a pastorate in New York City, then went to Chicago to occupy

---

[42] Channing Renwick Jeschke, "The Briggs Case: The Focus of a Study in Nineteenth Century Presbyterian History" (Ph.D. dissertation, University of Chicago, 1967), 83, 135, 150, 152, 157, 199; *National Cyclopaedia of American Biography*, 7:318-19, hereafter, *NCAB*.

[43] Jeschke, "Briggs Case," 231 (the quotation), 240, 275.

[44] Ibid., 185, 204, 215.

a professorship in the McCormick Presbyterian Seminary. Patton first won attention with his work *The Inspiration of Scriptures*, published on the eve of Presbyterian Reunion in 1869. This work defended the inerrancy of the original inspiration, while acknowledging that the missing original manuscripts create obstacles to discerning the exact nature of that inspiration. But in holding essentially for infallibility, Patton defended the doctrine that Briggs could not endorse.[45]

Patton's book won him attention, but the Swing heresy trial of 1874 embroiled him in controversy. David Swing was a Chicago Presbyterian minister, a former New School partisan, and an acknowledged liberal. His main point of contention was the doctrine of predestination, which he denounced. He believed it had no intellectual credence and that it had done irreparable harm to the Church and weakened the case against infidelity. Patton, who had become editor of the Chicago *Interior*, moved against Swing. He compiled thirty counts of heresy, and Swing was arraigned before the Chicago Presbytery. He was acquitted there, but Patton won an appeal and a decision against Swing in the Synod of Illinois.[46] Patton was Moderator of the General Assembly in 1881 and in 1884 assumed a joint appointment at Princeton Seminary and the college. The appointment of the renowned heresy hunter to Princeton College even gave rise to rumors that Patton had been chosen to moderate McCosh's liberal course at the school. The *Inter-Ocean* in Chicago thought Patton was going to Princeton "to keep it from heresy" and hoped that he would emerge as the "vindicator" of true theism there.[47] In the next years, Patton became the leading force against Briggs. He and Briggs debated the issue of revision in 1889, and Patton, now president of Princeton College, conceded that the Westminster Confession could bear revisions but went on to say that these should be extensions and clarification of its main ideas, not a modification of them. Patton dismissed the significance of German theology for American Presbyterianism and called for a renewal and sharpening of dogmatic theology. When Briggs was arraigned for a heresy trial, Patton was appointed by Moderator Henry Green of the Princeton Seminary to chair the Committee on Theological Seminaries, which would hear the evidence at the Detroit meeting in 1891. Patton, with plenty of help from his fellow

---

[45] Ibid., 37; Varnum Lansing Collins, *Princeton* (New York, 1914), p. 251.

[46] *New York Observer*, May 14, 1874, May 28, 1874, October 29, 1874; *NCAB*, 3:16.

[47] *Inter-Ocean*, December 19, 1883.

Princetonians, secured the defeat of Briggs by the American Presbyterian churches.[48]

Despite their loss in the Briggs case, Presbyterian liberals found a new identity and coalesced amid the opposition against them. One of the staunchest defenders of Briggs was Henry Van Dyke (1852-1933), later one of the major figures and symbols of the "New Princeton." Van Dyke's father was a Presbyterian minister and Moderator of the General Assembly in 1872. Henry planned to attend Rutgers in New Brunswick, where his grandfather had a place where he could live. But the father was impressed by the rising influence of McCosh and directed Henry to Princeton. He graduated in 1872, attended the seminary, and after 1876 pursued further study in Germany. That experience set Van Dyke on a liberal course that became more pronounced in the next years. He succeeded James Murray at the Brick Presbyterian Church in New York City, but maintained close connections with his alma mater. He helped to initiate a new Princeton Alumni group on Long Island, of which he was elected first president, and as a major fighter with McCosh for alumni representation, brought McCosh to the inaugural meeting. As the doctrinal issues flared in the 1880s, Van Dyke emerged as one of the leading liberals. He was "a convinced evolutionist," a strong opponent of the infant damnation doctrine, and little enamored of biblical literalism in theology.[49] Van Dyke despised the whole business of heresy trials, believing they drove the best minds from the church. He vigorously supported Briggs and sent him a sympathetic letter, saying, "What a farce a heresy trial is." Van Dyke blended his mild form of religion with his very popular literary efforts. He was a minor figure in the world of genteel letters and one of America's last spokesmen for literary idealism. In 1900 he became professor of English at Princeton, again succeeding Murray. His arrival further signaled the growth of Princeton from the evangelical style of the McCosh years to its scholarly, urbane, and genteel character under Patton and Wilson.[50]

Briggs's book of 1889, *Whither? A Theological Question for the Times*, published by Scribner's, contained his full case for the re-

---

[48] Tertius Van Dyke, *Henry Van Dyke: A Biography* (New York, 1935), pp. 125-26, 132; Jeschke, "Briggs Case," 284-86, 302, 307, 310, 321.

[49] Van Dyke, *Henry Van Dyke*, pp. 1, 9-11; *NCAB*, C:23-24; *Princetonian*, November 11, 1885.

[50] Roland Mushat Frye, "Henry Van Dyke: Many-Sided Litterateur," in *Sons of the Prophets: Leaders in Protestantism from Princeton Seminary*, ed. Hugh T. Kerr (Princeton, 1963), pp. 148-57.

vision of the Westminster Confession. McCosh entered the fray that year also when Scribner's published his *Whither? O Whither? Tell Me Where.* It was the first year of his retirement, but McCosh chose not to duck the compelling issues confronting his denomination. McCosh called himself a "conservative revisionist" and was not prepared to endorse heavy liberal inroads into Presbyterian thought. "We must not lower the standard to suit the sentiment of the day," he warned. Nonetheless, the question had to be faced. Did the Confession, as written and understood, express the true biblical message? McCosh said no. The charge levied by the Princeton Seminary group, that the liberals violated the true spirit of the faith, could be applied to them as well, McCosh said. Now McCosh even referred to "we New Light Men." (It is the first time, so far as I can tell, that McCosh emphatically sided with the New School group.) He also announced, that whereas he had up to this time not supported revision, the issue could no longer be postponed. Revisions were needed. McCosh asserted first that the Confession did not speak the true spirit of Scripture, that it was deficient in its declaration of the love of God and his "free offer of salvation." This remark clearly and precisely stated McCosh's opposition to Calvinism and demonstrated his remoteness from the seminary position. McCosh here endorsed the main strain of evangelical thinking in the nineteenth century, one that moved away from arbitrary damnation and placed salvation in the will of the believer. But McCosh also spoke as a teacher, one who had tried earnestly to steer as many of his students as possible into the ministry. His own students, he could testify, often found passages of the creed "knotty, crabbed, and hard to digest." Four students that he knew had changed their plans to enter the Presbyterian ministry because they could not live with the Confession. Furthermore, McCosh said, the Westminster Confession was a major deterrence to church unity.[51] Briggs had made the same point. McCosh wanted to defend the authority of Scriptures but asked, respecting the "orthodox" books on the subject, "Are they up to the scholarship of the day?" The question was scarcely complimentary to the seminarians of Princeton, and probably not a fair one. But McCosh was not polemical. He called for revisions, "a shorter and simpler creed," not a new one.[52]

[51] James McCosh, *Whither? O Whither? Tell Me Where* (New York, 1889), pp. 17-19, 21; idem, "The Good That May Come from Revision," *Independent*, March 15, 1890.

[52] McCosh, *Whither?*, pp. 32, 19.

McCosh entered into these Presbyterian disputes during the years of his retirement. He had laid down the burdens of office in 1888, after twenty years of service to Princeton. He considered himself almost successful. Princeton had become a university in all but name, and McCosh believed it was on the threshold of academic greatness. "So I retire," he said. "The College has been brought to the very borders, and I leave it to another to carry it over to the land of promise."[53] The school had grown considerably under McCosh, from sixteen to forty faculty members, and from 264 to 604 students. We have seen the indications of academic maturity at McCosh's Princeton and the means of his providing the college a new place in the larger society. It would have been informative, but perhaps inexpedient to chart all the details of McCosh's presidency. To do so would certainly establish that he was one of the most energetic and well-traveled college presidents of his century. Year after year McCosh was on the road, for one-day speaking engagements or for week-long presentations of a whole series of philosophical addresses. There were political trips, both to the New Jersey legislature, and to the nation's capital where once he lobbied with Congressmen to oppose federal support for state agricultural schools, bringing letters from Charles W. Eliot with him.[54] The trips to alumni organizations were frequent affairs, and McCosh covered the country as the number of organizations grew. A nationally known Presbyterian, McCosh appeared many times at local churches, and in the big cities he used the visits to make further contacts for Princeton. And still McCosh found time for numerous writings. Philosophy remained his greatest love and interest, but the public wanted his views on the critical issues in higher education too. He willingly provided them.

He willingly continued to teach also. The provisions of his retirement kept McCosh active in philosophy as he taught undergraduate courses and worked with several graduates in that subject at Princeton. He was indeed the grand old man of the campus. The snow-white hair, and the long, loose sideburns, still a McCosh feature, gave him every bit the appearance of the sage. He surely had the manners of one. McCosh remained a familiar figure at Princeton, and his daily walks around the campus became legendary. The old man, with derby and cane, carried his stooped frame along the path that is still known as McCosh Walk. And, like those

[53] Thorp, "Founding of the Graduate School," 3.
[54] See the McCosh-Eliot correspondence for 1873 in the "Charles W. Eliot Papers," Harvard University Archives.

James McCosh (about 1890)

of Kant in Königsberg, McCosh's habits marked the periods of the day. He spent the morning writing. At half past twelve precisely he stepped out for a stroll. He might be seen walking on Prospect Avenue, passing along McCosh Walk, or strolling through the campus to Nassau Street. He returned for lunch, napped for an hour, and spent the balance of the afternoon reading. Then came another walk before supper. Students who knew McCosh in these later years surely knew a friendlier man than the one who hid behind the severe exterior in years before. Many times he encountered students and joined them in their walks. Sometimes he stopped to watch students at their athletic endeavors, telling them that he once had great athletic prowess, and boasting of what he had done for sport at Princeton. And McCosh did remain an imposing figure. Students watched the stooped old man and concluded that he was lost in thought, trying to unravel some difficult philosophical knot. Then McCosh would strike his cane on the ground, and they knew that the problem was solved.[55]

Gradually McCosh's walks shortened. Into his seventies McCosh often strolled ten miles a day, but now his faltering steps demanded shorter and more careful efforts. Isabella McCosh opposed even these walks, for McCosh was greatly prone to falling. Students returning home one day with McCosh helped him from a spill, but as he looked up and saw his wife at the window, he whispered, "This is the second time, but I'll tell her it's the first."[56] McCosh was accustomed to strength and vigor, and his decline greatly saddened and frustrated him. In 1891 he wrote to a friend. "I have not bourne my retirement as well as I should [have]. There are works that I would like to do and I am fretted that I cannot do them. I feel at times my being *laid aside.*"[57] But McCosh was surrounded by friends and cheered by them. On his eightieth birthday, April 1, 1891, President Patton and the faculty called on McCosh and presented him with a large silver bowl from Tiffany's. It was a genuine surprise party, and more than a hundred of McCosh's former students had journeyed to Princeton for the celebration. First they presented him a gilded silver pitcher. Then the Princeton Club of New York unveiled a massive silver cup. Telegrams and flowers arrived, and a special collection of letters from ninety-six former students, in Britain and America, who had become teachers.

The next years, however, saw a noticeable weakening of the old professor. McCosh made his last public appearance at an educational conference at the Chicago World's Columbian Exhibition in 1893. Indeed, McCosh's mind remained alert while his body lost strength. His last letters are almost illegible, and he complained of stomach disorder and loss of sight. On Sunday, October 28, 1894, McCosh was at his usual place in the chapel for the last time. A few days later there were signs of serious weakening, and they remained noticeable for the next two weeks as McCosh was forced to remain in bed. As his condition worsened his family gathered from several places—Isabella, Dr. Andrew McCosh, Mrs. Alexander Maitland (Mary Jane McCosh), and Mrs. David Magie (Margaret Sarah McCosh). They were at his bedside the night of

---

[55] *Newark Daily Adviser*, November 19, 1894.
[56] Ibid.
[57] McCosh to "Dr. Roberts," May 12, 1891, in the McCosh Correspondence.

his death, Friday, November 16, 1894. The news quickly swept the campus, "and the students whom he had never taught, but who loved him, rang the bell at Nassau Hall to tell Princeton that Dr. McCosh was dead."[58] Newspapers the next day reported the event, and the *New York Tribune* commented in a manner that McCosh would perhaps have most appreciated: "To him more than any other man in its history, Princeton owes the reputation which it has to-day as a broad, unsectarian, progressive institution of learning." A few days later, academic dignitaries from many places arrived in Princeton. Amid buildings draped in black, they joined all members of the Princeton community to pay their last respects to the man who loved it.[59]

THIS WORK has been a study in cultural and institutional change. It has described the life and thought of one man, and has traced the institutional patterns that affected them. It has endeavored to demonstrate a continuity of thought and style that links McCosh's Scottish inheritance and his involvement in the religious life of that country to the course of American higher education and its particular unfolding at Princeton. But that full story is not yet told, and there is a discernible irony in its final chapter. Specifically, McCosh set in motion certain forces at Princeton that pursued a redefinition of the institution. He was unsuccessful in bringing those forces to their ultimate triumph at the school, as the defeat of the University Campaign symbolized. But after his death the McCosh generation at Princeton realized itself. It did so against strong opposition, the kind that McCosh had also faced. The result was one of the most remarkable academic coups in American history. There is no just assessment or appreciation of McCosh's career without some understanding of the events that transpired after his death.

Whither Princeton? That was the question as the board of trustees, faculty, and anxious alumni pondered the selection of McCosh's successor in 1888. Of course, only the trustees would make the final decision. McCosh's announcement of his retirement had been expected, and well before that fact speculation about a successor had circulated widely. Only two names, however, drew attention. One was Francis Landy Patton, and to many people the merits of his candidacy were obvious. Patton had emerged by this

---

[58] *Memorial Book of the Sesquicentennial Celebration of . . . Princeton University* (Princeton, 1898), p. 451.

[59] *New York Tribune*, November 17, 1894; *Princetonian*, November 21, 1896. The *Princeton College Bulletin*, 7 (1895), has many details of McCosh's funeral.

time as leader of the Presbyterian old guard, champion of the Princeton theology, and bloodhound of heresy. As the Briggs case became famous around the time of McCosh's retirement, Patton's appeal to the conservatives grew. He was the clear choice of those among the trustees who wanted to renew the link to the seminary, and longed to restore the safe and certain path of twenty years ago. Others opposed Patton for these same reasons. Scott stated that many of the alumni considered Patton a "narrow-minded bigot," who would undo what McCosh had achieved. These and others did not want a cleric to head the institution at all. They believed it was time to break completely from the identification with the Church and wanted no man in the presidency sporting the poke collar, white lawn tie, and black frock coat, as Patton did.[60]

Against the name of Patton, rivals pushed the name of William Milligan Sloane. The urbane and scholarly Sloane, brought to Princeton by McCosh, had emerged in the minds of many as the symbol of the new Princeton. He occupied the handsome stone residence Stanworth on a seventeen-acre site on Bayard Lane, soon to be the location of several splendid faculty homes and an indication of Princeton's new fashionableness. And those who supported Sloane saw themselves as the forces of a new Princeton. Robert Bridges wrote to Woodrow Wilson, saying "I am pretty sure that Prof. Sloane is the coming man for President of Princeton." And Bridges, Wilson's friend, spelled out the qualities behind Sloane's appeal. "He is . . . a good diplomat. I believe that his views as to the 'New Princeton' which we long for, are practically what you and I hold. He believes in gentlemanly scholars . . . he is opposed to pietism as such; he has a real admiration for scholarship, and is nothing of a prig." Bridges wrote to Wilson to encourage him to apply for what he hoped would soon be Sloane's vacated professorship. He should do so "if you hope to throw in your lot with the new Princeton."[61]

McCosh seems clearly to have preferred Sloane as his successor. But he was realistic, too. The board of trustees that had defeated the University Campaign and had overruled the plan for general fellowships was not likely to endorse such a man as Sloane. He supported another idea therefore. "At present," he wrote to James Mark Baldwin, "we are greatly anxious as to who is to be my

[60] William Berryman Scott, *Some Memories of a Palaeontologist* (Princeton, 1939), pp. 202-3; Thorp, "Founding of the Graduate School," 3-4.

[61] Arthur S. Link, ed., *The Papers of Woodrow Wilson* (Princeton, 1966-), 6:360; 5:631-34, hereafter, *WWP*.

successor. The older men want a minister and have fixed on Dr. Patton. The younger men wish [Sloane], but he cannot be carried in the Board of Trustees. There is now a proposal to have Dr. Patton made President and Professor [Sloane] made Vice-President. I am favorable to this plan. It will keep both men here. It will reconcile both parties."[62] But the trustees did not wish to reconcile both parties. They elected Patton to the presidency and made no allowance for a second man in office. McCosh pledged Patton his support for the good of the college. "I am to support Patton in every way," he wrote to Baldwin. He wanted Sloane to be vice-president, "but could not carry it. I hope Dr. Patton may turn out to be as practical a man as he is a powerful dialectician." But Patton did not. Others, like Scott, watched the selection and lived, "to my lasting regret," as Scott said, to see the results.[63]

Francis Patton was an enigmatic man. His was a first-rate mind, but he was no man for leadership. A general consensus, one that includes those who tried to be charitable to him, says that Patton simply left things to drift at Princeton, or at least left them to others. With respect to the whole academic routine, and to all the unlovely details of running a college, Patton was simply indifferent and lazy. His reports to the board of trustees were brief and imprecise. Often unprepared, he would speak off the cuff, and eventually the trustees had to request more formal reports.[64] Woodrow Wilson, arriving in Princeton in 1890, wrote to Frederick Jackson Turner and borrowed from Greek mythology in describing Patton's style. "We are under the reign of 'King Log' rather than 'King Stork' here, so far as our president is concerned."[65] Wilson's remarks on Patton in other places, however, add up to a contradictory assessment, one that characterizes the general impression Patton made. He had fine qualities, but fatal flaws. At one point Wilson described him as "colourless, disagreeable Dr. Patton." But he said on another occasion that Patton was "an extraordinary man intellectually . . . a man most liberal too in his whole mental outlook, outside church battles." He even said he was a good man to work with, and "I mean to make my praise of him unstinted."[66] James Mark Baldwin could be equally as enthusiastic. "For brilliant dialectic, incisive criticism, and sheer logical acumen, his lectures

---

[62] In James Mark Baldwin, *Between Two Wars, 1861-1921* . . . , 2 vols. (Boston, 1926), 2:202.

[63] Baldwin, *Between Two Wars*, 2:202; Scott, *Some Memories*, pp. 202-3.

[64] Thorp, "Founding of the Graduate School," 6.

[65] *WWP*, 10:52.   [66] *WWP*, 3:138; 7:62.

were a revelation and enchantment." Baldwin also considered Patton a liberal person, who told him he need have felt no constraints from the president in pursuing his work on evolution. Baldwin saw Patton as two persons in one—a Calvinist of the most thorough stripe in the pulpit, but a man of immense charity among the "sinners" of the world the rest of the week.[67] But returning to Wilson, perhaps the professor of political science spotted Patton's most important trait. "He is an extremely cautious man and feels perhaps overmuch the need of caution in the head of an institution representing a board of trustees and a constituency as conservative as ours."[68] That posture had profound results for the faculty.

Patton's lethargy could have positive effects. Certainly it left room for the activities and initiative of an ambitious faculty. And Wilson, for one, considered Princeton a place for ambitious people. To Robert Bridges he explained that he was going from Johns Hopkins to Princeton, even with a mediocre salary, because "it *is* Princeton—a big institution of the first class, with superior facilities for work, with the best class of students, and affording a member of its faculty a certain academic standing."[69] This was Wilson's view of his alma mater two years after McCosh. And Patton's slowness left room for others to manipulate. Alumni organizations endowed new chairs and placed their own candidates in them. Sometimes personal friends acted in a similar manner. Henry Van Dyke, Winthrop Daniels, John Bell Hatcher, and Bliss Perry, all distinguished faculty members, arrived at Princeton by these means.[70] But when pressure came from the Conservatives, Patton was likely to succumb. Thus when Wilson arrived as a professor at Princeton, Patton sent him a remarkable letter. He wanted to spell out to Wilson some of the "objections" that members of the board held against him. To some, Wilson's scholarship on politics was suspect, especially his theory of the state, which did not refer to its divine origins. Furthermore, Wilson won little favor from his "unqualified application of the doctrine of naturalistic evolution." You give much space, Patton told Wilson, to the influence of Roman law, but "you are silent with respect to the forming & reforming influences of Christianity." Patton wanted to warn Wilson, for his own good, "that the Trustees of the College mean to keep this College on the old ground of loyalty to the Christian

[67] Baldwin, *Between Two Wars*, 2:24, 56-57.
[68] *WWP*, 7:62.
[69] *WWP*, 6:528.
[70] Thorp, "Founding of the Graduate School," 7-8.

religion" and that Wilson must conduct his chair "under theistic and Christian presuppositions."[71]

One incident that reflected these attitudes, and a catalyst in the movement against Patton, was the affair surrounding Frederick Jackson Turner. Turner, a young historian at the University of Wisconsin, had won attention for his famous address of 1893, "The Significance of the Frontier in American History." Wilson, acting in the style encouraged by Patton's lethargy, took the initiative in exploring with Turner the possibility of his accepting an appointment. Wilson worked with some alumni and with John Grier Hibben and others on the faculty to promote the idea. Apparently, though, Wilson did not take to heart Patton's earlier letter to him. Turner was a Unitarian, but Wilson did not imagine that that fact could affect Turner's chances for a call from Princeton. Wilson blithely assured Turner: "I think I can say without qualification that no religious tests are applied here. The president and trustees are very anxious that every man they choose should be earnestly religious, but there are no doctrinal standards amongst us and I do not think that matter [the Unitarian factor] need embarrass" us. The sanguine letter further said of Patton, "he does not command or interfere." "I don't know of greater academic freedom anywhere."[72] But some of the trustees (Wilson named George Black Stewart, a minister, as one) were not prepared to preside over the appointment of a Unitarian at Princeton. Patton sensed their caution and became nervous. He told Cyrus McCormick, Wilson's friend, that he feared Princeton would lose financial support from its benefactors if such an appointment were made. Besides, the whole thing was not that important. Couldn't someone else just as easily fill the post?[73] Patton severely underestimated, in this issue, the ambitions of his faculty and its determination to bring the best scholars, of any kind, to Princeton. In 1898, this effort failed. Wilson felt angered and humiliated by the whole affair and sent his apologies to Turner.[74] But after this incident he and others were ready to fight.

In 1896 Princeton had celebrated its sesquicentennial anniversary. It was the greatest day of festivities since the inauguration of McCosh, and in splendor and ceremony probably outdid that event. For a particular element at Princeton, it was a special day for rejoicing, for an important symbolic victory had been achieved. For in its 150th year the College of New Jersey assumed the name of

[71] *WWP*, 6:527.
[72] *WWP*, 10:52-53.
[73] *WWP*, 10:498.
[74] *WWP*, 10:196, 201-2.

Princeton University. For many, this was a formal announcement to America and the world of higher education that Princeton believed it had joined the front ranks of universities. To these the change also signified a new identity for Princeton as first and foremost an academic institution, where teaching and advancement of learning in the widest sense were the governing purposes.[75] But furthermore, the change of title registered other important changes that had taken place since the retirement of McCosh eight years before. Now the faculty at Princeton swelled with McCosh students, fully twenty-four of fifty-three. Most of these had a general interest in McCosh's image of the modern university, and several had a resolve to carry it out. To them, "Princeton University" was particularly meaningful.[76]

Increasingly, as matters under Patton worsened, this group rallied around Woodrow Wilson, who emerged as a kind of floor leader for the young faculty. With this group, and with a loyal group of Wilsonians outside of Princeton, most from Wilson's class of 1879, Wilson guided a movement to get Princeton moving again. Indeed, there is something intriguing, even conspiratorial sounding in Wilson's notes for a dinner speech to a class of '79 banquet. Wilson, by then president of the college, referred to the cheering by his class when they had sat in the back row of Alexander Hall at the Sesquicentennial affair. Then Wilson remarked: "I knew as I thought about the occasion what it must all mean: I have but carried out the ideals and purposes formed amongst you in the old days of our first fellowship here: you know that I am trying to be what I promised you,—what we promised each other."[77]

Also among the gathering forces were new trustees. In the years after McCosh's departure, the ranks began to fill, slowly at first and then rapidly, with former students of McCosh, and among these, some close personal friends of Wilson. Seven men from the McCosh generation joined the trustees after 1888 (although Henry Van Dyke served only one year before assuming his professorship). Then, as we shall see presently, in 1900 the progressives finally secured direct alumni election of five trustee positions, and three of those selected were McCosh students, two of whom played a decisive role in bringing Wilson into office.[78] Wilson heard from

---

[75] See the *Princeton Sesquicentennial* for a colorful description of the celebration.

[76] Ibid., p. 3; Bragdon, *Woodrow Wilson*, p. 213.

[77] *WWP*, 10:189.

[78] *General Catalogue of Princeton University, 1746-1906* (Princeton, 1908), pp. 24-25. The two were Alexander Van Rensselaer and John David Davis.

Cyrus McCormick (son of the inventor of the reaper and one of the McCosh trustees): "Every one of the recent elections in the Board of Trustees is a hopeful sign, and augurs well for the broadest interests of Princeton University, and in the course of a reasonable time, I am confident that good results will be secured which will be exactly in harmony with the wishes which you and I have for Princeton's greatest advancement."[79] The new trustee group consisted in part of clerical persons, such as Melancthon W. Jacobus and Simon J. McPherson, who were sympathetic to Princeton's religious character, but with McCosh's tolerance and concern for scholarship. It also consisted of a more important group, wealthy Princeton alumni, such as McCormick, Cornelius C. Cuyler, James Bayard Henry, and Alexander Van Rensselaer, who had a more indifferent attitude toward religion. Still others, friends of Wilson particularly but also influential in the business world, took an interest in the events at Princeton and intervened for the forces aligning themselves against Patton. Edward Wright Sheldon (who had succeeded John A. Stewart at United States Trust) and Cleveland Dodge (later a trustee under Wilson in 1904) were most prominent.[80]

The letters of Woodrow Wilson clarify the means by which Wilson worked closely with these individuals for reforms at Princeton, and they document the politics of intrigue that set forces into operation against Patton. The letters also indicate Wilson's own admiration for McCosh and his appreciation of his former teacher's accomplishments at Princeton. "He found Princeton a quiet country college," Wilson said of McCosh, "and lifted it to a conspicuous place among the most notable institutions of the country. . . . He laid the foundations of a genuine university, and his own enthusiasm for learning vivified . . . the place."[81] Wilson's own academic record shows that he did his best work in McCosh's classes, in psychology and in the history of philosophy. But McCosh seems to have influenced Wilson most, not in any narrow academic sense, but in his educational philosophy and vision. Henry Wilkinson Bragdon, the fine biographer of Wilson's academic years, claims that Wilson's whole academic philosophy and practice, in regard to curriculum, mental discipline, the social life of students, and the place of the graduate school in the university, "followed lines laid down by his predecessor." Wilson's address at the Sesquicentennial,

---

[79] *WWP*, 10:495.
[80] Bragdon, *Woodrow Wilson*, pp. 275-76.   [81] *WWP*, 17:330.

where he spoke as the informal representative of the young faculty, reiterated in close detail the essential points of McCosh's inaugural address.[82] Andrew West, student of McCosh and colleague of Wilson, remarked, "Dr. McCosh founded the modern Princeton, and his pupil and successor has taken what he founded, developed it, and carried it along."[83]

The situation at Princeton had become somewhat ironic. Earlier, the reformer McCosh had faced the opposition and interference of a conservative board. Now the cautious and conservative Patton met the displeasure of a younger generation that wished to set Princeton moving forward. Within the faculty, there were some who were ready to take matters into their own hands. In June 1897, a faculty committee consisting of Wilson, Scott, Brackett, and others, reported to the trustees. It made several charges against Patton, saying in essence that Princeton had no leadership and was seriously drifting. In calling Patton an excellent man "in the pulpit," it was really saying that in an administrative capacity he was a fish out of water. The committee wanted the immediate appointment of someone to assist Patton in the latter area, specifically, "an alumnus; of business capacity and habit." The report, in fact, did just about everything short of actually calling for Patton's resignation.[84]

This event coincided closely with the renewal of the alumni representation issue. Once again petitions came from the Princeton Club of New York City and from new alumni groups in the Midwest, organized by John David Davis, '72. This time the alumni had an easy time of it. With the approval of the trustees in 1900, the way was prepared for the election of alumni trustees. The new plan called for direct election of alumni trustees by established alumni groups, thus making available another area of influence for McCosh's former students. In fact, there emerged a ready alliance of this group with McCosh's contingent on the faculty. Among the trustees, Cyrus McCormick, with Wilson speaking in his ear, became the organizing power among the disenchanted. Collaborating with Wilson, Fine, and Brackett, McCormick worked with Jones and Pyne on the board, and together they schemed to take power away from Patton. In the meantime, amid loud laments about the serious deterioration of the graduate program, the trustees

---

[82] Bragdon, *Woodrow Wilson*, pp. 20-21, 285.
[83] Quoted by Bragdon, *Woodrow Wilson*, p. 314.
[84] *WWP*, 10:269.

appointed Andrew West the dean of the graduate school, giving him autonomous power for its operation.[85]

The final blow against Patton came with another committee report. In November 1900 the trustees, again in reaction to vociferous complaints, took under examination the state of the entire academic department. The board appointed a faculty committee to review the situation. Eight of the nine persons selected were former McCosh students, including Dean Samuel Winans, William F. Magie, Paul Van Dyke (brother of Henry), and West. When this University Committee on Scholarship reported in 1902, its news was bad, but not new. "The condition of scholarship among our students at the present time is one of demoralization," it said. It cited several weaknesses: easy courses, lack of structure in many students' programs, and a pervasive superficiality.[86] Surely Patton was not entirely, perhaps not even mostly, to blame for this situation. With a faculty consisting of nearly one-half former McCosh students, some of these, it would seem, must have been responsible for the lax conditions. But it is true that the emerging cabal against Patton consisted overwhelmingly of men reared in the McCosh ideals and style. Wilson, Hibben, Fine, Magie, and West were the best scholars in the group, and they were close personal friends as well.

Day by day into 1902 the forces conspired against Patton. Meetings, letters, and rumor all created an atmosphere of intrigue, in one of the most bizarre stories of American academia. Patton gave no hint that he was prepared to step down, at least not unless things were made quite comfortable for him. McCormick wanted to take radical action, but another trustee, though sympathetic, insisted on preserving Patton's dignity.[87] All this meant one thing—Patton would have to be bought out of office. The matter was carefully arranged and executed, and secretly maneuvered. Money came from at least sixteen people, some of them trustees, others interested outsiders and supporters of Wilson, for whose advantage, it was clear, the whole affair was planned. The money gathered to purchase Patton's resignation, was, by the standards of the day, an immense sum. From David and Thomas Jones and Pyne came $5,000, from Cyrus McCormick, $4,000, from Dewitt C. Blair, Alexander Van Rensselaer, and Stephen S. Palmer $2,500 each.

[85] *WWP*, 12:200-201, 288-93, 319-30.

[86] *WWP*, 12:201-2, 331-39.

[87] *WWP*, 12:321. James Waddell Alexander is writing to Cyrus McCormick, April 7, 1902.

Others giving at least $500 included John A. Stewart, Alberta Pyne Russell, Cornelius C. Cuyler, James Bayard Henry, John D. Davis, Henry W. Green, James W. Alexander, and John J. McCook.[88] On June 9, 1902, Patton resigned, and Stewart, who had nominated James McCosh to the presidency thirty-four years before, put the name of McCosh's student Woodrow Wilson before the trustees. Wilson was duly elected, and all those trustees who were students when Wilson was at Princeton (they included Pyne, McCormick, Jacobus, Henry, Cuyler, and Jones), were instructed to inform Wilson of the news.[89] At Princeton, the McCosh generation had come to power.

Thus, by the aid of others, McCosh's work at Princeton bore fruit in the years after his death. At the end of his presidency in 1888, he could count many successes, but he had met disappointment when conservative reaction defeated his last campaign. With the removal of Patton, the forces that had most stubbornly resisted McCosh relinquished their controlling hold of the college. Princeton had acquired a new academic character and a new reputation in American higher education. But McCosh, nonetheless, would have seen no unmixed blessing here. Evangelical and democratic Princeton was dying even before he left, and he had had something to do with that fact.

The change was most visible in student life. By his energetic and moralistic efforts, McCosh had driven class rivalries and the vicious secret societies out of existence. But these were rerooted underground, and a new institution of student life sprang up in their place—the eating clubs of Princeton. Ivy Club appeared in 1879, followed by Cottage, Tiger Inn, Cap and Gown, Colonial, and Elm. Soon Prospect Avenue displayed handsome, stately homes, where elegant dining rooms, libraries, and billiard halls gave elegance to the leisure life of affluent, pipe-smoking collegians.[90] In 1885 Dean Murray reported a bad omen in the appearance of private servants for some students and feared they set unworthy standards of emulation for the others.[91] There were other signs of changing student tastes. Chess, even at the intercollegiate level, attracted wide interests, and gentlemanly tennis replaced football and baseball as the favorite sport of Princetonians.[92] In religious identifi-

---

[88] *WWP*, 12:474.   [89] *WWP*, 12:401.
[90] Bragdon, *Woodrow Wilson*, p. 272; Thomas Jefferson Wertenbaker, *Princeton: 1746-1896* (Princeton, 1946), pp. 324, 358-59.
[91] TM, February 12, 1885.
[92] *Princetonian*, November 11, 1886; *Nassau Lit*, '06, n. pag.

cation, the student body remained largely Presbyterian, but was supplemented increasingly by Episcopalians.[93] And most revealing, perhaps, Princeton, ironically through McCosh's own efforts, had become a college whose students came overwhelmingly from private boarding schools. Lawrenceville dominated, but others contributed. In 1909, 78 percent of Princeton's undergraduates were prep schoolers, compared to 65 percent at Yale, and 47 percent at Harvard.[94] And in such an environment of prosperity and comfort, the old evangelical style was simply uncongenial and unfashionable. It was gone, in fact, even before McCosh left. President Patton, it has been said, once remarked that he presided over the finest country club in America.[95] Of course religion did not wholly die at Princeton, but it did become formal and prescribed. McCosh would have counted as loss the evaporation of the older religious ways.

The life of James McCosh thus symbolizes the transformation of culture, in Western civilization generally, and in the intellectual and institutional life of the United States. He was the last great voice of the Scottish philosophical tradition, but no mere echo of its major trumpets. While he championed its tenets against its traditional rivals and carried the long warfare against empiricism into the celebrated battle with John Stuart Mill, McCosh always demonstrated versatility. He merged the Scottish system with the evangelical movement of the nineteenth century, and his synthesis unquestionably forestalled a bitter conflict of religion and science. McCosh's version of the Scottish philosophy demonstrated that these elements could live in relative peace at Princeton and elsewhere and ease the transition from the older collegiate ways to the modern university era. McCosh's cautious receptiveness to the new intellectual era of evolution and modern science further proved his usefulness in this transition. By no means, of course, was McCosh a member of the new intellectual order, but he was an inspiration and encouragement to many at Princeton who advanced beyond him. And above all, McCosh's career is a useful illustration of ideas in the American milieu. For he was first and foremost a philosopher, and secondarily a college president. But he seized the opportunity of history to translate a complex intellectual system into an insti-

[93] Summarized from the *Nassau Lit*, 1888 to 1906.
[94] James McLachlan, *American Boarding Schools: A Historical Study* (New York, 1970), p. 206.
[95] Bragdon, *Woodrow Wilson*, p. 272.

tutional style. That effort, we have seen, required that McCosh refashion the external relationships of Princeton College and bring into its institutional life the heterogeneous elements of pluralistic America. As a result, a sometimes confusing amalgam of unrelated individuals and groups was joined to a college's history by the medium of a philosopher's quest. For McCosh it was not an unflawed victory, but for Princeton it was an enduring legacy.

McCosh Bibliography

The following list of James McCosh's writings extends the bibliography prepared by Joseph H. Dulles for William Milligan Sloane's edition of *The Life of James McCosh* (New York, 1896).

Books

The Method of the Divine Government, Physical and Moral. Edinburgh, 1850. First American edition: New York, 1851.

Typical Forms and Special Ends in Creation. Edinburgh, 1855. With George Dickie. First American edition: New York, 1856.

The Intuitions of the Mind, Inductively Investigated. London and New York, 1860.

The Supernatural in Relation to the Natural. Cambridge and London, 1862.

An Examination of Mr. J. S. Mill's Philosophy; Being a Defence of Fundamental Truth. London and New York, 1866. The London title is: *A Defence of Fundamental Truth: An Examination of Mr. J. S. Mill's Philosophy.*

The Laws of Discursive Thought. London and New York, 1870.

Christianity and Positivism. New York and London, 1871.

The Scottish Philosophy, Biographical, Expository, Critical, From Hutcheson to Hamilton. New York, 1875.

The Emotions. New York and London, 1880.

Psychology: The Cognitive Powers. New York and London, 1886.

Psychology: The Motive Powers. New York and London, 1887.

The Religious Aspect of Evolution. New York, 1888.

First and Fundamental Truths. New York and London, 1889.

The Test of Various Kinds of Truth. New York and Cincinnati, 1889.

Our Moral Nature. New York, 1892.

Published Pamphlets, Essays, Articles

On the Use and Functions of Preaching and the Advantages of a Systematic Theology to a Preacher of the Gospel. Edinburgh, 1833.

Review of *The Work of the Holy Spirit*, by John Howard Hinton. *Edinburgh Christian Examiner*, 2 n.s. (1833), 831-41 and 3 n.s. (1834), 34-44.

Report and Address of the Old Church, Brechin, On the Subject of Intemperance. Brechin, 1841.
Does the Established Church Acknowledge Christ as Its Head? . . . Edinburgh, 1846.
A Tribute to the Memory of Dr. Thomas Chalmers, by a Former Pupil. Brechin, 1847.
Aids in Prayer: For the Use of the Young. Brechin, 1848.
"Typical Forms." *North British Review*, 15 (1851), 389-418.
"On the Method in Which Metaphysics Should Be Prosecuted." *Belfast Mercury*, January 13, 1852.
"Some Remarks on the Plant Morphologically Considered." *Transactions of the* [Edinburgh] *Botanical Society*, 4 (1853).
The Imagination: Its Use and Abuse. Belfast, 1854.
The Necessity for an Intermediate System of Education Between the National Schools and Colleges of Ireland. Belfast, 1854.
"Scottish Metaphysicians." *North British Review*, 27 (1857), 402-34.
"The Limits of Religious Thought Examined." *North British Review*, 30 (1859), 137-59.
The Shifting Scenes of Life: An Address to Youth. Brechin, [1859?].
"Sir William Hamilton's *Lectures.*" *North British Review*, 30 (1859), 532-61.
"Sir William Hamilton's Metaphysics." *Dublin University Magazine*, 54 (1859), 152-66.
"A Sketch of a Tour on the Continent of Europe, with Remarks on the Lower and Higher Educational Institutions of Prussia." Summarized in the *Proceedings of the Belfast Natural History and Philosophical Society.* Belfast, 1859.
The Ulster Revival and Its Physiological Accidents. Belfast, 1859. Also in *Evangelical Christendom*, 13 (1859), 368-75.
The Mental Sciences and the Queen's University in Ireland: Being a Letter to the Secretary of the Queen's University. Belfast, 1860.
"Present English Aspects of Life and Literature." *Evangelical Christendom*, 14 (1860), 461-67.
"Offenes Sendschreiben an die Kirchen Deutschlands." *Jahrbücher für Deutsche Theologie*, 6 (1861), 309-19.
"The Association of Ideas, and Its Influence in the Training of the Mind." In *Lectures Delivered Before the Dublin Young Men's Christian Association.* Dublin, 1862.
"The Scottish Philosophy." *British and Foreign Evangelical Review*, 12 (1863), 663-81.

The Present Tendency of Religious Thought Throughout the Three Kingdoms. Edinburgh, 1864.

"Introduction" and "Memoir, Supplement, and Questions." "Outlines of Moral Philosophy," by Dugald Stewart, in *Outlines of Moral Philosophy*, pp. 125-64. London, 1865.

"The Religious and Social Condition of the United States, as Gathered in a Summer Tour; with the Formation of an American Branch of the Evangelical Alliance." *Proceedings of the Evangelical Alliance* (1866), 15-24.

Christ the Way, the Truth, and the Life: A Sermon. London, 1867. Also Princeton, 1869. (Baccalaureate sermon.)

" 'Morality Independent of the Gospel' as Seen in England." *Evangelical Christendom*, 8 n.s. (1867), 461-63.

"Academic Teaching in Europe." In *Inauguration of James McCosh, D.D., LL.D., as President of the College of New Jersey . . .* , pp. 35-96. New York, 1868.

"The Art's Course in the Queen's University and the Queen's Colleges." Summarized in *Transactions of the National Association for the Promotion of Social Science, Belfast, 1867*, pp. 447-48. London, 1868.

The Duty of Irish Presbyterians to Their Church at the Present Crisis in the Sustentation of the Gospel Ministry. Belfast, 1868.

"Mill's Reply to His Critics." *British and Foreign Evangelical Review*, 17 (1868), 332-62; also in *American Presbyterian and Theological Review*, 6 n.s. (1868), 350-91.

"Moral Philosophy in Great Britain in Relation to Theology." *American Presbyterian and Theological Review*, 6 n.s. (1868), 5-20.

"On Compulsory Education." *Transactions for the National Association for the Promotion of Social Science, Belfast, 1867*, pp. 379-95. London, 1868.

"Recent Improvements in Logic in Great Britain." *American Presbyterian and Theological Review*, 6 n.s. (1868), 165-85.

"Farewell to the Presbyterian Church of Ireland." *New York Times*, June 26, 1868.

[Address.] Presbyterian Board of Education. *Proceedings* (1869), 19-23.

"Hopkins' 'Law of Love and Love as a Law.' " *New York Observer*, April 15, 1869.

"Answer to Dr. Hopkins." *New York Observer*, June 24, 1869.

"Dr. McCosh's Summation." *New York Observer*, September 23, 1869. (Final rejoinder to Hopkins.)

"The Evangelical Alliance." *Biblical Repertory and Princeton Review*, 42 (1870), 455-65.

"Introduction." In *Outline of Sir William Hamilton's Philosophy*, ed. J. Clark Murray. Boston, 1870.

Lessons Derived from the Plant. Princeton, 1870. (Baccalaureate sermon.)

"Dedication Address: The New Gymnasium." *Presbyterian*, January 22, 1870.

[Address.] In *Addresses Delivered in Reference to Free High Schools Before the Legislature of New Jersey . . .* , pp. 3-9. Trenton, 1871.

"Renan's Life of Jesus." In *Questions of Modern Thought*, Philadelphia, 1871, n. pag.

Unity With Diversity in the Works of God. Princeton, 1871. (Baccalaureate sermon.)

"Body and Mind." *Independent*, April 6, 1871.

"Materialism." *Independent*, April 27, 1871.

"Darwin's *Descent of Man*." *Independent*, May 4, 1871.

"The Support of Ministers." *New York Observer*, May 4, 1871.

"Sustentation of the Ministry." *New York Evangelist*, May 4, 1871.

"Competitive Examinations." *Presbyterian*, September 30, 1871.

Faith in Christ and Faith in Doctrine, Compared and Contrasted. Princeton, 1872. (Baccalaureate sermon.)

"On Prayer." *Contemporary Review*, 20 (1872), 777-82.

"Old College Customs in Danger." *New York Ledger*, January 6, 1872.

"Crisis of the Sustentation Fund." *New York Evangelist*, March 28, 1872.

"Prayer and Inflexible Law." *Independent*, December 5, 1872.

"Berkeley's Philosophy." *Presbyterian Quarterly and Princeton Review*, 2 n.s. (1873), 3-30.

"Notice of Dr. Burns." *Presbyterian Quarterly and Princeton Review*, 2 n.s. (1873), 337-41.

On Singleness of Eye. Princeton, 1873. (Baccalaureate sermon.)

"Presbyterians in Foreign Lands." In *The Tercentenary Book*, pp. 211-32. Philadelphia, 1873.

"Upper Schools." National Education Association, *Proceedings* (1873), 19-35; also in *International Review*, 1 (1874), 173-97.

"Obligatory Attendance at College Recitations." *New York Observer*, January 23, 1873.

"Sustentation of the Ministry." *Independent*, February 13, 1873.

"Dr. Guthrie's Early Ministry." *New York Observer*, August 7 and 14, 1873.

"A Marked Defect in Our Educational System." *New York Evangelist*, September 4, 1873.

"True and False Preaching." *New York Times*, September 8, 1873.

Living for a High End. Princeton, 1874. (Baccalaureate sermon.)

"College Regattas and Saratoga." *New York Observer*, February 19, 1874.

"The Sustentation Fund and Consolidation." *Presbyterian*, May 2, 1874.

"Federation of Presbyterians." *Evangelist*, September 24, 1874.

Ideas in Nature Overlooked by Dr. Tyndall . . . , New York, 1875.

"On Evolution." In *Wood's Bible Animals*, ed. T. G. Wood, pp. 649-77. San Francisco, 1875.

The Royal Law of Love. New York, 1875. (Baccalaureate sermon.)

"Does the Church Wish to Extinguish the Sustentation Fund?" *New York Evangelist*, April 1, 1875.

"Does the Church Wish Sustentation to Grow?" *Presbyterian*, April 3, 1875.

"The Church Must Now Settle the Sustentation Question." *Presbyterian*, April 17, 1875.

The Development Hypothesis: Is It Sufficient? New York, 1876.

"Is the Development Hypothesis Sufficient?" *Popular Science Monthly*, 10 (1876), 86-100.

"On Prayer." In *The Prayer-Gauge Debate*, pp. 135-44. Boston, 1876.

"Prepossessions For and Against the Supernatural: A Criticism of Dr. Carpenter." *Popular Science Monthly*, 9 (1876), 21-29.

The World a Scene of Contest. New York, 1876. (Baccalaureate sermon.)

"The Princeton College Communion." *New York Evangelist*, July 22, 1876.

Broad Churchism in Scotland. Glasgow, 1877.

"Discoveries in Science and Speculations in Philosophy." *Report of the Proceedings of the First Presbyterian Council* . . . , pp. 187-94. Edinburgh, 1877.

"Elements Involved in Emotions." *Mind*, 2 (1877), 413-15.

"Religious Aspects of the Doctrine of Development." *Report of the Proceedings of the First Presbyterian Council* . . . , pp. 264-71. Edinburgh, 1877.

"On American Preaching." *Evangelist*, September 27, 1877.

"An Advertisement for a New Religion." *North American Review*, 127 (1878), 44-60. (Signed "An Evolutionist.")

"Contemporary Philosophy: Historical." *Princeton Review*, 1 (1878), 192-206.

"Contemporary Philosophy: Mind and Brain." *Princeton Review*, 1 (1878), 606-32.

"A Criticism of the Critical Philosophy: A Reply to Professor Mahaffy." *Princeton Review*, 2 (1878), 889-915.

"Discipline in American Colleges." *North American Review*, 126 (1878), 428-41.

The Propriety of Acknowledging the Lord in All Our Ways. New York, 1878. (Baccalaureate sermon.)

"Confessions of an Agnostic." *North American Review*, 129 (1879), 274-87. (Signed: "An Agnostic.")

"Course of Study in the Academical Department of Princeton College." In *The Princeton Book* . . . , pp. 125-34. Boston, 1879.

"Final Cause, M. Janet and Professor Newcomb." *Princeton Review*, 3 (1879), 367-88.

"Herbert Spencer's 'Data of Ethics.' " *Princeton Review*, 4 (1879), 607-36.

"Law and Design in Nature." *North American Review*, 128 (1879), 558-62.

"Theologians of the Day,—Joseph Cook." *Catholic Presbyterian*, 2 (1879), 184-90.

"Criteria of the Various Kinds of Truth." *Princeton Review*, 6 (1880), 419-40; also in *British and Foreign Evangelical Review*, 30 (1881), 122-44.

"Development and Growth of Conscience." *Princeton Review*, 6 (1880), 138-44.

"How to Deal with Young Men Trained in Science in This Age of Unsettled Opinion." *Report of the Proceedings of the Second General Council of the Presbyterian Alliance* . . . , pp. 204-13. Philadelphia, 1880.

"The Importance of Harmonizing the Primary, Secondary, and Collegiate Systems of Education." National Education Association, *Addresses and Proceedings* (1880), 138-46.

"A Presbyterian College in America." *Catholic Presbyterian*, 4 (1880), 81-86.

"The Christian Knows No Man After the Flesh." *The Preacher and Homiletic Review*, 5 (1881), 434-44.

The Conflicts of the Age. New York, 1881.

"Development: Its Nature; What It Can and What It Cannot Do." In *Christ and Modern Thought*, pp. 60-76. London, 1881.

"On Causation and Development." *Princeton Review*, 7 (1881), 369-89.

"The Religious Conflicts of the Age." *North American Review*, 133 (1881), 24-42. (Signed: "A Yankee Farmer.")

"What Morality Do We Have Left?" *North American Review*, 132 (1881), 497-512. (Signed: "A New Light Moralist.")

Criteria of Various Kinds of Truth as Opposed to Agnosticism. Philosophical Series no. 1. New York, 1882.

"The Concord School of Philosophy." *Princeton Review*, 9 (1882), 49-71.

"The Scottish Philosophy as Contrasted with the German." *Princeton Review*, 10 (1882), 326-44; also in *British and Foreign Evangelical Review*, 32 (1883), 96-114.

Certitude, Providence, and Prayer. Philosophical Series no. 4. New York, 1883.

Development: What It Can and What It Cannot Do. Philosophical Series no. 3. New York, 1883.

Energy: Efficient and Final Cause. Philosophical Series no. 2. New York, 1883.

"On Manly Sports." *New York Ledger*, April 7, 1883.

Agnosticism of Hume and Huxley, With a Notice of the Scottish School. Philosophical Series no. 6. New York, 1884.

A Criticism of the Critical Philosophy. Philosophical Series no. 7. New York, 1884.

For Love's Sake: Being a Farewell Sermon Preached in the West Free Church, Brechin, August 24, 1884. [Brechin], 1884.

"Learning Worshipping Its King." *Pulpit Treasury*, 2 (1884), 241-42.

Locke's Theory of Knowledge, With a Notice of Berkeley. Philosophical Series no. 5. New York, 1884.

"The Origin of Evil." *Pulpit Treasury*, 2 (1884), 438-39.

"The Place of Religion in Colleges." *Minutes and Proceedings of the Third General Council of the Alliance of the Reformed Churches Holding the Presbyterian System*, pp. 465-80. Belfast, 1884.

"A Study of the Mind's Imagery." With H. F. Osborn. *Princeton Review*, 13 (1884), 50-72.

"Oversight of Students in Princeton College." *Evangelist*, April 17, 1884.

"The Course of Study in Princeton College." *Education*, 5 (1884-1885), 353-59.

Herbert Spencer's Philosophy as Culminated in His Ethics. Philosophical Series no. 8. New York, 1885.

The New Departure in College Education, Being a Reply to President Eliot's Defence of It. New York, 1885.

"What an American University Should Be." *Education*, 6 (1885-1886), 35-45.

"Preface to the American Edition." In Th. Ribot, *German Psychology Today: the Empirical School*. New York, 1886.

"The Providence of God." *Pulpit Treasury*, 4 (1886), 238-39.

"Realism: Its Place in the Various Philosophies." *New Princeton Review*, 2 (1886), 315-17.

Religion in a College: What Place It Should Have: Being an Examination of President Eliot's Paper, Read Before the Nineteenth Century Club, in New York, February 3, 1886. New York, 1886.

"What an American Philosophy Should Be." *New Princeton Review*, 1 (1886), 15-32.

"On Home Rule." *Evangelist*, April 22, 1886.

"Christian Philosophy." *Pulpit Treasury*, 5 (1887), 238-39.

"College Fraternities." *Academy* [Syracuse, N. Y.], (1887), 372.

Habit and Its Influence in the Training at School. Boston, 1887.

"Dabny's Refutation of the Sensualistic Philosophy: But What Next?" *Presbyterian Quarterly*, 2 (1888), 274-82.

"Relation of the Church to the Capital and Labor Question." In *Problems of American Civilization*. New York, 1888.

Twenty Years of Princeton College. New York, 1888.

"Robert Elsmere and His New Christianity." *New York Ledger*, December 29, 1888. Reprinted as "False Philosophy in Robert Elsmere." *Our Day*, 3 (1889), 13-16.

"Examination and Education." *American Supplement to the Nineteenth Century* (1889), 18-22.

Whither? O Whither? Tell Me Where. New York, 1889.

"Present State of the Evolution Question: Wallace and Weisman." *Independent*, October 3, 1889.

"Is There Final Cause in Evolution?" *Independent*, October 10, 1889.

"The Trials and Triumphs of the Teacher." *Independent*, November 14, 1889.

"Evils Arising from the Church Being Controlled by the State." In *Christian Thought*, ed. Charles F. Deems, pp. 1-6. New York, 1890.

John Witherspoon and His Times. Philadelphia, [1890].

The Prevailing Types of Philosophy, Can They Reach Reality Logically? New York, 1890.

"Recent Works on Kant." *Presbyterian and Reformed Review*, 1 (1890), 425-40.

"Federation of Churches to Secure that the Bible Be Preached to Every Creature." *Christian Union*, February 6, 1890; also in

Our Day, 5 (1890), 359-63; and *Church Review*, 17 (1890), 132-34.
"The Good that May Come from Revision." *Independent*, March 15, 1890.
"The Capacity of the Indian to be Educated." *22nd Annual Report of the Board of Indian Commissioners . . .* , pp. 67-70. Washington, D.C.: 1891.
"Federation of the Churches." *The Homiletic Review*, 21 n.s. (1891), 396-401.
"Reality—What Place It Should Hold in Philosophy." National Education Association, *Proceedings* (1893), 682-86. Reprinted as *Reality: What Place It Should Hold in Philosophy*. New York, 1894.
Philosophy of Reality: Should It Be Favored By America? New York, 1894.

ANTHOLOGIES

These collections include essays listed above.

Recollections of the Disruption in Brechin. [Brechin, 1842] *Philosophical Papers*. London, 1868.
The Conflicts of the Age. New York, 1881.
Realistic Philosophy Defended in a Series. Vol. 1. *Expository*. Vol. 2. *Historical and Critical*. New York and London, 1887.
Gospel Sermons. New York and London, 1888.

UNPUBLISHED MATERIAL

"History of Philosophy from Notes Taken in the Lecture Room of James McCosh, D.D., LL.D., President of the College of New Jersey" [by Andrew J. West] (1878). Princeton University Archives.
"Incidents of My Life in Three Countries." Typescript in the Princeton University Archives.
"Notes on Books." McCosh Papers, Department of Rare Books and Special Collections, Princeton University Library.

Index

Abbey Church (Arbroath), 71-72
Abbott, Frank, 319
Abbott, Lyman, 209n
Abelard, Peter, 149
Aberdeen, 22-23
Aberdeen Philosophical Society, 18n, 23
Aberdeen University. *See* Universities, Scottish, Aberdeen University
Absolute, 150, 154, 157; Sir William Hamilton on, 123, 153-54; and Herbert Spencer, 198
Absolute idealism, 121
Act of Separation and Deed of Demission, 87
Act of Supremacy, 8
Act of Union (1707), 14
Adam, Robert, 49
Affections: McCosh on, 106
Agassiz, Louis, 181n, 187, 205, 244; McCosh on, 194
Alexander, Archibald, 221, 308, 310
Alexander, James, 18
Alexander, James Waddel, 308, 347
Alumni, 297-300; and University Campaign, 327-28; and trustee representation issue, 345-46
American Bible Society, 222, 282, 307
American Home Mission Society, 222
American Mathematical Society, 290
American Philosophical Society, 287
American Presbyterian and Theological Review, 166
American Presbyterian Review, 310
American Society of Naturalists, 288
American Society of Palaeontologists, 287
American Theological Review, 315-16
Analogy of Religion (Butler), 53
Andover Theological Seminary, 240, 329
Angell, James B., 233
Anglicanism. *See* Church of England
Angus, 146

Antiquary, The (Scott), 23
Aquinas, Thomas, 170
Arbroath, 95-96; McCosh in, 71-78; described, 74
Archimedes, 152
Aristotelianism, 148
Aristotle, 119-20, 195, 197
Arminianism, 62
Arnold, Matthew, 67, 269
Associate Presbytery, 28
Astor, John J., 281
Astronomical Discourses (Chalmers), 52
Atheism, 68
Atwater, Lyman, 229, 239, 246n, 248
Auchterader case, 83-84
Augustine, Saint, 106
Ayr, Scotland, 33-34
Ayrshire, 33-34; characteristics of, 38-39; education in, 38

Bacon, Francis, 99n, 128, 139
Bain, Alexander, 317
Baldwin, James Mark, 243, 247, 278, 289n, 292, 294, 339; as student of McCosh, 288-89; on Patton, 340-41
Bancroft, George, 242, 311
Baptist Review, 315
Bascom, John, 209n, 233
Baumer, Franklin L., 166n
Baxter, Richard, 53
Beattie, James, 23, 25n, 117-18n, 136
Beecher, Henry Ward, 209n, 283
Belfast, xii, 111-14; McCosh in, 174-77
Belfast Town Mission, 175
Berkeley, George, 9, 24, 117, 120, 130, 145, 217, 292
Berkeley, Lowry E., 174
Berlin, University of, 240-41, 287, 290, 330
Bervie (Scotland), 91
Beza, Theodore, 7
Bible, 101; McCosh on, 106, 168;

Bible (*cont.*)
  McCosh teaches at Princeton College, 386-87
Bible and Colportage Society of Ireland, 174
Biblical Repertory and Princeton Review, 310
Bibliotheca Sacra, 315
Bisset, John, 28
Blackwood's, 57
Blair, Dewitt C., 346
Blair, Emma L., 308
Blair, Hugh, 17-18, 217
Blair, John, 304
Blair, John Inslee, 304, 308
Blair Academy, 304
Bonner, Robert, 260n, 283
Book of Discipline (first), 7
Book of Discipline (second), 6
Boorstin, Daniel, xii, 273
Boston, Thomas, 27-28
Botanical Society of Edinburgh, 188
Bothwell Brig, 39
Bowdoin College, 240, 244
Bowen, Francis, 225, 315-16, 350
Boyd, William, 38
Brackenridge, Hugh, 220
Brackett, Cyrus Fogg, 244, 247-48, 286, 345
Bragdon, Henry Wilkinson, 344
Brechin, Scotland, 78-79, 95, 99, 107; described, 78-79; McCosh in, 78-93, 99
Brechin Castle, 79
Breslau, University of, 241
Brick Presbyterian Church, 240, 333
Bridges, Robert, 339, 341
Bridgewater lectures, 53
Briggs, Charles Augustus, 330-34
Brody, Baruch, 25
Brontë, Charlotte, 67
Brontë, Emily, 67
Brougham, Henry, 26, 54, 56, 99n, 119
Brown, Thomas, 26, 45, 50, 57, 102, 106, 118-19, 121, 167; on causality, 119-20, 136, 160-61; Hamilton on, 122; McCosh on, 136; on mathematics, 136-37
Brownell, William Crary, 311
Brown University, 240

Buchanan, George, 6
Buckle, Henry, 28
Buile, John, 82
Bulloch, James, 65
Burns, James, 75
Burns, Robert, 29, 34, 38-39, 265; McCosh on, 29
Bushnell, Horace, 308
Butler, Joseph, 9, 17, 53, 167
Byron, Gordon George, 45

Calderwood, Henry, 178
Calvin, John, 7, 106, 270-71. *See also* Calvinism
Calvinism, 7, 10, 24, 55, 98, 101-2, 168, 219, 234, 277, 310, 341; and Hutcheson, 11, 12n; and Evangelicalism, 28, 67, 95; and McCosh, 95, 160, 168-69, 334; in Ulster, 176; at Princeton College, 220-21, 224, 268, 349, 353; at Princeton Theological Seminary, 221, 273. *See also* Westminster Confession
Cambridge University, 18n, 43, 59, 216, 287
Cameron, Henry Clay, 241
Campbell, George, 23, 25n
Cane Ridge revival, 221
Carlyle, Alexander, 17, 217
Carlyle, Thomas, 38, 99n, 150, 314
Carmichael, Gershom, 10, 16
Carnahan, James, 310
Carskeoch, 35-36
Carson, John, 35
Carstares, William, 19
Carter, Robert, 225, 307, 351, 354
Cathedral Church (Brechin), 78-79, 81, 85
Catholicism: in Scotland, 4-9; McCosh on, 149
Causality, 118, 160-62; McCosh on, 64-65, 102-3, 134-35, 160-62, 195-96, 319; Brown on, 119-20; Hamilton on, 124-25, 135, 160-61; Aristotle on, 195-96; Wright on, 469
Chalmers, Thomas, ix, xii, 26, 47-49, 71, 86, 259; in Glasgow, 45-46; and McCosh, 51-52n, 62; theological position of, 53n; and Claim of Right, 83; and Disruption, 87; and social reform, 102

Chambers, Robert, 100, 180n, 184n, 186, 318; career of, 181-83; religious views of, 183-84; and Hugh Miller, 184; and McCosh, 192-93, 207
Chambers, William, 181
Chambers' Edinburgh Journal, 183
Charles II, 8
Charnock, Stephen, 53, 149
Chicago, University of, 250
Christ (Jesus Christ), 68, 84, 95, 97, 209; place of, in the evangelical movement, 95-96; place of, in McCosh's sermons, 95-96, 98
Christian Examiner, 315
Christianity, 101-2, 148-49, 157, 177, 203, 341-42; and moral science, 166-68; and evolution, 207-11, 274-75. *See also* Christ
Christianity and Positivism (McCosh), 320
Church of England, 9, 14, 22, 42, 60-61; in Brechin, 78. *See also* Episcopalianism
Church of Ireland, 177n
Church of Scotland, 13-14, 20, 44, 66, 69, 89; and Patronage Act of 1712, 16; and Scottish Enlightenment, 16-17; McCosh on, 31; and evangelical movement, 28-29, 70, 77-78, 84-88; McCosh's work in, 75; and Disruption, 85-89; McCosh on authority of, 86; preaching in, 86. *See also* Presbyterianism; Reformation
Cicero, 99n
Claim of Right, 83, 89
Clarendon, earl of, 107
Clark, Jonas, 280
Clarke, Samuel, 9, 167
Clive, John, 55
Cockburn, Henry, 19, 26, 56, 58
Coleridge, Samuel Taylor, 67, 99n, 150, 167, 314
College of New Jersey. *See* Princeton College
Collier, Arthur, 120
Collocation, 190-91, 193-94
Columbia Theological Seminary, 278
Columbia University, 242, 268, 288, 296
Common sense philosophy. *See* Scottish philosophy

Comte, August, 99n, 100, 317, 352
Condillac, Etienne Bonnot de, 102, 131
Conscience. *See* Moral science
Consciousness: Hamilton on, 121-22; McCosh on, 128, 131-32
Cooke, Henry, 176, 179
Cooper, Anthony Ashley. *See* Shaftesbury, earl of
Cooper, Peter, 281
Cornell University, 233, 249
Cosmothetic idealism, 121
Cours de Philosophie (Cousin), 57
Court of Session, 83
Cousin, Victor, 57, 102, 106, 153-54, 167; on Locke, 139
Covenanters, 6, 28, 33, 61, 79, 84, 90
Cudworth, Ralph, 167
Cullen, William, 18, 55
Cuvier, Georges, 99n
Cuyler, Cornelius, 344, 347

Daniels, Winthrop, 249, 341
Dartmouth College, 240, 245
Darwin, Charles, 180-81, 191, 193-95, 203-7, 211, 274, 320; and teleology, 197n; and McCosh, 204-5, 207, 313-15. *See also* Darwinism; Evolution
Darwinism, 67, 289n, 317-18. *See also* Darwin; Evolution
David I, 79
Davie, G. E., 40-41, 129n
Davies, Samuel, 219
Davis, John David, 343n, 345, 347
Declaration of Arbroath, 73
Defoe, Daniel, 42
De Juri Regni (Buchanan), 6
Delitsch, Franz, 287
Democracy, 67
Descartes, René, 25, 121, 130, 167
Development. *See* Evolution
Dewey, John, 211, 320
Dialogues Concerning Natural Religion (Hume), 22
Dickens, Charles, 67, 283
Dickie, George, x, 189, 191, 205
Dickinson, Jonathan, 282
Discourses on Philosophy . . . (Hamilton), 115
Disruption: events of, 83-88; effects of,

Disruption (cont.)
88-89; McCosh on meaning of, 89-90
Dissenting academies, 216
Dissertation on Miracles (Campbell), 25n
Divine and Supernatural Light, A (Edwards), 64
"Doctrinal Attitudes of Old School Presbyterians" (Atwater), 239
Dod, Albert P., 299
Dod, Samuel Bayard, 299, 310
Dodge, Cleveland, 344
Does the Established Church Acknowledge Christ as Its Head? (McCosh), 86
Donaldson, Gordon, 7
Doon, Loch, 34
Doon, River, 33-34
Dorner, Isaac, 330
Drumclog, 39
Drummond, Andrew L., 65
Dublin Review, 177
Dubois-Raymond, Emil, 288
Duffield, Thomas, 238, 276
Duke, Benjamin Newton, 280
Dundee, 5
Dupree, A. Hunter, 181n
Dwight, Timothy, 36, 99n

East Church of Brechin, 78, 90
East Free Church of Brechin, 90-93
Eating clubs: at Princeton College, 347
Eaton, John, 90
Ecclesiastical Characteristics (Witherspoon), 32, 216
Edinburgh, 3, 5, 14, 25-26, 48-49, 55, 65, 71; H. Blair in, 17-18; T. Guthrie in, 77; Disruption in, 86-88
Edinburgh, University of. *See* Universities, Scottish, University of Edinburgh
Edinburgh Christian Instructor, 62
Edinburgh Review, 41, 54-55, 57, 59, 62, 119-20, 122, 183
Edinburgh Society for the Encouragement of Arts, Sciences, Manufactures, and Agriculture, 15
Edison, Thomas, 244
Education Act of 1803, 37
Edward III, 79
Edwards, Jonathan, 53, 64, 176, 219, 221

Elective system, 232; at Harvard, 234; at Yale, 235; McCosh on, 236-37
Elements of the Philosophy of the Human Mind (Stewart), 26
Eliot, Charles W., 233, 249, 250, 254, 268n, 280, 335; debates with McCosh, 46n, 233-37, 252-54
Elsin, William Thaddeus, 269
Emerson, Ralph Waldo, 315
Emotions. *See* Affections
Enlightenment, 24, 27
  in America, 216
  in France, 117, 172, 313
  in Scotland, ix, 3-4, 9-27, 30, 210, 215-16, 246n, 250; and religion, 9; social roots of, 15-16; and Church of Scotland, 16-17; and Robertson, 20; and Reid, 22-25; and D. Stewart, 25-27; McCosh on, 31-32, 106
Episcopalianism, 256, 259, 296, 347; and boarding schools, 303. *See also* Church of England
Erskine, Ebenezer, 27
Erskine, Ralph, 27-28
Essay on Justification (Witherspoon), 217
Essay on the Causes and Variety of Complexion and Figure in the Human Species (Smith), 218
Essays on the Active Powers of the Human Mind (Reid), 24
Essays on the Intellectual Powers of Man (Reid), 24
Essays on the Nature and Conduct of the Passions . . . (Hutcheson), 10
Established Church. *See* Church of Scotland
Ethics. *See* Moral science
Evangelical Alliance, 166, 176, 226, 244, 351
Evangelicalism, ix, 27, 47, 62, 66, 153, 166, 177n, 181, 215, 254; McCosh and, 28, 44, 49, 62-65, 71, 147, 168, 172-73, 176, 193, 210, 293; and Hamilton, 61-62; and Calvinism, 67; and Victorian age, 67-68; and social and economic reform, 68-70, 81-82; and intellectual life, 70; in Arbroath, 74; and Headship principle, 84-85; in Brechin, 84-93; and patronage, 86;

Index

and Bible, 95; and preparation for salvation, 97; and philosophy, 106; and Scottish universities, 125n; and Hugh Miller, 186; and Witherspoon, 217; in America, 219, 222; and World Alliance of Reformed Churches, 329. *See also* Revival of 1876
Evidences of Christianity (Paley), 53
Evolution, ix, 180-211, 244, 292-93; at Princeton College, 274-79
"Evolution of Self-Consciousness" (Wright), 319
Examination of Mr. J. S. Mill's Philosophy, An (McCosh), 115, 317
Examination of Sir William Hamilton's Philosophy, An (Mill), 115, 138, 315

Factory Bill, 70
Faculty psychology, 102, 231
"Fairport," 73
Faithful Narrative of the Surprising Work of God (Edwards), 176
Faraday, Michael, 99n
Ferguson, Adam, 15, 26
Ferrier, James, 58, 129
Fettercairn (Scotland), 91
Fichte, Johann Gottlieb, 126, 150, 156
Fifth Avenue Presbyterian Church, 282-83
Final causes. *See* Teleology
Fine, Henry Burchard, 287-88, 345-46
First Principles (Spencer), 159, 196
Fiske, John, 319
Flower, Elizabeth, 322
Flushing Institute, 303, 322
Foote, Alexander Leith Ross, 78, 85, 88-89
Footprints of the Creator (Miller), 187
Fourdoun (Scotland), 91
Franklin, Benjamin, 152
Free Church Central Organization, 90
Free Church Magazine, 69-70, 91, 100
Free Church of Scotland, ix, xii, 70-71, 78, 88-90, 215-16, 250, 253, 258-59, 279; preaching in, 93; and Hugh Miller, 186
Free Church University, 175
Freiburg, University of, 184n, 289
Freneau, Philip, 220
Frothingham, Arthur, Jr., 291

Gay, Peter, 21
General Assembly (Presbyterian): Church of Scotland, 70, 85-88; Free Church of Scotland, 91; in Ireland, 175; in America, 221-22, 259
Geological Society of North America, 287
German philosophy, 57, 59, 116, 131, 153, 155, 160
German universities: Hamilton on, 59-69; McCosh on, 232
Germany: McCosh visits, 225; McCosh recommends lower school system of, 301
Gibbon, Edward, 20
Gibbon, Lewis Grassic. *See* Mitchell, James Leslie
Gillispie, Charles Coulston, 180n
Gilman, Daniel Coit, 230, 240, 249
Gladden, Washington, 311
Glasgow, 24-28, 31-35, 40, 46-47, 65, 231, 250; described, 42-44; Chalmers in, 52
Glasgow Chemical Society, 18
Glasgow University. *See* Universities, Scottish, Glasgow University
Glenisla (Scotland), 72
Glorious Revolution, 90
Godkin, E. L., 311
Goethe, Johann Wolfgang von, 188
Göttingen, University of, 240
Grant, Ulysses S., 284
Gray, Asa, 206n
Great Awakening, 216, 219-20
Greeley, Horace, 283
Green, Ashbel, 222
Green, Charles E., 304
Green, Henry Woodhull, 227, 332, 347
Green, John Cleve, 282-83, 304
Green, William Henry, 227-28, 304
Gregory, John, 23, 118
Gregory, Margaret (Mrs. Reid), 23
Grey, John Hamilton, 42n
Guthrie, Alexander, 75, 93
Guthrie, Ann, 87
Guthrie, Isabella. *See* McCosh, Isabella Guthrie
Guthrie, Thomas, 66, 72, 75-77, 187, 224; character and personality of, 77; in Edinburgh, 77n, 84; McCosh friendship with, 77, 93-94; on Bre-

Guthrie, Thomas (*cont.*)
  chin, 78; and Disruption, 84, 86-88; on evangelical literature, 86
Guthrie family, 77
Guyot, Arnold Henry, 244, 248, 264, 286-87

Hamilton, duke of, 15
Hamilton, Sir William, ix, 4, 47, 49, 54, 62, 67, 115-16, 118, 120, 130, 136, 140, 147, 150, 157-58, 167, 175, 197n, 232, 316; early career of, 55-57; review of Cousin, 57; at University of Edinburgh, 57-62; character and personality of, 58-59; and McCosh, 59n, 62, 115, 132-33, 153-55, 159n, 162-63, 175; and Moderatism, 60-62, 83-84; on Scottish religion, 60-62; on T. Guthrie, 77; on consciousness, 121-24; opposes representative theories of knowledge, 122; and Scottish philosophy, 122; and philosophy of the unconditioned, 123, 125n, 153-55; on causality, 124-25, 135, 160-61; on knowledge of substance, 129; on mathematics, 137; Mill on, 138-39; and Kant, 151n; on the Infinite, 153n, 164n; on the Absolute, 153-54, 153n; on God and religious belief, 154-55; Mansel's interpretation of, 155-57; works of, at Harvard College, 315
Hanna, William, 175
Harper, William Rainey, 250
Hartford Courant, 283
Hartley, David, 117, 140, 167
Harvard College, 233-37, 245, 249, 254, 268, 280, 287, 291, 295, 300, 302, 328-29; philosophy at, 312-15; religion at, 329
Hatcher, John Bull, 341
Hauy, René-Just, 152
Hayes, Rutherford B., 302n
Headship principle: and evangelical movement, 84-85; McCosh on, 86
Hegel, Georg Wilhelm Friedrich, 156, 321
Heidelberg, University of, 241, 287
Helmholtz, Hermann von, 288

Henry, James Bayard, 344, 347, 374
Henry, Joseph, 223, 243-44, 246
Henry, Pooley Shuldham, 179
Hibben, John Grier, 291, 342, 346
Hinton, John Howard, 62-63, 95
History of the American People (McMaster), 242
Hobbes, Thomas, 106, 167
Hodge, Archibald Alexander, 226, 275, 330-31
Hodge, Caspar Wistar, 277
Hodge, Charles, 223, 226, 273, 275n, 287, 308, 310; at McCosh's inaugural, 230; on evolution, 274-75
Holmes, Oliver Wendell, 268
Holmes, Oliver Wendell, Jr., 319
"Holy Fair, The" (Burns), 30
Home, Henry, Lord Kames, 15
Home, John, 217
Homer, 44
Homologies, 191-92
Hopkins, Johns, 280
Hopkins, Mark, 302
Horner, Francis, 54, 119
Houghton, Walter, 67-68
House of Commons, 83
Howe, John, 102
Hume, David, 4, 13, 15, 17, 18n, 23, 45, 99n, 106, 117-18, 124, 129-30, 145, 154n, 167, 172, 198, 314; and Scottish Enlightenment, 20-22; McCosh on, 21; influences Brown, 119-20; compared to Mill, 140
Hunt, Theodore Whitefield, 240
Hutcheson, Alexander, 10
Hutcheson, Francis, 4, 10-13, 16-17, 21, 24, 27, 32, 104n, 217, 246; moral philosophy of, 10-12; on religion, 10-12; influence of, 12-13; and McCosh, 13, 105-6, 173
Hutton, James, 184n
Huxley, Thomas, 67, 204n, 274, 287

Idealism, x, 116, 120-23, 138, 140, 149-51, 178, 232, 314-15; Hamilton on, 122-23; McCosh on, 126, 151, 321. *See also* German philosophy
Immutability of Truth (Beattie), 18n
Infinite, 153n, 154, 162-65
"Influence of Darwin on Philosophy,

Index

The" (Dewey), 221n
Inquiry into the Mind on the Principles of Common Sense (Reid), 24
Inquiry into the Origin of Our Ideas of Beauty and Virtue (Hutcheson), 10
Inspiration of Scriptures, The (Patton), 332
Intuitional realism, 114, 125-37, 147, 149, 160, 163-65, 170
Intuitions of the Mind . . . (McCosh), x, 115, 125, 318, 321; reviewed, 177

Jacobus, Melancthon W., 344, 347
James I, 8
James II, 8
James V, 4-5
James, William, 320-21
Jameson, Robert, 50
Jardine, Henry, 26, 41, 55
Jeffrey, Francis, 26, 41, 54, 56, 119
Jesus Christ. *See* Christ
John (New Testament), 95
John C. Green School of Science, 245-46, 282
Johns Hopkins University, 233, 249, 290, 341
Johnson, Alexander, 242
Johnson, Samuel, 292
"Jolly Beggars, The" (Burns), 30
Jones, David, 345-47
Jones, Thomas, 346
Jordan, David Starr, 224n
Jouffroy, Théodore-Simon, 99n, 102, 106

Kames, Lord. *See* Home, Henry
Kant, Immanuel, x, 24, 57, 59, 106, 119, 123, 125n, 129-31, 134, 145, 147-48, 150-51, 154, 158, 159n, 178, 314-16, 321, 335; and Hamilton, 122; and McCosh, 126, 132n, 133, 135-36, 148, 321; on the soul, 129; on causality, 160-61
Kargé, Joseph, 241
Kenneth II, 79
King's College. *See* Universities, Scottish, Aberdeen University
Kirkmichael (Scotland), 71
Klein, Felix, 289
Knox, John, 5-6, 17, 33, 37, 51, 84, 93, 95; and educational reform, 7; and Scottish Reformation, 7-8

"Last Irish Grievance, The" (Thackeray), 112n
Lawrencekirk (Scotland), 91
Lawrence Scientific School, 245
Lawrenceville School, 297, 304-5, 347
Lecture on Limbs (Owen), 191
Lectures on Metaphysics and Logic (Hamilton), 115, 139
Lectures on the Philosophy of the Human Mind (Brown), 119
Lee, Charles, 200
Lee, Henry, 200
Leibniz, Gottfried Wilhelm von, 152
Leipzig, University of, 242, 287, 289, 294
Leslie, Sir John, 50, 52
Lesy, Michael, 75
Libbey, John M., 310
Libbey, William (father), 282
Libbey, William (son), 266, 282, 288
Liberal theology, 209
Library meetings, 289, 291-94
Life of James McCosh, The . . . (Sloane), 34n
Limits of Religious Thought Examined, The (Mansel), 116, 155
Lochlee (Scotland), 91
Locke, John, 4, 25, 126, 132, 139, 167; McCosh on, 145
Lollards of Kyle, 33
Low, Seth, 268
Lowell, James Russell, 311
Luther, Martin, 7
Lyell, Sir Charles, 50, 99n

Macaulay, Thomas Babbington, 249
McClymonts, 35
MacCoise, Erad, 34
McCook, John J., 347
McCormick, Cyrus, 342, 344-47
McCormick Seminary, 297, 332
McCosh, Alexander Guthrie, 93, 270
McCosh, Andrew (father of James), 35-37
McCosh, Andrew (son of James), 93
McCosh, Andrew James (son of James), 176, 269, 337

McCosh, Isabella Guthrie, 93, 269-71, 337
McCosh, James: author of *The Scottish Philosophy*, 3; on Reformation reforms in education, 7; and moral discipline in ministry, 7, 82; and Headship principle, 8, 86; on Shaftesbury, 10-13, 104n, 105-6, 173; on Moderatism, 13, 45-47, 63, 69, 85-86, 105; on Patronage Act of 1712, 16; on Scottish philosophy, 19, 31-32, 54, 147-48; on Hume, 21-22; on Turnbull, 22; on Aberdeen school, 23; on Locke, 25; on Reid, 25, 118, 128, 134; on D. Stewart, 26-27, 128-29; on Scottish Enlightenment, 27; and Evangelicalism, 28, 63, 70-71, 84-88, 105, 253-57, 329; and Burns, 29-30; birth of, 33; autobiography of, 36n; ancestry and family of, 34-35; early life of, 36-40; at Glasgow University, 40-47; at University of Edinburgh, 47-62; and Welsh, 50, 77n; and Chalmers, 51-54; and Edwards, 53, 64, 176; and Puritanism, 53, 64; and Hamilton, 55-62, 115, 131-34, 158, 159n, 160-62, 164n, 175; review of *The Work of the Holy Spirit*, 62-65; on causality, 64-65, 102-3, 160-62, 195-96, 319; in Arbroath, 71-78; and Guthrie, 75-77; in Brechin, 78-93, 107; and temperance, 80-81, 254; and Disruption, 85-93; in the Free Church, 88-93; and Isabella McCosh, 93, 269-71, 337; children of, 93, 176, 269, 337; gospel sermons of, 93-99; writes *Method of the Divine Government*, 99-100; and Calvinism, 101, 333-34; mental philosophy of, 102-3, 127-38; moral philosophy of, 103-5, 166-74, 200-202, 246-47n; appointment to Queen's College, Belfast, 106-7; at Queen's College, 112-13; on Queen's College curriculum, 113-14; relation to Scottish school, 114-16; on Brown, 119; on modern philosophy, 125-26; on intuitions, 127-38; and Kant, 131, 132n, 133, 148, 321; on space and time, 132-34, 163-65; on mathematics, 137-38; and Mill, 138-45, 167-73; religious philosophy of, 147-53, 157-66; on Christianity's relation to philosophy, 148-49; on German idealism, 150-53; and Mansel, 156-60, 163n; and Spencer, 159, 195-202; and Ulster Revival, 176-77; and disestablishment of the Church of Ireland, 177n; appointment to Princeton College, 178, 215, 227-29; and evolution, 187-211, 274-79, 292-93; and Chambers, 184; and Hugh Miller, 187-88; and morphology, 188-89; and Dickie, 189-90; and collocation, 190-91, 196; on homologies, 191-93; and Darwin, 193-95, 204-8, 313-15; on evolution and Christianity, 207-11; tours United States, 224-27; inaugural address at Princeton College, 229-33; debates Eliot, 235-37, 252-53; academic reforms at Princeton College, 237-49; and W. Wilson, 248-49, 264-65, 278, 344-45; and religion at Princeton College, 249-59; relations with students at Princeton College, 253-57, 259-60, 286-91, 323-24, 343-44, 346; Sustentation Plan of, 258-59; personality of, 260-71; raises money for Princeton College, 281-86; and graduate study at Princeton College, 286-91; library meetings of, 291-95; and Princeton College trustees, 295-97, 325-27; and Princeton College alumni, 296-30, 326-27; and feeder schools for Princeton College, 300-306; and his publishers, 306-10; and the *New Princeton Review*, 310-11; in American philosophy, 312-13, 316-22; and enrollment crisis at Princeton College, 322-23, 328-29; and University Campaign, 326-27; and Westminster Confession, 333-34; retirement of, 335-37; death of, 337-38; his choice for his successor, 338-40
McCosh, Janet Nivan, 34
McCosh, Jasper, 34
McCosh, Jean Carson, 35, 176
McCosh, John, 35

Index

McCosh, Margaret Sarah, 176, 269
McCosh, Mary Jane, 93
McCosh, Samuel Walker, 43
McCrie, Thomas, 84, 175
McFarlane, James J., 72
Mackensie, James Cameron, 304
Mackensie, John, 177
Mackintosh, James, 106
McLachlan, James, 303
Maclean, John, 224, 227, 262, 310
McMaster, John Bach, 242, 311
McPherson, Simon, 297, 344
Madison, James, 220
Magee, William, 99n
Magie, Mrs. David. *See* McCosh, Margaret Sarah
Magie, William Francis, 287, 346
Maitland, Mrs. Alexander. *See* McCosh, Mary Jane
Malebranche, Nicholas, 117
Malthus, Thomas, 54, 99n
"Man was Made to Mourn—A Dirge" (Burns), 30
Mansel, Henry, 57, 99n, 115-16, 146n, 150, 159-60, 162, 312, 315; religious philosophy of, 156-57; and McCosh, 157-58, 162, 163n; on causality, 160-61
Marischal College. *See* Universities, Scottish, Aberdeen University
Marquand, Allan, 290-91, 294
Marquand, Henry, 302
Marshall, Stephen, 53
Martin, Luther, 200
Materialism, 128, 140, 147; McCosh opposes, 113-14; in moral science, 170; Hugh Miller opposes, 186
Mathematics: debate over, 136-38
Matthews, Shailer, 209n
Maule, Fox (the younger Panmure), 79
Maule, Thomas (Lord Panmure), 79, 91
Maurice, H. D., 155
Maybole (Scotland), 35
Mechanics' Institutes, 183-84, 186; in Brechin, 81-82, 107
Melville, Andrew, 6-7, 19, 61, 84
Menmuir (Scotland), 91
Metaphysical Club (Cambridge, Mass.), 319

Metaphysics: at Glasgow University, 45; McCosh on, 148. *See also* German philosophy; Idealism
Methodism, 68, 70
Methodist Quarterly Review, 315, 317
Method of the Divine Government, The (McCosh), x, 58n, 100-107, 115-16, 134, 157, 159, 307
Michigan, University of, 233
Mill, James, 26, 140, 167
Mill, John Stuart, 57, 67, 99n, 115-16, 119-20, 125n, 135, 138, 155, 167, 193, 315-17, 347; on Hamilton, 138-39; and sensationalism, 138-40; and McCosh, 138-45, 167-73; on innate ideas, 139-40; on the permanent possibilities of sensation, 142-43; on the mind, 143-44; and moral science, 170-71; on the self, 238; Bowen on, 316; and Wright, 318
Miller, Howard, 219
Miller, Hugh, 58n, 70, 99n, 175, 181, 189, 275; career of, 184-86; on evolution, 187; and McCosh, 187-88, 194
Miller, Samuel, 221-22, 310
Mission and Tract Society, 308
Mitchell, James Leslie, 91
Moderatism, 16-17, 24, 32, 48, 66, 71-72, 98, 181, 210, 215, 240, 250; F. Hutcheson's influence on, 12-13; rivalry with Evangelicalism, 27-28; McCosh on, 31, 62-65, 69, 85-86, 94, 106; and Witherspoon, 32, 217; at Glasgow University, 45-46; and Chalmers, 51-54; at St. Andrews University, 52; and Hamilton, 61-62
Modern Erastianism Unveiled (Bisset), 28
Monboddo, James Burnett, 15
Monro, Alexander, 18
Moody, Dwight Lyman, 256-57, 269
"Moral Philosophy in Great Britain in Relation to Theology" (McCosh), 166
Moral science: McCosh on, 103-6, 166-74, 201-2; and Spencer, 200-201; and Witherspoon, 217; and S. S. Smith, 218; and Harvard College, 313-14
Morphology, 188-89

Muhlenberg, William Augustus, 303
Munsell, O. S., 316
Murchison, Sir Roderick, 181n
Murdoch, William, 43
Murphey, Murray G., 322
Murray, Hamilton, 257
Murray, James Ormsbee, 240, 325, 333, 347
Museum of Natural History, 283
Musgrave, George W., 277
Mylne, James, 42, 52, 55
My Schools and Schoolmasters (Miller), 184

National Covenant of 1637, 8
Natural realism, 131, 166; and Hamilton, 120-22
Natural Theology (Chalmers), 53
New Directions in American Intellectual History, xii
Newman, John Henry, 67, 70
New Princeton Review, 310-11, 321
Newton, Sir Isaac, 99n
New York Ledger, 283
New York Sabbath Committee, 307
Nixon, John Thompson, 299
North, Christopher. *See* Wilson, John
North American Review, 310, 315
North British Review, 70, 157, 178
Norton, Charles Eliot, 291, 311
"Notes on Books" (McCosh), 99

Observations on Man (Hartley), 117
O'Connell, Daniel, 111
Old Greyfriar's Church, 77
On the Archetype and Homologies of the Vertebrate Skeleton (Owen), 191
Origin of Species, The (Darwin), 180, 203
Ormond, Alexander T., 291
Orris, S. Stanhope, 241
Osborn, Henry Fairchild, 247, 287-88, 294, 296
Outlines of Moral Philosophy (Stewart), 25
Outlines of Philosophical Education (Jardine), 41
Owen, John, 53, 106
Owen, Richard, 181n, 192-94, 205; on homologies, 191-92

Oxford University, 18, 43, 155, 216, 287; Hamilton at, 55, 59

Packard, William Alfred, 240
Paine, Thomas, 263
Paley, William, 53, 100, 190-92, 204n
Palmer, Stephen S., 346
Palmerston, Henry John Temple, 26
Panmure, Lord. *See* Maule, Thomas
Pantheism, 147-48, 153
Paris, University of, 288
Parish schools, 37-38, 70
Parker, Mungo, 78, 92
Pater, Walter, 67
Patna (Scotland), 33, 35, 39
Patronage Act of 1712, 16, 28, 39
Pattison, Mark, 70
Patton, Francis Landy, 225, 288, 325; early career of, 331-32; chosen McCosh's successor, 338-40; characteristics of, 340-42; movement against, 342-46
Paul (New Testament), 95
Paulsen, Friedrich, 287
Peirce, Charles Sanders, 320
Perry, Bliss, 341
Phelps, Austin, 329
Philadelphian Society, 256-57
Phillipson, Nicholas, 14, 15n
Philosophical Series (McCosh), 309
Philosophy of the unconditioned, 57, 115, 122-25, 147
Physiological psychology: McCosh's interest in, 126, 294-95
Pictish Chronicle, 79
Plan of Union, 221-22
Plato, 102, 127, 148, 152
Playfair, John, 49, 99n, 184n
Poem on the Rising Glory of America (Brackenridge and Freneau), 220
Political Science Quarterly, 311
Popular Rhymes of Scotland (Chambers), 182
Porter, Noah, 230, 233, 235, 308
Positive Philosophy, The (Comte), 100
Positivism, 178
Practical reason, 148, 158
Pragmatism, 320
Presbyterian Hospital, 283
Presbyterianism, 18n, 33, 36, 42, 55, 216, 222-24, 347; Hamilton on, 60-

Index

62; in Ireland, 111-12; in America, 218-20, 239, 272, 276; New School ("New Light"), 219, 221, 225, 331-32, 334; Old School ("Old Side"), 219, 223, 226, 229, 238-39, 273, 276-77, 310, 331, 347; and McCosh, 258-59, 279, 310-11, 329-35; and boarding schools, 304. *See also* Church of Scotland; General Assembly; Reformation

Presbyterian Quarterly and Princeton Review, 310, 330-31

Presbyterian Quarterly Review, 223

Presbytery of Ayr, 71

Presbytery of Brechin, 75, 78

Prime, Irenaeus, 228

Princeton, New Jersey, 229-30

Princeton College, x, xiii, 4, 40, 46, 66, 88, 93, 98; McCosh's invitation to, 178, 215, 227-29; history of, 216-24; McCosh at, 228-311, 322-38; after McCosh, 338-49

Princeton Contributions to Psychology, 294-95

Princeton Review, 315

Princeton Theological Seminary, 221-24, 230, 239, 243, 273, 275n, 278, 290, 297, 299, 307, 310, 329, 330-34, 339; and Briggs case, 331-33

Princeton University Press, 308

Principles of Psychology (James), 320

Protestantism, 149, 153. *See also* Church of Scotland; Presbyterianism; Reformation

Psychological Review, 287

Pufendorf, 10

Puritanism, 70, 94, 97, 149, 222; and Chalmers, 53; and Evangelicalism, 67-68. *See also* Edwards, Jonathan

Pyne, Moses Taylor, 276, 296-97, 345, 347; and University Campaign, 327

Queen's College, Belfast, x, 50; McCosh at, 88, 112-14, 139, 178-79, 188; McCosh appointed to, 107; establishment of, 111; McCosh's inaugural address at, 112-13; curriculum of, 112

R. L. & A. Stuart Co., 283

"Ragged schools," 77

Ramsay, Allan, 15

Rationalism, 151-52; Mansel on, 156; McCosh on, 157; in moral science, 167

Raymond, George Lansing, 243

Realistic Philosophy (McCosh), 197, 321

Recapitulation theory, 183, 187

Reconstruction in Philosophy (Dewey), 211n

Reformation, Protestant, 4-9, 79, 90; Hamilton on, 61. *See also* Church of Scotland; Presbyterianism

Reformed theology. *See* Calvinism

Reid, Thomas, ix-x, 4, 18n, 21, 57, 95, 106, 117, 120, 122, 124, 129, 134, 139, 145, 167, 217, 313-14; career of, 22-25; on Scottish religion, 24; on speculative philosophy, 116; McCosh on, 116, 118, 128-29; on Hartley, 117; realism of, 118; on belief in mind, 128n; on causality, 134; and Hume, 134n

Religious Aspects of Evolution (McCosh), 309

Revivalism. *See* Evangelicalism

Revival of 1876, 255-56

Riehl, Alois, 289

Roberts, William Charles, 299

Robertson, William, 15, 17, 21, 217

Robert the Bruce, 34

Rockefeller, John D., 280

Romanticism, 166n, 191; McCosh on, 151, 153, 157

Roosevelt, Theodore, 311

Rosemary Street Church, 175

Round Tower (Brechin), 79

Rousseau, Jean-Jacques, 4

Royal College of Sciences, 287

Royal Commissions, 59; and Scottish universities, 40

Royal Society (London), 189, 288

Royal Society of Edinburgh, 20

Sabbatarianism, 272; and McCosh, 79

St. Andrew's Church, 87

St. Andrews University. *See* Universities, Scottish, St. Andrews University

St. David's Church, 50

St. Giles Church, 87
Sandford, Daniel K., 44
Sankey, Ira, 256
Schelling, Friedrich Wilhelm Joseph von, 150, 154, 156, 164n
Schleiermacher, 99n, 148
Scotch-Irish Society, 283
Scots Confession, 7
Scott, Sir Walter, 26, 45, 48, 57, 73
Scott, William Berryman, 261, 264, 276, 287, 294, 325, 339-40, 345
Scottish Ballads and Songs (Chambers), 182
Scottish Jests and Anecdotes (Chambers), 182-83
Scottish philosophy, ix, xi, 25n, 128, 130, 147, 149, 250, 310; and Reid, 22-25, 128; and McCosh, 106, 129-30, 147, 160, 174; at Queen's College, 113; and Hamilton, 121-22, 125; and D. Stewart, 129-30; and Witherspoon, 218; and Harvard College, 313-14
Scottish Philosophy, The . . . (McCosh), 3, 13, 118, 175, 320
Scribner, Arthur Hadley, 308-9
Scribner, Charles, Jr., 308-9
Scribner, Charles, Sr., 307-8
Scribner, John Blair, 308
Scripture. *See* Bible
Seceders, 27, 89
Secret societies, 262-64
Sedgwick, Adam, 181n
Select Club (Edinburgh), 15, 20
Shaftesbury, earl of, 9-11, 16-17
Shakespeare, William, 17, 252
Sheffield Scientific School, 245
Sheldon, Edward Wright, 344
Shields, Charles Woodruff, 239
Slavery, 222, 224-25
Sloane, William Milligan, 241-42, 286, 294, 304; edits McCosh autobiography, 34n; as possible successor to McCosh, 339-40
Smith, Adam, 13, 15, 17-18, 24, 43
Smith, Caleb Green, Jr., 304
Smith, Henry Boynton, 308, 316, 330
Smith, Samuel Stanhope, 217-18, 221-22
Smith, Sydney, 26, 54, 119

Smollett, Tobias, 42
Social Statics (Spencer), 196
Society for the Promotion of Collegiate and Theological Education in the West, 222
Socrates, 152
Space: Hamilton on, 123; McCosh on, 132-33
Spencer, Herbert, 146, 159, 195, 199n, 254, 274; McCosh on, 159, 198, 321-25; on religion and science, 196-97; and evolution, 197, 208; on mental behavior, 199-200; and moral philosophy, 200-201
Stanford, Leland, 280
Starr, Moses Alan, 291
Stearns, William A., 268n
Stevenson, John, 17, 26, 217
Stewart, Dugald, ix, 4, 21, 31, 54, 57, 106, 116, 118, 167, 217, 313-14; career of, 25-27; McCosh on, 26-27, 128-29; on sensation, 128-29
Stewart, George Black, 342
Stewart, John A., 228, 281, 344, 347
Stewart, Matthew, 13, 25-26
Stoicism, 62
Stonehaven (Scotland), 91
Stowe, Harriet Beecher, 307
Straiton (Scotland), 34, 36
Stuart, Robert L., 283
Stumpf, Carl, 287
Sunset Song (Mitchell), 91
Supernatural in Relation to the Natural, The (McCosh), 116
Swing, David, 332
Synod of Angus and Mearns (Church of Scotland), 75
Synod of Angus and Mearns (Free Church), 91
System of Logic (Mill), 139, 145, 167
System of Moral Philosophy, A (Hutcheson), 10-12

Tanfield Hall (Edinburgh), 87
Taylor, Jeremy, 99n
Taylor, John, 99n
Teleology, 191; in Chambers, 183-84; and McCosh, 192-94; and Spencer, 197; Darwin rejects, 203
Temperance, 222; and Evangelicalism,

68-69; and McCosh, 80-81, 254
Tennent, Gilbert, 219
Thackeray, William Makepeace, 112n
Theological Society, 49
Theory of the Earth (Hutton), 184n
Ticknor, George, 303
Time: Hamilton on, 123; McCosh on, 132-34
Toryism, 53
Traditions of Edinburgh (Chambers), 182
Transcendentalism, 315, 317. *See also* Idealism
Treatise on Human Nature (Hume), 21
Treatise on Regeneration (Witherspoon), 217
Trevor-Roper, Hugh, 222n
Trinity University, 18n
Tübingen, University of, 243
Tulane, Paul, 280
Turnbull, George, 22-23
Turner, Frederick Jackson, 342
Turner, Jonathan Baldwin, 260
Tyndall, John, 274
Typical Forms and Special Ends in Creation (McCosh and Dickie), x, 189-94, 203-5

Ulster Revival, 176
Union Theological Seminary, 330-31
Unitarianism, 234, 316-17, 342; and Harvard College, 313-15
United States Trust Co., 281-82
Universities, Scottish, 6, 9, 15n, 19, 42-44, 216; Royal Commissions at, 40-42; Hamilton on, 59-60; and evangelical movement, 70
  Aberdeen University (King's College, Marischal College), 18, 22, 78, 182, 189; Reid at, 23
  Glasgow University, 10, 18, 21, 26, 38, 40, 42, 55; McCosh at, ix, xi, 44-47, 264; F. Hutcheson at, 10-13; Reid at, 24; student life at, 46; Witherspoon at, 217
  St. Andrews University, 7, 18, 23, 39, 106; Chalmers at, 52
  University of Edinburgh, 18-20, 57, 65; McCosh at, ix, xi, 47-63, 66, 70, 99; H. Blair at, 17-18; classical education at, 19;

D. Stewart at, 26-27; student life at, 49; Hamilton at, 57-62; Brown at, 118-19; Ferrier at, 129; McCosh seeks appointment to, 175; Witherspoon at, 217
University Campaign, 326-27
Utilitarianism, 67-69, 125, 200-201; McCosh opposes, 106; and Evangelicalism, 127
Utilitarianism (Mill), 167

Vanderbilt, Cornelius, 280
Van Dyke, Henry, 240, 248, 278, 311, 341; and Briggs case, 333
Van Dyke, Paul, 346
Van Hise, Charles R., 249
Van Rensselaer, Alexander, 343n, 344, 346
Vestiges of the Natural History of Creation (Chambers), 100, 180, 183, 318
Veto Act, 61
Veysey, Laurence, xii
Victorian Frame of Mind, The (Houghton), 67
Victorianism, 67
Voltaire, François Marie Arouet de, 4
Von Baer, Karl Ernest, 181n

Warfield, Benjamin, 275, 331
Warfield, Ethelbert D., 268
Watt, James, 43
Welsh, David, 50, 70, 77n, 186; and Disruption, 87
Werner, Abraham Gottlob, 50, 184n
Wertenbaker, Thomas, 221
Wesley, John, 28
West, Andrew, 266, 291, 344, 346
West Church (Brechin), 82, 89, 107; and Disruption, 89. *See also* Cathedral Church
Westminster Confession, 8, 20, 219, 223, 332; McCosh on, 334
What Is Darwinism? (Hodge), 274
What Is Revelation? (Maurice), 155
Whatley, Richard, 99n
Whewell, William, 99n
White, Andrew Dickson, xi, 233, 249, 278

Whitefield, George, 221
Whitehall (Scotland), 35
Whither? A Theological Question for the Times (Briggs), 333
Whither? O Whither? Tell Me Where (McCosh), 334
Will: McCosh on, 102-3, 106
Williams, E. T., 278
Williams College, 243
Williamson, John Franklin, 286
William the Lion, 73
Wilson, John, 57
Wilson, Woodrow, 264, 278, 290-91, 311, 339, 341; as student, 248-49; and McCosh, 264-65, 278, 344-45; on Patton, 340; Patton admonishes, 341-42; and F. J. Turner, 342; leads faculty against Patton, 342-45; appointed president of Princeton College, 346-47
Winans, Samuel Ross, 291, 346
Wisconsin, University of, 233, 249, 342

Wishard, Luther, 257
Witherspoon, John, 4, 17, 32, 219-20, 221, 228, 314; career of, 216-17
Witness, The, 70, 186
Woodrow, James, 278
Work of the Holy Spirit in Conversion, The (Hinton), 62
World Alliance of Reformed Churches, 329
Wright, Chauncey, 318-20
Wundt, Wilhelm, 289, 294
Wundt Club, 294

Yale College, 36, 231, 233, 235, 245, 268, 295, 300, 328
Yale Report of 1828, 233, 235
Young, Ann, 82
Young, Charles Augustus, 244-45
Young Men's Christian Association, 257, 282

LIBRARY OF CONGRESS CATALOGING IN PUBLICATION DATA

Hoeveler, J   David, 1943-
   James McCosh and the Scottish intellectual tradition.

   Bibliography: p.
   Includes index.
   1. McCosh, James, 1811-1894.   2. College presidents—New Jersey—Biography.   3. Princeton University—History.   I. Title.
   LD4605 1868.H63   378'.111 [B]   80-8553
   ISBN 0-691-04670-0